MAGNIFICENT DELUSIONS

MAGNIFICENT DELUSIONS

Pakistan, the
United States, *and an* Epic History
of Misunderstanding

· · · · ·

Husain Haqqani

PublicAffairs
New York

Editorial production by *Marra*thon Production Services.
www.marrathon.net

BOOK DESIGN BY JANE RAESE
Set in 12.5-point Bembo

Library of Congress Control Number: 2013948306
ISBN 978-1-61039-317-1 (hardcover)
ISBN 978-1-61039-409-3 (INTL. HC)
ISBN 978-1-61039-410-9 (INTL. PB)
ISBN 978-1-61039-318-8 (e-book)

FIRST EDITION
2 4 6 8 10 9 7 5 3 1

To my late parents
Saeeda and Saleem Haqqani,

and my wife,
Farahnaz Ispahani,

for their lifelong love, support,
and encouragement

Contents

A doubtful friend is worse than a certain enemy.
Let a man be one thing or the other,
and we then know how to meet him.

—Aesop, *Aesop's Fables*

MAGNIFICENT
DELUSIONS

Introduction

Over the last two decades US–Pakistan relations have often been described as America's most difficult external relationship. Although the two countries have been nominal allies dating back to Pakistan's independence in 1947, their relationship has never been free of friction. Even in its heyday during the 1950s and 1960s, the US–Pakistan partnership was far from an alliance based on shared values and interests; instead, each of the two partners was always preoccupied with confronting different enemies and pinning different expectations to their association.

Pakistan's motive in pursuing an alliance with the United States is driven by its quest for security against its much larger neighbor, India. Pakistan has repeatedly turned to the United States as its most significant source of expensive weapons and economic aid. Although, in the hope of winning US support for Pakistan's regional aims, Pakistani leaders have assured US officials that they share the United States' global security concerns, Pakistan has been repeatedly disappointed because the United States does not share Pakistan's fears of Indian hegemony in South Asia.

For its part, the United States has also chased a mirage when it has assumed that, over time, its assistance to Pakistan would engender a sense of security among Pakistanis, thereby leading to a change in Pakistan's priorities and objectives. The United States initially poured money and arms into Pakistan in the hope of building a major fighting force that could assist in defending Asia against communism. Pakistan repeatedly failed to live up to its promises to provide troops for any of the wars the United States fought against communist

......

forces, instead using American weapons in its wars with India. Furthermore, US hopes of persuading Pakistan to give up or curtail its nuclear weapons program or to stop using Jihadi militants as proxies in regional conflicts have similarly proved futile.

Three American presidents—Dwight D. Eisenhower, John F. Kennedy, and Lyndon B. Johnson—have asked the question: What do we get from aiding Pakistan? Five—Jimmy Carter, George H. W. Bush, Bill Clinton, George W. Bush, and Barack Obama—have wondered aloud whether Pakistan's leaders can be trusted to keep their word. Meanwhile in Pakistan, successive governments have spent a lot of time trying to figure out how to maintain Pakistan's freedom of action while depending on US aid. But neither country has changed its core policies nor have they given up the hope that the other will change.

The US-Pakistan relationship has depended largely on cordial ties between leaders and officials who have often misunderstood each other's intentions and limitations. Whereas Pakistanis have often benefited from the American tendency to ignore history and focus only on immediate goals, Americans have often assumed that building up Pakistan's economic and military capacity provides them leverage even after periodically finding out the limits of US influence. And both sides have their own stereotypes about each other, traceable back to Pakistan's emergence as an independent country.

During that period, soon after emerging from British India's bloody partition in 1947, Pakistan's leaders confronted an uncertain future for their new country. When most of the world was indifferent to Pakistan as the potential homeland of South Asia's Muslims, India antagonized Pakistan without compromise or compassion. Because of this, soon after independence Pakistan's founding fathers, encouraged by some British geostrategists, decided that they would continue to maintain the large army they had inherited even though the new nation could not afford to pay for it from its own resources and did not immediately face a visible security threat. Given Pakistan's location at the crossroads of the Middle East and South Asia and its relative proximity to the Soviet Union, Pakistanis assumed that the United States would take an interest in financing and arming the fledgling new state. Thus, the gap in expectations between American and Pakistani leaders that has bedeviled their relationship over the last sixty-five years should have been apparent right at the beginning, when Pakistan's founding father and its first governor-general, Muhammad Ali Jinnah, asked the United States for a $2 billion aid package in September 1947, but the United States gave Pakistan only $10 million in assistance that first year.

International relations thinkers like Hans J. Morgenthau and George Kennan did not see Pakistan's value to the United States as an ally. After all, Pakistan's primary concern, competing with India for regional influence, was not a strategic concern for the United States. But after Dwight D. Eisenhower was elected president in 1952, his secretary of state, John Foster Dulles, embraced the idea that Pakistan could be influenced into sharing US strategic concerns in exchange for weapons and aid.

Primarily because of geopolitical considerations, the United States has enlisted Pakistan as an ally on three occasions: during the Cold War (1954–1972), the war against the Soviets in Afghanistan (1979–1989), and the war against terrorism (2001–present). In each instance the US motive for seeking Pakistani alliance has been different from Pakistan's reasons for accepting it. For example, after the Soviet invasion of Afghanistan the United States saw an opportunity to avenge the Vietnam War and bleed the Soviet Red army with the help of Mujahideen, militant Islamist radicals trained by Pakistan's Inter-Services Intelligence (ISI) and funded by United States' Central Intelligence Agency (CIA). Pakistan, however, looked upon the military action in Afghanistan as a Jihad to be used as the launching pad for asymmetric warfare that would increase its clout against India.

Since my days as a student at Karachi University, I found the anti-American narrative that was prevalent all around me difficult to believe. I spent many hours at the American Center Library, reading books and articles that exposed me to different perspectives of historic events. Unlike my colleagues, I could see through the absurdity of conspiracy theories.

When student protestors burned down the US embassy in Islamabad in 1979, I was a student leader allied to Islamists on my campus.

*****

A huge demonstration was organized at short notice, with university buses commandeered to transport protestors to the US consulate in Karachi. Several student speakers urged the mob to burn down the consulate, and the mob was ready to do so until I was called on to speak. My speech, citing the Quran and demanding that ascertainment of facts precede action, saved the US consulate (and its library) from meeting the same fate as the embassy in Islamabad.

Later, as a journalist, I covered the anti-Soviet Afghan war, observing firsthand the flow of US arms to the Mujahideen. My first foray into government was as adviser to Nawaz Sharif, who, in 1989, aspired to become prime minister of Pakistan. I accompanied Sharif on his introductory visit to the United States as opposition leader. Once Sharif became prime minister, I acted as his liaison with US media and diplomats before we parted ways quietly after differences of opinion.

In 1992 Pakistan's support for Jihadi groups nearly caused it to be designated a state sponsor of terrorism. I worked with Prime Minister Benazir Bhutto, who, in 1993, succeeded Sharif's first government and worked to fend off that label. My close association with Bhutto resulted in my own incarceration toward the end of the second Sharif government (1997–1999), and my opposition to General Pervez Musharraf's military dictatorship forced me to exile to the United States a few months after 9/11.

Over all these years I have seen Americans make mistakes in their dealings with Pakistan as well as in their overall foreign policy. Nonetheless, I have always been convinced that the United States remains a force for good in the world. Pakistan has benefited from its relations with the United States and would benefit even more if it could overcome erroneous assumptions about its own national security and role in the world. Instead of seeking close security ties based on false promises, Pakistan must face its history and diversity honestly, and it should be neither dependent on nor resentful of the world's most powerful nation.

As Pakistan's ambassador to the United States from 2008 to 2011, I sought to overcome the bitterness of the past in order to help lay the foundations for a long-term partnership. I studied the relations between the United States and its other partners so as to figure out why almost all post–World War II US allies have found prosperity and stability through this partnership, whereas Pakistan has not. But major power centers in my own country resisted my vision of a broader US-Pakistan partnership rooted in mutual trust.

Instead of appreciating my efforts to redefine the US-Pakistan relationship through an honest appraisal of past mistakes, Pakistan's security services saw me as working for American rather than Pakistani interests. Through the media I was falsely accused of helping the CIA expand its network of spies in Pakistan, and my remarks about the transactional nature of past ties were distorted so as to suggest that I had described Pakistanis as beggars. In the end I was forced to resign amid fabricated charges that I had sought help from the US military through a dubious American businessman of Pakistani origin in order to avert a coup.

But the willingness of my countrymen to believe the worst about their ambassador reflects a deeper pathology. Instead of basing international relations on facts, Pakistanis have become accustomed to seeing the world through the prism of an Islamo-nationalist ideology. Even well-traveled, erudite, and articulate Pakistani officials echo this ideology without realizing that holding tight to these self-defeating ideas makes little impact on the rest of the world; the gap is widening between how Pakistanis and the rest of the world view Pakistan.

Somehow, halfhearted and time-limited transactions rather than an honest dialog over shared interests seem to be the default pattern in US-Pakistan relations. For instance, as stated above, I found the two countries working toward very different outcomes in Afghanistan. I fear that the prospect of their alliance may end in acrimony once again.

The reemergence of democracy in Pakistan offers the hope that Pakistanis will someday be able to debate their national interests realistically and alter their national priorities so as to align more with those of the United States. If, however, the propaganda and the political strategies of the powerful Pakistani military continue to hold sway, alienation from the United States will remain inevitable. Additionally, Pakistanis are not likely to alter their priorities solely as part

......

of a bargain involving aid and arms from the United States. Moreover, both countries are wrong when they assume that even as they act at cross-purposes, they will eventually succeed in persuading the other of their own respective points of view.

Since its independence in 1947, Pakistan has debated its raison d'être. A vocal and powerful minority insists that the country was created to be an Islamic state, a semitheocracy governed by religious principles defined by those who support that vision. And in response to Pakistan's insecurity toward India and the fear of this much larger neighbor culturally if not politically reabsorbing Pakistan, many otherwise modern, educated generals, judges, and politicians have embraced this Islamist paradigm.

Because of this, Pakistan's short history as a nation has witnessed the demonization of many secularists as foreign collaborators and enemies of the national ideology. Furthermore, the country has failed to sustain economic growth, which has increased during times of cooperation with the United States, only to come to a halt during periods of estrangement. Pakistanis have seldom pondered why, after six decades of alliance with the United States, the country has not been able to build the kind of economy that other US allies such as South Korea and Taiwan have managed to create for themselves.

American critics of Pakistan point out that Pakistan has always pursued its own agenda, which seldom coincides with American interests, yet it repeatedly seeks US aid and arms without keeping the commitments it makes to acquire that assistance. As a result, the list of American grievances is long: Pakistan developed nuclear weapons while promising the United States that it would not; the United States helped arm and train Mujahideen against the Soviets during the 1980s, but Pakistan chose to keep these militants well armed and sufficiently funded even after the Soviet withdrawal in 1989; and, from the American perspective, Pakistan's crackdown on terrorist groups, particularly after 9/11, has been halfhearted at best.

The relationship between the United States and Pakistan is a tale of exaggerated expectations, broken promises, and disastrous misunderstandings. The discovery of Osama bin Laden in Pakistan in May 2011 further and significantly undermined any hope of convincing

Americans that Pakistan was an ally, albeit one with its own concerns and difficulties.

Many have noted that radical Islam, Pakistan's military, and US-Pakistan relations have shaped Pakistan's history, and I have spent most of my life at the intersection of these three critical elements. As a Pakistani, I feel that my country cannot forever depend on external factors for its survival and progress and that my compatriots need to set aside their contrived narrative and face the harsh facts of recent history. Conversely, Americans must realize that their policies toward Pakistan have helped neither the United States nor Pakistan's people.

In his 1842 book *American Notes*, Charles Dickens described Washington, DC—a purpose-built capital—as a "City of Magnificent Intentions." In this way Islamabad is similar to Washington, DC, as it is a new city with no history before the 1960s, when wheat fields and bushes were cleared in order to establish it as Pakistan's capital. And though these two cities' histories may parallel each other, Washington's magnificent intentions and delusions have often clashed with those of Islamabad. This book is an account of that clash. Although I have been witness to some critical events in US-Pakistan relations, this is not intended to be a personal memoir.

Chapter One

False Start

One month after Pakistan's creation as an independent state in August 1947, the country's founder and first governor-general, Muhammad Ali Jinnah, sat down at his stately residence in Karachi, the Flagstaff House, for an interview with *Life* magazine reporter and photographer Margaret Bourke-White. His followers revered the charismatic Jinnah as the Quaid-e-Azam, the Great Leader. But his detractors blamed him for the violent partition of British India that had carved out the subcontinent's northwestern and northeastern provinces into a new Muslim-majority British dominion.

Most American journalists covering the events leading to Indian and Pakistani independence were less than sympathetic to the idea of Pakistan, and Bourke-White was no exception. But Pakistanis deemed her magazine particularly prejudiced against their newly born country because *Life*'s sister publication, *Time*, had derided Jinnah as the "Pooh-Bah of Pakistan," dismissed the country as "the creation of one clever man, Jinnah," and described Pakistan's birth as "a slick political trick" when compared to the "mass movement" Mohandas Karamchand Gandhi led for India's independence.[1]

After asking probing questions about Jinnah's plans for the new nation's constitution, Bourke-White sought his views of relations with the United States. Jinnah replied that "America needs Pakistan more than Pakistan needs America." He then told her: "Pakistan is the pivot of the world, as we are placed," and went on to state, "the frontier on which the future position of the world revolves....Russia is not so very far away." He spoke of America's interest in arming Greece and Turkey and expressed the hope that the United States would pour money and arms into Pakistan as well.

In response to these answers, Bourke-White wrote disapprovingly: "In Jinnah's mind this brave new nation had no other claim on America's friendship than this—that across a wild tumble of roadless mountain ranges lay the land of the Bolsheviks. I wondered whether the Quaid-e-Azam considered his new state only as an armored buffer between opposing major powers."[2]

This account of Pakistani thinking within weeks of its creation offers perspective into the vagaries of US-Pakistan relations over the last six-and-a-half decades. Amid frequent Pakistani charges of American betrayal, few Americans remember that Pakistan initiated the US-Pakistan alliance primarily to compensate for its economic and military disadvantages.

At the time when Jinnah described Pakistan as a country that was the "pivot of the world," the United States had given little thought to the new nation and its possible role in international security. Although the US embassy was the first diplomatic mission to open for business in Karachi, fewer people staffed the building than the number posted in the US embassy in Cuba at that same time.

Oblivious to American disinterest, however, Pakistanis had high expectations of one of the world's two superpowers. Bourke-White wrote that government officials would say to her: "Surely America will build our army" and "Surely America will give us loans to keep Russia from walking in." But neither she nor the Pakistani officials she spoke to saw signs of Soviet infiltration. "They would reply almost sadly," she said, "as though sorry not to be able to make more of the argument. 'No, Russia has shown no signs of being interested in Pakistan.'"

Several months before Jinnah sat down for his interview with Bourke-White, he had addressed American diplomats about his expectation that the United States should help Pakistan build its economy and military in return for Pakistan mobilizing Muslim nations against the Soviet Union. At that time, May of 1947, the country was

* * * * *

still an idea, and discussions about partitioning India had not yet concluded when Jinnah sat down for a one-and-a-half-hour meeting with Raymond Hare of the State Department's Division of Middle Eastern and Indian Affairs as well as Thomas Weil, second secretary at the embassy in New Delhi.

According to the two diplomats' account of the meeting, Jinnah told them that the establishment of Pakistan was "essential to prevent 'Hindu imperialism' spreading" into the Middle East. In his vision the Muslim countries "would stand together against possible Russian aggression" and would look to the United States for assistance.

But Americans wondered how Pakistan could be an American ally without a shared interest. They pointed to "frequent jibes" against US "economic imperialism and dollar diplomacy" in *Dawn*, the newspaper Jinnah founded to advance the cause of Pakistan. Jinnah responded with an explanation that foretold Pakistan's future interaction with the United States, stating that the *Dawn* editors "simply reflected" the attitude of Indian Muslims in general toward America, and he "added jokingly 'they had to make a living'." He said that he realized that the US government was "probably open minded" about Pakistan; nonetheless, "most Indian Muslims felt Americans were against them." Jinnah cited two reasons for this view: first, he said, "because most Americans seemed opposed to Pakistan," and second, because the "U.S. government and people backed Jews against Arabs in Palestine."[3]

Jinnah's expectation of US aid for Pakistan, American officials' concerns about anti-Americanism, and Bourke-White's cynicism about Pakistani objectives around the time of the country's inception together seem like the prologue to a story with many repetitions. The *Life* correspondent discerned in Pakistan a persistently voiced "hope of tapping the US treasury," which led her to wonder "whether the purpose was to bolster the world against Bolshevism or to bolster Pakistan's own uncertain position as a new political entity."

Ultimately, in Bourke-White's opinion, "it was more nearly related to the even more significant bankruptcy of ideas in the new

Muslim state—a nation drawing its spurious warmth from the embers of an antique religious fanaticism, fanned into a new blaze."[4]

✦

THE FIRST ANTI-AMERICAN demonstration in Pakistan was reported from Karachi in May 1948. In the years that followed, during the 1950s and 1960s, mobs continued to attack US official buildings in Pakistan. In 1979 a hostile crowd burned down the US embassy in Islamabad—the only US embassy to ever be completely gutted because police did not arrive in time to protect it. The September 1982 issue of the *Journal of Conflict Resolution* carried an article by Pakistani civil servant Shafqat Naghmi in which he analyzed keywords used in the Pakistani press between 1965 and 1979 and subsequently found evidence for widespread anti-Americanism dating back to the beginning of the study.

But this roller-coaster ride of US-Pakistan relations cannot be understood without understanding the circumstances of Pakistan's creation, the worldview of its elite, and the miscalculations by both American and Pakistani leaders that have made the two countries military allies amidst mistrust and without really being friends.

✦

THE EMERGENCE OF Pakistan as an independent state in 1947 was the culmination of decades of debate and divisions among Muslims in British India regarding their collective future. After British rule was consolidated in the nineteenth century, Muslims found themselves deprived of the privileged status they had enjoyed under the Muslim Mughal empire that had dominated South Asia since 1526. Some of the Muslim leaders embraced territorial nationalism and did not define their collective personality through religion. As opposition to British rule grew, these leaders called for the Muslim population to participate fully in the Indian nationalist movement led by the Indian National Congress of Gandhi and Jawaharlal

Nehru. But others felt that Muslims had a special identity that ethnic and territorial nationalism, centered primarily on the Hindu majority in India, would erase over time.

Coalescing in the All-India Muslim League and led by Muhammad Ali Jinnah, these *Muslim nationalists* (as opposed to *Indian nationalists* in the secular Indian National Congress led by Gandhi and Nehru) asserted that India's Muslims constituted a separate nation from non-Muslim Indians and, because of this, demanded the creation of a separate country in areas with a Muslim majority.

British India's Muslim-majority provinces lay in its northwest and northeast, leading to Pakistan comprising two wings that were separated by India until December 1971, when the eastern wing became the new state of Bangladesh.

Pakistan's creation represented the general acceptance of the two-nation theory—that Muslims and Hindus constituted two distinct nations in view of their unique experience in India—a theory that had been periodically articulated long before the formal demand for a Pakistan state in 1940 but had never been fully explained in terms of how it could be applied. Although the creation of Pakistan was intended to save South Asia's Muslims from being a permanent minority within India, it never became the homeland of all of South Asia's Muslims.

One-third of the Indian subcontinent's Muslims remained behind as a minority in Hindu-dominated India even after the 1947 partition. The other two-thirds now live in two separate countries, Pakistan and Bangladesh, confirming the doubts that some expressed before independence about the practicality of applying the two-nation theory. In return for gaining one country of their own, the Muslim "nation" was effectively divided into three separate states.

Until the end of the Second World War, the Indian struggle for independence had received little attention in the United States; instead American interest had focused on the countries flanking the Pacific and Atlantic oceans. Although India had been crucial to Britain's war effort, it was less significant for American policy. Nonetheless, the United States set up a diplomatic presence in Delhi in 1941, and a Special Representative of President Franklin D. Roosevelt arrived in 1942.

These American officials sympathized with the demand for Indian independence, leading to strong disagreement with British colonial officials. But US sympathy with the anticolonial sentiment in the subcontinent did not translate into sympathy for Muslim separatism, which most Americans dealing with India found impractical.

According to Special Representative William Phillips, President Roosevelt thought that the idea of partitioning India "sounded terrible" when the British chargé d'affaires, Sir Ronald Campbell, first mentioned it to him. "It reminded the President of the experience of the American civil war," Phillips recalled. Although Phillips found Jinnah to be "brilliant" and was "personally attracted to him," he could not agree with the leader's views. "The more I studied Mr. Jinnah's Pakistan," he concluded, " the less it appealed to me as the answer to India's communal problem, since to break India into two separate nations would weaken both and might open Pakistan, at least, to the designs of ambitious neighbors."[5] From the American perspective, the notion of a significant minority seeking separation rather than safeguards for itself opened doors for perennial conflict. Postcolonial nations all over the world would fragment as a result of similar separatist demands.

The relatively sparse commentary in the US media reinforced the officials' views. Tom Treanor, reporting for the *Los Angeles Times* in March 1943, wrote, "Every instinct will persuade you that there shouldn't be a Pakistan, which means the secession of the Mohammedan portion of India from the Hindu portion." In his view "Only an old-school Southerner who thinks Appomattox was a shocking bad show could go for Pakistan." Treanor described Jinnah as "the greatest secessionist since 1865" and suggested that "Jinnah is just an old die-hard South Carolinian at heart who believes Jeff Davis ought to have been President."[6]

For supporters of the Pakistan movement, such comments reflected America's lack of empathy and further fueled the sense of insecurity and isolation that had drawn many of them to demand

Pakistan's creation in the first place. From their point of view Jinnah was a combination of George Washington, Thomas Jefferson, and Abraham Lincoln. He had created a country, not divided a nation. To this day Americans tend to know and admire Mohandas Karamchand Gandhi, seen as an apostle of peace, far more than they recognize Jinnah.

This contrasts significantly with the Pakistani characterization of Jinnah as "a man of ideals and integrity"[7] with "extraordinary qualities of vision."[8] University of California historian Stanley Wolpert would later observe that "Few individuals significantly alter the course of history," and "Fewer still modify the map of the world. Hardly anyone can be credited with creating a nation-state. Mohammad Ali Jinnah did all three."[9] For Pakistanis, this comment would supersede the opinions of Americans who disparaged Jinnah during his life.

Almost four decades after Pakistan's birth Wolpert pointed out that Jinnah "virtually conjured that country into statehood by the force of his indomitable will." Wolpert recognized Jinnah's "primacy in Pakistan's history," saying that it "looms like a lofty minaret over the achievements of all his contemporaries in the Muslim League." But during the 1940s there was little American sympathy for "conjuring" a new Asian country based on religion.

After the end of World War II Jinnah made a major effort to explain the idea of creating a Muslim state to American officials and to win them over to his argument. Consul general in India, John J. Macdonald, sent a detailed telegram to Secretary of State George C. Marshall after meeting Jinnah on March 5, 1947, at his residence in Bombay. According to Macdonald, Jinnah said he was "anxious to hear" about the American reaction to the British proposal to transfer power to "responsible Indian hands not later than June 1948."

Jinnah reportedly said that "he could understand the American public's surprise as well as impatience with India for not finding a solution to its political problems following Britain's offer of Independence." However, Jinnah felt that "news regarding Indian problems in the American press is influenced by false propaganda." The consul general noted that Jinnah blamed the "highly efficient propaganda organization" of the Indian Congress Party for turning Americans against Pakistan—a suggestion the US official tried to repudiate.

More significantly, Jinnah, the leader of the All-India Muslim League, shared with Macdonald his disappointment and frustration with the lack of international support for the Indian Muslims' demand for a separate homeland. He spoke of a reception for him in Cairo upon his return from London earlier in the year, where "a group of prominent Egyptians" told him that, their warmth for a brother Muslim notwithstanding, they "found his policy annoying." The Egyptians accused Jinnah of being "in league with the British instead of working for Indian independence," a charge that he vehemently rebuffed. The Indian Muslims' Quaid-e-Azam (Great Leader) was offended that fellow Muslims outside the subcontinent failed to support his lofty cause.

"He told the accusing group that if the Indian National Congress really wanted to test his sincerity regarding his desire for Indian independence, they should agree to Pakistan," Macdonald reported. After this agreement Jinnah "would immediately accept the responsibility placed upon him for taking the necessary steps to establish a constitutional government." The cable quoted Jinnah as saying, "I would be the first to go down to the Gateway of India to wave farewell to the British." It went on to describe Jinnah's principal argument for dividing the subcontinent.

As narrated by Consul General Macdonald: "The Muslims, according to Mr. Jinnah, cannot accept the idea of united India because in doing so they would merely be substituting a Hindu Raj for the British Raj." Jinnah described suggestions of a compromise as "foolish," saying there was no basis for it. In his view the "difference in culture, religion and way of life between the Muslims and Hindus precludes any possibility of a compromise."

Jinnah asked why "a hundred million Muslims should become a minority in a Hindu dominated Government" and argued that "safeguards for a minority in a united India were worthless because in the event of an appeal by the minority the accused would sit as the judges of the accusers. The only recourse left to the Muslims in such an eventuality would be an appeal to the United Nations."[10]

· · · · ·

Jinnah's discussion with the US consul general revealed the difficulty he faced when attempting to persuade people outside the subcontinent, including Muslims, of Pakistan's raison d'être. Although Jinnah and most of his colleagues were not known for religious observance, they were espousing a vague Islamo-nationalism that others saw as an ideology that could easily become the basis for more pietistic demands. And as feared, once Pakistan was finally created, the insecurities about Muslim identity in the modern era that led to its creation were absorbed into the identity of the new state, and the bombast about Hindu imperialism and threats to Islam carried on into India-Pakistan relations and how Pakistanis view international affairs.

After all, Pakistan was not just to be a country; it had become a cause. But the outward secular and westernized orientation of the Pakistani elite confused westerners. They assumed that Pakistan's leaders shared Western values and were simply trying to win the hearts of their followers by appealing to religious sentiments. As such, American and British policy makers did not see saying one thing to a domestic and another to a foreign audience as a problem. But this habit had serious consequences, including religious violence in the run-up to Pakistan's independence and the large-scale expulsion of non-Muslims from the Pakistan region.

Once the country had emerged, it encountered difficulty when attempting to reconcile its professed tenets with the demands of pragmatic political and economic considerations. As a result, throughout the country's history Pakistanis have been divided between those who want a greater role for religion in the nation's collective life and those who do not. On the one hand, Islam is described as the uniting factor for Pakistan's disparate ethnicities; on the other, it is also the basis for polarization and sectarian divisions.

Pakistan's independence movement was relatively short. It began with the All-India Muslim League's demand for separate Muslim states in 1940 and ended with the announcement of the partition plan in June 1947. The original demand was for multiple independent states of Muslim-majority provinces of India. The idea of a single Pakistani state evolved later.

*****

Although Pakistan was to be created in the areas where Muslims were a majority (referred to as Muslim-majority provinces), its strongest support and most of its national leadership came from regions where the Muslims were a minority (Muslim-minority provinces). Muslims from the minority provinces were better educated and had greater representation in the British Indian civil services and the military's officer corps than did their coreligionists in the majority provinces. Recognizing this, the original demand for Pakistan did not envisage any mass transfer of populations. After all, one-third of India's Muslims were to remain behind in India after the partition, and privileged Muslims who were not from territories belonging to the new state were to govern Pakistan.

Initially, the call for Pakistan resonated with Muslims in the minority provinces, whereas the landed Muslim gentry of the majority provinces supported provincial parties. Although the Muslim League belatedly won over local notables in the provinces that were to constitute Pakistan, it could not build consensus among its leaders over the new country's future direction. In February 1947, a few months before independence, Khwaja Nazimuddin, who later became Pakistan's second governor-general as well as its second prime minister, candidly told a British governor that "he did not know what Pakistan means and that nobody in the Muslim League knew."[11]

This echoed Nazimuddin's discussion with the governor of Bengal, Richard Casey, in September 1945. Casey recorded in his diary that he asked Nazimuddin many questions about Pakistan. "Very little has been discussed or worked out by them," the Englishman lamented, referring to the Muslim League leaders. In another meeting with Nazimuddin, Casey shared his view that the Muslim League had "had only the most cursory examination and thought given to" the consequences of India's division. "I believed that they relied too implicitly on their leader, Mr. Jinnah—and that, apart from whatever thought he may have given to the subject, I did not believe that any other Muslim had really applied himself to the study of the many problems involved," he wrote.[12]

Sir Bertrand Glancy, the governor of Punjab, the other major province designated to be part of Pakistan, shared similar anxieties

......

about Jinnah's scheme. Glancy revealed his concerns about the logic of the demand for Pakistan in a secret letter to the viceroy, Field Marshal Archibald Wavell, written in August 1946, ahead of elections that would choose India's future leaders. "I must confess that I am gravely perturbed about the situation, because there is a very serious danger of the elections being fought, so far as Muslims are concerned, on an entirely false issue," he wrote.

"Crude Pakistan may be quite illogical, undefinable and ruinous to India and in particular to Muslims," Glancy went on, "but this does not detract from its potency as a political slogan. The uninformed Muslim will be told that the question he is called on to answer at the polls is—Are you a true believer or an infidel and a traitor?" Glancy presciently warned that the Muslims would be swayed by "the false and fanatical scream that Islam is in danger" and that "if Pakistan becomes an imminent reality, we shall be heading straight for bloodshed on a wide scale."[13]

But the lukewarm British efforts at reconciling the Congress and the Muslim League between the end of the war in 1945 and until 1947 proved ineffective. The Congress leadership failed to guarantee safeguards acceptable to a majority of the Muslim elite. Even if the demand for Pakistan was initially a negotiating stratagem to ensure protections for the Muslim minority in a post-British India, the idea of it had moved millions of Indian Muslims into expecting a separate country. While devoting their energies to pleading for it, Muslim leaders had made no preparations for running that separate state.

Franchise in the 1946 election was limited by several qualifications, such as college education, service in the British government, and property ownership. Thus, only the most elite 15 percent of the population had the right to vote. As a result, the Muslim League swept the Muslim electorate on the basis of the demand for Pakistan, leaving little option for the British but to accede to partition. Issues such as the new nation's constitutional scheme, the status of various ethnolinguistic groups within Pakistan, and the role of religion and theologians in matters of state were barely discussed during the election campaign. No one knew how revenue would be raised, and there was no mention of the future state's foreign policy.

One possible explanation for the ambiguity is that the demand for Pakistan was an instrument with which to bargain for greater political leverage for India's Muslim minority.[14] By leaving future plans unspecified, some argue, Jinnah was trying to mobilize the broadest possible support for his position, which was open to change depending on the circumstances.

Nevertheless, following independence Pakistan has developed a clear national ideology and narrative that today is explicitly outlined at all levels of schooling. But during the years leading up to its creation Pakistan meant different things to different people. For some the country was to be a Muslim-majority state where greater economic opportunities would open up for Muslims without competition from non-Muslims; others envisioned a utopia resembling the Muslim empires that dominated the Middle East from the seventh to the twelfth centuries.

Those who looked upon Jinnah as their great leader found a coherence in his exhortations that others dismissed as just clever arguments. Tom Treanor, for example, wondered how Pakistan would help protect the 25 million Muslims who would be left behind in India after Pakistan was created. Jinnah argued, "Because 25 million of my people must suffer should I sacrifice the other 75 million. Should I?"

Jinnah and his lieutenants offered little beyond sharply crafted statements and speeches to explain the idea of Pakistan. "Pakistan is not the product of the conduct or misconduct of the Hindus," Jinnah explained. "It had always been there, only they were not conscious of it. Hindus and Muslims, though living in the same towns and villages, had never blended into one nation; they were always two separate entities."[15] To this day Pakistani schoolchildren are taught that the roots of Pakistan go back to the arrival of the first Muslim conqueror in the subcontinent in 712 AD.

"We are a nation," Jinnah argued, "with our own distinctive culture and civilization, language and literature, art and architecture, names and nomenclature, sense of values and proportion, legal laws and moral codes, customs and calendar, history and traditions, aptitudes and ambitions, in short, we have our own distinctive outlook

......

on life and of life. By all canons of International Law we are a nation."[16] But the Muslim League still did not offer any book-length elaboration of the idea of a separate Muslim homeland and how recognizing Muslims as a separate nation in the subcontinent would work in practice.

The party's official newspaper, *Dawn*, carried polemical pieces about the poor prospects for Muslims under future Hindu domination. These served as exhortations to Muslims to press their claim for separate statehood. But there was virtually no discussion of tough questions about economics, national security policy, and potential interethnic conflict, all of which remained unanswered before independence. This pattern of avoiding details of policy persisted even after Pakistan had appeared on the world map.

Soon after independence differences between East and West Pakistan and ethnic differences among Pakistanis surfaced, but these were papered over with religious grandiloquence. Pakistan was officially described as *Mamlakat Khudadad*, Persian for "Divinely Granted State." Soon prominent individuals within the government mooted proposals for adopting Arabic as the national language and of changing the script of the Bengali language from its Sanskrit base to an Arabic-Persian one.[17] Within a few years the president of the Muslim League, Chaudhry Khaliq-uz-Zaman, announced that Pakistan would bring all Muslim countries together into Islamistan—a pan-Islamic entity.[18]

None of these developments within the new country elicited approval among Americans for the idea of India's partition. The *New York Times* saw the dislocation of millions resulting from partition as a "great tragedy" and attributed it to "the insistence of the Moslem leaders on the partition of an economically homogenous territory along religious lines." In an editorial the paper argued that "Four hundred million people in both Dominions are paying a high price for a division that is hardly understandable to countries where the political principle of separation of church and state is firmly established."[19]

Bourke-White, among others, questioned whether Jinnah had given much thought to the human cost of partition, stating, "More Muslim lives had been sacrificed to create the new Muslim homeland than America, for example, had lost during the entire Second World War." She also found disturbing that, one month after the country had been created, Jinnah was unwilling to share details of his plans for it. When she asked about the future, all Jinnah said was, "Of course it will be a democratic constitution; Islam is a democratic religion." Asked to define what he considered democracy, Pakistan's founder declared, "Democracy is not just a new thing we are learning. It is in our blood. We have always had our system of zakat—our obligation to the poor."

Jinnah's frequent assertion that "Our Islamic ideas have been based on democracy and social justice since the thirteenth century" often drew applause from his Pakistani followers, but this mention of the thirteenth century troubled Americans. Bourke-White noticed that Pakistan's leaders were unwilling to discuss how they would transition from a feudal order to a modern democracy. There had also been no serious discussion of the relationship between "true Islamic principles" and the new nation's laws. All Jinnah told Bourke-White was that the constitution would be democratic because "the soil is perfectly fertile for democracy."

The two-nation theory, the founding premise of Pakistan, had little appeal outside of Pakistan, just as few outside of Northern Ireland (Ulster) Protestants find the two-nation theory in Ireland appealing. Despite this, in anticipation of independence, Jinnah sought support from other Muslim-majority countries. In 1946 he told a conference in Cairo: "It is only when Pakistan is established that Indian and Egyptian Muslims will be really free. Otherwise there will be the menace of a Hindu Imperialist Raj spreading its tentacles right across the Middle East."[20] But arguments about a "Hindu imperialistic power" suffusing "the British imperialistic power" did not impress the Arab audience.

British Prime Minister Clement Atlee voiced the international consensus at the time when he told the House of Commons of his hope that "this severance may not endure." He hoped that the proposed dominions of India and Pakistan would "in course of time, come together again to form one great Member State of the British Commonwealth of Nations."[21]

⋯⋯

During the same debate in the British Parliament, the secretary of state for India, Lord Listowel stated his expectation that "when the disadvantages of separation have become apparent in the light of experience, the two Dominions will freely decide to reunite in a single Indian Dominion, which might achieve that position among the nations of the world to which its territories and resources would entitle it."[22]

Jinnah's rhetoric about "a Hindu empire" rising out of the dust of the British Raj had inflamed Muslim passions in India as had statements about the impending "end of Islam in India, and even in other Muslim countries."[23] But outside the subcontinent's inveigled context it meant little and moved few. Soon after independence Pakistan found that some Muslim countries chose to side with India once the Hindu-Muslim division was presented as a Pakistan-India conflict.

During this time most of the Arab world was going through a nationalist awakening. Pan-Islamic dreams involving the unification of Muslim countries, possibly under Pakistani leadership, had little attraction. Likewise, within Pakistan ethnolinguistic nationalism remained alive, challenging the idea of religion-based nationhood within a few months.

Meanwhile, some American observers tried to figure out Pakistan's emerging strategy for survival as a new state. On the one hand, Pakistan sought Western aid and arms to compensate for its initial lack of resources; on the other, it sought to define its nationhood through Islam, pursuing leadership of the Muslim world. "Jinnah's most frequently used technique in the struggle for his new nation had been the playing of opponent against opponent," Bourke-White wrote scathingly. "Evidently this technique was now to be extended into foreign policy. Not only the tension between the great powers but the Palestine situation as well held opportunities for profiting from the disputes of others. Pakistan was occupied with her own grave internal problems, but she still found time to talk fervently, though vaguely, of sending a liberation army to Palestine to help the Arabs free the Holy Land from the Jews."[24]

The *Life* reporter also found it strange that Pakistan's leaders found time to comment on distant issues such as Palestine while there were serious difficulties at home: millions of refugees from India awaited settlement, there was little money in the treasury, and the emigration of Sikh and Hindu merchants out of Pakistan had resulted in a deficit of capital available for investment. But amid all this, "Muslim divines began advocating that trained ex-servicemen be dispatched" in the "holy cause" of Palestine. Bourke-White noticed that *Dawn*, the official government newspaper, condemned the "Jewish state" and "urged a united front of Muslim countries in the military as well as the spiritual sense," with one editorial asserting, "That way lies the salvation of Islam."[25]

Foreign criticism of the very idea of Pakistani nationhood heightened Pakistan enthusiasts' commitment to the new country. A national narrative emerged about the origins and purpose of Pakistan that simultaneously fed paranoia about global conspiracies to eliminate Pakistan soon after its inception. In this way, developments during the first two years of Pakistan's existence as an independent state foreshadowed the path the country was to take in subsequent decades. Pakistan actively sought to become a Western ally, on the one hand, and embraced anti-Western Islamist vocabulary, on the other. Economic and military necessity forced Pakistan to seek an international patron in the United States, whereas an inadequately defined Islamic nationalism made shunning the idea of being that patron's client equally necessary.

The ambiguity about Pakistan's raison d'être that had served well during the struggle for statehood led to internal disharmony soon after its creation. Jinnah and his subordinates had rallied India's Muslims on the basis of perceived threats to their Islamic way of life, but Pakistan's leaders were Westernized individuals not known for religious learning or practice. Soon after partition, the more religious Pakistanis started clamoring for the state to be run in accordance with Islamic Sharia law. Jinnah tried to clarify that the new country was intended as a homeland for Muslims but would not have a role for religion in its governance.

In a landmark inaugural address before Pakistan's constituent assembly on August 11, 1947, Jinnah declared that "in course of time Hindus would cease to be Hindus and Muslims would cease to be

Muslims, not in the religious sense, because that is the personal faith of each individual, but in the political sense as citizens of the State."[26] About a year later, in its commentary on his death, *Time* magazine lamented that "the inflammatory preachings of Jinnah the agitator would live on, but the occasionally restraining hand of Jinnah the politician had been removed."[27]

After his death in September 1948 Jinnah's successors faced difficulty convincing their countrymen that Pakistani nationalism could be completely secular. To maintain the momentum generated during the political campaign that led to Pakistan's independence, the country's first prime minister, Liaquat Ali Khan—often referred to only as "Liaquat" due to the common occurrence of his last name, Khan—introduced the concept of a national ideology. With this, Pakistan's Islamic identity would be an "ideological safeguard" protecting its territorial integrity and preventing internal disputes and disruption. Khan went on to describe Pakistan's ideology as the Islamic way of life, rooted in "faith, tradition and belief which has been a part of man's heritage for over thirteen hundred years."[28] He argued that this ideology had unified the Indian Muslims in seeking Pakistan and would likewise enable Pakistan to emerge as an effective, functional state.

Parallel to the emphasis on Islam as a national unifier ran the argument that Hindus were eager to avenge centuries of Muslim rule over the subcontinent and sought to eliminate Muslim identity. Although communal violence during partition had equally affected Hindus, Sikhs, and Muslims, Pakistani officials and writers chose to present that violence as being targeted only at Muslims. Liaquat described the mayhem as the sacrifice of India's Muslims for the creation of Pakistan, as an editorial in *Dawn* claimed that "hundreds of thousands" of Muslims "were forcibly converted to Hinduism almost simultaneously with the attainment of independence by the Hindus after a thousand years of slavery."[29]

Jinnah delivered a speech that called for religion to be relegated to the private domain, but his words had little effect on the passions that had been aroused in the populace to create Pakistan, emotions that were continuously reinforced to consolidate its statehood after independence. A year after it was delivered, the government republished Jinnah's inaugural speech but excised the portion that spoke of citizens ceasing to be Muslims or Hindus in a political sense. After all, Pakistan was soon on its way to becoming an Islamic state, not just a homeland for Muslims seeking to avoid being a permanent minority in post–British India.

The need to justify their country at an ideological level was only one part of the challenge Pakistan's founding fathers faced; they also needed resources to sustain the country. Although some men like Liaquat and Abol Hasan Ispahani gifted some of their property to the new state and had no plans of returning to India, for several years after independence some of Pakistan's elite acted as if their country was temporary. For instance, Jinnah told India's Prime Minister Nehru, through India's ambassador to Pakistan, that he wanted his house in Bombay kept in good condition so that he could retire there.[30] Pakistan's first ambassador to India, Muhammad Ismail, assumed his responsibilities without migrating to Pakistan and at one point claimed that he had not ceased to be an Indian national by becoming Pakistan's diplomatic representative.[31] And well-to-do Muslim politicians and officials went back and forth, trying to figure out where their careers might prosper more; some wanted to become Pakistani without losing the benefits of being Indian. It took several years for Pakistan to define its citizenship laws in regard especially to migrants or Indian refugees.

The partition plan provided only seventy-two days for transition from British rule to full independence, and communal rioting consumed most of that time. The hasty drawing of boundaries, division of civil and military services, and apportioning of assets were particularly detrimental to Pakistan. As one Pakistani official later put it, Pakistan, "unlike India, inherited neither a capital nor government nor the financial resources to establish and equip the administrative, economic and military institutions of the new state."[32]

Pakistan also had virtually no industry, and the major markets of its agricultural products were in India. The non-Muslim entrepreneurial class that had dominated commerce in the areas now constituting Pakistan either fled or transferred its capital across the new border. Uncertainties about Pakistan's survival as well as communal violence further exacerbated this flight of capital, shrinking the already narrow revenue base of the new country. Further, the Reserve Bank of India held the Pakistan government's monetary assets, and given the atmosphere of hostility between Congress and Muslim League partisans, the division and transfer of assets was by no means a smooth process.

Pakistan's earliest government officials feared their new country's economic strangulation and saw a "Hindu design to force Pakistan to its knees." The Congress party that led independent India had opposed the idea of Pakistan, so its leaders were certainly not eager to help the new state. Indian assurances that their reluctant acceptance of partition did not reflect a desire to undo it by force were not believed in Pakistan.

Upon partition Pakistan had received 30 percent of British India's army, 40 percent of its navy, and 20 percent of its air force. Its share of revenue, however, was a meager 17 percent, leading to concerns about the new state's ability to pay for all its armed forces. Within days of independence Pakistan was concerned about its share of India's assets, both financial and military. India's decision to delay transferring Pakistan's share of assets further increased the bitterness of partition.

Gandhi, the father of modern India, recognized the importance of containing that bitterness in India-Pakistan relations. Because of this, he went on a fast in January 1948, demanding that Pakistan's share of the monetary assets be paid. But the terms of the partition did not fully satisfy Pakistanis. They felt—and the new state's leaders exacerbated this—that the Indians as well as the British had deliberately created additional problems for the new country while dividing the assets and especially in demarcating the border.

Among the contentious issues born out of the partition was that of the princely state of Jammu and Kashmir. Pakistanis expected the Kashmir region, given its Muslim majority, to be rightfully part of the new Muslim-majority country. When that did not happen, a sense of grievance immediately took root. This provided grounds for Pakistan's leaders to convert the Hindu-Muslim divide of the

......

prepartition era into a permanent Pakistan–India rivalry and justified retaining Pakistan's large military inherited from colonial rule and expending the bulk of the country's meager resources on defense. It also further fed the sense of Muslim victimhood that had led Muslims to demand Pakistan in the first place.

During the British Raj 562 princely states had retained varying degrees of administrative independence through treaties with Britain that had been concluded during the process of colonial penetration. Jammu and Kashmir was one of them. The treaty relationships conferred "paramountcy" on the British and, in most cases, control over defense, external affairs, and communications. But the end of the Raj marked the end of paramountcy, and at the time of partition the British asked these states' rulers to choose between India and Pakistan, taking into consideration geographical contiguity and the wishes of their subjects.

Because of Kashmir's contiguity with Pakistan and its Muslim majority, Pakistan's leaders anticipated that it would join the new Muslim country. But the state's ruler at the time of partition, Maharajah Hari Singh, a Hindu, sought to retain independence even though a segment of his Muslim subjects wanted Kashmir to join Pakistan.

Some scholars argue that Indian Prime Minister Jawaharlal Nehru, had thought through a grand strategy for the princely states, including a design to ensure that Jammu and Kashmir would be a part of the independent Indian Union. Having a Muslim-majority state in India would also help highlight that country's secular character. For the exact opposite reason, however, Pakistan needed Kashmir to prove the rationale for partition.

Most Pakistani leaders and scholars as well as some Western authors implicate the last British Viceroy, Lord Louis Mountbatten and members of his staff in a plot to draw the partition boundary so that Kashmir would abut both India and Pakistan. Further, under the partition plan the province of Punjab was to be divided between India and Pakistan on grounds of contiguity and its religious majority. The Boundary Commission, led by British judge Sir Cyril Radcliffe, awarded two Muslim-majority *tehsils* (subdivisions) in

Gurdaspur district to India, providing overland access to Kashmir from India. Had the map of the Punjab been drawn differently, Kashmir could have ended up with road access only to Pakistan and a natural mountainous frontier with India, which would have precluded any effective Indian claim on the princely state.

But the chaotic condition of government in the newly born state of Pakistan left little room for planning grand strategy. Pakistanis felt that the Boundary Commission cheated them. The concern about the future of Kashmir was addressed by supporting the pro-Pakistan All Jammu and Kashmir Muslim Conference, which led an agitation against the Maharajah. Pashtun tribesmen were hastily trained in Pakistan's Northwest Frontier Province to enter Kashmir, with support from Pakistani military officers.

The fact that a British general headed the new Pakistani army limited the scope for a declaration of war against the ill-equipped forces of a British-allied Maharajah. The Indians, however, sought support from Kashmir's most popular Muslim leader at the time, Shaikh Abdullah, who did not share Jinnah's vision of Pakistan.

Thus, Pakistan's first move in Kashmir was to announce Jihad by unofficial forces. An unconventional war was started on the assumption that the Kashmiri people would support the invading tribal *lashkar* (unstructured army) and that the Maharajah's forces would be easily subdued. Little, if any, thought had been given to the prospect of failure or to what might happen if the Indian army got involved in forestalling a Pakistani fait accompli.

However, the Kashmir Maharajah did seek Indian military help and signed the Instrument of Accession with India to secure military assistance. India's prime minister, Jawaharlal Nehru, sent in Indian troops to fend off the Azad (Free) Kashmir forces. The Indian army then secured the capital, Srinagar, and established control over the Kashmir valley and most parts of Jammu and Ladakh before a UN-sponsored cease-fire.

The battle over Kashmir so early after independence transformed the ideological confrontation between Muslims and Hindus of which Jinnah often spoke into a military conflict. Within months of independence Pakistan was at war with India. To this day Pakistan disputes

Hari Singh's accession to India, arguing that it was not the result of a voluntary decision and that he was not competent to accede to India because he had signed a standstill agreement with Pakistan earlier.

Ideologues argued that Pakistan should put off normal relations with India "until and unless the Kashmir issue has been settled."[33] By and large this stance has endured ever since. As a result, the state of virtually permanent war with India helped Pakistan's British-trained generals and civil servants establish their dominance over politicians who lacked any real experience in government.

In addition to Kashmir the issue of Pashtunistan, involving Afghanistan, further justified Pakistan's maintenance of the inherited large military. During the nineteenth century Britain and Russia competed for influence in Central Asia in what came to be known as the "Great Game" of espionage and proxy wars. Britain feared that the Russian empire would expand southward, threatening its control over India, the "jewel in the British crown" that had been progressively acquired at great expense over more than a century.

The two empires settled on recognizing Afghanistan as a buffer between them, thus saving them from military confrontations with each other. Previously, the British had lost precious lives in their effort to directly control Afghanistan. But by accepting a neutral and independent Afghan Kingdom, they sought to pass on the burden of subduing some of the lawless tribes to a local monarch, albeit with British economic and military assistance.

In 1893 a British civil servant, Sir Mortimer Durand, drew Afghanistan's frontier with British India, which representatives of both governments agreed upon. The border, named the Durand Line, divided Pashtun tribes living in the area intentionally so as to prevent them from becoming a nuisance for the Raj. On their side of the frontier the British created autonomous tribal agencies that British political officers controlled with the help of tribal chieftains whose loyalty was ensured through regular subsidies. The British used force to put down the sporadic uprisings in the tribal areas but generally left the tribes alone in return for stability along the frontier.

Adjacent to the autonomous tribal agencies were the "settled" Pashtuns who lived in towns and villages under direct British rule.

Here, too, the Pashtuns were divided between the Northwest Frontier province (NWFP) and British Balochistan, which did not enjoy the status of being a full province under British rule. Although Muslim, the Pashtuns generally sided with the cause of anti-British Indian nationalism and were both late and reluctant to embrace the Muslim separatism of the All-India Muslim League's campaign for Pakistan.

Pashtun leader Abdul Ghaffar Khan launched the *Khudai Khidmatgaar* (Servants of God) movement, known as the Red Shirts because of their uniform, and supported the Indian National Congress. In fact, the association between the Red Shirts and the Congress was so close that Ghaffar Khan became known as the "Frontier Gandhi." Even when the 1946 election saw the emergence of the Muslim League as the representative of Muslims throughout British India, Ghaffar Khan's Red Shirts and the Congress remained the dominant political force among Pashtuns and controlled the elected provincial government in Pakistan's northwest.

When the creation of Pakistan appeared inevitable, Ghaffar Khan demanded that the Pashtun areas be allowed independence as "Pashtunistan," a demand that the British did not accept. A referendum was subsequently held in NWFP, which Ghaffar Khan and his supporters boycotted, leading to the region's inclusion in Pakistan.

But soon after Pakistan's independence Afghanistan voted against Pakistan's admission to the United Nations, arguing that Afghanistan's treaties with British India relating to Afghan borders were no longer valid because a new country was being created where none existed at the time when these treaties were signed.

Further, Afghanistan continued to demand the creation of Pashtunistan because it would link the Pashtun tribes living in Afghanistan with those in the NWFP and Balochistan. There were also ambiguous demands for a Baloch state "linking Baloch areas in Pakistan and Iran with a small strip of adjacent Baloch territory in Afghanistan."

From Pakistan's perspective, these calls for separate states amounted to splinter groups demanding the greater part of Pakistan's territory and was clearly unacceptable. But the Afghan demand failed to generate international backing, and Afghanistan did not have the military means to force Pakistan's hand. At the time Afghanistan had a population of twelve million and a small military, which could not constitute a threat to Pakistan. It did not press its claim at the United Nations and instead established diplomatic relations with Pakistan.

The overall feeling of insecurity Pakistan's leadership felt about the future of their fledgling state nevertheless accentuated the possible threat from Afghanistan. The demand for Pashtunistan became part of the combination of perceived security threats that required Pakistan's military buildup, which would need to be backed by great power alliances.

Although India publicly did not support the Afghan claim, Pakistan's early leaders could not separate the Afghan questioning of Pakistani borders from their own perception of an Indian grand design against Pakistan. But Indian leaders, especially Nehru, sought to allay Pakistani fears with public comments affirming India's acceptance of Pakistan. In a speech in March 1948 the Indian prime minister explained that "there is no going back in history" and that India had no desire to "strangle and crush Pakistan and to force it into a reunion with India."

Nehru asked, "If we had wanted to break up Pakistan, why did we agree to partition? It was easier to prevent it then, than to try to do so now after all that has happened." In his view it would be "to India's advantage that Pakistan should be a secure and prosperous State with which we can develop close and friendly relations." He went on to declare that if he were offered the chance to reunite India and Pakistan, he would decline because "I do not want to carry the burden of Pakistan's great problems; I have enough of my own."[34]

India's secretary general for external affairs, Sir Girija Shankar Bajpai, told the US State Department that "India had no desire to eliminate Pakistan as an independent state or to reincorporate into an Indian union the territories now held by Pakistan."[35] Recognizing that political reunion was "most unlikely in the foreseeable future," the Indians expressed the hope for an understanding on joint defense of the Indian subcontinent and possibly a customs union. This reflected Nehru's vision of a "closer association" coming out "of a normal process and in a friendly way which does not end Pakistan as a state but which makes it an equal part of a larger union in which several countries might be associated."[36]

But none of this changed minds in Pakistan. The country's elite had started defining its national interest solely in ideological terms, with its primary goal to secure itself against India. Ensuring Kashmir's inclusion in Pakistan and resolving the Pashtun question were declared as crucial to completing the process of Pakistan's creation. In this way, settling the unfinished business of partition took priority over everything else.

But Pakistan was already short of resources. It needed even more funds to finance the large army it had inherited; an army that was now needed to remain battle ready for the permanent conflict with India. Within a few months of independence the army was on the road to becoming the most powerful political actor in the country; its institutional requirements took priority over all other national needs. Prime Minister Liaquat Ali Khan proudly told troops of the 144 Brigade in Lahore on April 8, 1948, that their government had allocated 75 percent of its budget for national defense.[37]

Moreover, international skepticism about Pakistan's viability and the paucity of resources did not deter its leaders from seeking Western support for the new country, for both its army and its claim over Kashmir. A few months before Pakistan's creation, Jinnah had told General Hastings Ismay, chief of staff to the last viceroy of India, Lord Louis Mountbatten, that "Pakistan could not stand alone" once the British left. Jinnah felt the need for a superpower ally, even before any shots had been exchanged between the Pakistani and Indian armies in Kashmir. Ismay reported his conversation with Jinnah to Mountbatten: "Russia had no appeal for them. France was weak and divided; there remained only England and America, and of these the former was the natural friend." According to Ismay, Jinnah had joked that "Apart from anything else, the devil you know is better than the devil you don't."[38]

* * * * *

This acknowledgement of the need for Western support for Pakistan differed significantly from Jinnah's earlier stance while discussing Pakistan's defense with the British and Congress leaders. The US ambassador in London, John G. Winant, reported to the US secretary of state in February 1946 that Jinnah had been reluctant to commit to joint defense plans for the subcontinent. When Gandhi had apparently raised the question of Pakistan's integration in a common defense plan, according to Winant, "Jinnah had replied that 'his people' looked to linking up with the Arab states."[39]

As independence drew closer, the Muslim League leaders realistically reevaluated their desire for close association with the Arab world. Perceived ideological affinity notwithstanding, there could be no expectation of effective military cooperation from Arab countries. None of them had an armaments industry nor were they known for maintaining high-quality military training establishments. At the time the Arab states also did not have foreign currency reserves that Pakistan could tap for imports.

Jinnah and most of his lieutenants knew Britain well, but Britain's capacity to get the new country on its feet was limited. The British empire was exhausted from the recent world war, which had left the United States and the Soviet Union as global superpowers. Most of Jinnah's lieutenants had never traveled to the United States and knew little about American politics or history. Recognizing this need prior to the partition, Jinnah had urged a Cambridge-educated scion of a prominent merchant family, Mirza Abol Hasan Ispahani, to tour the United States in the mid-1940s to drum up support for an independent Muslim state in South Asia. In a November 1946 letter to Jinnah, Ispahani explained what he knew of the American psyche. "I have learnt that sweet words and first impressions count a lot with Americans," he wrote. "They are inclined to quickly like or dislike an individual or organization."[40] Ispahani later became Pakistan's first ambassador to the United States.

The British realized that their own influence in their former colony would depend on American interest in the region. During a private luncheon with US Ambassador to India, Henry F. Grady, on

July 2, 1947, British Viceroy Mountbatten suggested that the United States should announce its intention of establishing diplomatic relations with Pakistan at an early date. While reporting the suggestion to Washington, Grady added his conclusion that Mountbatten saw an early American commitment of diplomatic representation in Karachi "as an aid to him in his negotiations with Jinnah."[41]

The Americans deferred to the British and hastened the process of establishing ties with Pakistan. The US embassy was the first to open in Karachi, then Pakistan's capital, and US diplomats found access to senior Pakistani leaders relatively easy. After his arrival Paul Alling, the first US ambassador, realized that undoing partition was unrealistic. In a discussion between American ambassadors to India, Pakistan, and Burma, Alling agreed with Ambassador to India Grady that "it is unlikely that the two nations could get together" as they were before partition. He advised that US policy should focus on "good neighborliness rather than unity."[42]

Even a cursory glance at official records of exchanges between Pakistanis and Americans from these early years reveals Pakistan's almost exclusive focus on US military and economic aid. The unconstrained seeking of aid intensified when, after Ambassador Grady's luncheon with Viceroy Mountbatten, formal talks began regarding a US diplomatic presence in Pakistan. Grady reported that Jinnah had been "most cordial, expressed great admiration for the U.S. and said he was hopeful [the] U.S. would aid Pakistan in its many problems."[43]

A few months later Grady was also the first US diplomat to realize that the United States had to be careful when navigating the treacherous waters of India–Pakistan relations. "Indians are very jealous of everything we do for Pakistan," he told his State Department colleagues. "I am constantly questioned on this point in India. If we made a loan to Pakistan, India would resent it unless we gave the same to India. This applies to all matters right down the line."[44]

The United States did not want to choose between a partnership with India or one with Pakistan. Washington was preoccupied with postwar European and Japanese reconstruction as well as the evolving strategy of containing Soviet communist expansion. But this did not stop Pakistanis from demanding attention as the world's largest independent Muslim country. The most frequent visitor from Karachi to Washington was the Pakistani finance minister, Ghulam Muhammad, who came "seeking aid for the new state."[45]

The elite in Pakistan's capital at the time, Karachi, were relatively few and often interconnected. The landed gentry from Pakistan's various provinces had bought or taken over large mansions Hindu businessmen had left behind when they migrated to India. Many of these Pakistani elite represented their districts in the Constituent Assembly that doubled as Parliament. Muslim civil servants and military officers, largely from India, had taken over positions of responsibility in makeshift offices. A few businessmen, often migrants from India, were also prominent.

And American diplomats mingled among these influential people and often found them making identical arguments about Pakistan's future and the ways in which the United States could help the new country. Joseph S. Sparks, who as vice-consul in Karachi, was hardly a policy maker, reported his conversation with local Muslim League leader Yusuf Haroon, a prominent businessman and part owner of *Dawn*, the quasi-official English newspaper. Pakistan was keen on having a foreign policy that was independent and different from India's, and it counted on American help and assistance, Haroon had told Sparks.[46]

Then, less than a month after independence, on September 7, 1947, Jinnah declared at a cabinet meeting: "Pakistan [is] a democracy and communism [does] not flourish in the soil of Islam. It [is] clear that our interests [lie] more with the two great democracies, namely the UK and the USA rather than with Russia."[47] His words were immediately conveyed to American diplomats in Karachi, who duly reported them to Washington. Four days later, on September 11, Jinnah announced in another cabinet meeting that it was important for the United States and the West to ally with Pakistan against the Soviet Union.

"The safety of the North West Frontier [is] of world concern and not merely an internal matter for Pakistan alone," Jinnah said, hinting that the Soviet Union was already hostile to Pakistan. According to him it was "significant to note that Russia alone of all the great countries has not sent a congratulatory message on the birth of Pakistan." But the argument he cited as evidence of Soviet hostility could equally have demonstrated Soviet indifference. After all, at this point there were no relations between Pakistan and the Soviet Union, and there had been no diplomatic or media reports of Soviet ill feeling toward Pakistan. Thus, Jinnah's comment that Soviets had failed to send a congratulatory message was directed at the United States.

Consequently, having taken a position in America's favor, Pakistanis expected the United States to understand their economic and military needs and to offer generous financial support. Also in early September Finance Minister Ghulam Muhammad met with Charge d'Affaires Charles Lewis to discuss the dollars and cents aspect of potential US assistance.[48]

These early requests for aid took the the United States aback somewhat, particularly as Washington did not share Karachi's view of Pakistan's centrality to US strategy. Although Pakistanis thought their offers of cooperation with the United States merited immediate attention and return benefits, US officials saw no urgency to embrace Pakistan. Pakistani officials' expectations were clearly disproportionate to US diplomats' assessments of Pakistan's value.

But Pakistani expectations were not limited to American financing of their new state. Landlords in Karachi wanted American diplomats to rent their properties and pay in dollars. A job with the US embassy, as driver, clerk, or translator, was much sought after, and store owners pursued Americans as preferred customers. During a quiet picnic with US Ambassador Paul Alling, Jinnah and his sister Fatima suggested that the ambassador buy their property, the magnificent Flagstaff House, for his embassy. Alling politely informed the governor-general that the embassy had already obtained another property. The ambassador then sent Jinnah a gift of four ceiling fans after he complained about Karachi's sweltering heat.[49]

In subsequent decades, especially after the collapse of the Soviet Union in 1991, Pakistanis have often complained that the United States failed to reward Pakistan for its contributions during the Cold War. But in 1947–1948 Pakistan had yet to do anything for America,

· · · · ·

yet it still expected huge inflows of US cash, commodities, and arms. There was little discussion among Pakistanis about possible reductions in the size of the army that it inherited from the British so as to lower the fiscal deficit.

Furthermore, Pakistani leaders prioritized the political necessity of avoiding Indian dominance over the economic need to retain regional markets for agricultural products. They also rejected ideas of a customs union or closer economic cooperation with India. Instead, Pakistan's leaders convinced themselves that they deserved special consideration from America, and thus they devoted their energies to securing aid from US leaders.

But Pakistan's most pressing economic problem related to its external reserves. Around the time Ispahani presented credentials as ambassador in Washington, Jinnah sent Mir Laik Ali, a former adviser to the princely state of Hyderabad, on a mission to Washington to seek a $2 billion loan. Ostensibly the money was needed for "the relief and rehabilitation of refugees who have entered Pakistan in a destitute condition from India." However, US officials politely informed the Pakistani emissary that the US government was "not authorized to extend foreign credits for a comprehensive program of this magnitude without prior Congressional approval and appropriation."[50] Furthermore, the State Department was not willing "to recommend such Congressional action." US officials then advised Laik Ali to identify projects that "might qualify for financing by the Export-Import Bank or ultimately by the International Bank."

The US government responded to this first specific plea from Pakistan for financial assistance with $10 million in funding from the War Assets Administration—0.5 percent of the original request. A detailed request for military equipment met a similar fate.

In October–November 1947 Pakistan asked the United States to provide $170 million for Pakistan's army, $75 million for the Air Force, and $60 million for the Navy. Pakistan wanted the United States to help it maintain "a regular army of 100,000 to consist of one armored division, five infantry divisions partly motorized, and a small cavalry establishment" as well as help with payment of personnel. It asked for twelve fighter squadrons (150 planes), four fighter

·····

reconnaissance squadrons (70 planes), three bomber squadrons (50 planes), four transport squadrons (50 planes), and four training wings (200 planes) as well as four light cruisers, sixteen destroyers, four corvettes, twelve coast guard gunboats, and three submarines.

Upon receiving the military shopping list, officials at the State Department and the Pentagon concluded that "Pakistan was thinking in terms of the US as a primary source of military strength and that this would involve virtual US military responsibility for the new dominion."[51] But the United States was not ready to accept this responsibility. "We may defeat our own purpose if by extending assistance to any country in this area we alienate the friendship of one or more of the other South Asian powers," explained an internal US government report. A few months later a British government request for transfer "from British lend-lease stores to the Government of Pakistan, of 5,198,000 rounds of 0.30 caliber and 1,091,000 rounds of 0.50 caliber ammunition" was also turned down.

President Harry Truman concurred with the views of Secretary of State George Marshall, who was also supported by Secretary of Defense James Forrestal, to impose an informal arms embargo on both India and Pakistan while they fought their war in Kashmir. The Truman administration had determined that it was not in America's interest to insert itself in the middle of the India–Pakistan conflict. To avoid publicity, however, the United States did not impose a formal embargo.[52]

Moreover, the United States viewed India as the region's natural leader. State Department and Pentagon officials wrote in a report, "India is the natural political and economic center of South Asia and aid given to the peripheral countries would have to be adapted to conditions in India."[53] Pakistanis who sought parity with India and were totally averse to any suggestion of India's regional preeminence, however, did not share this view.

Thus, the United States had flatly refused to embrace the plan for sustaining Pakistan economically and militarily through large amounts of aid. There were no buyers in Washington for the conception of the new country as the "pivot of the world," as Jinnah had described it. This should have led Pakistan to reevaluate its hopes for a lucrative relationship with the United States. But Pakistan's leaders did not disclose the details of the United States' rejection of their requests for assistance to Pakistan's people for fear that it would undermine the Pakistani national morale or even encourage India to join forces with dissidents within Pakistan so as to break up the country. Maintaining the people's hopes for US aid and the prospect of strength and prosperity was important while Pakistan struggled to get on its feet.

Pakistan made the demand for aid from rich countries to poorer ones an important plank of its foreign policy. This helped form the widely held view within the country that donor countries were obligated to provide aid that should not be tied to political or policy issues. Pakistani delegations at international conferences emphasized this position.

For instance, in November 1947 Ispahani, while leading Pakistan's team to Havana, Cuba, for the UN Conference on Trade and Employment, insisted that the charter of a future international trade organization must "unambiguously" provide for aid for the world's "undeveloped nations, which comprise the majority of the world."[54] But the chief US delegate found the demand unreasonable and likely to sow dissension instead of expanding trade.

Then the Pakistani employers' delegation to the International Labor Organization Conference in San Francisco went even further. They asked for "some sort of Marshall Plan"[55]—the American plan to help Europe rebuilt after World War II—for Pakistan. Prime Minister Liaquat Ali Khan told the United Press in an interview that the United States should initiate an aid package similar to the Marshall Plan to benefit the Middle East and Pakistan.

Other voices in Karachi soon joined the chorus. "Every country in the earlier stages of its development has needed assistance from outside," argued one columnist. "Countries in the Middle East are no exception to this rule, and it is the duty, and should be the privilege, of more advanced countries, and particularly the USA to assist them," he elaborated.[56] Although Pakistan was a South Asian country, its appeals for assistance were based on describing it as an extension of the Middle East.

......

However, not everyone in Pakistan agreed with the clamor for US aid. Bengali politicians from the country's eastern wing proposed normal relations with India so that Pakistani farm products could continue to be sold in their traditional markets. Reducing the tensions that the partition had generated would also enable a reduction in the massive defense budget. Left-wing intellectuals also warned that dependence on US assistance might lead to "economic subjugation" and "political tutelage to America."

"Whatever foreign aid Pakistan accepts must be on terms of its own choosing," the left-wing *Pakistan Times* opined in one of its many editorials. "If American dollars are not available on these terms our country must look elsewhere for help."[57] The Pakistani left's proposed strategy for industrial development was to seek machinery and technical help from Eastern Europe and to adopt austerity at home. Limiting conflict and reducing military spending were also deemed important. But the emerging Pakistani elite did not find the notion of austerity appealing, nor did they consider trimming the military to levels Pakistan could afford.

Then, instead of revisiting the wisdom of their original bet, Pakistan's founders doubled down on seeking alliance with the United States as the source of economic sustenance and military maintenance. Thus, Pakistan initiated elaborate efforts to persuade the United States of Pakistan's value and usefulness as an ally. Pakistani politicians and diplomats charmed Americans in Karachi as well as Washington with their hospitality, during which Pakistani representatives dangled the fear of the young country's people turning against the United States, intelligence about Soviet threats in the region, and offers of military bases and listening posts as instruments to secure American attention.

In addition to Ambassador Ispahani's early observation that Americans respond well to "sweet words and first impressions," Pakistanis had also figured out that US diplomats read the local press carefully and reported back to Washington everything they heard or read where they were assigned. Americans like being liked, Pakistanis thought, so if reports filter into Washington that some Pakistani officials deeply admire the United States, it could favorably influence American policy toward the country. Thus, Pakistani officials missed no opportunity to highlight Pakistan's support for the United States. Local newspapers often ran articles to induce guilt among American diplomats for not being helpful to a struggling nation whose leaders were so favorably disposed toward this superpower. Foreign Minister Zafrulla Khan made this argument when he said that the "well-known friendship of Pakistan toward the U.S. and Pakistan's obvious antipathy to the Russian ideology would seem to justify serious consideration by the US government of the defense requirements of Pakistan."[58]

The Muslim League media also raised the specter that Pakistan may turn against the United States if its needs were not met. In addition, Pakistan tried to balance its Islamo-nationalist aspirations with its pursuit of a Western alliance. That tension came to a head in May 1948, when three thousand protesters mobbed the US Embassy in Karachi, protesting American recognition of the state of Israel. The United Press reported that "Leaders climbed on window ledges of the Embassy and shouted their protests against recognition of Israel inside. American officials rigged up a loudspeaker and Ambassador Paul Alling, through an interpreter, promised to convey the Pakistani sentiment to Washington."[59]

As American diplomats in Karachi pondered the implications of the protest, they concluded that supporting the pro-US government was key to containing anti-American sentiment. No one suspected that the demonstrations could be part of an orchestrated effort to seek American attention.

★

JINNAH'S SUCCUMBING TO tuberculosis in September 1948 jolted Pakistan, leading many analysts around the world to speculate about the future of the country that he had created. Given that Jinnah was a towering personality and his death was indeed a huge loss, concern about its impact on the future of Pakistan was not entirely unfounded. A wire service report from Reuters stated that US diplomatic sources were wondering whether "Mr. Jinnah's disappearance from the political scene would weaken Muslim determination to maintain the partition of India."

This anonymous report stirred an emotional reaction that US representatives abroad were not accustomed to. *Dawn* responded with an indignant editorial titled, "To the Americans," which questioned American diplomats' "pitifully inadequate" understanding of the "conception of Pakistan." Instead of responding to the quoted remark as commentary, *Dawn* reacted as though it were an insidious conspiracy. "Far from weakening the Muslim determination to maintain the partition of the Indo-Pakistan subcontinent," the editorial fired back, "the demise of the Quaid-i-Azam will strengthen it a thousand fold. That's our last word to the world."[60]

Realizing that the remarks from US diplomatic sources had touched a raw nerve, the US embassy in Karachi responded, explaining that "the editorial [in *Dawn*] was based on 'erroneous interpretation'." *Dawn* ran the embassy's clarification along with another editorial, this time titled, "From the Americans." Although the editor accepted the American clarification, he likewise claimed that the altercation had "made clear to all whom it may concern that Pakistan public opinion will not tolerate any attempt by any quarter to question the firmness of our faith in the future of our country."[61]

That a simple speculative comment should elicit such reaction indicated Pakistanis' prickliness about observations of the country's viability. In the six decades since this first Pakistani claim that a single remark in a news report somehow amounted to an attack on Pakistan's integrity, American officials would have to issue many more clarifications, explanations, and apologies. This first angry riposte foretold the rage Americans could expect if they questioned Pakistan's view of events and the nation's sense of self.

Following Jinnah's death, a *Time* magazine article titled, "That Man," described Pakistan's founder as a "man of hate" and "the best showman." It accused Jinnah of being double-faced, stating, "He would stalk into meetings wearing his 'political uniform'—native

• • • • •

dress with a black astrakhan cap—and whip the Moslems into a frenzy. Sometimes, in his fury, his monocle would pop out of its socket. After meetings, he would go home, change to Western clothes and be again the suave Western lawyer." *Time* then suggested that "Jinnah's passing might release a new wave of fanaticism which even he would have opposed" and "that his political heirs might seek the final solution for insolvent, disorganized governments: war."[62]

The Pakistani media's reaction to this article was ferocious. The Urdu press claimed that the article reflected American malice against Pakistan, and an English-language article by Ghulam Moinuddin, a senior civil servant, described the news magazine as "American gutter press" and suggested that "Some wretched malicious Hindu must have said these things to [the] *Time* Correspondent in India and he swallowed it and so did his editor at home."[63]

Reflecting what would become a pattern of psychological warfare aimed at US diplomats, policy makers, and journalists, Moinuddin's rebuttal then became personal: "Why does this type of American behave so towards us? What wrong have we Muslims or Pakistanis done to them? A friend who has been in America suggests to me that the sex life of some of the American reporters in New Delhi and some American female editors in the land of sexy "dates" may have something to do with it. Another friend suggests that all this is due to Jewish money and influence."[64] Pakistani public opinion was being shaped against the United States long before US foreign policy provided Pakistanis a reason for anti-Americanism.

An implicit threat then followed Moinuddin's ad hominem attack. The people who have maligned our leader, he contended, were the same people who "malign the Russians. No Russian newspaper has slandered us so. They seem to be lots more decent that way." In other words, if Americans did not learn to respect Pakistan and its people, Pakistan would turn to the Russians, who had not hurled any criticism or insult toward this new country. The Soviet Union, however, had not changed its conduct (or lack thereof) with Pakistan: not only had the Soviets not criticized Pakistan or its founder; they in fact had yet to show any interest whatsoever in the world's most populous

Muslim country carved out of the British Raj. Pakistan was eager to play the Soviet card when seeking American attention, but to do that they needed Moscow's interest.

Based on the State Department's assessment that India was the more important of the two new dominions, President Truman sent an invitation in mid-1949 for Prime Minister Nehru to visit Washington. Pakistanis saw this as a slight; they expected to be treated at least equally to India. Liaquat, in particular, had invested heavily in developing rapport with US diplomats, but now he felt he had nothing to show to the Pakistani people for his pro-American stance. There had been no progress in Kashmir, aid had failed to flow, and now the Americans preferred Nehru over him as their first South Asian state visitor.

Liaquat's efforts, however, had not been in vain. In his book *The United States and Pakistan, 1947–2000: Disenchanted Allies*, career diplomat Dennis Kux detailed how American diplomats in Karachi admired "the small band of overworked, highly motivated, and idealist civil servants who struggled to establish their new country." Further, junior diplomats had access to government leaders, including Liaquat, and were invited to social functions without regard to rank or status. "The gregarious prime minister enjoyed entertaining at his home, at times asking American guests to remain for late-night jazz sessions, during which Liaquat enthusiastically beat the drums," Kux noted. "It was hard for the embassy staff not to empathize with the Pakistanis and their view of the troubles with India over Kashmir and other issues."[65] But the assessment in Washington was clearly different. Thus, US diplomats' personal ties with their Pakistani counterparts possibly caused Pakistanis to hold exaggerated expectations that were crushed when Nehru received precedence over Liaquat in Washington.

Liaquat then decided to respond to what he saw as an American snub by pretending to turn to the Soviet Union, even though Pakistan had no formal relations with the other world superpower at this time. Pakistan's ambassador to Iran, Raja Ghazanfar Ali, leveraged his personal ties with his Soviet counterpart in Tehran to seek an invitation for Liaquat from Moscow. The ambassador arranged a meeting between Liaquat and the Soviet charge d'affaires, Ali Aliev, at dinner, where Liaquat conveyed his interest in visiting the Soviet Union. Aliev managed to secure an invitation, which was transmitted and accepted through Ambassador Ghazanfar Ali in Tehran.[66] Soon after the invitation Pakistan and the Soviet Union established diplomatic relations.

Although the Soviets did nothing to arrange a trip and Liaquat never went to Moscow, the news of an invitation had the desired result. Soon after Nehru's visit to Washington, Truman approved an invitation for Liaquat that George McGhee, assistant secretary of state for Near East Asia, delivered before the year's end during a visit to the region. The first Pakistani official to meet McGhee, Finance Minister Ghulam Muhammad, told him that the United States had to appear to treat Pakistan at par with India; it was "of the utmost importance," McGhee related, that Liaquat was accorded a reception equal to what Nehru received.[67]

Muhammad also attempted to convince the United States of the importance of creating an Islamic economic bloc, an idea Jinnah originally introduced. McGhee responded by pointing out that Islamic countries' economies were not complementary. Thus, cooperation between countries producing more or less similar goods from primitive agricultural economies, he elaborated, would not yield substantial gains.

"I did not believe that religion in itself provided a basis for a separate economic grouping," McGhee wrote later. He also noted that Muhammad shared details of his speech at the recent Islamic economic conference hosted by Pakistan but that he had edited out anti-Western statements he had made. The American diplomat did not call out the Pakistani official on that doublespeak, instead holding out the promise of economic aid.

The visiting US Assistant Secretary of State then told a press conference in Karachi that the "U.S. is becoming increasingly aware of the importance of Pakistan and of our relations with Pakistan." This resulted in again kindling Pakistani officials' hopes of becoming an American ally. But others were not convinced. *Pakistan Times* ran a cartoon of McGhee as a Yankee spider wearing a black top hat and

* * * * *

smoking a cigar in his web as he attracted Pakistani leaders to their fate, whereas the *Civil and Military Gazette's* cartoon showed Uncle Sam offering Pakistan an empty hat labeled "Foreign Policy," while India was given a hat full of trade agreements and dollar loans.

✦

MEANWHILE, PAKISTAN STARTED preparing for Liaquat's trip by creating military shopping lists. Ghulam Muhammad along with Defense Secretary Iskander Mirza undertook most of this preparatory work. Both Muhammad and Mirza were civil servants who later became heads of state and played a crucial role both in US-Pakistan relations as well as in Pakistan's subsequent evolution as a national security state.

Mirza sought Sherman tanks, tank spare parts, radar equipment, and recoilless guns, among other things, preferably as direct aid because the country could not afford to spend its limited hard currency reserves on acquiring these commercially. He was aware that the United States had been reluctant in the past to supply Pakistan with military materiel and assumed this was because "America was doubtful of Pakistan's attitude towards communism."[68] In his view, if only Liaquat would clearly spell out where Pakistan stood in the East-West conflict, the Americans would almost certainly loosen their purse strings.

But the State Department's forty-one page briefing memorandum for the White House ahead of the Liaquat visit offered a very different picture. "The entire South Asian region is of relatively secondary importance to the US from a military point of view," it pointed out, adding that one possible value of Pakistan might be as location for US aircraft in event of war with the Soviet Union. But the memorandum emphasized the need not to openly voice the United States' lack of interest in the region "since it negates our oft-expressed interest in helping the region for economic reasons."[69]

Consequently, as the Pakistanis were overemphasizing their commitment to the anti-Communist cause to secure American interest, the Americans were likewise pretending to be attentive even though their interest was less than what they publicly stated.

This brief for the president explained that "Liaquat was well disposed toward the US and 'Western ways'" but had to contend with "strong local opinion which still considers western nations imperialistic." America's relations with Pakistan were basically friendly, it said, while listing US policy on Palestine, "leniency towards India in the Kashmir dispute," and "favoring India at the expense of Pakistan" as irritants. According to the brief, Pakistan's economic requests thus far had "seemed impracticable," and the United States could not "make available to Pakistan any large quantity" of military equipment because other countries facing greater threats than Pakistan needed that equipment.

On May 3, 1950, Truman and several cabinet members received Liaquat and his beautiful wife, Ráana, when they arrived at Washington's National Airport. They stayed in the United States for a full three weeks, one week less than Nehru's four-week trip almost a year earlier. In Washington there was the full range of formalities associated with state visits: a formal state dinner; addresses to the two houses of Congress, though not a joint session; a press conference at the National Press Club; a dinner hosted by the secretary of state and a reception given by Ambassador Ispahani.

The *Washington Times-Herald* covered the secretary's white-tie dinner on its social pages, boasting the headline, "Came and Conquered." Separately, Assistant Secretary of State McGhee was impressed by Liaquat's ability to consume alcoholic drinks, forbidden by Islam, without appearing to have drunk at all. But Liaquat's social successes in Washington had to be kept a secret from his own people back home.

Only a few months had elapsed since the prime minister had committed his government to making Pakistan's constitution subservient to Islamic values. His ability to hold his drink, impressive in Washington, would have destroyed his reputation in Karachi with the mullahs who supported his *Objectives Resolution* in Pakistan's legislature. The resolution declared that Pakistan would be an Islamic state run by men according to God's law. "He was a big, strong, confident man with considerable international stature," McGhee enthused, saying that he found Liaquat to be "a man you could do business with."[70]

The personal qualities of Liaquat and his wife—"he brimming with smiles and she bursting with energy and exuberance"[71]—overcame difficult political questions. Liaquat criticized the United States at the University of Chicago, saying that it "was interested only in the possibility of a war with the U.S.S.R. and not in the peace of the world." He wanted America both to increase its aid for the people in the East and to play a more active role in Kashmir, "the most dangerous dispute facing the world today." But these remarks were deemed insignificant, and McGhee described them as attempts to assuage neutralist public opinion in Pakistan.

McGhee, the official who was responsible for policy toward South Asia, formed favorable impressions of both Muhammad and Liaquat. "They understood how much help they needed if their new state was to survive their keen competition with India and make a go of it," the assistant secretary noted. He liked that the Pakistanis sought US aid on US terms and promised support to help the United States build defenses against global communism. To McGhee and some others in the administration, "Compared with the wishy-washy neutralist Indians, they were a breath of fresh air."[72]

But there was little substantive discussion on Pakistan's wish list, and Liaquat generated a lot less enthusiasm in Washington than Nehru had. The Senate lacked a quorum when the Pakistani leader arrived to address it, and the proceedings were delayed by half an hour.[73] Further, according to Kux, Truman did not even have a business meeting with the prime minister, and a session between Secretary of State Dean Acheson and Liaquat scheduled for after the state dinner "did not take place because the State Department protocol officer failed to inform the Pakistanis." Although Secretary of Defense Louis Johnson and Chairman of the Joint Chiefs of State General Omar Bradley met Liaquat at the Pentagon for functional meetings, they merely noted Pakistan's interest in obtaining arms instead of giving even a nominal response.[74]

......

The Pakistani spin on the visit, however, was markedly different. The visit was meant partly to bolster Liaquat's prestige at home and partly to keep alive the anticipation of American largesse, which was necessary in order to maintain national self-confidence. *Dawn* described the meetings with Johnson and Bradley as "secret" and implied that Pakistan's request for arms was being seriously considered. Liaquat ostensibly made the argument that military assistance "would serve the interests of the entire free world." He "stressed his nation's strategic position and the fighting qualities of her anti-Communist Muslim warriors."[75] In response to these reports, there was great excitement in Karachi. Pakistan's media ran details of every event the prime minister attended, such as a dinner at International House New Orleans, and depicted it as a breakthrough in winning American hearts and minds.

Liaquat's decision to visit the United States for three weeks when he had not undertaken a similar long trip to any of the Muslim countries was criticized by Islamists and others, who wanted to focus Pakistan's external relations on the Islamic world. Pakistani diplomat Samuel Martin Burke offered an explanation for the relatively long duration of the visit. After the formalities of Washington, Liaquat had spent the rest of his visit introducing Pakistan to Americans, which was necessary because "the real reasons for the establishment of Pakistan were not sufficiently understood abroad." Pakistan, Burke argued, was seen as "a backward theocratic state as compared to a forward-looking secular India."[76]

And Liaquat had encountered several reminders of Americans' ignorance about Pakistan. When introducing Liaquat to the US Senate, Vice President Alben S. Barkley described him as the prime minister of Pakistan, "which originally was a part of India." A British embassy cable wryly wondered whether the Pakistani prime minister had succeeded in convincing US policy makers of Pakistan's importance. "Mr. Liaquat Ali Khan probably learnt more about America than Americans learnt about Pakistan," the cable noted. According to the British diplomat writing the cable, at a luncheon a California businessman asked Liaquat "whether the blank space between the two parts of Pakistan as shown on the menu card was Africa."[77]

·····

Although the American media covered Liaquat favorably, there were fewer stories about his visit than there had been about Nehru's earlier sojourn. The *New York Times* described his anticommunist statements as "heartwarming" and saw them as a "pledge that the Pakistanis will stand and be counted among those who are devoted to freedom, regardless of the cost."[78]

In a Foreign Policy Association meeting in New York, Liaquat elucidated Pakistan's security needs in relation to India while also declaring unequivocal opposition to communism. "There have always been certain sections of opinion in India which resented the birth of Pakistan," he said, adding, "if they accepted it they did so with strong mental reservations."[79] According to Liaquat, even after the creation of Pakistan, its territorial integrity was constantly under threat. But the creation of Pakistan would not lead to instability in Asia, as many people believed, but instead to stability. Pakistan could be a useful ally for the West, and the United States should grasp the hand of friendship that Pakistan was extending.

Liaquat emphasized Pakistan's key strategic location in Asia with its eastern wing bordering Burma, making it a part of Southeast Asia. In addition, Pakistan's western wing bordered Iran and Afghanistan and was thus important with respect to any "communications to and from the oil-bearing areas of the Middle East." His argument was simple: if Americans helped with Pakistan's existential challenges, Pakistan could help protect American strategic interests in both Southeast Asia and the Middle East. Earlier in the trip, during his press conference at the National Press Club, Liaquat was asked how large an army he envisaged for Pakistan. He replied that this depended on "this great country of yours. ... If your country will guarantee our territorial integrity, I will not keep any army at all."[80]

In response, George Kennan, counselor of the State Department, decided to reply candidly to Liaquat's plea for America to assume responsibility for Pakistan's security. After Liaquat's speech at the Foreign Policy Association, Kennan said that the United States had to act with "great prudence and restraint and observe the utmost care not to enter into relationships which might become the subjects of misunderstandings either here or in the partner-country or elsewhere."

• • • • •

Kennan's message was clear: Pakistan should not pin inflated hopes to the United States. "We want our friends to understand the complexities of our situation and to refrain from expecting us to do things which we cannot do," Kennan went on. "You will note I say our friends must not expect us to do things which we cannot do. It is no less important that they should not expect us to be things which we cannot be."[81] But the overall success of the prime minister's visit prevented Kennan's message from being fully understood in Pakistan. Defense Secretary Mirza and others supposed that military aid would now be forthcoming.

Coinciding with Liaquat's visit to America, North Korea began its invasion of South Korea, leading to the Korean War. Pakistan then supported the US effort to send troops to Korea under the UN flag and even lobbied Arab states in the United Nations on Washington's behalf. When Secretary of State Dean Acheson thanked Ispahani for Pakistan's support[82] officials in Karachi immediately saw an opportunity to ask for military equipment as payoff for Pakistani support. But Ispahani warned Mirza in a letter that Mirza was being "overly optimistic."

Advising realism, Ispahani wrote, "We have had in the past promises for the sympathetic consideration of our demands but unfortunately none of them have so far borne fruit. I shall therefore, be pleasantly surprised if anything materializes on this occasion as well." Commenting on Mirza's request to ask the Americans for two hundred latest-type tanks, Ispahani observed, "Your optimism really startles me. Those are still on the top secret list and have not yet been made available to even the Atlantic Pact countries."[83]

The Pakistani embassy in Washington had a clearer idea of the conditions that the United States might attach if it agreed to provide arms for the Pakistani military. Pakistan, Ispahani explained, would most likely have to limit the use of American weapons to legitimate self-defense and guarantee that it would not undertake any act of aggression against any other state. Mirza saw no problem with the conditions. "Pakistan will be expected to help with her armed forces in a situation like Korea where the UN asked the nations for armed help against North Koreans," Mirza retorted. "But in the view of what has happened in the past, Pakistan can limit her help to declarations in favor of the UN."[84]

As the war in Korea began, the United States sought troops for the war from several countries, including Pakistan. Based on Liaquat's conversations during his trip, the Pentagon considered Pakistan a prime candidate for providing a contingent for the UN force assembled under the command of General Douglas MacArthur. Indeed, the only reference to Pakistan in Truman's *Memoirs* relates to MacArthur's discussion about the countries from which he expected to draw troops.

These American requests in turn created a false impression in Karachi. Liaquat and his team overestimated the American need for Pakistani soldiers. Liaquat told Ambassador Avra Warren that if the United States needed Pakistan's help, it should reciprocate by helping Pakistan in its disputes over Kashmir and Afghanistan. "Liaquat said bluntly that now is the time for decision," Warren reported to Secretary of State Acheson. Pakistan would move with the Americans "not only in Korea but also in [the] Middle East and to commit themselves irrevocably" to issues of interest to the United States, but the "US must give him a commitment that will assure his people."

Liaquat then offered "one or more division for use in Korea out of seven now under arms" in return for US support "against Nehru's defiance of the UN with the threat of a rigged election in Kashmir this summer." According to Warren, Liaquat also wanted the United States to "bring our influence to bear" in Afghanistan and put an end to what Liaquat described as "the Pashtun nonsense." US Ambassador Warren sympathized with Liaquat's proposed quid pro quo and, in response, recommended strengthening the UN resolution on Kashmir and accepting the offer of a Pakistani infantry division for Korea. He also suggested that "we ask Liaquat what practical assistance he needs" for Pakistan's military and industrial posture "to assist in defense of Middle East from Commie aggression."[85]

But Acheson, known for being one of the "wise men" of the emerging US foreign policy establishment, wrote back, saying that the United States did not need Pakistani troops in exchange for "complete and unqualified support" on Kashmir and Pashtun issues.

Pakistan, Acheson replied, should send troops to Korea "as a responsibility" under the UN Charter and should not use it as a "bargaining tool." The United States would equip and maintain the Pakistani division in Korea but could not accept Liaquat's proposal. According to Acheson, aligning with Pakistan in its regional disputes would completely alienate India and Afghanistan and thus limit US freedom of action in dealing with "complex present and future issues in Asia."[86]

Pakistan had proposed a transactional relationship, but Acheson had turned it down. The decision reflected the State Department's annual policy statement, which identified relatively modest goals in US-Pakistan relations. It described, "the orientation of its government and people toward the US and other Western democracies and away from the USSR" as America's fundamental interest in Pakistan.

The US government understood that "Pakistan remains dependent upon outside assistance for defense and for economic development" and was willing to "assist Pakistan within the limits of our capabilities." But the United States gained no advantage by getting entangled in regional issues on behalf of Pakistan. The Truman administration also sought to discourage any notion of America having unlimited capacity or intention to assist Pakistan in its defense and development.

"If disruptive forces remain in check," the US policy statement predicted in 1950, "Pakistan will emerge after India as the strongest power between Turkey and Japan on the periphery of Asia." But it also said prophetically that the United States would have to "remind the Pakistanis that we are neither pro-Indian, pro-Israel nor anti-Muslim."[87]

Although Acheson and his colleagues preferred not to get involved in the India-Pakistan rivalry, India's refusal to support the West in the evolving Cold War continually annoyed them. For instance, India sided with the Soviet Union and communist China in opposing the Peace Treaty with Japan on grounds that it failed to provide for return of the island of Formosa (Taiwan) to China. Further, Indian Prime Minister Nehru did not support the US position on Korea, suggesting instead that if Beijing had its rightful representation in the UN Security Council, war could have been averted.

. . . . .

Acheson later observed in his memoirs that Nehru "was one of the most difficult men with whom I have ever had to deal."[88]

The United States' refusal of his conditional offer of support in Korea stunned Liaquat. Nonetheless, his government did not give up hopes of getting arms and political support from America to use against India and Afghanistan. Meanwhile, the urgency of US economic assistance for Pakistan in order to maintain the balance of payments eased somewhat as the global market price of principal commodities rose due to what came to be known as the "Korean War Boom," though the need for defense assistance persisted. Pakistani officials considered that a stronger anticommunist stance in Karachi was the right formula for getting what Pakistan really wanted from the United States.

Then, in October 1951, Liaquat was assassinated while addressing a public rally in the garrison town of Rawalpindi. The lone gunman was a disgruntled Pashtun, motivated by what he perceived to be the prime minister's un-Islamic attitude. The killing came on the heels of a coup attempt by disgruntled military officers earlier in the year, and this had been tenuously linked to a group of communist intellectuals. The officers seeking to overthrow the government wanted more robust military operations in Kashmir. Although he had sought arms for Pakistan's military ostensibly to fight communists, the two issues that cast a long shadow on Liaquat's time as prime minister were ultimately the Pashtun and Kashmir disputes.

Liaquat was Jinnah's undisputed successor, and his assassination left Pakistan without a unifying charismatic leader. Power passed into the hands of a group of civil servants led by Ghulam Muhammad and Iskander Mirza. This group had been most eager in pursuing the option of large-scale American aid as the means of consolidating the fledgling Pakistani state. Now that Liaquat was out of the way, they had a powerful ally in Sandhurst-trained General Muhammad Ayub Khan, who had become the first Pakistani to command its army after taking over from British general Sir Douglas Gracey. The enthusiasm Jinnah's campaign generated for Pakistan had by now begun to wane. The Muslim League splintered into factions, resulting in frequent changes of government ministers and increasing reliance on the military as the source of stability. The ill-defined ideal of a South Asian Muslim homeland was now mired in fractious feudal politics as generals and civil servants scrambled to put together plans for their country's security and prosperity.

Chapter Two

Aid, Arms, and Bases

On a warm Friday in June 1953 Pakistani and American dignitaries, flanked by an army band, assembled alongside the wharf in Baltimore Harbor. The SS *Anchorage Victory* was setting sail for Karachi with nine thousand tons of wheat, the first shipment of seven hundred thousand tons to be donated under the United States' Pakistan Wheat Aid Act. This came about after Pakistan faced two successive crop failures due to lack of monsoon rains and did not have hard currency to buy wheat on the international market.

The State Department had concluded that there was a real danger of famine in Pakistan, and a grant-in-aid from US wheat surpluses was considered the only practical way of preventing famine. Borrowing was an option, but Pakistan's ability to repay the loan without retarding economic growth was questionable.

So President Dwight D. Eisenhower asked the Eighty-Third Congress to authorize the administration to send up to one million tons of wheat to Pakistan, valued at $75 million. The Congress acted quickly to pass the Pakistan-specific law, and shipments began within two weeks of the president's request. "Everything about this action is commendable," said a *New York Times* editorial. It would "relieve distress in Pakistan" and would serve as "the mark of our friendly concern with the needs of others."[1]

On the Pakistani side, the semi-official *Dawn* described the American decision to provide wheat as "a noble gesture." But the paper

......

56

carefully avoided expressing gratefulness; instead, it insisted that Pakistan's food security could be guaranteed only after it had absorbed Kashmir and ensured control of the sources of rivers flowing into it. Although the famine that had just been averted had little to do with Kashmir, *Dawn* suggested that it did. The Americans had helped solve the immediate problem, but apparently they also needed to resolve the India–Pakistan dispute to earn true appreciation.[2]

Internal discussions within the Eisenhower administration had also focused on Pakistan's famine less as a humanitarian problem than as a political one. The US mission sent to Pakistan to examine the wheat shortage had concluded that "it was in the security interest of the US to extend food assistance to Pakistan at the earliest." In addition to averting the threat of famine, officials were concerned about "the possible political and financial collapse of the friendly government of an important and strategic country."[3]

The US ambassador, Avra Warren, had reported some time back that the Soviets were willing to barter four hundred thousand tons of wheat in exchange for Pakistani cotton and jute.[4] Although there had been no independent confirmation of this offer, the United States felt that keeping Pakistan in the Western camp was important.

The Wheat Aid Act marked the first major success in Pakistan's wooing of America. The election of Eisenhower, a Republican, as US president, aided Pakistan's relationship with the United States. Eisenhower was overall tougher about confronting the Soviet Union, and India's stubborn refusal to get drawn into the Cold War further helped Pakistan's case.

During the presidential election campaign Eisenhower aides had spoken of their plans for "bringing strategically situated Pakistan into the free world's defense system" and for "building a Pakistani army and eventually locating American airfields there."[5] Additionally, the new secretary of state, John Foster Dulles, saw the world in Manichaean terms. He did not know much about the subcontinent, but he did know that a willing ally was preferable to someone who preferred to sit on the sidelines of the great ideological conflict of the age. Dulles had told the *New York Times* soon after Eisenhower's election that "the strong spiritual faith and martial spirit of the

......

people" of Pakistan "make them a dependable bulwark against communism."[6]

But Dulles had been wary of India's leaders long before he became Eisenhower's secretary of state. British conservatives, many of whom saw India unfit for self-governance and a potential target for Soviet penetration after British withdrawal, heavily influenced his view of South Asia. Months before partition Dulles had told the National Publishers Association in New York that "In India, Soviet Communism exercises a strong influence through the interim Hindu government" led by Jawaharlal Nehru.

Ironically, the interim government Dulles criticized also included representatives of Jinnah's Muslim League. But Dulles had already made up his mind that the Muslims were inherently anticommunist whereas the Hindus were willing to let communism influence them. Because the US embassy in New Delhi rejected this suggestion, Secretary of State Marshall undertook to try to give Dulles "a more complete picture of the Indian situation."[7] Later developments proved that Dulles never got that complete picture and maintained the prejudice he had initially voiced.

Under Dulles's stewardship the Eisenhower administration moved from Truman's cautious policy of Soviet-power containment to a more aggressive anticommunism stance throughout the world. He and many others saw Asia as the major battleground against communist ideology. The Soviet satellites in Europe, he reasoned, had seen better days so they were predisposed to resisting Soviet influence. In Asia, however, the reverse was true; the Soviet system could be seen in poverty-ridden Asian nations as a better option.

"The Russian intruding into Europe is viewed as an Asiatic," remarked foreign affairs columnist C. L. Sulzberger, explaining how Dulles viewed the world. "The same Russian intruding into Asia comes as a European."[8] The United States had to make sure that Asian states did not succumb to the temptation of embracing communist ideology in a quest for superior social organization, modernity, and literacy, as the region's "illiterate, impoverished feudality" offered fertile ground for communism to advance. So the United States preferred allies who prioritized resisting communism to those who focused on changing living conditions at home, even if it involved doing business with the Soviets.

Muhammad Ali Bogra, who had succeeded Ispahani as Pakistan's ambassador to the United States, had seen an opportunity for Pakistan as he watched the US presidential election campaign in 1952. He calculated that Pakistan could secure economic and military aid by portraying itself as a frontline state in the battle against communism.

With this in mind, Bogra, the scion of a Bengali aristocratic family, arrived in Washington months before Eisenhower's election and ingratiated himself with the Republican elite. He went bowling with hard-line anticommunists and convinced them of Pakistan's anticommunist credentials. He also advanced the idea that Pakistan's army was the only army in the region willing to fight Soviet influence and incursions. That there was no significant Soviet influence in the region hardly mattered to men like Dulles, who were eager to implement their grand global strategy.

But Pakistan's domestic politics at the time were chaotic and byzantine. Ghulam Muhammad, the powerful former finance minister, was now governor-general. National elections had been postponed indefinitely, and political factions vied for influence in an environment of palace intrigue. Those in power were primarily concerned with the paucity of resources to run the government as well as to maintain the British-inherited army.

Along with Defense Secretary Iskander Mirza and the army commander, General Muhammad Ayub Khan, the governor-general concerned himself with securing economic and military aid for Pakistan more than other political concerns. Within months of Eisenhower's inauguration Governor-General Muhammad decided to appoint Bogra as prime minister, hoping that his standing in Washington would help with Pakistan's quest for aid.

Bogra was ensconced as prime minister when Dulles visited twelve countries in an attempt to rally Middle Eastern and South Asian countries in a global crusade against communism. The US secretary of state was received warmly in Pakistan, but felt that the Indians rebuffed him when they told him outright that they would not join

· · · · ·

any military alliance. Even before independence Nehru had declared that India would "keep away from the power politics of groups, aligned against one another, which have led in the past to world wars and which may again lead to disasters on an even faster scale."[9]

On several occasions Nehru tried to explain to American officials that his vision for India was one of nonalignment, not neutrality, in the US-Soviet struggle. Although his sister, Vijay Lakshmi Pandit, while serving as New Delhi's ambassador in Moscow right after independence, told her US counterpart that most Indian leaders knew that their "natural alignment" was with the West, Nehru recognized India's "relative impotence." He felt that a nation "still in swaddling clothes" should not talk about "military participation in event of war."

Pandit's view, which her brother shared, was that "India's role in the family of nations should be modest and relatively humble" until the nation had solved some of its basic internal problems.[10] Conversely, Pakistani leaders saw external alliances as a means of addressing their domestic issues. They were all too willing to privately discuss joining a US-led military alliance as long as assurances of arms and aid accompanied it. They also sought US support in Pakistan's conflicts with Afghanistan and India.

Without realizing the complexity of the issues involved, Dulles thought he could help Pakistan cut a deal with its neighbors. American officials also ignored the Pakistani government's policy of keeping discussions of alliance with the United States secret from the country's Parliament and media. The calculus of the Ghulam Muhammad-Mirza-Ayub trio was that they would bargain for the highest bidder for Pakistan's support. The absence of political support at home would serve as a convenient way of getting out of fulfilling promises to Americans as well as being the basis for renegotiating that price.

On his return, Dulles identified four sources of what he said was "fear, bitterness and weakness" in the Middle East–South Asia region. In addition to "the overwhelming poverty of the entire area," he felt that the United States could enlist the region's nations as allies after solving three quarrels: the Egyptian–British dispute over the

* * * * *

Suez Canal, the Arab-Israeli hostility, and the India-Pakistan dispute over Kashmir.[11] This view was somewhat simplistic, as history demonstrates that only one of the three has been resolved six decades later: after the failed Anglo-French-Israeli invasion of 1956, France and Britain no longer own the Suez Canal.

In addition to Dulles, eleven other US officials visited Pakistan over the summer of 1953. That year had also seen a massive decline in the world prices of cotton and jute, the two items that accounted for 85 percent of Pakistan's exports. Given the adverse economic conditions, the flurry of visitors from Washington bolstered Pakistan's hopes of tapping the US treasury. As the country's leaders had failed to make plans for dealing with economic crisis, "The Americans will soon rescue us" was also a formula for the country's ruling class's political survival.

The United States decided to supply wheat and avert famine in Pakistan soon after Dulles's first visit. Although the wheat was welcomed in Pakistan, it was not considered enough. From the point of view of Pakistan's army, one million tons of wheat was hardly adequate compensation for what it was being asked to do on behalf of the free world. The real prize would be military equipment, which the United States had not yet promised. Frustrated with the civilians' negotiations, Ayub decided to take matters in his own hand.

Just prior to when Muhammad, Pakistan's civilian head of state, and Zafrulla Khan, the foreign minister, visited the United States, Ayub also made a trip there.[12] He sought a "deal whereby Pakistan could—for the right price—serve as the West's eastern anchor in an Asian alliance structure."[13] Even though the Americans had arranged a series of visits to US military facilities for the Pakistan army commander, Ayub stormed into the office of Assistant Secretary of State Henry Byroade and said, "For Christ's sake, I didn't come here to look at barracks. Our army can be your army if you want us. But let's make a decision."[14]

However, by the end of its first year in office, the Eisenhower administration was seeking to reduce American involvement in military operations like those undertaken in Korea, and it aimed to do this by building up frontline states' military capability. The idea of a

Middle East defense organization was shelved in favor of creating a "Northern Tier of Defense" against Soviet expansion, with Iraq, Iran, Turkey, and Pakistan as its partners.

Each of these countries presented its own unique problems. Iran could not be included in such an arrangement until its left-leaning Prime Minister Mohammad Mossadegh was deposed. Iraq's weak monarchy and Turkey's Kemalist regime extracted their own benefits from the Americans. And in the case of Pakistan, the issue was overcoming India's objections.

Dulles and his brother Allen, who now headed the Central Intelligence Agency (CIA), saw Pakistan's usefulness primarily in terms of its geographic location, an opinion that resonated with the Pakistani leadership's own views. A National Intelligence Estimate (NIE) at the time argued that "given sufficient inducement, Pakistan would probably be willing to authorize Western use of Pakistan air and naval bases in wartime and possibly Western development of such bases in peacetime." Military aid was regarded as that incentive.

Moreover, the NIE argued that the United States would have to arm Pakistan if it wanted Pakistan to play a role in military operations such as the one in Korea. "Even with substantial Western military aid, Pakistan could probably furnish few if any troops for early employment outside the subcontinent in the absence of a comprehensive settlement with India," the CIA asserted. It noted that Pakistan's forces were "small even for their primary mission of defense of Pakistan's borders" but that the country could be "of potential military value to the West because of the strategically located airbases which it can provide."[15]

But Eisenhower was eager not to push India away while courting Pakistan. In a note to Dulles he pointed out that the subcontinent was "one area of the world where, even more than most cases, emotion rather than reason seems to dictate policy." He asked his secretary of state to be watchful "to see that we do not create antagonism unnecessarily." In his reply Dulles agreed, stating that with India and Pakistan, it was "difficult to help one without making an enemy of the other."[16]

The NIE addressed that problem by claiming that there was no likelihood of war between India and Pakistan. India-Pakistan relations were better than they had been at any time since partition, and India had "little desire to risk its present position" in Kashmir. In a major error of judgment, the NIE claimed, "Pakistan, with the weaker bargaining position, appears more willing to compromise and may eventually become reconciled to its inability to shake India's grip on Kashmir; there are already some signs that Pakistani emotionalism on the subject is beginning to subside."

The CIA recognized that Pakistan's apparent willingness to join US military arrangements for the region were "motivated largely by a desire to strengthen Pakistan's military position vis-à-vis India." But it assumed that Pakistan would be willing to provide troops for defending the Middle East in return for US assurances of securing its Indian borders. Pakistan's leaders would "drive as hard a bargain as possible and would almost certainly expect substantial military and economic assistance." But, the CIA believed, they would come around in the end and align their security policies with those of the West.

This assessment failed to take into account the effect on Pakistan's posture once they felt stronger after receiving US arms. After all, the weapons the United States gave to Pakistan for a future battle with the Soviet Union could easily be used in fighting India. But according to the NIE, even though Indian and Pakistani forces were lined up against each other, hostilities were not likely to resume. "India has virtually no incentive to risk a war," the CIA told the US government. "Despite past talk of a second round, Pakistan's leaders, particularly the military, appear to be convinced of the folly of attacking India's superior forces," it concluded, arguing that the likelihood of sharp reaction from the Western powers would deter Pakistan against such a move. In the years to come these calculations proved terribly wrong.

★

PAKISTANI LEADERS HAD concealed from their people the negotiations for US military aid in the possible exchange for bases. Maintaining similar secrecy, however, was not possible in Washington. The State Department had to seek appropriations for aid to Pakistan, and it had to share its reasoning for it with members of Congress. There were the inevitable leaks into the US media as well.

In Pakistan those who opposed allying with the West questioned their government's "stubborn refusal to discuss the vital question of Pakistan's possible association in a US-sponsored military pact." It was "symptomatic of their lack of respect for the Parliament and the people" wrote the *Pakistan Times*.[17] India also reacted strongly, leading to belated public comments from the Pakistan government on what it was seeking from the United States.

Governor-General Ghulam Muhammad denied that Pakistan intended to join US-led alliances or had offered to provide military bases. "Reports that my government is negotiating with the U.S. Government for military assistance in return for American bases in Pakistan are absolutely unfounded and baseless," he declared in a statement issued from London, where he was visiting at the time. He also said, "Pakistan will never be a camp-follower of anyone," implying that Pakistan's desired foreign policy was, like India, one of nonalignment.[18]

But the official statement was a blatant lie. That it was told should have rung alarm bells in Washington. If an agreement was reached on an arms-for-bases deal later, how would Muhammad explain his earlier perfunctory denial of its discussion? Keeping secret large-scale naval or air force bases, which was what Dulles sought, would be impossible. Thus, the Pakistani government obviously had no intention of providing the bases it was dangling in front of the Americans.

An opportunity to discuss the terms of an alliance presented itself when Vice President Richard Nixon arrived in Karachi as part of a twelve-country tour of Asia. Nixon traveled thirty-eight thousand miles over sixty-eight days, partly as a public relations exercise and partly because Eisenhower was willing to concede to his vice president a somewhat enhanced role in foreign affairs.

According to media reports at the time, the policy agenda for Nixon's trip included the possible rearmament of Japan, Korean reconstruction, the war emerging in French Indo-China, and the completion of "an agreement providing Pakistan with arms and the US with bases in Pakistan."[19] For this last item, the State Department advised in its preparatory memo for Nixon to avoid adopting "a patronizing tone" with Pakistani officials but to give "positive encouragement" to the governor-general and "especially Prime Minister" Bogra. The two leaders faced domestic challenges—Bogra had only recently gone on to become prime minister from his position as ambassador to the United States—and American support was meant to reassure them.

But Nixon's comments on Pakistan's domestic politics only accentuated the perception among Pakistan's elite that Americans pick whom to support in foreign countries and then ensure their success. Over the years the belief about Americans being veiled king makers has become only stronger.

Moreover, the State Department had advised Nixon to avoid discussing US military aid in specific terms. The vice president was to tell his Pakistani hosts that he had been away from the United States for some time and therefore was unable to address specific questions on the subject.[20] But once Nixon arrived in Karachi, he realized that military aid was one of the two subjects Pakistan's leaders wished most to discuss—the other was their commitment to fighting communism, which they declared they abhorred.

Nixon liked the anticommunism he encountered in Pakistan, especially as it contrasted with his experience in India, namely, their unwillingness to even discuss the notion that communism was the gravest threat to civilization. The Indians had lectured Nixon about global poverty and injustice, both of which, they said, Western colonialism has exacerbated. Conversely, the Pakistanis seemed eager to join the American-led ideological struggle.

In his memoirs Nixon described Nehru as "the least friendly leader" that he had met in Asia.[21] After returning to Washington he told the National Security Council (NSC) that "Pakistan is a country I would like to do everything for. The people have fewer complexes than the Indians."[22] Thus, Nixon's conclusion was that it would be "disastrous" if the United States failed to provide aid to Pakistan and "may force out the Prime Minister" who was America's friend. He had become convinced that, ideologically, Pakistan was an anticommunist bastion and would not go communist even if it received no US support.[23] His impressions were the result of conversations during a three-day visit, during which he met only people who had carefully choreographed what to say to him.

One sign that Pakistani officials had rehearsed their message came during Nixon's separate meetings with Governor-General Muhammad and Prime Minister Bogra. Muhammad "talked mostly about the military aid question, stating it was absurd to think of Pakistan attacking India with 40 million Muslims in India," reported US Ambassador Horace Hildreth, who was present during the meeting. If aid was provided, the governor-general said he would personally reassure Nehru "on any fears he might have of the intent of Pakistan in its use of military equipment."

Muhammad also emphasized that the Pakistani public now expected American aid. According to him: "Were the US not to grant aid now, especially in view of all the publicity, it would be like taking a poor girl for a walk and then walking out on her, leaving her only with a bad name." Hildreth could not help but notice that Bogra used the same analogy in his subsequent meeting with Nixon. To him this was a clear indication that "they put their heads together before seeing the Vice President and me."[24]

The Pakistanis had clearly won Nixon and Dulles over, but they were not the only ones influenced by their favorable view of Pakistani leaders. Admiral Arthur Radford, the chairman of the joint chiefs of staff, had also developed a personal friendship with army chief Ayub, whom he saw as someone "in a position to deliver the goods" and "willing to do so."[25]

The Americans were already eyeing bases in Pakistan that had not been guaranteed. The Pakistani approach so far had been to demonstrate that they were committed to the anticommunist cause, ask for resources and materiel for their military, and hint at the prospect of US bases. The likability of Pakistani leaders in comparison with the

· · · · ·

Indians rather than a hard-nosed assessment of policy had become the driving force in US-Pakistan relations. And the American embassy in Karachi had become indirectly involved in domestic politics by advancing the cause of pro-Western civil servants and generals against politicians who seemed to prefer alternatives, including nonalignment.

Ambassador Hildreth, a former Republican governor of Maine, argued passionately that rejecting Pakistan's request for military aid would have an adverse effect on Pakistan's government, and he considered the government's survival to be important for US interests. Hildreth thought that the advantages of Pakistan's contribution to Middle East defense outweighed the risk of adverse reaction in India. But he was unable to predict whether and to what extent Pakistan would, in fact, contribute to the American conception of Middle East defense.

But even as US officials were justifying possible military aid for Pakistan in return for naval and air bases, Foreign Minister Zafrulla Khan declared that "there have been no negotiations, nor attempts at negotiations, for an American-Pakistani military alliance." The Pakistan government was only making "inquiries for the purchase of arms," he told the Pakistani media, while allowing US media to publish reports about an alliance involving bases.

These denials, however, did not deter the optimists in Washington from expecting that aid would secure leverage for the United States in Pakistan. They continued to believe that Pakistan would turn around and fulfill America's expectations once military aid arrived. For these officials, the proposition was a simple equation: Pakistan will get money and weapons, the United States will get its bases, and Pakistan's problems with India and Afghanistan will diminish over time.

Ambassador Hildreth's sympathy for Pakistan was partly the result of his personal relationship with Iskander Mirza, who served as defense secretary, governor of East Pakistan, interior minister, and, eventually, governor-general and president during Hildreth's tenure (1953–1957) as ambassador. Mirza's son, Humayun, married Hildreth's daughter Josephine at a ceremony in Cumberland, Maine, which the groom's father was unable to attend because of a political crisis in Pakistan.

Around this time Governor-General Muhammad had dismissed Pakistan's Constituent Assembly and Parliament in what was described as a constitutional coup. Then, when a new legislature was put in place without elections, the country's affairs were completely in the hands of unelected nonpoliticians. This sequence of events opened itself to conspiracy theories, including one that focused on a few coincident events: Mirza's son had married the US ambassador's daughter, the legislature was dismissed around the time of their wedding, and Mirza rose spectacularly within the power corridors immediately thereafter.

Reading through the declassified documents of the era reveals that the Americans had not orchestrated the domestic developments in Pakistan, but the appearance of an American role in Pakistan's affairs had still been created. Moreover, the marriage of Hildreth's daughter to Mirza's son had not been part of some medieval marital alliance; if anything, Pakistanis were the ones who saw political and economic advantage in it. A year earlier Bogra had been brought from ambassadorship in Washington to become the prime minister so as to help secure aid from the Americans. Now Mirza's ties to Hildreth could also be tapped for the same purpose.

The British, who had better cultural and historic knowledge of the subcontinent than did the Americans, tried to warn the Americans against veering too close to Pakistan. Her Majesty's government also realized that arming any side in South Asia could aggravate an already emotive conflict. During a meeting with Dulles in Bermuda in December 1953, Foreign Secretary Anthony Eden conveyed London's doubts about the usefulness or wisdom of the United States inserting itself into the India-Pakistan situation.

Dulles informed Eden that the United States "definitely" wished to help Pakistan but had yet to decide on what arms to provide. Dulles needed fighting men in South Asia for his encirclement of Soviet communism, and the Pakistanis were ready to join the crusade. India, he said, did not have "the right not only to remain neutral herself but to prevent other countries from lining up with the West."[26]

Ultimately, then, Dulles ignored Eden's advice. The United States and Pakistan signed a Mutual Defense Assistance Agreement on May 19, 1954, under which the United States "was to make available equipment, materials, services or other assistance with such terms and conditions as may be agreed." The government of Pakistan agreed to use American weapons "exclusively to maintain its internal security, its legitimate self-defense or to permit it to participate in the defense of the area, or in the United Nations collective security arrangements and measures." In a sop to India, Pakistan affirmed that it "would not undertake any act of aggression against any other nation."[27]

The progovernment *Times of Karachi* described the significance of the aid as Pakistan's declaration of choice in the "ideological conflict that overshadows the world."[28] But both Pakistan's Islamists and the left wing criticized the agreement. On the one hand, the Islamists saw it as a betrayal of the Pan-Islamic ideal. They liked the idea of a stronger military but did not want restrictions on the purposes for which that military may be used. The leftists, on the other hand, resented the fact that Pakistan had become a member of the Western bloc, which would unnecessarily limit the country's international options; they feared Pakistan's militarization at the expense of development.

These opposing voices to close military ties with the United States helped Muhammad, Mirza, and Ayub voice a new argument to the Americans about their value as partners: if the United States failed to prop up Pakistan's Western-trained civil servants and military officers with economic and military assistance, Pakistan would fall under the leadership of either the mullahs or the leftists, a contention similar to one that these leaders had earlier made when seeking US wheat. At that time, the State Department had told the NSC that in the absence of US support, the "present government of enlightened and western-oriented leaders" could be replaced by those likely to be "far less cooperative with the West."[29]

* * * * *

✦

ALTHOUGH THE Mutual Defense Assistance Agreement enabled the transfer of US weaponry to Pakistan, Dulles still faced opposition to helping Pakistan militarily. US media and congressmen worried that supplying American arms to a country in conflict would fuel instability and regional discord. "The real danger in the Indo-Pakistan subcontinent is not so much from outside aggression as from unstable economies," argued one *Washington Post* editorial, adding that "India now devotes 45 percent of her budget to armament, and Pakistan 60 percent. Even if the US should attempt to assuage India's fears by offering her equal military aid, the result could hardly be other than to promote increased military expenditure in both countries."[30] Just as some predicted, soon after the possibility of military supplies to Pakistan opened, Pakistan's relations with both Afghanistan and India began to deteriorate.

Moreover, the major military challenge from communism was seen as coming from East, and not South Asia. Communism had run over China in 1949; by the early fifties the rise of the Viet-Minh in French Indo-China was presented as the new battleground in the East-West conflict. The South East Asian Treaty Organization (SEATO) was created in September 1954 to address the potential threats in Laos, Cambodia, and Vietnam. Dulles proposed including Pakistan in the organization because doing so helped its primary goal of securing military equipment for its armed forces; Pakistan joined SEATO. The only problem was geography: East Pakistan, with its eastern border with India and Burma, was distant from the region where SEATO was designed to provide security, whereas West Pakistan was even farther.

Columnist Walter Lippmann drew Dulles's attention to this irony in an exchange that provides insight into the flawed reasoning behind Pakistan's inclusion in American grand strategy. At a dinner party in Washington Lippmann questioned the efficacy of SEATO and told Dulles: "You've got mostly Europeans, plus Pakistan which is nowhere near Southeast Asia." The secretary of state retorted by saying, "I've got to get some real fighting men into the south of Asia.

· · · · ·

The only Asians who can really fight are the Pakistanis. That's why we need them in the alliance. We could never get along without the Gurkhas."[31]

Dulles was, of course, wrong, because the Gurkhas are Hindus from Nepal, not Pakistanis. Nineteenth-century British theories about the martial races of the subcontinent had obviously influenced Dulles's views. In an 1897 book, Lord Roberts of Kandahar had argued that certain ethnic groups in the subcontinent were natural warriors, whereas others were not. Pashtun and Punjabi Muslims from what is now Pakistan and the Gurkhas were both listed as martial races. Thus, the US secretary of state had embraced the thesis but had forgotten its details. When Nehru snubbed him, he became convinced that Pakistani Muslim warriors would better safeguard America's interest in the region. A racialist concept British officers used as their guide when recruiting troops for a colonial army thus exercised undue influence in US foreign policy during the 1950s.

Dulles soon found out that any hopes he had of seeing Pakistan's martial Muslims fighting alongside Americans against the communists would not be fulfilled before Pakistani demands for gratis military equipment had been met. An American team under Brigadier General Harry Meyers was sent to Pakistan to determine Pakistan's military needs from a technical standpoint. The team's assessment that at that stage, $29.5 million in equipment would be enough for Pakistan's military was far below Pakistani expectations.

No one in the US government at that time knew that Pakistan's senior-most generals held several meetings at army headquarters, commonly called the GHQ, in Rawalpindi to war-game for the Meyers team visit. The meeting's participants included three men who would later serve terms as Pakistan's president.

Between them, Iskander Mirza, Ayub Khan, and Yahya Khan (then only a brigadier) ruled Pakistan for sixteen years, from 1955 to 1971. They had expected the Americans to turn on the spigot of aid immediately after the Mutual Assistance Agreement and Pakistan's membership in SEATO. Their plan involved impressing their superpower ally with their political commitment to its global cause, followed by presenting the visitors with a list of military items they

......

sought from the United States, which they hoped would be provided soon.

Based on minutes in GHQ archives, "Note that the name of India is never to be used, even in internal discourse," says an account of the meeting. "This would be fatal and would ruin the prospects of getting any assistance from the USA."[32] In addition to concealing any intention of using US-supplied weaponry against India, the meeting's participants were to ensure that every Pakistani who met the Americans spoke with one voice. The meeting's premeditations were to be treated as a state secret. The group met at least three times before meeting the American delegation.

Face to face with the US team, General Ayub welcomed them with a speech about Pakistan's commitment to the anticommunist cause and the country's strategic location. Pakistan offered to fill the "power vacuum in the Middle East" that the end of British rule in the Indian subcontinent created. He also spoke of the Soviets' "covetous eye" and US dependence on Middle Eastern oil. But the mid-level Pentagon officials were not policy makers; they were in Pakistan for a technical study and did not have the mandate to promise large quantities of US weaponry.

Disappointed Pakistani civilian and military leaders separately approached their respective American interlocutors. They said that Pakistan could not afford to accept US military assistance at low levels, and the military aid program should not become known as "mere token." That, they argued, would discourage other countries from becoming US allies. "Disillusionment within Pakistan" would threaten the government that had staked its future on the bold decision of allying with the West.

The United States, Pakistani leaders argued, should be prepared to treat Pakistan like Turkey—with liberal defense support and direct contributions to the sustenance of its forces. Otherwise, making the Pakistani public understand Pakistan's alliance with the United States would be impossible.[33] This led even the normally supportive US Ambassador Hildreth to observe that though there was some merit in the Pakistani government's viewpoint, "they always overstate their virtues."

......

After all, the Pakistanis were effectively saying that US aid to Pakistan had to be massive to be useful. Only after Pakistan received large doses of aid would it be able to do something in return for the United States. Moreover, there should be no expectation that the government's popularity at home would legitimate its foreign policy with the United States. The sense of security and prosperity that American aid would provide was instead supposed to help legitimize the Pakistan government.

Somewhat irate, Dulles decided to privately address the "exaggerated expectations of certain Pakistan officials which have been self-stimulated and publicized without any US encouragement." He told his ambassador in Karachi to remind his interlocutors of "Pakistan's own responsibilities."

Dulles explained that it was not within the financial capabilities of the United States to create a "well balanced expanding economy" merely with the support of "massive financial donations"; instead, Pakistan's people and leaders had to build it largely through their own efforts. He also asked that "there should be no misconception in Pakistani minds" that US assistance "is without cost or effort to our people" or that "U.S. resources are unlimited."[34] Although this may have been the first time that one of the American leaders most supportive of aid to Pakistan was forced to explain political facts of life to Pakistani leaders and officials, it was by no means the last.

Dulles went on to explain that Turkey had received priority because it was a "vigorous self-reliant ally," geographically contiguous to the Soviet Union, "under direct and immediate threat," and prepared to "take its stand and defend its territory regardless whether it received US assistance." Turkey, therefore, could not be compared to Pakistan: Ataturk's Western orientation was unambiguous, and the Turks had given military bases as part of NATO and had suffered more than seven hundred fatalities fighting alongside the Americans in Korea.

But this clarification did not change Pakistan's perspective that it could draw unlimited American support only if the Americans realized Pakistan's strategic importance. The generals and bureaucrats in Karachi concluded that they needed the prospect of a more

......

immediate communist threat in order to get the Americans to act. So Prime Minister Bogra met Dulles in Washington soon after this communication and reiterated Pakistan's demand for greater military aid. Dulles attempted once again to convince him that alliance with the United States was not the silver bullet for Pakistan's problems.

The most significant discussion between Bogra and Dulles during their meeting related to their differing interpretations of their respective military obligations. Dulles stressed the anticommunist character of SEATO, underscoring that Pakistan should not expect SEATO support in its conflict with India. The United States had made that clear at the outset, and for the Pakistanis to continue expecting that the US position would change was unfair and unrealistic.

"We could not say, nor could we ask the U.S. Senate to accept the concept," Dulles said, "that any dispute in the area would be considered a threat to the peace and security of the U.S." Bogra retorted that Pakistan was only one nation among the treaty signatories that might fear aggression from a noncommunist country. According to him, the US view of the treaty "tended by implication to condone aggression from a non-communist country." But this argument amounted to virtually renegotiating the terms of the treaty on the basis of a signatory's expectation.

The Pakistani prime minister spoke emotionally of the risks that Pakistan had incurred in its relations with India, Afghanistan, and the USSR as a result of aligning with the West. These risks to the country as well as to its leaders could not be justified for "only $30 million of military assistance from the U.S." Bogra seemed to suggest that the United States needed to make the alliance worth Pakistan's while by increasing the quantum of aid.

The US secretary of state remarked that he had "thought Pakistan had taken its anticommunist stand because it was the right one, not just to make itself eligible for certain sums of dollar aid."[35] An alliance needed a shared concern or shared enemy, Dulles averred, but Pakistan had chosen to become an ally by playing on a shared concern while seeking weapons to deal with an enemy that the Americans did not share. The allies simply could not agree.

......

This marked the beginning of the argument that American and Pakistani officials have had several times in the six decades since then. Both sides have been reluctant to say to each other that in relations between nations, each side must calculate its own costs. In this case, the Americans had failed to get a commitment on bases, whereas the Pakistanis had not negotiated the amount of aid beforehand. Even as transactional relationships go, this was one based on too many assumptions and insufficient clarity.

Further, the Americans were basing their policy toward Pakistan on their impressions of the people that ran the country instead of analyzing their policies. On his return from a trip to Pakistan at the beginning of 1955, Admiral Radford spent considerable time during his briefing to the State Department on his views of the various individuals within the Pakistan government. The Governor-General Muhammad, the admiral said, was "a very sick man, and might drop off at any time. If he does go, there was certain to be a struggle for power within the country." Radford saw General Mirza as "the number two strong man," but in his opinion "the best man was General Ayub."

The minutes of the meeting reflect the US obsession with personalities at the expense of trying to understand the Pakistani leaders' view of Pakistan's national interest. Hearing Ayub's praise from Radford, the State Department's John Jernegan remarked that he did not know Mirza, but "the specialists in the Department think that General Mirza, who definitely expects to be Prime Minister one day, is more competent than General Ayub." The minutes go on: "The Admiral said that that very well might be, but as far as honesty and directness is concerned, Mirza was no match for Ayub." Radford then opined that "Pakistan was a potential ally of great importance" and that "from the military point of view, they have a trained armed force which no other friendly power can match, not even the Turks."[36]

Amid all this discussion of Pakistan, there was no consideration whatsoever of Pakistan's unwillingness to spare its troops for Western alliances without first resolving its disputes with India. The State Department officials demonstrated even less understanding of the

. . . . .

debate about Pakistan's raison d'être that was holding the country back from writing a constitution.

The leaders the Americans preferred were the ones responsible for putting off popular elections; no steps were being taken to reform the economy or improve productivity, and the new country's national identity was being shaped around hatred of India and vague appeals to Islamic sentiment. All of these developments had implications for the future, but none of them received much attention from American diplomats and generals at the time.

It was the Pentagon's assistant secretary for international security affairs, H. Struve Hensel, who finally asked some tough questions. After he visited Karachi, he wrote that US civilian and military officials did not have "any clear idea of the part Pakistan was expected to play in the defense of the Middle East." Military men like Radford wanted to increase Pakistan's military strength, "but no one seemed to know precisely why except that Pakistanis obviously make reliable fighting soldiers."

Hensel pointed out that Pakistan regarded the Indian threat as much more serious to Pakistan than the threats from communist Russia or communist China. He saw this in the way the Pakistan army was deployed along the Indian border, and all its tactical and strategic planning centered on prioritizing India-related problems. Under what circumstances would Pakistan spare troops for the defense of the Middle East? he asked. "If it is thought that Pakistan can contribute to the defense of Southeast Asia," he observed, "it should be remembered that practically all of the military strength of Pakistan is concentrated in West Pakistan."

Apart from questioning the premises on which US engagement with Pakistan was based, Hensel also questioned the excessive coziness between American and Pakistani officials. He noted that Ambassador Hildreth had shared the details of anticipated aid for Pakistan over the next three years with Pakistan's prime minister in an aide-memoire. Even if Hildreth's disclosure was a mistake, it had effectively converted a dollar figure still under discussion in Washington into a firm commitment. Hensel remarked that any modification of the amount or the time over which it would be disbursed would now result in dissatisfaction.[37]

But this voice of dissent within the Pentagon did not carry enough weight to dissuade Dulles and Radford from continuing to see their relations with Pakistani leaders as an investment that would bear fruit over time. More than a year after Pakistan joined SEATO there had been no progress in securing a "centrally positioned landing site" for possible operations against the USSR and China. Although Ayub had enticed Washington with possible offers of bases "if the price was right," as it turned out the right price was an American guarantee of Pakistan's security against India, which was not as easy for Washington as Pakistani officials made it sound.

By the end of 1955 the American alliance with Pakistan had resulted in relations between India and the Soviet Union warming considerably. Pakistan had joined Britain, Iraq, Iran, and Turkey in the Baghdad Pact, which the United States had initially not joined. Nehru then visited Moscow that June. In fall, Soviet leaders Nikita Khrushchev and Marshall Nikolai Bulganin traveled to India, Afghanistan, and Burma—all three countries then neighboring Pakistan.

Khrushchev chose Srinagar, the capital of Kashmir, as the location at which to make comments against American plans for building bases in Pakistan close to Soviet territory. He likely chose Srinagar as the place to make that statement deliberately; after all, the USSR wanted Pakistan to know that it had lost Soviet support for Kashmiri self-determination now that Pakistan had allied with America. Pakistan's prime minister responded by denying flatly that Pakistan had any intention of *ever* allowing *any country* to establish bases.

This led Hildreth to approach Mirza, who was now governor-general and head of state, for clarification. Pakistan had continually sought US support in return for bases, Hildreth reminded Mirza, as he also expressed puzzlement with the unequivocal declaration that Pakistan would never give any bases. The ambassador had completely overlooked the fact that Mirza's predecessor as governor-general, Ghulam Muhammad, had issued a similar statement a couple of

......

years earlier. This kind of ignorance of relatively recent history has remained a constant of American interaction with Pakistani leaders.

In his meeting with Hildreth, Mirza responded by keeping the American's hopes alive, expressing impatience with the "Prime Minister's over-caution." But he said that it was untimely for the United States to seek bases until it had "shown more support for Pakistanis on Kashmir" and backed the Baghdad Pact. Instead of accepting that Pakistan was unlikely to grant bases to the United States, Hildreth told the State Department that Pakistan might be trying to trade US adherence to the Baghdad Pact as a precondition for the use of Pakistani bases.[38]

By the time the pact was renamed the Central Treaty Organization (CENTO) in 1959, the United States joined the Baghdad Pact countries, including Pakistan, in bilateral military agreements. Yet the prospect of Western naval and air bases in Pakistan did not materialize. The United States could not secure Kashmir for Pakistan, and without that, Pakistan would not offer the United States what it sought. As a result, US economic and military assistance trickled into Pakistan at a rate much slower than that sought by Pakistan's leaders.

The United States had committed itself to providing Pakistan with equipment and training for five and a half new divisions at a cost of $171 million. But Ayub employed creative methods to get an increase in the dollar figure. He altered the numerical strength of each Pakistan army division to be able to claim that the amount of money was insufficient for the target force levels. Before American tanks were delivered, the Pakistan army speculated that the tanks would wear out quickly without tank transporters or railway flat-cars. Having provided the tanks, then, the Americans had to pay for them to remain usable. Requests for additional expenses for fuel and motor transport as well as grumbling about a shortage of motorized battalions, reserves, and troop accommodations followed.[39]

By 1957 many people, including President Eisenhower, wondered what American purpose was served by ballooning military aid to Pakistan. Lippmann wrote in a column that it was "fiction" that the United States was arming Pakistan "to defend the Middle East against the Red army." This fiction had "earned us the deep suspicion of India." In Lippmann's view Dulles had based US foreign policy to "escape from reality."[40]

Hans J. Morgenthau, the well-regarded scholar of international relations, raised similar doubts. "Pakistan is not a nation and hardly a state," wrote Morgenthau in an article in the *New Republic* titled "Military Illusions." "It has no justification in history, ethnic origin, language, civilization, or the consciousness of those who make up its population. They have no interest in common, save one: fear of Hindu domination. It is to that fear, and to nothing else, that Pakistan owes its existence, and thus far its survival, as an independent state." He also derided the geographic and political distance between East and West Pakistan: "It is as if after the Civil War Louisiana and Maryland had decided to form a state of their own with the capital in Baton Rouge. In fact, it is worse than that."

Morgenthau also questioned the rationale of arming and equipping the Pakistan army in the hope of using it against the Soviet or Chinese communists. "Against whom and how is an army likely to fight, which is built upon so tenuous a political foundation?" he wondered. "Only extraordinary wisdom and political skill" could keep Pakistan together, he wrote, and it was "not to be found among the politicians of Karachi." Morgenthau saw it difficult how "anything but a miracle, or else a revival of religious fanaticism" would assure Pakistan's future. He predicted that Pakistan's government "might well need its army to maintain its rule over the two disparate territories of Pakistan."

According to Morgenthau's clear analysis, geography allowed the Pakistan army to conduct military operations against only two countries: Afghanistan and India. But "While the Pakistani army could easily take care of Afghanistan and might perhaps be able to defend West Pakistan against India at the price of the surrender of East Bengal, such capabilities are obviously meaningless in view of the overall political and strategic situation on the continent of Asia as it appears from the vantage point of the United States." A local war between Pakistan and one or the other of its neighbors did not necessarily

......

affect America's vital interests. "By allying ourselves with Pakistan, we have alienated India which is infinitely more important than our ally," he pointed out.[41]

The benefits of the alliance were questioned in Pakistan as well, albeit from an opposite perspective. One example was the Pakistani media reaction to any suggestion that the Western powers would not take sides in South Asian disputes. The British Foreign Office announced before a meeting of the SEATO Council that the anticommunist alliances were not concerned with the India-Pakistan dispute over Kashmir or the Pashtunistan issue between Pakistan and Afghanistan. This announcement created uproar in Pakistan. Politicians and editorial writers criticized the "lack of Anglo-American support for Pakistan in its disputes with India and Afghanistan."[42]

Pakistani diplomats also repeatedly told their American counterparts that their government encountered difficulty explaining to its people its alliance with the West without an American promise of support against India. For instance, visiting finance minister Amjad Ali told US officials that Pakistan's alliances were "operating to the detriment of Pakistan." The government was being criticized for failing to contribute to unifying the world's Muslims and for being unable to succeed in resolving the Kashmir dispute in Pakistan's favor.

Ali's suggestion was that the United States could help its ally by enabling it to argue that Pakistan had gained strength in relation to India by becoming America's partner. American officials quickly reminded him that Pakistan had previously said that it had joined US-led alliances to defend the free world against communism. Pakistan had given assurances it was not acquiring US arms to fight India. Ali's American hosts then explained to him that public statements about Pakistan's military buildup being aimed at India would erode support among Americans for the aid program.[43]

The back and forth on the subject became even more intense after a 1958 coup. Days before the coup, leaders of the Muslim League, supported by Islamic parties, had started calling for Jihad against India over Kashmir. Westerners saw this not as a sober policy recommendation but instead as oratory designed to "exercise a powerfully unifying influence within the country."[44] While imposing martial law, Mirza had cited those "screaming for war with India" as being among the negative influences that martial law was intended to counter. Ayub had attempted to sound reasonable when he told the press, soon after removing Mirza and taking power for himself days later, that "Once there is a solution of the canal waters and the Kashmir disputes, we have no other grouse against India."[45] Ayub spoke of Kashmir and the issue of sharing waters from the network of canals the British had built for irrigation in the divided Punjab province as solvable problems and did not describe India as an existential threat to Pakistan. But soon it was apparent that anxiety about India would be invoked with even greater passion than before.

Even before becoming Pakistan's all-powerful ruler, Ayub had expressed concerns about the need to define and consolidate Pakistani national identity. The country needed a new narrative of its history and a strong nationalism. Ayub adapted the ideology of Pakistan to mean demonization of India's Brahmin Hinduism and a zealous hostility toward India.

A strong stance against India, Ayub thought, would help in "liberating the basic concept of our ideology from the dust of vagueness." Thus, the nation would unite against India. Militarism would help overcome the difficulty Pakistan's unique origins posed. Ayub wanted to change what he described as Pakistan's foundational dilemma: Until 1947, he wrote, "our nationalism was based more on an idea than on any territorial definition. Till then, ideologically we were Muslims; territorially we happened to be Indians; and parochially we were a conglomeration of at least eleven, smaller provincial loyalties."[46]

Western diplomats in Karachi saw Ayub as a modernizing reformer. As a British-trained general, he could be expected to defer to economic experts, minimize the role of divisive politicians, and isolate the clerics. So they took his anti-India assertions with a pinch of salt.

For the benefit of Americans, Ayub tried to connect his anti-India stance with his anticommunism. He told a US delegation early in his long administration that "one of India's aims was to get the United States out of Asia."[47] If only the United States and Britain coerced India, he reasoned, then it would be forced to concede Pakistan's fair demands about canal waters and in Kashmir. But if the United States refused to help Pakistan defend itself against India, Pakistanis would turn against the United States, and this would cause the United States to lose both Pakistan and India.

Even though the martial law regime tightly controlled debate and discussion within Pakistan, that did not stop Pakistani officials from invoking the argument about anti-American public opinion. Occasionally American officials responded by pointing to the manner in which that opinion was being created. They observed that the Pakistan government made little effort to explain to the public its motives for pursuing alliances. Anti-Western propaganda, however, was often unleashed precisely so Pakistani officials could argue that the United States had to support Pakistan against India so as to preserve its alliance with them. Few Pakistanis knew how much their country and its armed forces had become dependent on US assistance.

Ayub and members of his military regime were very conscious of the need to manage a positive image in the United States. Aziz Ahmed, a Cambridge-educated career civil servant, arrived in Washington in March 1959 and tried to persuade any American who would listen that Pakistan faced a serious military threat from India. In a meeting with Secretary of Defense Neil McElroy he conveyed Ayub's concern that "influential circles of the intelligentsia, some legislators, and to some degree the general public" in the United States were becoming unsympathetic to Pakistan's security needs.

Ahmed observed that many Americans commented that Pakistan was "supporting armed forces in excess of her needs at the expense of sorely needed economic development." He then went on to suggest that "the ordinary Pakistani" was likely to interpret this criticism as reflecting American hostility. After all, the Indian army was much stronger than that of Pakistan and could mount an offensive against Pakistan in ten days. "It would be almost impossible to convince those Pakistanis living near the Indian border that any reduction in the strength of the Pakistan Army was a reasonable course of action," he stated.

· · · · ·

The ambassador pointed out that Pakistan had not received from the United States, either privately or publicly, any assurances guaranteeing her territorial integrity. He then dwelt at some length on how it was "very difficult for the ordinary Pakistani" to understand why the US press criticized Pakistan. Ahmed implied that US officials should help mitigate criticism of Pakistan by informing American journalists of Pakistan's difficulties as well as its value to US security.[48]

Browsing through media reports at the time, it seems that the Pentagon undertook background briefings in response to the ambassador's request. Some positive reports and editorials followed, especially in the *New York Times*. But generally Americans continued to wonder whether they were getting their money's worth by aiding Pakistan's military. The reverse question was being asked in Pakistan. If Pakistan would gain nothing in its conflicts with India and Afghanistan, why should it commit itself to the US-led military alliances?

The answer, of course, was that alliance with the United States was the only way of securing crucial military equipment as aid. Between 1954 and 1959 $425 million in American aid had been pumped into Pakistan's military. Pakistan's army received Patton tanks, modern artillery, howitzers, and state-of-the-art communications and transportation equipment. The Air Force was armed with F-86 jet fighters that could effectively defend against an attack across Pakistan's borders. The only ships added to the Pakistan navy since 1947 were used American vessels transferred mostly as grants.

This was on top of $855 million in economic assistance over the same period. But the Pakistanis still felt they were not getting enough of the items on their wish lists fast enough, just as American officials realized they were giving too much to Pakistan in return for too little. The issue came to a head when Eisenhower questioned his own administration's Pakistan policy at an NSC meeting. The president observed that having Pakistan as a military ally was proving costly.

A very large proportion of total US assistance at the time was allocated to Pakistan's military. Eisenhower said that the United States

......

was "doing practically nothing for Pakistan except in the form of military aid," which "was perhaps the worst kind of a plan and decision we could have made." Describing it as "a terrible error," the president wondered why the United States was "hopelessly involved in it." He also commented that the United States had "the same damned problem with Turkey" and that America's "tendency to rush out and seek allies was not very sensible."

Interestingly, Eisenhower recognized intellectually that "in some instances the neutrality of a foreign nation was to the direct advantage of the United States." If the option of buying an ally with aid had been exercised in case of India, "there wouldn't be enough money in the United States to provide the support that India would require as an ally of the United States," he exclaimed.

The president confessed that he did not quite know what to do about the military program for Pakistan, so he proposed that "some skillful negotiator ought to try to induce the Pakistanis themselves to suggest changes in this military assistance program over a period of time." The State Department told him that it wanted "to work toward some reduction of our military assistance program in Pakistan while avoiding serious political repercussions."[49]

Thus, the American honeymoon with Pakistan had started to go sour. Dulles's policy toward the Middle East had not been particularly effective. Gamal Abdel Nasser had emerged as the strongman of Egypt, and his anti-Western and anti-Israeli idiom was finding increasing favor among Arabs. Pakistan's pro-Western leaders wanted to persist with their strategy of building their military and maintaining their economy with American funds, but there was no will to rally public opinion behind that strategy. The Pakistani people continued to be fed a steady diet of anti-India and Pan-Islamist slogans that had been the staple since partition.

Pakistan found itself distrusted by Arabs as well as by two crucial neighbors, Afghanistan and India. Its leaders also failed to read correctly the extent to which the United States was committed to spending money on Pakistan's security and economic well-being. Moreover, the Pakistani and American definitions of security were very different. Pakistan measured its security in terms of militarily defeating India and securing territory in Kashmir that it felt had been cheated from them in 1947. Conversely, the United States was content with seeing Pakistan protect its international borders and stave off a communist insurrection if one ever happened.

✦

TEN YEARS HAD PASSED since Pakistan's founding when James M. Langley, owner and editor of the *Concord Monitor* in New Hampshire, arrived in Karachi as the new US ambassador. Langley was one of the earliest supporters of Eisenhower's nomination as the Republican candidate for president in 1952, and Eisenhower rewarded that support and loyalty with the ambassadorial appointment soon after beginning his second term as president. Langley was not part of the emerging national security establishment and was, therefore, able to look at Pakistan with relative detachment.

Six months into his job the new ambassador realized that US aid was the only thing that kept Pakistan going. In detailed reports and letters to the State Department, Langley shared his impressions and analysis of Pakistan. He wrote about the economic, military, and psychological dimensions of what he described as "the Pakistan problem."

According to Langley, a "small thinking elite," including the army's officer corps, ran the country, while the masses were restricted to preserving their "inadequate South Asian standard of living." The army, "with its excellent morale and fine equipment," had become the country's "safe anchor," but relying primarily on the army as "the framework of the Pakistan state" was "questionable statesmanship," he argued.

In Langley's opinion the overall situation in Pakistan was deteriorating. The country was dysfunctional, and the United States was inadvertently exacerbating that dysfunction with its support for a militarized Pakistan. He pointed out that "Military strength, without a sound economic and political base, does not constitute real strength in South Asia or elsewhere." The editor-turned-ambassador wanted Americans to rethink their approach to this ally.

......

The problem that Langley spoke of related to Pakistan's lack of internal cohesion and the unending personal and factional rivalries that plagued the country's politics. After much debate the Pakistani leadership had finally written a constitution in 1956. The document combined Westminster-style parliamentary democracy with Islamic pronouncements. But whereas India had held two national elections since independence, Pakistan had yet to hold one.

Nehru was unifying India by recognizing its diversity. British-created Provinces were broken into states within the Indian Union based on ethnicity and language. In one such state, Kerala, an elected communist government had taken office. Conversely, Pakistan tried to impose unity from the top down. The British provinces were eliminated to create one unit in West Pakistan and another in the east.

After initially insisting on Urdu as the sole national language, Bengali had been grudgingly accepted. But other languages were removed from schools and offices. Politicians from some ethnicities were labeled as enemies of the state. East and West Pakistan were drifting apart. The prospect of integrating the nation on religious basis had met its first challenge during sectarian disturbances in Lahore in 1953. Mainstream Muslim sects had rioted to demand that the Ahmadiyya sect be legally declared to be non-Muslim. Defining who was or was not a Muslim would open Pandora's box.

In the midst of ideological arguments and grandiloquence about restoring Islam's lost glory, Pakistan's leaders tended to ignore fundamental economic realities. Even though 65 percent of the country's revenue went toward military spending, Pakistan still needed aid to pay for expensive equipment. Land reform and modernization of agriculture were totally ignored. Instead of utilizing aid as the means to an efficient, self-sustaining economy for the future, Pakistan's government considered aid to be a substitute for revenue.

Six prime ministers had held office within the country's first decade, with one more to come within weeks of Langley's missive to Washington about the "Pakistan problem." Although Mirza and Ayub had been the continuity figures in frequent cabinet reshuffles, eventually even they fell out with one another. Within two years of its adoption Mirza abrogated the Constitution and then imposed martial law in 1958.

Ambassador Langley seemed to read the signs for Pakistan's perilous path ahead within months of his arrival. He proposed that the United States should give greater weight "to developing Pakistan as a strong viable ally" instead of concentrating on building up its military in the hope of using it against the communist bloc. "In Pakistan," he remarked, "We have an unruly horse by the tail and are confronted by the dilemma of trying to tame it before we can let go safely." Langley realized that the "horse we assumed to be so friendly has actually grown wilder of late" and that America's enticements had not been enough to persuade Pakistani leaders to alter their course.

In a candid letter to the State Department, the US ambassador posited the question: "I wonder if we have not collectively developed certain generalizations about Pakistan and then proceeded to accept them as gospel truth without sufficient periodic scrutiny?" He cited the oft-repeated statements about Pakistan, "that Pakistan constitutes a cornerstone of U.S. policy in this part of the world, that Pakistan is the anchor of the Baghdad Pact, and of SEATO, that the Paks are strong, direct, friendly and virile, and that Pakistan constitutes a bulwark of strength in the area." He expressed concern that the positive aspects of the US-Pakistan relationship would be wiped out because of "deterioration in many aspects of Pakistani life."

Many of the issues Langley raised in 1957 have resurfaced with alarming regularity over subsequent years. He spoke of the "increasing level of unproductive expenses (military and government operating costs) and a decline in the productive part of the budget" that erased the gains resulting from foreign assistance. "Unfortunately," Langley wrote in a particularly prescient paragraph, "I fear that our past generosity in helping out our friends has too often permitted them to avoid grasping the nettle and facing their problems with the required spirit of urgency and determination." He described as "wishful thinking" the view that Pakistanis were pro–United States and pro-Western.

Langley's conclusion was that Pakistan's military establishment needed to be "appreciably trimmed." Military expenses were such a drain on the economy that US aid served only "to maintain precarious living standards." The man in the street could not be expected to appreciate benefits of aid because he could not always feel them, he argued. In any case, the US military program in Pakistan was "based on a hoax," according to the ambassador. "The hoax" was that it was related to the Soviet threat.

In Langley's assessment Pakistan's forces were "unnecessarily large for dealing with any Afghan threat over Pashtunistan." Furthermore, Pakistan's concentration of forces along the Indian border made it impossible for Pakistan to provide any troops for American use in the Middle East. "Pakistan would be of little use to us should perchance worse come to worst and India go communist," he elaborated, adding that "even though India is undoubtedly less vulnerable to events in Pakistan, the larger country would hardly profit from a complete breakdown of the embryonic structure of political democracy in Pakistan."

"One of the most disturbing attitudes I have encountered in the highest political places here," Langley concluded, "is that the United States *must* keep up and increase its aid to Pakistan, and conversely, that Pakistan is doing the United States a favor in accepting aid, in addition to the Pakistani pro-Western posture in the Baghdad Pact and SEATO and the United Nations, when actually these postures are in part dictated by Pakistani hatred for India." Langley did not expect gratitude could be bought in Pakistan any more than anywhere else, "but I do believe that the U.S. is entitled to a reasonable degree of respect," he asserted.[50]

In hindsight, it appears that the former owner-editor of a small town New Hampshire newspaper had understood the emerging trends in US-Pakistan relations rather well. But neither his insights nor the questions the president, among others, raised immediately altered the course of American policy. Radford's favorable personal disposition toward Ayub ensured the Pentagon's support for continuing military assistance. Instead of asking for naval and air bases, the United States now settled on seeking an NSA listening post to be located in Pakistan's northwest. In January 1958 Ambassador Langley was asked to discuss with Pakistani leaders the details of the proposal. The negotiations resulted in a ten-year lease, beginning in summer of 1959, for the United States Air Force to set up a "communications facility" at Badaber, ten miles from Peshawar, near the Afghan border.[51]

The air force communications station provided cover for an NSA-run major intercept operation. The Central Asian Republics of the Soviet Union were not far from Peshawar, which was also the headquarters of Pakistan's air force at the time. The United States expected to monitor signals from Soviet missile test sites in addition to intercepting other communications from Soviet Central Asia. The Badaber facility was manned by Americans, who also had access to the air force base at Peshawar for U-2 spy plane flights, but its existence was kept secret from the Pakistani public.

The Badaber facility drew attention within months of becoming operational. The Soviets shot down one of the U-2s operating from Peshawar inside their territory and captured its pilot, Francis Gary Powers, who had bailed out after his plane was hit. The incident on May 1, 1960, resulted in the collapse of the four-power Paris Peace Conference a fortnight later. Khrushchev announced that he knew the espionage mission had originated in Pakistan. After the CIA station chief in London, where Ayub was at the time, informed him of the incident, Ayub shrugged it off, saying he had expected something like this while agreeing to the grant of basing rights.[52]

Ayub did not see the base as a provocation for the Soviets and did not calculate the potential risk of Soviets drawing closer to India or Afghanistan as a result. The fact that the base's existence had angered the Soviet Union could only enhance Pakistan's leverage with the United States. Pakistan could now ask for even more aid on the grounds of potential Soviet retaliation. If the Americans responded unfavorably to Pakistani requests, the termination clause of the lease agreement could be invoked for effect.

The other countries that served as the launching point of the U-2 aircraft were all important US allies. Pakistan had now joined a relatively exclusive club comprising Turkey, Norway, Japan, and West

Germany. Pakistan's military leaders saw this as a good opening for enhanced military and intelligence ties; Ayub and others around him saw it as a major attainment. Around the same time that the lease for the Badaber communications facility was signed, Pakistan also put in a request to replace its one hundred F-86 aircraft with the more sophisticated F-104 supersonic Starfighter planes for its air force at no cost to Pakistan.[53]

The Badaber listening post would, for the time being, silence those within the Eisenhower administration who were asking, "What is the US getting from aiding Pakistan?" It would have the additional advantage of forging closer ties between Pakistan's Inter-Services Intelligence (ISI) agency and the American intelligence community. Pakistan had finally become useful for the United States and, thus, could ask for more weapons to deal with the threat its leaders saw from India.

Making the case for Pakistan's strategic benefits as a US ally had proved difficult. For every American persuaded of Pakistan's value as a partner, there were several who questioned the alliance's benefits. Once Americans started receiving intelligence through a location in Pakistan, the CIA could be trusted to argue that the country was significant for US national security.

Bureaucrats often think only in terms of their immediate needs and requirements, and tactical issues always trump strategic vision. The Badaber listening post and U-2 staging site enabled Pakistan to offer the Americans something in the realm of tactical advantage. Big-picture arguments such as those that Lippmann, Morgenthau, or Langley made were now going to be lost for some time.

★

IN DECEMBER 1959 Eisenhower traveled to Pakistan, Afghanistan, and India for the first-ever visit to the subcontinent by a serving American president.[54] All three countries received him enthusiastically. Eisenhower wrote in his memoirs that India was the magnet that drew him to the region. After all, following an initial flirtation, India's ties with China had somewhat deteriorated, and nonalignment notwithstanding, India had worked with the Americans to support the Tibetan revolt led by the Dalai Lama's supporters. Eisenhower sought to build bridges between India and Pakistan in the hope that both would become America's partners in containing communism.

Upon Eisenhower's arrival in Karachi, Ayub and his administration spared no effort in trying to convince him that Pakistan was America's dependable ally. The hospitality was impeccable. The city was decorated with bunting and illuminated at night to mark the US president's visit. A musical fountain was built near the president's house where he was to stay. As 750,000 flag-waving Pakistanis lined the streets, Ayub and the US president drove fifteen miles from the airport into downtown Karachi. For the final mile, they rode in an open, horse-drawn carriage to Ayub's official residence, with a cheering crowd surrounding them the entire way.[55] The American president could not help but be charmed.

During his discussions with Ayub Eisenhower tried to persuade the Pakistanis to rationalize their military buildup. After Eisenhower's reelection he had told the NSC that a skillful negotiator was needed to do just that. But in long discussions with Ayub he discovered how difficult that negotiation could be. In Delhi Nehru had explained away the India-Pakistan hostility as a result of Pakistan's lack of stable roots; Ayub spoke of it in terms of inherent Indian animosity toward Pakistan. For Ayub, the only acceptable way forward was American intervention on Pakistan's side in redressing the injustice over Kashmir at the time of partition.

Eisenhower inquired about possible solutions of the Kashmir dispute. If India and Pakistan could come to an agreement on the waters dispute, protecting Pakistan's vital interest in the matter of irrigation, why not withdraw troops on both sides in Kashmir, "putting aside the question of who had political control of Kashmir" for the moment? Ayub replied by trying to play on America's concern over China. China claimed parts of Kashmir, Ayub explained, and if forces were withdrawn altogether, it was "almost certain that the Chinese would simply move in and take over. Other points of Kashmir would fall to the communists."[56] Kashmir could neither be demilitarized nor made independent, according to Ayub.

......

The visiting president then asked if there could be "permanent division of Kashmir generally along the present armistice lines." Ayub responded that this would not be possible. Among other reasons, he said, it would mean that India would be within fifteen miles of Pakistan's vital communications system. Eisenhower also tried to ascertain the validity of Pakistan's claim that Kashmir had to be part of its territory in order to ensure the supply of rivers flowing into Pakistan from Kashmir.

Eisenhower wondered whether it was necessary for Pakistan physically to possess the land from which the waters of the rivers originated. After all, he pointed out, several countries, including the United States and Canada, had arrangements for the assured flow of waters. But Ayub refused to accept that what applied to other nations could apply to India and Pakistan. The problem here, Ayub explained, was "the lack of confidence" because "India had taken away rivers that should belong to Pakistan and upon which Pakistan's life depended." Eisenhower did not press his point. He could have pointed out that only one out of the six major rivers flowing into Pakistan as part of the Indus system actually originated in Kashmir.

Ayub then proceeded to make his case with emotional bromides: "Pakistan should not be exposed to unnecessary dangers; if it should go down, American influence in all of Asia would diminish or disappear," and "Pakistan was a strong bulwark against communism; that was in fact the reason why it was the victim of the most vicious communist and neutralist propaganda."[57] Eisenhower could say little but to acknowledge that the United States had sturdy allies in Pakistan and Turkey.

Ayub then proceeded to argue that if Pakistan did not receive American support, the Chinese would inevitably overwhelm Pakistan as well as India. This argument was ingenuous, at best, because Pakistan had already started exploring close ties with China, a fact that the American government knew. But during his meeting with Eisenhower Ayub wanted to make the case for modernizing the Pakistani military with American money. Raising the specter of a Chinese threat to the subcontinent was a good way of doing that.

·····

After complaining about Soviet and Chinese flights over Pakistani territory "and the inability of the Pakistan Air Force to do anything about them," Ayub asked for F-104 aircraft. Eisenhower said that he was not sure about giving F-104s and asked whether F-100s might not be adequate. A US general traveling with Eisenhower commented that the F-100 was a good plane and had recently been provided to the Germans. But Ayub insisted that the F-100 was obsolete, and "it would be a mistake for Pakistan to have anything that would soon be out of date."[58] He also asked for radar equipment, anti-aircraft artillery, Nike-Ajax missiles, and sidewinders.

Turning to Afghanistan, Ayub made an implicit plea for Pakistan to be seen as that country's effective protector. Afghanistan had "no intrinsic strength," he said, and "no economic resources and no military power." The country was created as a buffer because of a clash of interests during the nineteenth century between the Russian and British empires. It was now surviving by playing the United States against the Soviet Union.

Ayub also claimed that Afghanistan was getting enormous quantities of aid from the Soviet Union. "Afghanistan was completely sold to the Soviet Union," he alleged, though he offered no evidence to support his allegation. "Soviet aid totaled $610 million, of which $441 million was for military purposes," he said. The United States should threaten to cut off aid to Afghanistan and support Pakistan against it. Eisenhower observed that if the situation in Afghanistan was so far gone, he did not understand why the Afghans were so anxious for him to come to Kabul. Ayub responded by suggesting that the Afghans "intended to deceive President Eisenhower into believing that continued American aid was in the interests of the United States."[59]

The most interesting part of the Eisenhower-Ayub exchange came, however, when Ayub said that "the Afghans were not Muslims nearly as much as they were opportunists."[60] This provided an insight into the emerging mindset in Pakistan. Afghans had been Muslim for longer than several ethnic groups in Pakistan. A large part of what is now Pakistan was part of the Afghan Kingdom until 1893,

......

when the British severed it. Pakistan had come into being only twelve years earlier, whereas Afghanistan had been a country for centuries. But in 1959 Pakistan's military dictator felt that he could dismiss his country's northwestern neighbor as an opportunist and as insufficiently Muslim.

Eisenhower heard the other side when he went to Kabul and Delhi. During two formal meetings the US president told Nehru that he had "a favorable impression of General Ayub's sincerity of purpose and his desire to live at peace with India and to bring about a settlement of the problems presently affecting relations between the two countries." He "offered to do anything that might be considered helpful" but clarified that he should not be seen as a mediator.

According to the Indian prime minister: "Pakistan is a nation created out of opposition to things—chiefly Indian independence—and would have remained under Britain if India itself had not forced through its own independence."[61] He described the relationship between the two countries as "peculiar," hinting that outsiders, such as Americans, could neither understand nor address its complexity.

Indians and Pakistanis, Nehru explained, were essentially the same people, and there were deep cross-border ties. He cited the example of the chief of protocol in the Indian Ministry of External Affairs whose brother had until recently been secretary general of the Pakistan Foreign Office. Even though cousins were generals in both armies, that had not helped diminish a contrived feeling of animosity. Nehru said that he thought a better feeling was developing between India and Pakistan; bitterness had diminished. But, he said, it could "be inflamed again by demagogues at any time since the people could be quickly aroused."[62]

During Eisenhower's visit the Indians made the point that the American aid program reduced the likelihood that Pakistan would normalize relations with India. Equipped with US weapons, the Indians argued, the Pakistanis felt they could take on India and win. Nehru also spoke of his apprehension of "a stab in the back" from Pakistan while India was reacting to the Chinese threat. The president referred to the conditions in the terms of contract in mutual security programs for all countries, assuring Nehru that "the U.S.

......

would never permit Pakistan to employ military equipment received from the U.S. for aggressive purposes against India."[63]

Eisenhower added that Pakistan and other countries receiving aid were dependent on the United States for ammunition. They could not carry on aggressive action for more than a week without US support, which would be immediately stopped in such situations. He spoke of "convincing assurances given by President Ayub that the last thing his government would wish would be to attack India in light of the fact that the real danger to both countries came from the Sino-Soviet bloc." Eisenhower then expressed that Ayub had impressed him as "progressive, forward-looking and deeply concerned with the welfare of his people."

Within a few years each one of his statements was put to the test. Pakistan initiated war with India a few years later, and the military action lasted seventeen days, at least ten days more than Eisenhower had anticipated. Pakistan reacted to an American arms cutoff by turning to the Soviet Union and China. Widespread rioting against his rule all over Pakistan challenged Ayub's progressive credentials. But at the time the assumptions Eisenhower shared with Nehru shaped American policy.

As he recalled his three-week trip through Europe and South Asia, Eisenhower must have realized that he had disagreed with Ayub on all substantive issues. He had not found the Indians bent upon Pakistan's destruction, and the Soviets had not run over Afghanistan.

But Eisenhower liked Ayub, so the details of Ayub's views did not change the American president's impression of him. This became clear when Eisenhower met with Generalissimo Francisco Franco of Spain in Madrid on his way back to the United States. Reviewing his trip, Eisenhower spoke of America's "starry-eyed and academic types of liberals" who "criticized General Ayub when he seized power via a military coup." But the US president felt that "one can see everywhere in Pakistan improvements and a quite happy attitude."

In Eisenhower's opinion Pakistan's progress was "demonstrated by the huge crowds of friendly people who turned out in Karachi" to welcome him. He did not, however, explain how a huge welcoming

......

crowd attested to the progress of the country's multitudes; after all, it could as easily have pointed to people not having much to do or the authoritarian regime's ability to generate a gathering. But Eisenhower felt that "The whole Pakistani nation was strongly anti-Communist," and that alone was enough to make him very fond of it.[64]

However, the US government found no evidence that Pakistan faced an immediate Soviet threat or that the Soviets supported an aggressive Afghan posture against Pakistan. There was also no evidence of China preparing to militarily assert its territorial claims against Pakistan.[65] Nonetheless, the Eisenhower administration approved a phased program to modernize the country's air force anyway. Orders were soon placed with the Lockheed Corporation for the first squadron comprising twelve planes of the F-104 Starfighter high-performance supersonic interceptor aircraft on behalf of Pakistan, paid for with US funds.

By the end of Eisenhower's term as president the United States had helped Pakistan's army equip four infantry divisions and one and a half armored divisions, including M-47 Patton tanks. Barracks had also been built with US money for twenty-five thousand troops as well as new cantonments at Kharian and Jhelum. The United States had provided twelve vessels for the Pakistan navy, including destroyers and minesweepers. The Pakistan air force had received six squadrons of aircraft, including three fighter-bomber squadrons and one squadron each of interceptor day fighters, light bombers, and transport planes.

★

THE ELECTION IN 1960 of John F. Kennedy as president of the United States led to closer ties between India and the United States. Even as a Democratic senator from Massachusetts, Kennedy had questioned America's embrace of Pakistan at the expense of close ties with India. In an article in *Foreign Affairs*, he had called for a reassessment of "those American aid programs which have reflected an ill-conceived and ill-concealed disdain for the 'neutralists' and 'socialists'."[66] For Kennedy, neutralism and socialism in India's democracy represented "the free world's strongest bulwarks to the seductive appeal of Peking and Moscow."

Liberal economist John Kenneth Galbraith arrived as ambassador to India soon after Kennedy's inauguration. He spoke effusively about democratic India being America's natural partner. This led to strong protests from Pakistan that a neutral nation was being given preference over an American ally. By now Ayub had consolidated control over Pakistan's media through a Ministry of Information and Broadcasting, through which media criticism was easy to generate or turn off for political effect. Conscious that the Americans responded to how they were perceived, a major media offensive was launched against the Indo-American entente.

The government-owned *Morning News*, for example, lambasted the Kennedy administration for wooing Nehru. Ignoring Eisenhower's munificence toward Pakistan, an editorial in the paper argued that the new president had only "accentuated the tendency" of Eisenhower to court those whom Moscow supported. "America obviously does not want to be left behind in the race to woo Pandit Nehru," it said, sarcastically referring to the Indian leader with his Brahmin title. "In fact, Mr. Kennedy has scored a lead over Khrushchev by conferring upon the Indian Prime Minister the mantle of leadership of Asia and Africa," wrote the editorialist, echoing the sentiment in other newspapers.[67]

Officials chimed in with suggestions of a possible conspiracy, which they knew to be false. Bogra, serving as Ayub's foreign minister, claimed that the United States had "deceived Pakistan" as far back as 1951 by entering into a secret treaty with India.[68] Coming from someone who served as a poster boy for US-Pakistan alliance during the 1950s, this conspiracy theory was bound to gain traction.

Thus, Pakistani public opinion was fully mobilized against the possibility of Americans preparing to desert Pakistan. Veiled threats of Pakistan turning to China and the Soviet Union for its security accompanied the criticism. This ran contrary to Eisenhower and Nixon's beliefs about Pakistanis being inherently anticommunist.

The *New York Times*, which had editorially supported the alliance with Pakistan during the Dulles years, now dismissed Pakistan's

......

objections to improved American ties with India. "Pakistan's dissat-
isfactions with the United States are as much psychological as anything else,"[69] observed an editorial. But these Pakistani protests did
have the effect of tempering the Kennedy administration's handling
of Pakistan while it strengthened relations with India.

Vice President Lyndon B. Johnson traveled to the region in the
spring of 1961. His mission was not only to generate good will for
the United States but also to persuade the Indians and Pakistanis that
their policies need not be a zero-sum game. Just ahead of his visit,
Ayub had appeared willing to provide troops for a multinational
force for Laos, where a communist insurgency threatened the US-
backed government. Johnson sought a firmer commitment during
his meeting with Ayub, only to hear the Pakistani president explain
how American victory against communism depended on American
willingness to help Pakistan against India.

Ayub said that "Pakistan did not want the United States to fail—
it wanted it to win against the Soviets. The US battle was Pakistan's
battle." But, he argued, the United States was not deploying its great
power effectively. If the United States did not use its power, it hurt
Pakistan, he claimed, adding that "The power of the United States
was much greater than at times the Americans seemed to think."[70]
Ayub wanted the United States to use its power "to influence
Nehru," and this alone could ensure the defense of South Asia. He
spoke of the "threat to India" from the Soviets and from the Chinese
communists, saying that only good relations between Pakistan and
India could save India from communism.

This first discussion with Ayub was a lesson for Johnson in how,
for Pakistanis, even the conflict in Laos was less about global communism than it was about their dispute with India. Ayub stressed
that Nehru only wanted American economic assistance and the assurance of help if he should get into difficulties with the Chinese.
"He would never help the United States," he said of Nehru, and
suggested that the United States should use its leverage with India
to force a change in its policies. Once again, Ayub emphasized Pakistan's willingness to help America but only after its military had
been provided "more equipment and more mobility."[71]

......

Looking back, it seems that Ayub's script for conversation with American leaders seldom changed. He spoke to Johnson passionately about Kashmir just as he had briefed Eisenhower eighteen months earlier. He then repeated himself when he met Kennedy in Washington later that summer. Following up on his earlier offer, the United States had asked Pakistan to prepare a battalion to send to Laos. But at that time Ayub said that he had concluded "a battalion could do nothing but get itself lost." He would rather send a brigade so that "it could fight well as a more integrated group."[72]

But according to Ayub, Pakistan could not discount the threat on its borders with India and Afghanistan. If only the Americans pressured India, he argued as before, it would give in to Pakistani demands over Kashmir. Then Pakistan would be free to join the Americans in defending the free world. Kennedy retorted that he did not believe the Indians were going to march on Pakistan; they already had what they wanted in Kashmir. Ayub responded by saying that "the point was that India wanted to neutralize all Pakistan." In answer to Kennedy's question of how that would help India, Ayub said that it was clear from the Indian army deployments that they regarded Pakistan as enemy number one.

The discussion that followed reflected the huge gap in Pakistani and American thinking over regional issues. According to the record of the conversation, Kennedy said he could understand India's desire, especially Nehru's, to hold on to what they had in Kashmir. He could also understand India's force being placed there to keep out Pakistan, which had irredentist feeling. But Ayub insisted that Kashmir was a test. "If India should settle with Pakistan on Kashmir, it would mean India wanted to live at peace with Pakistan," he argued. Ayub described Kashmir as the manifestation of India's hostility toward Pakistan.

Kennedy explained that the United States had supported India not with the expectation that India would support US policies but instead because it was in the interest of everyone to save India from collapse. He acknowledged difficulties in dealing with Nehru, who had been around a long time, and he did not know how the United States could pressure him. "We could not even bring Chiang

*****

99

Kai-shek, whom we had helped more than anyone, to do what we saw was in his own interest," he pointed out.

But Ayub proceeded to paint the picture of an embattled India on the verge of a communist takeover piecemeal. According to him, the Chinese communists had an army of one-half million troops in Tibet, ostensibly to control a population of two million. These troops were not far from Calcutta, which was the base of communism in India and could act in concert. Ayub predicted that India was bound to break up in fifteen to twenty years, and the "key to the defense of the subcontinent was Pakistan." Once again the leader of the newest country in the region was pontificating on the lack of viability of a historically older entity.

Kennedy, like Eisenhower before him, wondered what both sides could agree to in the Kashmir dispute. Ayub replied that Nehru had shown no disposition to yield anything beyond the cease-fire line in Kashmir. Pakistan, he said, would have no objection to India taking Jammu, with some adjustments of the border. "Pakistan's people are getting fed up," Ayub remarked, adding that this was the reason they sometimes talked of working more closely with China. When Kennedy asked what Pakistan might want from China, Ayub said Pakistanis wanted nothing of China, adding that he would "like to see it go to hell. But the Pakistani people were anxious to do something about Kashmir."[73]

Kennedy promised that he would make a major effort with Nehru when the Indian prime minister came to Washington later that year. He wanted Ayub to know that even if he did not succeed, he would try. Ayub asked if the United States would support Pakistan if this effort failed and Pakistan brought the matter to the United Nations. Kennedy promised that the United States would support the UN resolutions—a promise he later kept. As with Eisenhower, Ayub also spoke critically of Afghanistan and asked Kennedy for US support in keeping the Soviets out of Afghanistan.

Thinking that personal goodwill would help change Ayub's stance, Johnson invited him to his ranch in Texas. Because the vice president had been warmly received in Pakistan, he decided that equally warm hospitality would convince Ayub that Americans had Pakistan's best interests at heart. In this effort, Air Force officers and men stationed at a nearby base complained that they were ordered to appear with their families to augment the crowd on Ayub's arrival. When reports of that complaint reached the media, an Air Force public relations officer said the men weren't ordered to show up but instead were encouraged to do so. A colonel even advised the press that reporting on the episode would be unpatriotic.

But the incident nonetheless attracted a critical editorial in the *Chicago Tribune*, arguing that international relations needed to be founded upon reality, not illusion. "It is no service to Pakistan or President Ayub to lead his countrymen or him to believe, contrary to fact, that the presence here of the Pakistani president has filled the American people with joyful excitement," the paper said. "That is simply not true." The paper cautioned that the "faked appearance of enthusiasm" for Ayub in Texas could lead the Pakistanis to believe that their exaggerated expectations have the support of American public opinion. But, the article stated, "the Pakistanis are destined to be disappointed."[74]

Ayub's optimism did, in fact, rise as a result of his visit. Although Kennedy had refused to back away from his agenda of closer ties with India, Ayub had returned home with assurances of continued military and economic assistance. There was also the possibility of an American role in resolving the Kashmir dispute. In a somewhat overconfident mood, Ayub decided to get tough first with Afghanistan, shutting down Afghan consulates in Pakistan and demanding that Afghanistan close its own within two weeks. American diplomats got worried about the prospect of Soviet involvement and scurried to help deescalate tensions. Ayub kept pressing for similar American diplomatic efforts between India and Pakistan. Earlier, the dispute over irrigation waters had been resolved with the US-backed Indus Waters Treaty, signed in 1960, which enabled Pakistan and India to share the six rivers flowing into Pakistan from the north, with the World Bank providing funding for Pakistan to build dams and storage capacity. The Americans saw the Indus Treaty as a great success of rational problem solving in the subcontinent. They would have liked a similar approach in Kashmir.

......

Kennedy sought the advice of "the best and brightest" that he had assembled around him, but none of them seemed convinced of the case for getting more deeply involved on Pakistan's side. McGeorge Bundy, the national security adviser, had tasked Robert Komer, a fifteen-year CIA veteran, with evaluating the developments in South Asia. Many saw Komer as the model of what novelist John LeCarre described as an "intellocrat"—an intelligence man, armed with information, commanding a theater of war from his desk. Komer's acerbic memoranda and arguments during the Vietnam War earned him the nickname "Blowtorch Bob."

Komer wrote a comprehensive memorandum for Bundy on US-Pakistan relations, arguing that Pakistan's exclusive focus on India militated against its usefulness as an ally against China or the Soviet Union. "Our basically different views on how to deal with the Afghan, Kashmir, and Indian problems have been apparent in the series of exchanges the New Administration has had with Ayub," he wrote. "Ayub's main concerns are Pakistan's position versus Afghanistan and especially India," Komer added, concluding that Pakistan viewed its alliance with the United States "primarily as insurance against Indian and Afghan threats, and as a means of leverage."[75]

The American official sympathized with Pakistan's concerns "as the weaker power on the subcontinent, fearful of eventual Indian attempts to reunify it." He also saw some merit in Pakistan's case on Kashmir and Pashtunistan. "But to the extent Ayub uses his alliance tie to push us into supporting his forward policies vis-à-vis India and Afghanistan," Komer observed, "he forces us into a position which runs contrary to our larger strategic interests in the area."

In his view Americans tended to lean over too far in their concern, "lest we offend a staunch ally." They had failed to get across to Pakistan the limitations on, as well as the benefits from US support. Ayub seemed to think that the United States was "so attached to him as an ally that he can pursue his own aims with renewed vigor, and drag us along with him." But other than "some highly important facilities," the United States had received nothing from showering largesse on Pakistan "except a paper commitment to SEATO and

CENTO on which it is hard to see how Ayub could effectively pay off in more than peanuts."[76]

"Blowtorch Bob" concluded that "Pakistan's chief preoccupation will long remain India," but if the United States had to choose among the countries of the subcontinent, "there is little question that India (because of its sheer size and resources) is where we must put our chief reliance." Although the Ayub regime was seen as more "pro-Western" than the Indians, it was "questionable whether most Pakistanis are really less neutralist than Indians."

Komer posed the question that many have asked frequently since: "Are we more interested in a Western-oriented weak ally or a strong neutralist India able to defend its own national interests (which happen to broadly coincide with ours)?" Inverting Jinnah's postulate that had guided all Pakistani governments in their policy toward the United States, he remarked, "In the last analysis, Pakistan needs the U.S. connection more than we need it." In essence, Washington needed to stop "showering" Pakistan with aid and deal with it on a more realistic basis.

Although Kennedy himself agreed with some of Komer's arguments regarding military aid, his administration still supported economic assistance. As a result, Pakistan received $169.1 million in development aid in 1961 and $403.4 million in 1962. But the US president was "dubious about giving more jets" to Pakistan and "was extremely reluctant to give any new commitments" of military aid. He even asked, like Eisenhower, why the United States got into multiyear commitments about providing specific weapons systems to countries like Pakistan in the first place.[77]

Pakistan's military had become totally dependent on American equipment obtained as aid, whereas India bought weapons from multiple sources. But that balance was seriously upset when, in October 1962, India went to war with China along their disputed Himalayan border. The United States then initiated an urgent air shipment of military supplies to India. The US-supplied materiel included antipersonnel mines, machine guns and their ammunition, mortars, and radios.[78]

· · · · ·

Although these were aimed at reinforcing Indian resistance against the Chinese communists, Pakistan immediately protested against what it described as the American arming of India. As an American ally, Pakistan claimed, it had a right to be consulted before supplying weapons to its enemy. There was clamor in the Pakistani media for the government to take advantage of India's misfortune and settle the Kashmir issue by force. "All this talk of the Chinese being the aggressors is Washington-brewed tommy rot," *Dawn* claimed in an editorial designed to arouse religious and racial passion. The trouble had been stirred "at the instigation of India's White patrons in Washington, London—as well as Moscow," it said.[79] This was an unsophisticated conspiracy theory, based on the notion that the West and the Soviets might be enemies in other parts of the world but in the subcontinent they were acting in concert to support Hindu India against Islamic Pakistan.

Pseudonymous articles appeared in newspapers, describing Nehru as Hitler and calling for Pakistan to play a lead role in confronting India's "expansionism."[80] Members of Pakistan's National Assembly, dominated by Ayub supporters in the Muslim League, called for revisiting Pakistan's association with SEATO and CENTO, which were described as being against Pakistan's national interest. Ayub approached his American friends with the plea that he would face a popular uprising even though elements within the government were fueling the potential uprising.

In Washington the National Security Council saw the India-China conflict in global strategic terms. "The Pakistanis are going through a genuine emotional crisis as they see their cherished ambitions of using the US as a lever against India going up in the smoke of the Chinese border war," Komer synopsized. According to him: "Their plaint about lack of consultation is mere cover for this (if we'd 'consulted' with the Paks, instead of notifying them, we'd still be arguing about Kashmir)."

The United States needed to be patient and understanding with Pakistan, said Komer, but there was "no need to apologize." In his analysis any attempt to compensate Ayub for American actions vis-à-vis India would result in postponing the long-needed clarification of the United States' position. This was "a time when we've never had a better excuse for clarifying" the US position to Pakistan, he pointed out.

Komer reasoned that Ayub would not likely be willing to risk Pakistan's relationship with the United States. "He may be a prisoner of Pak public emotions in this case," but "even Ayub has found that a hard line often works well with us." The CIA veteran thought that the Pakistanis will eventually realize that they get far too much from their US tie to be able to do without it. "So if we can weather the current shock, we should be able to hold on to our assets in Pakistan, while still emerging with the sub-continent-wide policy toward which we aim," he concluded.[81]

After the initial negative noise, Ayub sat down with British minister for commonwealth relations, Duncan Sandys, and W. Averell Harriman, US assistant secretary of state for Far Eastern affairs, to discuss their proposal for India-Pakistan discussions on Kashmir without preconditions. Ayub turned down the idea of direct dialog with Nehru but accepted a meeting between cabinet-level representatives from both countries.

Harriman noted that he and Sandys had made it plain to Ayub that Pakistan's demand for a plebiscite in Kashmir could not be fulfilled and that the Vale of Kashmir, controlled by India, "could not be transferred to Pakistan." But the Indians understood that "they had to make certain concessions beyond the present cease-fire line," though the Americans and the British could not assure Pakistan of the nature of these concessions. Ayub accepted this situation, according to Harriman, and "recognized that the negotiations on Kashmir might last a considerable time." From America's perspective, however, it was positive that India and Pakistan would now start talking.[82]

The negotiations began soon and lasted six rounds. India designated its minister for railways, Swaran Singh, a good-humored Sikh politician, as its negotiator. Pakistan's representative was Zulfikar Ali Bhutto, the charismatic scion of a land-owning Sindhi family, who served as minister for natural resources in Ayub's cabinet. Both men went on to become their country's foreign ministers. Bhutto also attained wide popularity in Pakistan when he dissociated with Ayub and was elected prime minister once the country held national elections years later.

Ayub had decided to move Pakistan's capital from Karachi to a new city, Islamabad, which was to be built near the garrison town of Rawalpindi. Until the construction of Islamabad was completed, Rawalpindi would serve as the interim capital. The Indian delegation arrived in Rawalpindi for the first round of talks two days after Christmas in 1962. That very day Pakistan announced that it had reached an agreement with China to settle their boundary, which involved Pakistan giving a part of Kashmir to China. For the Indians, this represented bad faith on the part of Pakistan. An assurance from Ayub that the timing of the announcement was inadvertent saved the talks. But the discussions still went nowhere.

During the course of negotiations India offered changes in the cease-fire line that would have added fifteen hundred square miles to Kashmir's territory controlled by Pakistan. But the Pakistani negotiators rejected the proposal because it would still leave an overwhelming Muslim population of Kashmir under Indian rule. The British and the Americans proposed third-party mediation, which India rejected. Kennedy had thus kept his promise to Ayub to try to address the Kashmir dispute. Secretary of State Dean Rusk reported after traveling to both countries that "there is little evidence of a desire in either Pakistan or India to work hard toward a general reconciliation which would involve major concessions on Kashmir."[83]

According to Rusk, "Nothing less than a Franco-German type of reconciliation is likely to work. India is more ready for this than Pakistan; the latter appears most reluctant to ease pressures on Kashmir by discussing or agreeing on other questions prior to a Kashmir settlement." Rusk seemed to have understood the heart of the matter. "Pakistan pretends to be convinced that India has never accepted partition and seeks the disappearance of Pakistan,"[84] he observed.

✦

THE ASSASSINATION OF John F. Kennedy on November 22, 1963, shocked the world. But it also affected US-Pakistan relations. Johnson's priorities as president related to domestic matters. In foreign policy he tended to defer to the national security professionals. Bundy, the national security adviser, and Robert McNamara, the secretary of defense, led Johnson into an expanded war in Vietnam. John McCone, director of central intelligence, and Lieutenant General Gordon Blake, director of the National Security Agency, were instrumental in persuading the president of Pakistan's indispensability in intelligence gathering.

In a meeting with Bundy and McCone on November 30 Johnson brought up the question of Pakistan. McCone spoke of the intelligence community's view that the relationship with Pakistan was "of the greatest importance." They did not want efforts at regional balance to jeopardize the operations of the Communications Intercept facility at Badaber. Johnson expressed the "greatest of confidence in Ayub" and voiced the feeling that Ayub had drifted away because of "the thought that we would abandon him in favor of India." He directed his team that this should be "corrected in a most positive manner."[85]

The Johnson administration's overtures encouraged Ayub to believe that Americans had reverted to recognizing Pakistan's importance as an ally. Only months beforehand the United States had been upset with Pakistan's decision to start civilian flights to and from China. In response, the United States had held back a $4.3 million loan for airport improvement over this China-Pakistan civil aviation agreement, which provided China air travel access to the noncommunist world for the first time.[86]

Regular flights had started between Canton and Shanghai in China and Karachi and Dhaka in Pakistan. The *Chicago Tribune* cited Pakistan's decision as an example of the limits of foreign aid as leverage in America's relations with other countries. "Not even a two billion dollar handout was able to keep one Asian ally in line," it lamented.[87]

When Johnson attempted to offer reassurance that Pakistan would not be abandoned in favor of India, Ayub interpreted that as a signal that American aid would not be interrupted on account of Pakistan's continued engagement with China. Acting on this misunderstanding,

Ayub went on to tell General Maxwell Taylor, chairman of the joint chiefs, that the United States should stop its aid to India, as it would not be used against communist China but instead to intimidate smaller neighbors. The United States "held Pakistan's interests too cheap," he said, telling Taylor that "we will fight for this land of ours."[88] Taylor interpreted that as reiterating Pakistan's willingness to fight communism. In fact, Ayub was talking about fighting the Indians.

Ayub had settled on a three-part strategy: he kept protesting to the Americans regarding their aid to India while also continuing to seek US military assistance, he deepened Pakistan's ties with communist China, and he prepared to settle the Kashmir dispute by force, based on the assumption that the United States, because of its reliance on the Badaber Intelligence base, would not cut off military supplies to Pakistan.

In a letter to Johnson, Ayub laid out the argument against military aid to India. "This aid imperils the security of Pakistan, your ally," Ayub wrote. "It prevents an Indo-Pakistan rapprochement over Kashmir which immobilizes the bulk of their armed forces in a dangerous confrontation," he went on. According to Ayub, American aid to India "must lead to an arms race between India and Pakistan and thereby place a crushing burden on their economies. Surely this is no way of preventing the inroads of communism into the subcontinent—if this is the United States objective. On the contrary, it would facilitate them."[89] Ironically, all of these arguments could be reversed to make the Indian case against American aid to Pakistan.

Ayub's single-minded focus on India and Kashmir annoyed Johnson, who decided to share his opinion with the Pakistani ambassador, Ghulam Ahmed, after receiving the Pakistani president's letter. Johnson told the ambassador that he did not share "Ayub's feeling that because the United States has helped India, Pakistan should ignore its alliance obligations." Johnson did not think it would be in Pakistan's interest to leave the alliances, but that would have to be Pakistan's decision. He "expressed great admiration for President Ayub and great affection for the people of Pakistan," but he also realized that the two countries were coming "to the point at which we would all have to re-evaluate the condition of our relationship."[90]

Johnson also told the American ambassador to Pakistan, Walter P. McConaughy, that he was distressed that "such an old and valued ally of ours as President Ayub should want to give the attention he has given to Communist China." He wanted McConaughy to tell Ayub that America was "having all sorts of trouble with China in Southeast Asia right now."

In his discussion with McConaughy Johnson asked the question that both his predecessors had asked: he wondered how much the United States was getting for the very large amounts of aid it was giving to India as well as Pakistan. According to McConaughy's notes of the meeting: "The President said that when Ayub was willing to send men to Laos, he thought our aid was worthwhile. But now that the Pakistanis refused to help us in Viet Nam, he didn't know whether we were getting very much for our money."[91]

Johnson was not the only one frustrated by the course of US–Pakistan relations; Ayub had also started talking of reconsidering ties with the United States. When demonstrations against the Vietnam War outside US government buildings in some Pakistani cities turned violent, the Pakistani media had taken an extremely anti-American turn. Further, the fact that police showed up late or failed to act against the demonstrators made Americans wonder if this was not a coincidence. The discussion between McConaughy and Ayub that followed summed up the weariness of both sides.

The US ambassador spoke of the Chinese communist challenge, stating that the "Chinese communist shadow would be even longer and more ominous than the Soviet one for the next few years." As the reported North Vietnamese attack on an American Navy vessel in the Gulf of Tonkin had occurred only a few days earlier, the United States thought it was "entitled to ask our allies and indeed every free country to stand up and be counted in the current dangerous confluence of events." McConaughy expressed disappointment that Pakistan had "not yet seen fit to make even a token non-strategic contribution in Viet Nam." Ayub confirmed that

Pakistan would not be able to contribute in Vietnam because of its "vulnerability" in relation to India.

McConaughy asked Ayub how a token contribution in the non-military field would represent any enlarged political or military commitment. Ayub's response—that his "people would not understand"—elicited an angry retort from the career American diplomat. If the people did not understand, he replied, "It would be because of the conditioning they had received in recent months from official and other public news media."[92]

At this time Ayub also conveyed to the United States his intention to "re-examine" Pakistan's tie to SEATO. He told McConaughy that Pakistan had never had a deep intrinsic interest of its own in SEATO anyway. Pakistan had joined in 1954 only as a cooperative gesture to the United States and was now "embarrassed by her current inability to pull her weight in the organization because of liabilities nearer home," he explained.

The State Department read this as a reflection of two already apparent trends in Pakistan's foreign policy: the country was pulling away from alliances and it was trying to narrow its relationship with the United States to bilateral interchange. But if Pakistan revised the terms of its relationship, the United States would naturally do the same. Americans interacting with Ayub at the time saw no realization among Pakistani officials that there would be consequences for Pakistan if they were to back out of alliance commitments.[93] Ayub and other Pakistani leaders had succeeded in repeatedly getting the Americans to give aid without asking for an immediate return, which had made them oblivious of the possibility of the United States turning around and someday saying, "No."

Little had obviously changed since the days of the Korean conflict, when Pakistan's leaders had made a similar argument. Since then the United States had invested heavily in increasing the size of the Pakistani armed forces, which, by the summer of 1964, had reached a strength of around 250,000 troops. Economic, military, and food aid to Pakistan between 1950 and 1966 totaled $5 billion. Large loans from international financial institutions such as the World Bank and the Asian Development Bank provided additional capital during

······

Ayub's decade of direct military rule, leading to GDP growth averaging 5 percent annually.

But for Ayub and his generals, supported by many civilians, this was not enough. Pakistan had to secure its rights in Kashmir before and above all else. Because the Americans were unwilling or unable to ensure that the Kashmir dispute resolved in Pakistan's favor, Pakistan would use the means available to it, including those the Americans provided ostensibly for a different enemy. The calculus in Rawalpindi was that the Indian military was relatively weak, especially after the conflict with China, and Pakistan was stronger than it would likely be in the future. American-made Patton tanks and F-86 and F-104 aircraft were superior in quality to the equipment in the Indian arsenal. If Pakistan could get "a military-induced solution to the Kashmir imbroglio," now was the time.[94]

The death in 1964 of Nehru, the only prime minister India had since partition, provided Ayub with an opportunity to test his theory that India might break up within fifteen to twenty years. In what was named "Operation Gibraltar," Pakistan helped exacerbate Muslim unrest in the Indian-controlled parts of Kashmir. Ayub's strategic minds had developed the doctrine of "irregular warfare" as a tool for "reducing the crucial nature of the initial battles of Pakistan."[95] Under this doctrine armed infiltrators were sent into Kashmir in August of 1965, hoping to ignite a wider uprising.

If everything went according to plan, Pakistan's regular forces would enter Kashmir triumphantly in "Operation Grand Slam." The Indians would then either sue for peace or the US-led international community would force a settlement of the Kashmir dispute in favor of Pakistan. But the plan had a critical flaw: it did not take into account the possibility that India may widen the conflict along Pakistan's international borders, denying Pakistan victory in Kashmir and forcing it to defend its own territory. Ayub had also misread the likely American reaction.

Robert Komer described the situation for the US president in his usual colorful style. "Kashmir is still bubbling merrily and could blow up," he wrote on August 29, 1965. "U Thant [the UN secretary general] fears the whole 1949 ceasefire agreement may collapse. He wanted to report blaming the Paks for starting the mess, but the Paks threatened to withdraw from the UN if he did. Nor are the Indians too eager to take Kashmir to the UN lest the whole question of its status be reopened (which is what the Paks want)."[96]

The American ambassador to India, Chester Bowles, anticipated Indian retaliation and urged that the United States pressure Pakistan, "lest they be encouraged to think they are getting away with the game." In addition, Komer referred to intelligence reports that "both the Kashmir infiltration and the earlier Rann of Kutch affair are part of a 'well-organized plan' to force a Kashmir settlement." The Rann of Kutch had been an India-Pakistan battleground a few months earlier, and the United States had helped refer that dispute about demarcation of borders to international arbitration. The Americans had clandestinely obtained the Pakistani military plan and knew that it had been shared with the Chinese.[97]

Although his advisers asked for robust intervention to prevent a full-blown India-Pakistan war, Johnson decided that it would be better for the United States to sit it out. Secretary of State Rusk shared with the president his fear of communal rioting in Kashmir and across the subcontinent. He suspected that millions could be killed and wanted the United States to make every effort to stop the fighting. "The Pakistanis had started the current affair with a massive infiltration of several thousand men," Rusk told Johnson, adding, "Then the Indians crossed the Ceasefire Line in a mop-up operation, especially to pinch off a dangerous salient."[98] According to him, the Pakistanis had escalated the conflict by throwing in their regular army to cut the road to Srinagar.

Johnson said he wanted to be very cautious about anything the United States said. "First, both sides wanted us to threaten them so they could be martyrs," he observed. "Second, both would use US equipment if they needed it, regardless of what we said." His proposed solution was to ask Britain or someone else to talk to both sides while the Americans should "get behind a log and sleep a bit." The president said he had found out over the last few months how little influence the United States had with the Pakistanis or Indians. Rusk felt that the United States had to remind both the Indians and

· · · · ·

the Pakistanis that American arms were not for the purpose of fighting each other.[99]

On September 6 India retaliated by widening the war along Pakistan's international border, forcing Pakistani troops to defend the cities of Lahore, Kasur, and Sialkot. Pakistan's dreams of "liberating" Kashmir had gone up in smoke—now it was a question of defending Pakistan. In discussions with American diplomats, Ayub acknowledged that the war had begun as a result of Pakistan's forays in Kashmir, but this did not stop him from seeking American intervention on behalf of Pakistan and the Pakistanis from feeling aggrieved when its Western allies did not help it in war.[100]

As was often the case, the Pakistanis debated their American interlocutors, invoking history selectively. The Americans did not see this as the time to remind the Pakistanis that they had failed to fire a single bullet against any communist army, even after receiving massive military assistance ostensibly to fight communism. There was no mention of Pakistan's past refusal to provide even nonmilitary support in Korea, Laos, and Vietnam, but instead considerable discussion about America's obligations.

In a long argument Foreign Minister Bhutto told the US ambassador that the Americans had a commitment to defend Pakistan if it was attacked. Treaties bound the United States to stop India from attacking Pakistan, he argued, refusing to accept US attempts to secure a UN-sponsored cease-fire as a substitute. According to Bhutto, the United States needed to take action for a final settlement of the Kashmir issue.[101]

In fact, Pakistan had budged little from the stance that Ayub had repeatedly adopted during talks with American officials. In almost all his conversations with Americans he had focused exclusively on asking for military aid and demanding Western intervention on behalf of Pakistan for a Kashmir settlement. During the war a Canadian diplomat asked the Pakistani president what he wanted. He replied, "We want Kashmir but we know we can't win it by military action. If only you people would show some guts, we would have it."[102]

From the US point of view there was no commitment to assist Pakistan in a war it had initiated. The United States saw itself as

......

doing Pakistan a favor by seeking an early end to the war. The Americans were clear that they did not want to be dragged deeper into the India-Pakistan quagmire. As soon as the war began, Rusk sent a personal message to McConaughy and Bowles, warning them that both India and Pakistan would make a major effort to gain US support, and both could be expected to cite their disappointment and resentment toward the United States.

The ambassadors and their staffs "should be ready to explain firmly but sympathetically why the U.S. is not moving in to partici-pate in the way each might wish," Rusk directed. The United States would ignore resentment and recrimination. "We are being asked to come in on the crash landing where we had no chance to be in on the take-off," said the secretary of state, pointing out the futility of joining that exercise.[103]

The United States suspended supplies of arms to both India and Pakistan, causing disappointment in Pakistan because of the coun-try's greater dependence on American weapons. Foreign Minister Bhutto told McConaughy that this was "an act not of an ally and not even that of a neutral. Rather, it was an act which would be of net benefit to the Indian side."[104] In an emotional plea Bhutto asked the United States to cut off economic assistance to India, including food aid, until "India terminated the aggression against Pakistan."[105]

McConaughy maintained that the United States did this to pre-serve Pakistan as well as the subcontinent as a whole. He attempted to convey as diplomatically as possible US disenchantment with Pakistan, which had started a war in the hope of dragging in the United States without prior discussion. Ayub's finance minister, Muhammad Shuaib, conveyed the Pakistani president's desperation for a "gesture" that would enable him to reject Chinese overtures and remain an American ally. The United States' refusal to side with Pakistan against India seemed "designed to push me toward the Chi-nese," Ayub was quoted as saying. "I don't want to sit in the Chinese lap, and I won't do so if it can be avoided. But if U.S. can't give me any help, I'll have no choice." Ayub wanted "an authoritative U.S. statement attaching responsibility to India" for starting the war and a public statement that America would use its influence to effect a Kashmir settlement in Pakistan's favor.[106]

Rusk's response to the plea was unequivocal: the United States would support a cease-fire and any negotiations acceptable to both parties on the cause of their conflict. "Once the firing is stopped and President Johnson is convinced that renewed US assistance will be used to help the people of Pakistan and not to support military adventures," said the secretary of state, "close and mutually helpful relations between the U.S. and Pakistan can quickly be restored."[107]

The war ended in a stalemate seventeen days after it started, denying Pakistan the military advantage it had hoped to seek. That had several consequences, each of them important for Pakistan's future. First, based on the notion that the United States had not come to Pakistan's aid despite being its ally, it bred anti-Americanism among Pakistanis. Second, it linked the Pakistani military closer to an Islamist ideology. Religious symbolism and calls to Jihad were used to build the morale of soldiers and the people. Third, it widened the gulf between East and West Pakistan, as Bengalis felt that Ayub's military strategy had left them completely unprotected. Fourth, it weakened Ayub, who lost America's confidence without being able to score a definitive victory against India.

Pakistan's state-controlled media generated a frenzy of Jihad, extolling the virtues of Pakistan's "soldiers of Islam." There were stories of gallantry, of divine help, and of superhuman resistance. The legend of a suicide squad "of dedicated soldiers who acted as live mines to blow up the advancing Indian tanks" became popular, along with tales of "green-robed angels deflecting bombs from their targets."[108] The state told the Pakistani people that they had been victims of aggression and that the aggression had been repelled with the help of God.

Official propaganda convinced the people of Pakistan that their military had won the war. Pakistan had occupied 1,600 square miles of Indian territory, 1,300 of it in the desert, whereas India secured 350 square miles of Pakistani real estate. But the Indian-occupied Pakistani land was of greater strategic value, located near the West

Pakistani capital, Lahore, and the industrial city of Sialkot as well as in Kashmir. Moreover, although Pakistan had held its own against a larger army, it came out of the war a weakened nation.

The US-Pakistan relationship had lost its initial strength, Kashmir was still unsettled, and inattention from the central government was upsetting the Bengalis in East Pakistan more than ever. Domestic factors were also causing unrest in Sindh and Balochistan. Ayub decided to turn to the Soviet Union to host the postwar peace conference, which was eventually held in Tashkent in January 1966. He went to Washington before going to Tashkent so as to ensure that the United States would not interpret his moves as hostile. At Tashkent Ayub agreed to swap the territory both sides seized in the recent war.

Brought to believe that the war had ended in a Pakistani victory, the public could not understand why Pakistan had to give up any territory it had won. Nor did the Tashkent agreement make any mention of Pakistan's demand for a plebiscite in Kashmir, and the people were led to the question why, if Pakistan had scored a military victory, there had neither been territorial gains nor the promise of a future favorable settlement. Bhutto resigned from the cabinet and led Ayub's critics to suggest that political surrender at Tashkent had converted a military victory into defeat.

The United States observed and documented the attacks on its consulates and information centers in the wake of the war. As a result, there was a general decline in support and sympathy for Pakistan throughout the US government. Meanwhile, in Pakistan conspiracy theories were on the rise. An article in London's *Telegraph* claimed that the CIA had started the India-Pakistan war to get rid of Ayub; US intelligence suspected that Bhutto had been behind that story.

In a document titled "Pakistani Gamesmanship," Komer listed for National Security Adviser Bundy events that pointed toward an orchestration of anti-Americanism. "Our Pak friends have sent pictures to Turkey of the way the Karachi mob damaged our USIS installation (show Turks how to deal with US facilities?)," he said sarcastically. Then he pointed out that the mob in Karachi carried handbills containing the *Telegraph* article. Komer also spoke of a newspaper story in Pakistan that the Pakistani government had placed. The story claimed that "the State Department instructed the US press to play down Indian defeats in an effort to make [US] Congress think that India could stand up to China."[109]

Also significant for Komer was an intelligence report that Bhutto had distributed among Pakistani officials: three hundred copies of the book *The Invisible Government*, written by journalists David Wise and Thomas Ross. The book detailed the CIA's clandestine operations in several countries, including Iran. It contained previously un-published information about the Badaber facility near Peshawar. If Bhutto had, in fact, distributed copies of the book among officials, this meant that he wanted to question Pakistan's secret relationship with US intelligence. If the allegation of his role in distributing the book was false, however, someone in Pakistan's establishment was gunning for him and feeding false information about him to the US embassy.

According to Komer, the US embassy in Pakistan doubted that Pakistan's government had "an exaggerated idea any longer of the importance of Peshawar [Badaber] to the U.S., since the recent record of our aid hold-ups must convince them that they can't use Peshawar as a decisive lever." Although six smaller US intelligence installations in Pakistan had been closed down "because of petty ir-ritations," the embassy did not fear closure of the Badaber base. Komer, more realistic than the embassy, thought that the Pakistanis were convinced the intelligence facilities they hosted were much more important and, thus, would use it as a lever soon. In his view the United States would not be able to convince the Pakistanis "to play ball unless we confront them continually with the prospect of losing all U.S. support."[110]

But the US intelligence community was not willing to risk their Badaber communications intercept facility. As such, they were partly instrumental in convincing Johnson to offer Ayub further food aid when the two met in December 1965 for the first time after the war. The American president spoke to the Pakistani dictator as if nothing had gone seriously wrong. Reviewing the meeting with his advisers, Johnson said he thought that Ayub was much chastened. "He had gone on an adventure and been licked," Johnson said, adding that he hated to see a proud man humble himself so. He saw Ayub "subdued, troubled, pathetic and sad."[111]

Johnson asserted that he understood Ayub's difficulties. "Ayub felt hemmed in by powerful neighbors on all sides—China, Russia and India," he remarked. Johnson observed that at home the Pakistan president had his domestic problems with the Bhutto group and others, but "Ayub seemed almost to have a psychosis about India." Ayub had apparently told Johnson that "I know you won't believe it but those Indians are going to gobble us up."[112] Johnson had replied that if they tried this, the United States would stop them. The US president emphasized how close he felt to Ayub. He said he understood Ayub—his fears and his problems.

Ayub had managed to take Johnson into confidence before letting the Soviets help shape the postwar peace. Once again the personal feelings of an American leader about a Pakistani one had saved the relationship. But Ayub never shared the extent of Pakistan's dependence on the United States with the Pakistani people, nor did he acknowledge that the war against India was a blunder. He published a book titled *Friends, Not Masters*, which served both as his memoirs and a statement that he had sought friendship with the West, which in turn sought to act as Pakistan's masters.

The book helped exacerbate Pakistani anger against the United States. In it Ayub acknowledged that "the objectives which the western powers wanted the Baghdad Pact to serve were quite different from the objectives we had in mind." But he argued that Pakistan had "never made any secret of our intentions or our interests" and that the United States knew Pakistan would use its new arms against India. This feigned version of events was also fed to the public through the media.

People were told that India attacked Pakistan and the United States stabbed Pakistan in the back by withholding crucial military materiel. The Pakistani people were not told that Pakistan's alliance treaties with the United States did not apply to war with India or that the 1965 war had, in fact, started because of Pakistan's attempt to militarily change the status quo in Kashmir.

······

The United States, Komer pointed out, had helped Pakistan build its independent position through $5 billion in support. It stopped a war Ayub started "just in time to save the Paks." But all that the United States got in return was "a bit of quite valuable real estate"— a reference to intelligence listening posts. Pakistan had shut down some of these installations, and four were still closed at the time of Komer's comments. Apparently Pakistan had not informed the Americans about getting MIG aircraft and tanks from China before the war. Komer concluded that "if there's any history of broken moral commitments, it's on the Pak side—not ours."[113]

In less than two years Johnson's personally favorable disposition resulted in Pakistan's military approaching the American embassy with a fresh request for arms and munitions. Defense Minister Admiral Afzal Rahman Khan spoke at length on the subject with Benjamin Oehlert, a former Coca-Cola executive who had arrived as ambassador in July 1967. "Next to President Ayub," the admiral told Oehlert, "the military establishment" was America's best friend in Pakistan. The country's economic circumstances did not permit buying tanks and other much-needed equipment for the military. The army badly needed two hundred new tanks, he said, so it would be a good idea if the US ambassador sat down "in cool of evening over couple of scotch-and-sodas" with Ayub to discuss how the Americans could resume military supplies in return for retaining the Badaber base.[114]

After the war with India Ayub had tried to obtain arms from several sources, including the Soviet Union and France, but no one seemed to be able to meet Pakistan's military needs on the type of terms on which Pakistan had become accustomed with the Americans. The Pakistanis had found that the global arms market was a tough place. No one, except the Americans, offered weapons as aid or on relatively easy financial terms. Although the United States had resumed the supply of ammunition and spare parts in April 1967, Pakistan was having difficulty buying major items like tanks and planes.

For the United States, the decision was difficult. It had armed Pakistan in the past after Ayub's assurance that the Pakistan army would become theirs. But the Pakistanis had not used those weapons to fight any American enemy; instead, they had gone to war against a friend of the United States, India. Removing the arms embargo without a change in Pakistan's policy sent the wrong message to all American allies, many of whom had their own local disputes to settle.

Rusk realized "the temptation to try to 'buy' an assured future for the Peshawar facility with one or two hundred tanks." But he also knew that linking "military supply policy with Peshawar" would encourage "intolerable pressures from Government of Pakistan for more and more hardware."[115] Thus, the Pakistani officials' request was politely turned down. When Johnson stopped over in Karachi for refueling while on his way back from a trip to Australia and Thailand, Ayub reiterated the request along with a plea for vegetable oil and wheat. Johnson immediately agreed to the food aid and promised to help Pakistan get the tanks from a third party, possibly Turkey.[116]

The United States delivered on the food aid, but getting the tanks through third parties proved difficult. The Pakistanis decided to up the ante and served notice on April 6, 1968, for vacating the Badaber Intelligence Facility upon the expiration of its lease on July 17, 1969. The formal notice of termination did not surprise the Americans; it was the likely way for Pakistan to open negotiations about possibly renewing the lease. But the notice was delivered shortly before the expected arrival in Pakistan of Soviet Prime Minister Alexei Kosygin, a coincidence the Americans found interesting.

The Pakistani officials who delivered the notice gave the US ambassador a long speech about how the base disrupted Pakistan's relations with China and the Soviet Union without bringing any significant benefit to Pakistan.[117] Although the agreement to grant the base to the United States had been kept secret from the Pakistani public, the decision to end the lease was made public even before discussions between the two sides had been completed.

Johnson, still confident that his personal ties with Ayub could change things, wrote a personal letter to the Pakistani president seeking continuation of the intelligence facility. The letter said that the Pakistani decision to prematurely announce its position had "surprised and disturbed" him and that, too, "because of threats and demands by another power." It pointed out that the intelligence facility helped US security "as well as the security of many other nations" and reminded Ayub of "the close relationship that has existed for so many years between our two countries."

This relationship, Johnson said, had been manifested in America's "contribution of more than $3,500,000,000 in aid to Pakistan." He had obviously used the numerals for effect before asking for "a reasonable withdrawal period" to lessen the impact of the facility's closure. Johnson ended the letter with the words: "I do not think, old friend, this is too much to ask."[118] Ayub wrote back, and there was some further discussion, including the possibility of giving the Americans some more time in return for the two hundred Patton tanks. In the end, however, the Badaber Communications Intercept Facility stopped being operational well before its lease expired. The base was formally handed back on the day of the expiration of its lease.

The US alliance with Pakistan, beginning with SEATO, had satisfied neither country. The reason Pakistan accepted the arrangement was obvious to everyone: the country was short of resources and it had inherited a large military establishment that it sought not only to retain but also to expand. American critics of the relationship objected more to what journalist Selig Harrison described as the American decision to "subsidize Pakistan as a permanent garrison state with a military capability swollen out of all proportion to her size."[119]

Chester Bowles, the American ambassador to India, offered a plausible explanation for US decision making in relation to Pakistan. He attributed American policy toward South Asia as the product of "sending important personages to this area who have no knowledge of the forces at work here." Unfamiliar Americans, Bowles said, "come convinced that all Asians are 'inscrutable' products of the 'inscrutable East'!"

But Pakistan's British-trained elite were "Asians who argue the advantages of an olive over an onion in a martini and who know friends they know in London," he argued. This created a mirage for

· · · · ·

American policy makers. "Here at last are Asians who make sense, who understand our problems, who face up to the realities, who understand the menace of whatever may worry us at the moment," Bowles observed critically. "And so we agree to more F-104s or C130s or whatever may be currently required as political therapy to ease wounded Pakistani feelings."[120]

✦

AYUB RESIGNED FROM the presidency in March 1969 after several months of violent demonstrations against his government. Instead of transferring power to the speaker of the National Assembly, a Bengali, as was required by the constitution he himself had imposed seven years earlier, Ayub returned the country to martial law. The army chief, General Yahya Khan, became Pakistan's president and chief martial law administrator, ruling by decree and without a constitution.

Yahya organized Pakistan's first open elections in December 1970, and these were followed by a brutal civil war in East Pakistan.

Chapter Three

A Split and a Tilt

D uring Richard M. Nixon's successful campaign to become the thirty-seventh president of the United States, Pakistan was not mentioned at all; the Vietnam War was the major foreign policy issue during the 1968 elections. But Nixon did feel a strong attachment to Pakistan, so much so that he visited Pakistan within the first few months of his presidency. Pakistan was also his country of choice as the intermediary when opening relations with China. And it was in defense of Pakistan that he described Indian Prime Minister Indira Gandhi as "a bitch" and an "old witch." Not to be left out, Nixon's national security adviser, Henry Kissinger, likewise made the unusual remark: "The Indians are bastards anyway."[1]

These remarks came about in response to Gandhi's visit to Washington in November 1971, at the height of the East Pakistan crisis. At that time Pakistan's military was forcefully suppressing protests following the country's first election. The Bengali-led Awami League had won the election, but the West Pakistan–based military regime had accused the party of seeking secession with Indian help. After much brutality in East Pakistan, international opinion had aligned against Pakistan. Threat of another India-Pakistan war loomed.

Nixon and Kissinger made these remarks during a conversation in the Oval Office that also involved the president's assistant, H. R. "Bob" Haldeman. The exchange was being recorded for posterity, and its transcript is now available in the Nixon archives. The president had met Gandhi a day earlier and was scheduled to meet her again after his meeting with Kissinger and Haldeman. He was reviewing the previous day's discussion.

"I raised my voice a little," Nixon acknowledged. Kissinger, Nixon's national security adviser, advised him to be "a shade cooler today," explaining that "even though she was a bitch, we shouldn't overlook the fact that we got what we wanted." The president had warned Gandhi to stay out of West Pakistan even if Pakistan's military collapsed in East Pakistan, and the message had been conveyed, Kissinger pointed out, in such a way that Gandhi could not claim that "the United States kicked her in the teeth."[2]

A few days later Nixon and Kissinger spoke again about trying to prevent an Indian attack on West Pakistan. They discussed plans to send an American aircraft carrier into the Bay of Bengal as a deterrent to the Indians. "We're in the position," Kissinger said, "where a Soviet stooge, supported with Soviet arms, is overrunning a country that is an American ally." Kissinger saw this as an opportunity to find out if America could scare a country like India. "If we can still scare somebody else," he said, noting that there was less than a fifty-fifty chance of that happening, "it may open the Middle East solution."[3] Kissinger was testing America's ability to influence medium-sized powers such as India through bluff. If India could be scared, he seemed to suggest, the much smaller countries of the Middle East could also be forced to comply with US demands without using force.

The plan did not work, however, as India calculated correctly that the Americans would not be willing to get into a shooting war. In the same conversation Nixon expressed irritation over China's refusal to get involved. "Boy, I tell you," he exclaimed, "movement of even some Chinese toward that border could scare those goddamn Indians to death." But by the very next day the president had tired of working so hard at intervening on Pakistan's behalf.

Kissinger informed him that Soviet leader Leonid Brezhnev had written a letter proposing negotiations between West and East Pakistan. However, even though mediation could avert bloodshed, Pakistani leaders did not want to be told what to do. Nixon recognized that "The partition of Pakistan is a fact" and asked, "Now the point is, why then, Henry, are we going through all this agony?" Kissinger replied, "We're going through this agony to prevent the West Pakistan army from being destroyed" because "the world's psychological balance of power" was at stake. The United States could not allow a Soviet ally to defeat an American ally.[4]

In the end most of Nixon's and Kissinger's exertions proved futile. On December 16, 1971, Indian forces marched triumphantly into Dhaka, the capital of East Pakistan, where Pakistan's army laid down its arms. Ninety thousand Pakistani troops, civilian officials, and allies became prisoners of war. East Pakistan now proclaimed itself the independent Peoples Republic of Bangladesh, and it soon received international recognition.

After initial hesitation, the United States recognized Bangladesh. But Pakistan refused to recognize Bangladesh for over two years, though it eventually relented. Although the United States, with Soviet help, had prevented India from overrunning West Pakistan as well, it received no gratitude for its efforts. The Indians claimed that they had no plans of doing that anyway, whereas the Pakistanis resented the United States for not stepping in to help save the country's eastern wing.

The chain of events that led to Pakistan's bifurcation had begun with Ayub's removal from power. Although the United States had lost its intelligence base near Peshawar, some Americans still wanted to retain their alliance with Pakistan—Nixon and Kissinger foremost among them. Their attachment to Pakistan, based on an expectation of support in global strategy, is what had led the United States to support West Pakistan's army. But "the tilt"[5] brought no advantage to the United States, nor did it serve Pakistan well. American support gave Pakistan a sense of false confidence, which encouraged Pakistani leaders to march into a blunder and then persist with folly. If this had not been the case, Pakistan may have negotiated a settlement with politicians from East Pakistan. But it didn't.

★

THE PROCESS OF Pakistan's breakup had started much earlier than 1971 and was largely a function of domestic politics. Protests broke out against Ayub's government in the fall of 1968, after he had ruled for a decade. Multiple factors contributed to the unrest: economic growth had stalled after the 1965 war with India, American aid had declined to a third of what it had been, and conditions on loans from the International Financial Institutions became somewhat stringent. As a result, economic disparities between East and West Pakistan and among different classes had become the subject of political agitation. The people were tired of dictatorship and demanded change.

Pakistan's traditional political parties, which Ayub had sidelined, coalesced into an alliance to demand his ouster. The Awami League (AL), led by Shaikh Mujibur Rahman, referred to as Mujib because of the commonality of his last name, was gaining ground in the East with its calls for greater rights and autonomy for Bengalis. It drew its strength from Bengalis' widespread resentment over being treated as second-class citizens in a country where they constituted the majority of the population.

In West Pakistan Ayub's former foreign minister Zulfikar Ali Bhutto had formed the Pakistan People's Party (PPP) with a socialist manifesto, and this tapped into his personal popularity. He also benefited from nationalist sentiment generated in the aftermath of the war against India, especially in the Punjab region, from which most of Pakistan's soldiers and civil servants were traditionally recruited.

Before the outbreak of the street protests Mujib had been jailed over allegations that he had conspired with Indian intelligence to pursue East Pakistani secession. Then, soon after violent protests started in both wings of Pakistan, Bhutto was also imprisoned under preventive detention laws. By the time the two were released, both of them had become heroes in their respective parts of the country.

Initially Ayub's administration tried to put the demonstrations down with force. However, Ayub had suffered a stroke, which his subordinates had chosen not to reveal to the public, and by the time he was well enough to start making decisions himself, the situation had spiraled out of control.

·····

A CIA assessment noted "a steady deterioration of Ayub's political base" by February 1969, shortly after Nixon's inauguration. The Pakistani president had previously relied on the military, the Civil Service, the business community, and the landowners for support, providing an aura of stability after years of political chaos, contributing to Ayub's political longevity. Now, however, widespread rioting had damaged that aura beyond repair.

According to the US appraisal, Ayub had justified "his highly centralized and at times dictatorial rule" by making "frequent use of the widespread fear that India will try to reincorporate Pakistan into the Indian Union." This tactic was still "one of Ayub's few remaining psychological weapons," but his survival depended solely on "the loyalty to the regime of the nation's armed forces."[6] A few days later another intelligence assessment said that the army did not seem to "have the stomach for the violence that would seem necessary to restore order."[7] Pakistan was in for a "prolonged period of adjustment," the State Department's Bureau of Intelligence and Research predicted, and "the country will be fortunate if it emerges from this period of stress as a single entity."[8]

Finally, Ayub resigned on March 25, but not until after imposing martial law and handing power over to army commander General Yahya Khan. Both men claimed that the military had a legal and constitutional responsibility to defend the country not only against external aggression but also from internal disorder and chaos.[9] This transfer of power from one general to another thus amounted to a determination that the Pakistani military was the final arbiter in political matters. The *Economist* magazine described Ayub's ouster and replacement by Yahya Khan in an editorial titled "Tweedle Khan Takes Over."[10] Most international observers saw Yahya's regime as a continuation of Ayub's. Yahya did not change the foreign and domestic policies that Ayub had pursued for over a decade, and the West Pakistani elite, mostly ethnic Punjabis, continued to dominate the new government as they had the previous one.

The chaos that led to Ayub's ouster was related exclusively to Pakistan's internal politics. Although he had been a good friend to the United States until toward the end of his regime, Ayub had erred when he sought domestic strength solely through external relations. He failed to understand his diverse people's aspirations, imposing unity rather than nurturing it by recognizing his nation's differences. Obsessed with his belief in West Pakistan's martial races being superior to the Bengalis, Ayub treated East Pakistan particularly badly.

Conversely, Yahya did not fully follow in Ayub's footsteps by presenting himself as a savior for Pakistan; instead, he announced his intention to hold elections for an Assembly, open to all political parties, that would write a new constitution for the country. He wanted the politicians to maintain "the integrity of Pakistan and the glory of Islam"[11]—an allusion to the national ideology that had evolved since the days of Liaquat. He also said that he wanted to retire after transferring power to civilians, which blunted opposition that he might otherwise have faced for being Pakistan's second successive military dictator.

It would have made sense for the United States to take a step back so Pakistan could resolve its internal discord on its own, but some US policy makers still saw Pakistan solely through the prism of the Cold War. In particular, Kissinger told Nixon that the return to normalcy in Pakistan after Ayub's resignation depended on East Pakistanis accepting martial law.

According to Kissinger, violent reaction in East Pakistan to "a virtual coup by the West Pakistani establishment which has long dominated the country" could make the situation in the east wing dangerous. Although evidence did not suggest that any foreign country played a role in the recent internal disturbances, the national security adviser nonetheless concluded that opportunities for foreign meddling, "especially by the Communist Chinese," would increase.[12]

The Pakistani military also made no effort to pause, reflect, and change the basis of Pakistan's ties with the United States and deliberated even less over what had caused the country's disharmony. Within days of Yahya's ascent to power, Pakistan's military was pressing the United States to restore military assistance. The deputy martial law administrator and commander of the navy, Vice-Admiral Syed Muhammad Ahsan, represented Pakistan at President Eisenhower's funeral in April, using the opportunity to explain to US of-

· · · · ·

ficials the circumstances of imposing martial law and the new junta's intentions as well as to plead for renewed military aid.

Ahsan told State Department officials that it would be dangerous for the United States to withhold arms from Pakistan because doing so might force the country to "get involved with others" who might be "inimical to U.S. interests." Pakistan could not afford "expensive purchases in Western Europe," Ahsan said, going on to argue that this was a psychologically important time for the United States to invest in Pakistan's new leaders, who needed weapons for internal security and to "keep their troops from becoming disgruntled."[13]

But the US embassy in Pakistan was not sure which way the wind was blowing. It asked Washington to weigh the advantages or otherwise of supporting the new government that "may or may not win support of [the] populace and may or may not become [a] repressive force" in order to maintain a strong central government. Although West Pakistanis, especially those from the Punjabi ethnic group, dominated the country, the Bengalis from East Pakistan constituted a majority of Pakistan's population. US diplomats from Dhaka, in East Pakistan, were already reporting the wide gulf that had opened between the two wings of the country.

During this period of major changes in Pakistan, Benjamin Oehlert was serving his last few weeks as US ambassador. In a cable to the State Department he observed that the principal reasons for imposing martial law were to prevent East Pakistan from "obtaining national political power proportionate to population."[14] Experience had shown that aid had given Americans considerable access in Pakistan, even if it did not help change the country's policies. Consequently, Oehlert proposed supporting Yahya and his military regime "to expand leverage of our assistance." In his view, this could help Pakistan by increasing the chances of an American-backed political solution to its internal schism.

Secretary of State William Rogers visited Pakistan in May and met Yahya as well as other members of his junta. He was told that martial law had saved Pakistan from chaos, that elections would soon be held, and that a civilian government would come after a constitution was written. Insisting that he was a soldier who would return to soldiering after holding elections, Yahya laid out the case for aid. Pakistan was making economic progress, he said, adding that its economic progress could be cited as "vindication of the U.S. philosophy of assistance."[15]

When the subject turned to Pakistan's demands for sophisticated weaponry, Yahya argued that Pakistan needed them for its security. But Rogers questioned Pakistan's threat perception and wondered if it was indeed based on reality. He hinted that Pakistan faced problems at home that needed attention. But Yahya seemed more interested in Pakistan's international role, expressing familiar concerns about Afghanistan and India as well as communist subversion. He assured Rogers that Pakistan had no intention to leave SEATO and CENTO and that it remained committed to its alliance with the United States.

The Nixon White House soon decided that it would resume assistance, including military aid for Pakistan, as soon as it could overcome international and domestic anxieties about doing so. Kissinger told Pakistan's ambassador in Washington, Agha Hilaly, that the US president had "a very warm spot in his heart for former President Ayub Khan and for Pakistan." He assured the new government that the United States held "deep concern for Pakistan's interests and responsiveness to Pakistan's requirements," though he was not sure how that concern might translate into dollars.[16] This heartened Yahya, as did Nixon's decision to visit Pakistan as part of a round-the-world tour that summer.

For Nixon, Pakistan was only one stop in an Asia-wide trip. He started his journey on July 23, 1969, by observing the splashdown and recovery of the *Apollo 11* spacecraft from the deck of the USS *Hornet*, followed by an overnight stop in Guam. He traveled to the Philippines, Indonesia, Thailand, and India and then made an unannounced stopover in South Vietnam before arriving in Pakistan. The American president's journey continued on to Romania, and after a brief stopover in England to meet with Prime Minister Harold Wilson, he returned to the United States on August 3.

For Yahya, however, Nixon's arrival in Pakistan amounted to receiving the American stamp of approval. He needed it in order to reassure key Pakistani constituencies—especially the army—that the

......

United States would continue paying some of the country's bills even after Ayub was gone. Thus, Yahya gave Nixon a welcome in Lahore comparable to the one Eisenhower received in Karachi ten years earlier.

While Nixon was there, the Pakistani team made a strong pitch for greater aid. The Pakistani foreign secretary even told Nixon that Pakistan's need for a deterrent to India was so critical that it was content with getting weapons that the United States considered obsolete for its own military. Yahya complained that the United States no longer considered Pakistan its "most allied ally"—a term Eisenhower had used—any longer. "We are still allies," Yahya said, while offering the assurance that Pakistan wanted to move beyond its disagreements with the United States that followed the 1965 war. Nixon agreed that what happened under previous leaders in both countries could now be put behind them. The two countries "will be on [the] up-and-up with each other,"[17] he declared.

Nixon's attitude toward Pakistan was influenced, at least in part, by his desire to engage with communist China. Whereas Kennedy and Johnson had vehemently opposed Pakistan's close ties with Beijing, Nixon hoped to take advantage of them. During the presidential election campaign Nixon had pointed out that, considering its size and significance, China could not be ignored. And as someone with devout anticommunist credentials, he believed he could reach out to China without inviting criticism about being soft on communism. Pakistan, with an equally strong anticommunist reputation, could be a valuable partner in the venture.

Since 1955, in the absence of diplomatic relations, China and the United States had interacted through their ambassadors in Warsaw. They had effected little progress except an agreement over repatriation of citizens of the two countries who had been stranded as a result of the communist victory in China in 1949. That agreement was implemented with the help of the British Embassy assisting Americans in Beijing and the Indian Embassy helping the Chinese in Washington.

But the Warsaw Talks involved the State Department bureaucracy, whereas Nixon envisioned a bold approach, going directly to

......

China's top leaders. He had already sent private signals through US ambassadors in Warsaw and Paris, but these signals did not result in a major breakthrough. The Chinese could not publicly accept that they were doing business with the United States because even after the communist victory in China's mainland, the Americans still recognized the defeated nationalist Chinese government, limited to the island of Taiwan since 1949, as the legal representative of all of China. The communist Chinese wanted the United States to recognize their government's legitimacy before open negotiations took place. The Nixon administration had to be mindful of the powerful Taiwan lobby and the strong anticommunist sentiment in the United States.

During his round-the-world tour Nixon brought up China with Yahya as well as Romanian leader Nicolae Ceaușescu. Both dictators had access to China's premier, Zhou Enlai. If they could verbally convey Nixon's desire for normalizing ties with China, he could possibly put a deal in place before announcing it. A more public negotiating process, such as one involving the US State Department, could result in media leaks and the prospect of the anticommunist sentiment scuttling a deal before it was made. Nixon wanted to present Americans and the Taiwanese government with a fait accompli by announcing an agreement with China rather than opening debate over whether a bargain was desirable.

H. R. Haldeman, the US president's chief of staff at the time, recorded in his diary after Nixon's trip that Nixon saw Yahya as "a real leader—very intelligent—and with great insight into Russia-China relations." According to Haldeman, Nixon thought that Yahya could be a "valuable channel to China" and even the Soviet Union.

Although Nixon and Kissinger had not yet charted in detail their course for a thaw with China, Nixon's suggestion that Pakistan could act as a bridge between the two superpowers pleased Yahya and other Pakistani officials. After Ayub's decision to end the lease of the Badaber intelligence base at Peshawar, which had been meant to show the Americans how much they needed Pakistan, Pakistan's usefulness had diminished in American eyes. Now, however, if Pakistan could be the channel through which the Americans reached China, it would be important again. Acting as the United States' intermediary with China could compensate for the loss of influence Pakistan endured when it closed the US intelligence facilities.

Soon after Nixon's trip Yahya started preparing for his new role as facilitator of dialogue between China and the United States. But he did not realize the complexities of US domestic politics, which Nixon and Kissinger had hoped to circumvent. As a result of Yahya's indiscretion, an American diplomat in Pakistan informed the State Department that Yahya was "apparently debating" whether to communicate Nixon's desire for better relations through the communist Chinese ambassador "or whether to wait until he sees Zhou Enlai, probably some months hence."[18]

Kissinger asked Harold "Hal" Saunders, a trusted member of his team, to ensure that the discussions over China were treated strictly as a White House matter; the State Department and normal channels of diplomacy were not to be involved. Saunders, a PhD from Yale University who had served on the National Security Council staff since the Johnson presidency, met with Hilaly, the Pakistani ambassador, telling him that Nixon "did not have in mind that passing this word was urgent or that it required any immediate or dramatic Pakistani effort."[19]

The US president, Saunders explained, regarded reaching out to China "as important but not as something that needs to be done immediately." Kissinger was to be the sole point of contact on this matter, and the State Department did not need to know, he conveyed. "What President Nixon had in mind," Saunders told Hilaly, "was that President Yahya might at some natural and appropriate time convey this statement of the US position in a low-key factual way."[20] Yahya was scheduled to travel to China at the beginning of 1970, and that would be the appropriate time to convey Nixon's message.

Once Kissinger conveyed the need for secrecy as well as the importance of dealing exclusively with the White House, Pakistani officials felt reassured that they had been charged with a major undertaking. Therefore, they immediately asked for some payoff for their country in economic and military assistance, renewing their previous request for planes and tanks. Nixon wanted to help but could not do so without overcoming congressional skepticism.

After Pakistan's 1965 war with India, Congress had passed two amendments to the Foreign Assistance Act that forbade arming "underdeveloped countries" with "sophisticated weapons." The Conte-Long Amendment (named after Congressmen Silvio Conte, a Republican, and Clarence D. Long, a Democrat, both from Maryland) also required reducing US economic aid to such countries by the amount that they used their own resources for such purchases. However, the president could waive this restriction if he determined that a military sale was "important to the national security of the U.S."

Another amendment, sponsored by Senator Stuart Symington of Missouri and passed by Congress, directed the president to cut off US economic aid to any developing country that excessively diverted its resources to military expenditures. Congress, therefore, made it known that it did not want the United States arming either India or Pakistan. Consequently, if Nixon wanted to transfer any American weapons to Yahya as a favor, he would have to make a waiver for Pakistan that he would justify on grounds that US national security was at stake.

Nixon wanted to provide weapons to Pakistan as a reward for its help in reaching out to China, but he could hardly declare that publicly, especially as, at that stage, the entire China initiative was being kept secret from the American public. So Kissinger turned to Saunders to find a way out. Saunders, in turn, wrote a detailed memorandum on the options available to the administration, pointing out that America's "main interest is in the political and economic evolution of South Asia and not in the development of its military strength."

According to Saunders, "the political and economic evolution of India and its ability to defend its Himalayan frontier" was the greater US priority. "Our concern with Pakistan is that its political and economic evolution in the near term be constructive enough not to disrupt India's," he wrote. Saunders was suggesting that the principal US interest in helping Pakistan ought to be to prevent Pakistan from disrupting India—a goal that could not be achieved by enhancing

Pakistan's military capabilities. His analysis for the Nixon administration in 1969 differed little from "Blowtorch Bob" Komer's for Johnson in 1965. Similar assessments had also been provided to Presidents Truman and Eisenhower.

But any evaluation that Pakistan was less important than India was anathema to Pakistani leaders. So Saunders did not examine the possibility of giving up on Pakistan altogether, though he did wonder whether "going back into full-scale military aid would sufficiently further US interests to outweigh the disadvantages" and warned that arming Pakistan again "could strengthen Indian sense of political reliance on the USSR."[21] He then proposed a way out: Pakistan could be given a one-time waiver for some planes and tanks while conditions should be imposed that assuaged India's concerns.

But these recommendations were not good enough for Kissinger. In a handwritten note he shot back: "Hal—The President wants action not study. When are the tanks moving? When will the lawyers decide? Please get me quick answers."[22] Once Yahya had conveyed Nixon's message to Zhou Enlai and the positive Chinese reply had been communicated back, there was even greater urgency to offer Pakistan some recompense. Not surprisingly, the State Department, not fully informed about the China initiative and Pakistan's role in it, fought back.

"We do not have overriding political or security interests in South Asia which require us to get back into the arms business," observed acting Secretary of State Elliot Richardson in a memorandum to the president. Richardson, who resigned as attorney general a few years later rather than carry out Nixon's orders during the Watergate controversy, at the time was a rising star in the Nixon administration. And he saw no justification for supplying weapons to any country on the subcontinent. After all, both India and Pakistan had sufficiently strong militaries, the Indians were capable of withstanding a potential Chinese attack, and the prospects of Indo-Pakistan hostilities seemed remote.

According to Richardson, "India is relatively more important to our interests than Pakistan." Furthermore, he expected that there would be a sharp reaction from India if the United States changed its policy and resumed supplying weapons to Pakistan. "If we can please only one of the two countries, we should lean toward India, the larger and more influential power," he declared unequivocally. "Pakistan's unhappiness will be containable. It will continue to maintain good relations with us as a political offset to its relations with the USSR and Communist China and because we are Pakistan's largest aid donor."[23]

The State Department also recommended to maintain the status quo and retain the arms embargo for South Asia. But Richardson realized that Nixon felt "some obligation to President Yahya" that might "take the form of providing some military equipment or some economic development related help." He expressed the hope that any gesture toward Pakistan would not mark a significant departure from existing policy. In response, the State Department recommended a one-time exception to the embargo and supported the sale of six F-104 fighter aircraft to Pakistan, planes that Pakistan had asked to purchase.

Kissinger asked officials at the State Department to review their recommendation. He told assistant secretary of state for Near Eastern and South Asian affairs, Joseph Sisco, that Nixon "feels morally obligated to do something" for Yahya. Kissinger then proposed that the United States offer a military aid package to Pakistan that included seven B-57 bombers and the tanks that Pakistan had been requesting for some time.

Sisco informed Kissinger that those additions would make "a defensive replacement package" seem more offensive and would "have more effect in India." He felt that adding six B-57s could be justified as a replacement of old planes, but more tanks would have an "unfortunate psychological effect." After bargaining with the State Department on behalf of the Pakistani military, Kissinger explained, "Our worry is that this package is so small they will consider it an insult."[24]

Although willing to offer more weapons to Pakistan in discharging what Nixon considered a moral obligation, the White House was not completely ignorant of the views of Pakistan's generals. Kissinger had learned firsthand during a conversation with the West

Pakistan governor, Air Marshal Nur Khan, that Pakistan was ready to stumble into another war as it had done earlier. Nur Khan, known for his intellect and professional competence, came from a district in Punjab that was home to many of Pakistan's military men. He had been the chief of the air force and was a quintessential member of Pakistan's establishment.

In their meeting in Lahore in August 1969 Nur Khan had told Kissinger that Pakistan realized it could not take Kashmir by force, but there was no reason for Pakistan to cease its support for Kashmiris, which, according to Nur Khan, was now limited to propaganda. The air marshal said he could see why the United States and the other great powers would want the Kashmir problem to be settled, but he could see "no reason why Pakistan would benefit from such a settlement."

Nur Khan offered a succinct explanation of Pakistan's strategic vision. "In the present situation Pakistan obviously is not going to get what it wanted," he said to Kissinger, as a settlement would require appeasement of India, which in turn "would formally declare Pakistan's second class status in the subcontinent." Consequently, waiting for an opportunity to arise that would force India's hand in Kashmir while increasing its own military preparedness would serve Pakistan better. Nur Khan also made it clear that Pakistan needed additional US aircraft to maintain its military balance with India.[25] He effectively told Kissinger that Pakistan was in a permanent state of war with India over Kashmir and had no interest in resolving the conflict through talks. Pakistan did not want to be seen as less important or less powerful than India; equal status with India took priority over solving specific issues such as Kashmir.

In Kissinger's mind Pakistan's readiness to go to war again with India was not enough to deter him and Nixon from resuming arms supplies to Pakistan. Yahya's value as an ally lay in creating an opening for US ties with China, and that mattered more, as did the need to outmaneuver the Soviet Union in South Asia. Although neither India nor Pakistan were likely to go communist any time soon, Nixon's team constantly thought about the need to deny the Soviets influence in Pakistan. Thus, when Yahya scheduled a visit to Moscow

. . . . . .

in June 1970 Kissinger rushed to convey to him Nixon's willingness to sell a substantial amount of military hardware that Pakistan had requested.

Pakistan would now be able to get a twelve-aircraft squadron of tactical fighter aircraft (F-104Gs or F-5s) or six replacement F-104As. Kissinger explained that their intent was to enable Pakistan to reactivate its F-104A squadron, either by replacing planes lost and bringing it up to strength or by trading in the old planes and reestablishing the squadron with new aircraft. In addition, three hundred armored personnel carriers and four advanced design naval patrol antisubmarine aircraft would be supplied. Seven B-57 bombers would replace B-57 aircraft the United States had previously supplied but had been lost through attrition.

Kissinger told Hilaly that "the President wanted President Yahya to know that this has been done on the basis of his personal intervention and personal interest." Hilaly noted the word "sell" and asked whether credit could be discussed. Pakistan simply did not have the money to buy the equipment, but Kissinger's team had been working on the assumption of a cash sale. Given the congressional opposition as well as restrictions imposed by the Foreign Military Sales Act, offering credit to Pakistan would be difficult.

If Kissinger had expected appreciation from Pakistan, none was forthcoming. Hilaly pointed out that there were no tanks on the list. Kissinger explained that the White House had tried to introduce tanks into the package but realized that "this could wreck the whole arrangement"; the furor that might have arisen in Congress could have produced further amendments to the Foreign Military Sales Act or the later appropriations legislation, making "any kind of arrangement impossible." According to Kissinger, it was important to first establish the principle that the United States will continue to supply military equipment to Pakistan before moving forward.[26]

Yahya's response was somewhat better than Hilaly's. Joseph Farland, a lawyer who had arrived in Pakistan as US ambassador soon after Yahya's coup, informed the Pakistani president of the decision. Farland, a West Virginia Republican who owned a coal mining company, had previously served as ambassador in the Dominican Republic and Panama and had a reputation for pursuing unconventional methods of diplomacy. In Pakistan this had translated into regular informal meetings with key public figures, including Yahya and his inner circle. "Yahya immediately exclaimed that he was deeply pleased and appreciative of the president's action," Farland reported to the State Department. "Yahya said the president's decision is not only a gesture of friendship, but also evidence that the U.S. understands Pakistan's problems and difficulties," he continued. But the idea of cash sales did not cheer the Pakistani president. "Pakistan is broke and everyone knows it," he told Farland, adding that the United States knew that better than anyone else.

According to Farland, Yahya said "he valued above all the friendship and support which President Nixon's decision evidenced." He did not want to get into a detailed discussion of the package that had been offered, but the Pakistan army "badly needed to replenish its tank inventory" and would have to continue to seek supplies. "Yahya left me in no doubt," Farland summarized, "that he was sorry we had been unable accommodate Pakistan on tanks, to which they obviously attach great importance."[27]

Subsequently the Pakistani leader explored ways to get around the cash-payment framework. Yahya asked Farland about the possibility of "substantial concessions on prices" and "concessions on timing of payments." He said that he and his government would face a very difficult situation if Pakistan was unable to pay for US equipment that it required and desired and that the Americans had offered to sell.[28] The deal was, for Pakistanis, as much a matter of national prestige as a question of securing equipment for their armed forces.

Nixon and Yahya got a chance to speak directly when Yahya visited the United States for the twenty-fifth anniversary celebrations of the United Nations. Each president had one major issue on his mind: Nixon was uneasy about the slow pace of his outreach to China, and Yahya was troubled by the difficulty in procuring American arms, which he needed in order to retain the Pakistani military's respect even more than to confront India.

Kissinger took notes of their meeting in the Oval Office. "Yahya is tough, direct, and with a good sense of humor," observed

......

Kissinger. "He talks in a very clipped way, is a splendid product of Sandhurst and affects a sort of social naiveté but is probably much more complicated than this."[29] That apparently made it easier for Nixon to treat Yahya as a personal friend instead of approaching him as the head of state of an ally that had drifted away.

The US president began the conversation by blaming congressional opposition for "difficult times in our relationships with our allies" and assuring Yahya that "we will stick by our friends." Nixon said, "There is a psychosis in this country about India" before promising that "We will keep our word with Pakistan." Nixon's comments about India animated Yahya, as did the words "we will work with you" and "we will try to be as helpful as we can." Yahya said somewhat poetically, "We were surrounded by enemies when we became friends. We are no longer surrounded by enemies but we will still remain friends."

Neither leader addressed directly the objections that most Americans raised about military supplies to Pakistan, but Yahya wanted Nixon to know that he would not strengthen the American president's congressional critics by simultaneously seeking weapons from the Soviet Union. If Pakistan really felt threatened by India and needed weapons for its defense, closing other options for acquiring them would not make sense. "We are a sentimental people and we will never do anything to embarrass you," Yahya declared, meaning that Nixon's gesture of support had earned him personal goodwill in Pakistan. Nixon responded, "Your people are too proud to do a thing like that," appreciating that Pakistan chose being an American ally over the nonalignment India had adopted.

But then Yahya set aside his pride and added, after expressing approval for the recent military assistance package, an additional request for economic aid. The Aid to Pakistan Consortium, organized by the World Bank, was scheduled to meet in the near future, he explained. The Japanese prime minister, Eisaku Sato, had apparently told Yahya that the amount of Japanese aid to Pakistan would depend on whether the United States would agree to a significant contribution. Nixon then turned to Kissinger and, according to Kissinger, "ordered me to do what I could to encourage assistance to Pakistan."[30]

......

The Pakistani president also updated Nixon on Pakistani domestic politics. General elections were scheduled for December 7, he said, adding a swipe at Bhutto for accusing Yahya of waiting to cut a deal with India and selling out Pakistan. "It was absurd the levels to which political opponents would stoop," Kissinger reported Yahya as saying.

In response, Nixon proposed "a strong Presidency as in France" for Pakistan. Yahya said, "Without it Pakistan would disintegrate. Our people like the Parliamentary system only because they have been ruled by Britain for so many centuries, but they cannot make it work and they do not have the basic prerequisite, namely a two-party system; we have about 35 parties."[31]

Once he felt that Yahya was sufficiently confident of US support, Nixon gave him his assignment, beginning with the words: "I understand you are going to Peking." Nixon then declared, "It is essential that we open negotiations with China." He wanted Yahya to tell Zhou Enlai that the United States would not close ranks with the Soviet Union against China now that the Sino-Soviet rift was widening, and that the United States was also willing to send a high-level emissary to Peking "to establish links secretly."

Yahya said he had been told to establish secret links before and had communicated it to the Chinese. The Chinese had asked whether the United States was thinking of a hotline to Peking, similar to the one that existed to Moscow. Nixon categorically told Yahya that was not what he meant—the United States was willing to send ambassadors.[32] The significance of the message was not lost on Yahya: until now Yahya was conveying to the Chinese Nixon's desire for good relations, but now he could play an even more substantive role by providing cover for secret links involving a high-level emissary.

★

ON DECEMBER 7, 1970, Pakistan held its first general elections since its independence in 1947. With dozens of political parties in the fray, Yahya and his fellow generals had hoped for a fragmented result. The military had even worked behind the scenes to ensure "that the Constituent Assembly is so fragmented as to render impossible the drafting of a constitution."[33] Further, the military regime had tried to safeguard Pakistan's identity as an Islamic ideological state before allowing the people to vote. Propaganda through state-controlled media and changes in academic curriculum would forestall elected politicians' attempts to alter Pakistan's orientation fundamentally.[34]

Official media had projected the year-long election campaign, which officially began on January 1, as a battle between Islam and socialism.[35] As a result, Islamist vigilantes violently confronted their secular rivals on university campuses and in trade unions. Yahya's minister for information, Major General Sher Ali Khan, used a journalists' strike in April-May as an excuse to purge state and privately owned media of leftists and secularists. Cadres from the Islamist party, Jamaat-e-Islami, then replaced the purged journalists.

The well-funded Islamists confronted Bhutto's PPP in West Pakistan and the Awami League in the eastern wing. Judging by their visibility in the media, the Islamists appeared quite powerful. Their attacks on the PPP focused on the "un-Islamic lifestyle" of the party's popular leader and stooped so low as to allege that Bhutto's mother had been a Hindu. Further, the Awami League was accused of close ties with Bengali Hindus and was alleged to be funded by India.

But the ideological debates that Pakistan's military orchestrated attracted attention only in garrison towns and from religiously conservative urban intellectuals. For the rural masses bread-and-butter issues were more important. Here, the Awami League's promise of greater power for impoverished Bengalis and Bhutto's calls for income redistribution had tremendous advantage.

The Awami League got a further boost when a major cyclone followed by a tidal wave struck East Pakistan on November 12, less than a month before the election. Images of impoverished Bengalis uprooted from their homes in coastal areas served as a reminder of West Pakistan's neglect of the eastern wing. The US government worried about the tragedy's effect on Yahya's position, as Pakistan's government lacked the capacity to manage the situation. But Nixon worried that publicly giving too much aid or help may embarrass Yahya.

For rescue operations the United States provided six helicopters and fifty sixteen-foot motor launches, each with a carrying capacity of two tons, and $50 million in aid under various heads. Pakistan's request for fifty thousand tons of wheat was also immediately approved, though the staple food in East Pakistan was rice. Kissinger told Nixon that the United States had to maintain a subtle posture in providing disaster relief for political reasons as well as humanitarian ones. "The east-west issue within Pakistan is an extremely delicate one for President Yahya, especially in this election period," he explained. "A highly visible appearance that the U.S. was injecting its independent management would carry the implication that President Yahya's government in West Pakistan could not or would not effectively manage this situation in East Pakistan."[36] But the impression the US government sought to eschew could not be avoided. Bengalis concluded that they could not trust West Pakistani leaders or their Bengali cohorts any longer. On Election Day they overwhelmingly voted for the Awami League.

When the votes were counted, Yahya regime's expectations of a truncated Parliament were not fulfilled. The Awami League had won more than 72 percent of the popular vote in East Pakistan and ended up with 160 seats out of the 300 contested seats. Its uncontested winning of 7 seats reserved for women gave it a total of 167 seats in the 313-member National Assembly. Only two National Assembly seats from East Pakistan went to non-Awami League members. In the provincial assembly election ten days later, the Awami League secured 89 percent of the votes and won 288 out of 300 seats in East Pakistan.

In West Pakistan, Bhutto's Pakistan People's Party (PPP) won 81 out of 138 seats for the National Assembly, mainly in the provinces of Sindh and Punjab, and the addition of 4 seats reserved for women would take its tally up to 85. Its share of the popular vote, however, was 38.89 percent. Balochistan and the Northwest Frontier Province (since renamed Khyber-Pushtoonkhwa) gave a plurality to the Pashtun nationalist National Awami Party (NAP). The orthodox Jamiat

Ulema Islam (JUI), which had aligned itself with the left-wing parties instead of other Islamists, came in second in those two provinces. The conservative parties that the military covertly supported had fared poorly.[37]

The election results meant that Yahya and the military would not have a smooth ride when steering the country toward a constitution of their choice. Yahya had agreed with Nixon that Pakistan needed the steadying hand of a strong president. As he had told Nixon, he was skeptical about parliamentary democracy in a country with thirty-five parties because, he claimed, parliamentary democracy worked best in a two-party system. Although Pakistan now had two major parties, that did not augur well for Yahya or the military's vision for the country, as neither of the two major parties were likely to yield their mandate to a strong presidency.

The Americans were also not happy with the outcome. They had neither predicted nor prepared for it, and now they had to deal with a complex political situation. Even if Yahya remained in charge, he could not ignore Mujib and Bhutto, who had emerged as popular leaders of Pakistan's two wings. The State Department's director of intelligence and research, Ray Cline, interpreted the election results for the US government the very next day in a report titled, "Pakistan: Election Results Suggest Fresh Problems."[38]

"The Awami League's sweep, which may give it an absolute majority in the forthcoming Constituent Assembly," Cline's report said, "and the surprising victory of the PPP have called into question almost all of the speculations about the post-election period which preceded December 7." These speculations had projected a combination between the Awami League and West Pakistani centrists, which might have resulted in "needed accommodation between Pakistan's two wings on the key issue of provincial autonomy." But the prospect of accommodation had become more problematic.

The Awami League would now be tempted to press for "more autonomy than the West Pakistanis are prepared to accept," Cline cautioned. Even if Mujib understood the dangers of asking for too much, he might not be able to restrain his followers. "The emergence of Bhutto as a figure of substantial prominence" had also com-

......

plicated the situation. According to Cline's assessment, Bhutto's radical appeals were "anathema to the present establishment, and thus may raise fresh doubts in the minds of the regime as to the value of popular government."

Although Bhutto had avoided open criticism of the Awami League's demands for autonomy, Cline thought that "his proclivities" reflected preference for a strong center. Bhutto was "unlikely to join forces with Sheikh Mujib" on the issue of autonomy, but that would make Yahya the key to resolving any critical questions. Yahya knew he would have to work with Mujib, Cline explained, but he had supposed that "the present West Pakistani ruling elite would be well-represented" in the new legislature. Now, however, there were very few centrists who could "work with and control the Awami League leader and thus protect West Pakistani interests."

Before holding elections Yahya had insisted that the new Constituent Assembly must complete its work on a constitution within 120 days and that Yahya would have to approve the proposed constitution. Given the election results, Cline presciently observed that ending martial law and establishing a popular civilian government had become less certain. Further, he anticipated dire consequences if the future constitution did not include the Awami League's vision of adequate autonomy. "The Bengali reaction could well be secession," he warned.

Cline also spoke of the election's foreign affairs implications. Both the PPP and the Awami League favored balancing relations with the United States, the USSR, and China. Both also called for Pakistan's withdrawal from SEATO and CENTO. "Bhutto, however, has made much of Pakistan's relations with China," wrote the CIA veteran, adding, "There is every reason to conclude that, private disclaimers to the contrary notwithstanding, he would favor China at the expense of the United States."

He also noted that Mujib's and Bhutto's views diverged significantly in relation to the subcontinent. The Awami League leader favored decreasing tension and resuming trade with India. But in Cline's assessment, "Bhutto, reflecting both his own xenophobia and popular West Pakistani sentiment (including that of the military), urges a hard line toward India, frequently couched in inflammatory and irresponsible language."[39]

With all this in mind, American diplomats watched cautiously as Bhutto and Mujib started negotiating the new constitution. These negotiations dragged on for almost two months and remained inconclusive. In February 1971 Yahya belatedly scheduled the session of the Constituent Assembly for March 3 in Dhaka, the capital of East Pakistan, but later postponed it indefinitely, ostensibly on Bhutto's demand. The West Pakistani leader saw no point in attending the Assembly meeting until his party and the Awami League had agreed on the basic principles of the constitution. Bhutto and Yahya had most likely acted in concert, because no one in relatively privileged West Pakistan was prepared to cede power completely to the Bengali majority.[40]

Kissinger foresaw the fresh crisis emerging in Pakistan and told Nixon that it could have far-reaching implications for US interests in South Asia. He recognized that the main issue was the power relationship between East and West Pakistan, and he lamented that Mujib and Bhutto had failed to forge a consensus. But he saw the issue primarily from Yahya's perspective. "Yahya remains committed to turning his military government over to the civilian politicians," Kissinger wrote, adding that Yahya was not willing to "preside over the splitting of Pakistan."

The odds were increasing against the emergence of "a constitution acceptable to each of the major parties"—Mujib, Bhutto, and Yahya. Mujib was planning to "stick with his demands for the virtual autonomy of East Pakistan and if he does not get his way—which is very likely—to declare East Pakistan's independence." The Bengali leader had approached "U.S. and other diplomats to play a peacemaking role to avoid an East-West civil war if he does not get his way and makes a unilateral declaration of independence." The United States was being forced "to walk a very narrow tightrope."[41]

Kissinger noted that although the United States was not the controlling factor in the emerging situation, all major actors in Pakistan's unfolding drama were seeking its influence. "We do have some important interests, and our posture at this juncture is critical to how these interests will be protected in the future," he pointed out. The US position had been to support the unity of Pakistan, as the United States had been forced to state that position in response to some Pakistani politicians' charges that the United States was plotting East Pakistani secession.

Kissinger wanted Nixon to determine American policy when faced with a declaration of East Pakistani independence. He wondered whether the United States should adopt a more neutral stance toward Mujib, who was "basically friendly toward the U.S." This would hedge against the day the United States might have to deal with an independent East Pakistan.

The national security adviser realized that "there is very little material left in the fabric of the unity of Pakistan." But that reality was inconvenient because in his view, "the division of Pakistan would not serve U.S. interests."[42] He wanted to start contingency planning in order to protect US interests in the face of the growing possibility that East and West Pakistan would split. The worst-case scenario for the United States could be the emergence of two countries out of Pakistan, both opposing American interests. India was already closer to the Soviet Union than to the United States; the loss of Pakistan would mean that the Americans had lost all of South Asia.

While Kissinger sought Nixon's direction for dealing with the changing circumstances in East Pakistan, Ambassador Farland traveled to Dhaka and met Mujib. The Awami League leader was unwilling to join Yahya and his cronies in blaming Bhutto exclusively for the delay in convening the newly elected Parliament. Instead, he held the army responsible for trying to manipulate the situation to stay in power. "Those very people who had supported Ayub," he told Farland, had brought about the current situation.

According to Mujib, Bhutto's hard line toward East Pakistan was the result of "the help and leadership of certain West Pakistani military officers." Bhutto favored "excessive expenditures on military preparedness," precisely because of his ties to a section of the Pakistani military. He predicted that "the life struggle of Bangladesh would begin" when Bhutto called off all talks and the Constituent Assembly failed to meet because Yahya refused to summon it.

......

During his meeting with the US ambassador, Mujib made it clear that the eclipse of West Pakistani military leadership would not threaten US interests. He also denigrated "Bhutto's love for Communist China and his intransigent position vis-à-vis India," Farland reported. Mujib "reflected at length upon his anti–communist position and the dangers that China portended to the area." But what distinguished Mujib from West Pakistanis who had dealt with the United States since Pakistan's independence was his attitude toward India; he declared that Bangladesh needed to reestablish good relations with India and "reopen the historic trade routes in the area."

Mujib said he did not want separation; instead, he wanted "a form of confederation in which the people of Bangladesh would get their just and rightful share of foreign aid, and not a mere twenty percent." Products from Bangladesh constituted the main source of hard currency earnings for Pakistan, he argued, prompting him to ask, rhetorically, "How can Islamabad justify the crumbs which they have thrown us?"[43]

In effect, the Bengali leader was asking the United States to use its influence to redress West Pakistan's injustices against his people. His electoral mandate gave him the right to seek a constitutional arrangement his voters preferred. Mujib also wanted Americans to know that their past policy of supporting the West Pakistan army and its leaders had not turned him and the Bengali people against the United States. All Washington needed to do was take off its blinders and stop assuming that only through close ties with West Pakistani generals could American interests be protected.

Previously, American policy makers, beginning with Dulles, had looked at Pakistan only through the eyes of its "fighting men." But now they were confronted with Pakistan's internal contradictions that journalists and academics like Margaret Bourke-White and Hans J. Morgenthau had pointed out, only to be ignored: the subcontinent was on the verge of another partition, this time not on the basis of religion but on grounds of ethnicity. As an independent country Bangladesh would be more ethnically homogenous than either India or Pakistan. One language, a common culture, and a shared history would unite it. Islam would be the religion of

Bangladesh's majority, but unlike Pakistan, it would not be the basis of its nationhood. Regrettably, few Americans in government had paid attention to the Bengali perspective while allying with Pakistan's military leaders.

Most of Pakistan's generals belonged to the West Pakistani provinces of Punjab and the Northwest Frontier. They were ethnic Punjabis or Pashtuns. Some were from the Urdu-speaking minority that moved to Pakistan from northern India after partition. Pakistan's army was a product of the British concept of martial races, which had led the British in India to recruit soldiers only from certain ethnic groups. The British had not deemed the Bengalis a martial race, so Pakistan's army boasted very little East Pakistani representation.

In 1947 Bengalis constituted only 1 percent of the Pakistan army, and by the 1960s their number went up to only 7 percent.[44] In the officer corps the difference was sharper. Similarly, Pakistan's bureaucracy had far fewer Bengalis than it had West Pakistanis. In 1966 only 27,648 government officials out of a total of 114,302 belonged to East Pakistan.[45] Although East Pakistan was the country's major foreign exchange earner, it received a smaller share of federal investment. As a result, in 1970 West Pakistani per capita income was 61 percent higher than Bengali per capita income.[46]

East Pakistan had been seething with anger long before Mujib and the Awami League translated that rage into votes. But West Pakistani officers were unable to feel the depth of this sentiment in what can only be described as colonial hubris. The West Pakistani elite seemed willing to risk the division of the country rather than allow the Bengali majority to have a leading role in the country's governance.

Successive Pakistani leaders had tried to forge Pakistani nationhood on the basis of Islam and hatred of India, but the Bengalis resented the West Pakistani tendency to see their cultural affinity with Bengali Hindus as somehow un-Islamic. After all, their economic interests were more closely tied to India. With American assistance West Pakistan had achieved a degree of industrialization, which enabled West Pakistan to export cotton yarn and textiles to Europe, the United States, and Japan. Thus, East Pakistanis still preferred traditional trade patterns that had linked India, through Bengal, to Southeast Asia.

American journalists had reported on the East-West chasm in Pakistan, but US policy had completely ignored it. Pakistan is "an improbable country," the *New York Times* had pointed out on the eve of the elections. "Its two parts, the Bengali East and the Punjabi West are separated by culture, language, diet, temperament and a thousand miles of the unfriendly territory of India." The paper's reporter could see that the glue of Islam was "losing its hold" and that Pakistan was the rare country "where the majority region is the backward one." He quoted Mujib as saying: "If we are the majority, we are Pakistan."[47]

The December 1970 election had brought Pakistan's fissures to the fore. In response, West Pakistanis reacted with shades of ethnic superiority. Soon after the elections a general visiting Dhaka told his military colleagues: "Don't worry. We will not allow these black bastards to rule over us," a reference to the darker skin color of Bengalis compared to Pashtuns and Punjabis.[48] "The Punjab is finished, smashed," an industrialist told the *Times*. "Our country has gone to the dogs," he said, because "We will be ruled by Sindh and Bengal," a reference to the fact that Mujib was Bengali whereas Bhutto was an ethnic Sindhi.[49]

When Yahya announced that he would defer convening the legislature indefinitely, the Awami League responded by calling for civil disobedience. In response, for the next several days the military virtually lost control of East Pakistan to Awami League mobs. West Pakistani civilians were attacked as were central government buildings. Bangladesh flags replaced the Pakistani standard in the province. Government employees (including High Court judges) absented themselves from their offices. Mujib's residence became the new secretariat of Bangladesh, from where he issued directives to keep the Bangladesh economy moving. Millions of Bengalis joined rallies all over East Pakistan, singing the song "Our Golden Bengal."[50] Bangladesh had effectively seceded.

After a few days of armed preparation, during which three-way talks involving the Awami League, the PPP, and the army were arranged as subterfuge, Yahya ordered the army to crackdown on the

Bengalis. According to one Pakistani general, Yahya was assured that "short and harsh action" would cow down Mujib and his supporters. In the view of Pakistani generals, "killing of a few thousand would not be a high price for keeping the country together."[51] They saw Mujib as a "traitor" to Pakistan and were not prepared to negotiate with him further.

However, two important West Pakistani military officers did not support the decision to use force. The military governor of East Pakistan, Admiral Syed Muhammad Ahsan, and the military commander of East Pakistan, Lieutenant General Sahibzada Yaqub Khan, both argued that military measures would not change the political situation. Ahsan had been Yahya's representative at Eisenhower's funeral a couple of years earlier, and Yaqub later became Pakistan's ambassador to the United States and foreign minister.

US officials knew Ahsan and Yaqub well, so Washington should have heard their views. But the United States chose to stand by Yahya. A new military commander, Lieutenant General Tikka Khan, arrived in Dhaka in March 1971 to enforce national unity with US weapons supplied ostensibly to save South Asia from communism. Pakistani soldiers then confined foreign journalists to their hotels before starting "Operation Searchlight," a ferocious military action aimed at arresting and killing Awami League leaders. During this military operation at least ten thousand civilians were massacred within three days. There was a large Pakistani force already stationed in East Pakistan, but reinforcements and equipment were flown in from West Pakistan to bolster their strength.

The general officer commanding in East Pakistan, Major General Khadim Hussain Raja, summed up the army's attitude when he told an Awami League sympathizer within earshot of fellow officers: "I will muster all I can—tanks, artillery and machine guns—to kill all the traitors and, if necessary, raze Dhaka to the ground. There will be no one to rule; there will be nothing to rule."[52] Four days after the army operation began, Kissinger reported to Nixon that "Apparently, Yahya has got control of East Pakistan."[53]

The conversations between Nixon and Kissinger during this period provide insight into their thoughts on the approaching debacle.

·····

Kissinger noted, for example, that "all the experts were saying that 30,000 people can't get control of 75 million." He conceded the State Department experts' opinion could "still turn out to be true," but resistance in East Pakistan had crumbled for the moment, and the Pakistan government had managed to hide the gravity of the situation from the rest of the world. "The use of power against seeming odds pays off," he said. Nixon declared, "When you look over the history of nations 30,000 well-disciplined people can take 75 million any time."

"Look what the Spanish did when they came in and took the Incas and all the rest," the US president said. "Look what the British did when they took India." He failed to see the irony of invoking colonial parallels while discussing the use of force to keep a postcolonial state together. Kissinger acknowledged that Mujib was a moderate, but he and Nixon did not trust the Bengalis to be able to rule their own country. They feared an "unstable situation," that "radical groups" would gain strength.

As the Pakistan army used force to subdue East Pakistan, Kissinger admitted that "the Indians who one normally would expect to favor a breakup of Pakistan aren't so eager for this one."[54] Ahsan, who had conducted the elections as military governor, agreed with that assessment. He told US officials later that he did not believe in the theory that India engineered Mujib's electoral victory and subsequent stance on autonomy. "Prior to March at least, separation was not Mujib's intention," Ahsan observed. He also said that "India's position has, despite public outcry, been relatively moderate and its hands before the events in March were relatively clean."[55]

But soon after Operation Searchlight, Pakistan blamed India for the events in East Pakistan. Faced with Pakistan's military might, a large number of Awami League activists and East Bengali Hindus crossed the border into the Indian states of Tripura, Assam, and West Bengal. Defecting Bengali soldiers and officers from the Pakistan army soon joined them. These trained military men had preempted a Pakistani order to disarm and detain all ethnic Bengalis in the army.

Mujib had been arrested and taken to West Pakistan. But several other Awami League leaders had announced the formation of a

Bangladesh government in exile based in the Indian port city of Calcutta. India then asserted that hundreds of thousands of refugees had poured in, creating a refugee emergency. The Indian intelligence service, Research and Analysis Wing (RAW), started recruiting and training a guerrilla army from the refugee camps. Soon the Bangladesh *Mukti Bahini* (Liberation army) was methodically attacking the Pakistani forces throughout the country's eastern wing.

Pakistan rushed in further reinforcements, but this proved difficult because India had banned Pakistani aircraft from flying over its territory after a group of Kashmiris hijacked an Indian civilian airliner to Lahore. Aircraft carrying Pakistani troops had to fly a circuitous route over the sea, avoiding Indian territory, to get to Dhaka. This slowed but did not stop, as the flights brought in additional soldiers.

Pakistani soldiers were trained to fight in the continental climate of West Pakistan's border with India. Most of them had never set foot in East Pakistan and did not speak the Bengali language. In the tropical climate and heavily vegetated terrain of Bengal, they felt lost. Moreover, the Mukti Bahini not only had the support of the people, but its soldiers also knew their territory better. Pakistan alleged that regular Indian forces operated alongside the guerrillas, pretending to be part of the hastily raised liberation army.

Nixon and Kissinger agreed that the United States could not do much about the situation. "We should just stay out—like in Biafra," Nixon determined, referring to an earlier secessionist war in the African state of Nigeria that ended in the central government's military victory. Kissinger agreed. US involvement "would infuriate the West Pakistanis," but "it wouldn't gain anything with the East Pakistanis, who wouldn't know about it anyway." As for the Indians, Kissinger pointed out that the "Indians are not noted for their gratitude."[56] But the American media did not see the unfolding tragedy with similar nonchalance. The brutality of the Pakistan army shocked US diplomats on ground in Dhaka. "Here in Dhaka we are mute and horrified witnesses to a reign of terror by the Pakistan military," began a telegram to the State Department, signed by Archer Blood, US consul-general in East Pakistan. "Evidence continues to mount

.....

that the Martial Law authorities have a list of Awami league supporters whom they are systematically eliminating by seeking them out
in their homes and shooting them down."

Blood, a career foreign service officer, had titled his cable, "Selective Genocide." He warned that the "full horror of Pakistani military
atrocities will come to light sooner or later" and wondered why the
US government pretended to believe the Pakistan government's assertions that they were not taking place.

The US government had apparently been oblivious to cynical
manipulation, Blood said, even when its citizens were evacuated
from East Pakistan. The Pakistan government had insisted that the
Americans fly first from Dhaka to Karachi on Pakistan International
Airlines (PIA) aircraft before leaving the country. The United States
could have evacuated its citizens to Bangkok, which was geographically closer, but the Pakistanis denied permission for special military
flights because they wanted to earn revenue on the return flights
that were ferrying troops to the eastern wing.

Blood gave vivid details of massacres Pakistani troops had conducted and informed Washington that the army was supporting
non-Bengali Muslims in "systematically attacking poor people's
quarters and murdering Bengalis and Hindus." He further wrote that
the United States "should be expressing our shock, at least privately,"
to the government of Pakistan over "this wave of terror" the Pakistan
military directed against its own countrymen.[57]

In a second telegram Blood listed reports of carnage that US citizens present at the time in East Pakistan had provided. He said that
there was no armed resistance to the Pakistani military, which was
setting Awami League supporters' houses on fire before gunning
down people as they escaped from their burning homes. In an effort
to eliminate all sources of "intellectual ferment," the military was
killing Bengali university professors.

There were "reliable reports of troops engaged in looting homes
(beating those who object, including middle level government officials) and shaking down refugees." There had been incidents of "unprovoked firing by military on children and fishermen."[58] A third

cable, titled "Killings" spoke of the mass murder of students on university campuses.[59]

But this recounting of horror stories had little effect on senior US policy makers. Ambassador Farland opined that "Yahya was sincere in his efforts to bring about a political solution" to disagreements between East and West Pakistan, but "acts of insurrection" had forced his hand. Farland recognized the Pakistan army's "brutal, ruthless and excessive use of force" and shared the "indignation" and "sense of horror" Blood and other witnesses at the scene had felt. But in Farland's view government servants could not base their reaction solely on "righteous indignation."

Like Nixon and Kissinger, the US ambassador also wanted to stay quiet about the events in East Pakistan. He pointed out, smugly, that the use of force had not affected American property and citizens. For Farland, the matter was Pakistan's internal problem, because "the constituted government is using force against citizens accused of flouting its authority." He concluded that "deplorable as current events in East Pakistan may be, it is undesirable that they be raised to the level of a contentious international political issue."[60]

At this point nineteen of the twenty Americans posted in the US consulate at Dhaka decided to use the State Department's dissent channel to send what came to be known as the "Blood Telegram," named after Archer Blood. It concluded that a Bengali victory was inevitable, as was the establishment of an independent Bangladesh. "At the moment we possess the good will of the Awami League," Blood added to the draft of his political officer W. Scott Butcher. "We would be foolish to forfeit this asset by pursuing a rigid policy of one-sided support to the likely loser."[61]

The US officials, including the ironically named Blood and Butcher, wrote of their conviction that the US response to the tragedy in East Pakistan served "neither our moral interests broadly defined nor our national interests narrowly defined." They pointed to the US government's failure to "denounce the suppression of democracy" and its "bending over backwards to placate the West Pakistan-dominated government."

⁕⁕⁕⁕⁕

One of the cable's memorable lines read, "Our government has evidenced what many will consider moral bankruptcy, ironically at a time when the USSR sent President Yahya Khan a message defending democracy."

The day after the "Blood Telegram" arrived, seven specialists on South Asian affairs from the State Department's Near East Asia bureau, one from the Bureau of Intelligence and Research and another from the Agency for International Development, sent a letter to Secretary of State Rogers supporting the consulate staff's views. The telegram had significant influence within the US government, even though it did not result in a change in policy. After some effort to convince the consul-general that he and his colleagues were being overly emotional, Rogers recalled Blood to Washington on Nixon's orders.

But Blood was not the only one reporting indiscriminate slaughter. Several American journalists were expelled for describing the Pakistan army's carnage in their dispatches, including Sydney Schanberg of the *New York Times*. His final story from Dhaka, published in the paper on July 4, ran under the headline: "An Alien Army Imposes Its Will: East Pakistan."

"Doesn't the world realize that they're nothing but butchers?" Schanberg's story began, quoting a foreigner, "who has lived in East Pakistan for years," speaking of the Pakistan army. "That they killed—are still killing—Bengalis to intimidate them, to make slaves out of them? That they wiped out whole villages, opening fire at first light and stopping only when they got tired?"

Schanberg questioned the army's design of "Islamic integrity" for Pakistan. He cited a Westerner as saying, "It's a medieval army operation as if against serfs," adding that the West Pakistanis "will use any method just to own East Pakistan."[62] Later accounts from participating Pakistani officers, including Major General Raja, confirmed that thinking within the army.

Chester Bowles, the two-time ambassador to India, demanded that the United States discontinue all aid to West Pakistan, except food and medical supplies, and he blamed the United States for arming Pakistan in the first place. "The appalling struggle now going on in East Pakistan," Bowles pronounced, "is a further testament to the folly of doling out arms to 'friendly governments' with little regard for whom they are to be used against or for what reasons."[63]

Opposition to violence against the Bengalis soon became an international campaign, joined by politicians, human rights activists, and celebrities. Musicians, including former Beatles George Harrison and Ringo Starr, joined Indian sitar maestro Ravi Shankar in performing at two benefit concerts at the Madison Square Garden in New York for the victims of Pakistani atrocities. Other famous musicians, including Bob Dylan, Eric Clapton, and Leon Preston, joined the "Bangladesh Concert." The concerts raised mass awareness as well as $250,000 for Bangladesh, and recordings of the music continued to sell for years to come.

In his memoirs written years later, Kissinger confessed that the reports emanating from Dhaka put the administration in a tight spot. "The United States could not condone a brutal military repression," he said, admitting that there was "no doubt about the strong-arm tactics of the Pakistani military." He explained the Nixon administration's decision not to react publicly to the military repression in East Pakistan as necessary in order to protect "our sole channel to China."[64]

Writing in 1979, Kissinger conceded that "there was some merit to the charge of moral insensitivity" regarding US policy toward Pakistan. In 1971, however, Yahya's role as messenger to China trumped questioning his decision to unleash brutal violence against Bengalis. Two weeks after Yahya sent his army into action in East Pakistan, Farland reported that the Pakistan military controlled the province's major cities while the Bengalis held the countryside. He did not see the West Pakistan establishment as willing to "give up voluntarily what it has engaged to protect by the bayonet."

But the ambassador recognized that the Pakistan army would face major logistical and operational difficulties during summer, once the monsoons began. He was "extremely doubtful" that the government of Pakistan could regain its Bengali citizens' loyalty. Farland said that most Bengalis would see through the "Indian bogey," which had been invoked "to divert attention from West Pakistan's own deeds."[65]

......

Conversely, Saunders thought that the breakup of Pakistan was inevitable but not necessarily imminent.

By Saunders' calculation US interest was best served by ensuring that it maintained ties with all three entities in South Asia—Pakistan, India, and Bangladesh—and denying influence to China and the Soviet Union. The delay in Pakistan's breakup meant that the United States had some time with which to come to terms with the new political reality. Instead of "rushing to get on the Bengali bandwagon," the United States should help "a friend find a practical and face-saving way out of a bind."[66] In other words, America should advise Yahya, not admonish him. It should also start a general dialogue with India about the longer-term future of South Asia.

Based on Saunders' evaluation, Kissinger laid out for the president the United States' options. The first was to support Yahya without questions. This, however, was unlikely to save Pakistan from disintegration and would leave the United States without friends in the region after East Pakistan had formally become Bangladesh. The second was neutrality, which in effect leaned toward East Pakistanis because the rest of the world, including many Western nations, were lining up to support the Bengalis.

The third option, which Kissinger preferred, would lead the United States to help Yahya achieve a negotiated settlement. Nixon approved the last option and added a handwritten note on Kissinger's memo that read, "To all hands. Don't squeeze Yahya at this time." He underlined "Don't" three times.[67] This meant that US encouragement of a political agreement over the future of East Pakistan would not be accompanied by any pressure on Pakistan's military regime.

But Nixon and Kissinger did not realize the propensity of Pakistan's generals for self-deception. Yahya was under the impression that his plan of beating East Pakistan into submission was working. Farland reported after a visit to Dhaka that "Army officials and soldiers give every sign of believing they are now embarked on a Jihad against Hindu-corrupted Bengalis"[68] He did not say that the Pakistanis were interpreting the US refusal to pressure Yahya as a sign of support for Pakistan's Jihad against its own citizens.

......

In an address to the nation in June, Yahya asked the nation to express "gratitude to Almighty Allah" for the army's success in East Pakistan. After blaming external forces for the challenges Pakistan faced, Yahya had declared that "Every one of us is a *Mujahid*"—a holy warrior.[69] Although Pakistan had lost to India in previous wars, its military believed it could beat India if it tried to fight on behalf of the Bengalis. To add to its strength, the Pakistan army had recruited thousands of volunteers from Islamist groups in East Pakistan. These *razakaars* (volunteers) and Mujahideen terrorized critics of the Pakistani central state.

To Pakistani leaders, Indian protests over horrors in Bangladesh meant little and could be dismissed as a function of Indian unhappiness with the mere existence of Pakistan. Furthermore, strict censorship kept West Pakistanis from learning about their country's international isolation. Pakistan's economy was in tailspin, but it had recovered before. The lives of West Pakistan's elites had carried on, unperturbed by the violence in the country's distant Eastern wing. Now, only the United States had leverage to change Pakistani behavior without a full-fledged war. But Nixon had decided that the United States would not press Yahya in any way.

The Nixon administration also gave a wink and a nod to shipping war materiel to Pakistan under export licenses that had not been canceled despite the announced embargo. Administration officials admitted to Congress later that by October, $2.5 million worth of arms had been released despite the ban. The administration also encouraged the transfer of American-supplied jet fighters from Jordan and Libya to the Pakistani air force, in apparent violation of US foreign aid laws. The US General Accounting Office (GAO) also discovered that the Pakistani government diverted $10 million in US humanitarian aid to building military fortifications against India.[70]

Some members of Congress and the US media were criticizing Nixon for ignoring West Pakistani cruelties in East Pakistan when Yahya conveyed a message from Zhou Enlai to Nixon. Zhou said that China's government would be willing to publicly welcome Nixon or Nixon's envoy to move forward the US-China dialogue. After much internal deliberation Nixon decided that Kissinger

......

should travel to China first and that the visit should be secret. Once Kissinger had reached overall agreement with the Chinese, it would then be easier for Nixon to go public with his China initiative.

Yahya and Pakistan's Foreign Ministry made all the arrangements for Kissinger's trip to China. To maintain secrecy, Kissinger arrived in Pakistan and then disappeared from public view after feigning an illness. Farland informed journalists that the national security adviser had a severe stomachache and had been taken to Nathiagali, a mountain resort not far from Islamabad, to recuperate. A Pakistan Airlines plane flew Kissinger to southern China for a clandestine meeting, from July 9 to 11, 1971, with Zhou Enlai. There they arranged for Nixon's weeklong trip to China in February 1972, where they restructured long-strained Sino-American relations.

Hassan Zaheer was the senior-most West Pakistani civil servant in East Pakistan at the time. He later explained the link between Yahya's role as intermediary between China and the United States' and the army's overconfidence in relation to the civil war. "Although no one was very clear how the new development was going to help Pakistan extricate itself from the mess," he said, "the army's faith in the omnipotence of U.S. support was reinforced." Pakistan's Foreign Office "expected to be rewarded for services rendered, and started dreaming of a Washington-Islamabad-Beijing axis against the evil designs of its neighbor," India.[71]

The secrecy surrounding Kissinger's China trip meant that most people did not know the reason for Nixon's failure to reprimand Yahya over the Pakistan army's actions in East Pakistan. Indian Prime Minister Indira Gandhi was among those in the dark about this hush-hush diplomacy. In May she wrote a letter to Nixon describing "the gigantic problems which Pakistan's actions in East Bengal have created for India."

According to her, "Pakistan's war on the people of East Bengal and its impact on us in the form of millions of refugees" could not be separated. She claimed that, by May 12, 1971, 2,328,507 refugees had been registered, and more were pouring in "at the rate of about fifty thousand a day." The problem of providing shelter for the refugees would become complicated with the anticipated monsoon rains. "Apparently, Pakistan is trying to solve its internal problems by cutting down the size of its population in East Bengal," Gandhi said, adding that Pakistan was trying to change "its communal composition through an organized and selective program." She sought "the advice of all friendly Governments on how they would wish us to deal with the problem."

The Indian prime minister shared her conviction that "the loyalty of a people to a State cannot be enforced at gun-point" and cautioned that stifling the will of the people in East Bengal will eventually strengthen extremists. Referring to the long-running Marxist insurgency in West Bengal, Gandhi said that "the dangers of a link-up between the extremists in the two Bengals are real."

She concluded by requesting that "the power and prestige of the United States" be used "to persuade the military rulers of Pakistan to recognize that the solution they have chosen for their problem in East Pakistan is unwise and untenable."[72] But her plea had little effect in Washington. Although Kissinger had voiced fears soon after Ayub's ouster about Chinese communists taking advantage of the situation in East Pakistan, he did not react when Gandhi warned about Marxist gains because of the violence Pakistan's army had unleashed.

During the monsoon season both the influx of refugees into India and the fighting in East Pakistan intensified, as did international condemnation of Pakistan's actions. A World Bank mission told of death and destruction throughout the region, with one member of the mission describing the Bengali town of Kushtia, for example, as "looking like a World War II German town having undergone strategic bombing attacks, as a result of twelve days of 'punitive action' by the West Pakistani army." Ten members of the eleven-nation Aid to Pakistan consortium agreed to withhold aid to Pakistan. But the United States did not.[73]

Only ironically did Nixon realize the futility of Pakistan continuing to hang on to East Pakistan by force. During a meeting in the Oval Office Farland told Nixon that he was convinced that Yahya would fight to the bitter end. "He will commit suicide," Nixon remarked. Nonetheless, he still stuck to his original decision. Farland

......

and Kissinger agreed with the president when he said that the United States had to stand by its friend. All three thought that some deep-rooted hatred between Hindus and Muslims, rather than Yahya's unwillingness to accept the will of the Bengali majority, was fueling the conflict in South Asia.[74]

Years later, as he reminisced about his role as national security adviser, Kissinger wrote that he had tried to reason with Yahya during his stay in Pakistan for his secret China trip. He said he asked Yahya to put forward a comprehensive proposal to encourage refugees to return home and "to deny India a pretext for going to war." He also asked "Yahya and his associates" to admit the United Nations for relief efforts in East Pakistan and recommended the early appointment of a civilian governor.

"Yahya promised to consider these suggestions," Kissinger wrote. "But fundamentally he was oblivious to his perils and unprepared to face necessities. He and his colleagues did not feel that India was planning war; if so, they were convinced that they would win. When I asked as tactfully as I could about the Indian advantage in numbers and equipment, Yahya and his colleagues answered with bravado about the historic superiority of Moslem fighters."[75]

If the United States recognized the perils of Yahya's course, however, they did not tell him about the impending disaster. Nixon told British Foreign Secretary Alec Douglas-Home that Yahya had handled the situation "in a stupid way" as he also insisted that "He's a very decent man" and that the Indians were "hypocrites and sanctimonious." Nixon said he knew it was "inevitable" that Pakistan would "come apart," but the Indians were "deliberately trying to make it insoluble." He saw the danger that "a West Pakistani with a suicidal attitude will decide to have a fight," possibly in Kashmir.

Nixon saw his policy as one aimed at averting that war. Kissinger insisted that there had to be "a face-saving formula and a transition period." Although a few months earlier he had described Yahya as "a splendid product of Sandhurst," he now conceded that "He's not very bright." Nixon described Yahya as "a decent man, an honorable man." He also expressed to the British minister that he didn't think the British should have granted India and Pakistan independence so soon. "They just aren't ready, that's all," he concluded.[76]

★

INDIRA GANDHI could not ignore Nixon's refusal to lean on Pakistan as well as his unfriendly view of India. Before his covert trip to China through Pakistan in July, Kissinger had also visited Delhi. During this visit Indian leaders shared their ideas with the US official about a settlement in East Pakistan. Gandhi told Kissinger that she did not wish to use force and that she was willing to accept any suggestions that the United States may have. Kissinger informed her of the Nixon administration's efforts to establish a relationship with communist China gradually. He said that these were not directed at India and that they derived from America's global policy.

The Indian prime minister kept her counsel in relation to China. But she did press Kissinger on East Bengal, as the number of registered refugees who had come into India had risen to 6.8 million. She insisted that Pakistan had to create circumstances that would enable the refugees to return home. "The settlement must be between East Pakistan and West Pakistan," she said. "This is not an Indo-Pakistani problem. India would not have been involved except for the refugees." Kissinger promised to "use what influence we have to encourage a solution."

Gandhi tried to persuade Kissinger to recognize the need for more robust US involvement. She said that Pakistan has felt all these years that it will get support from the United States no matter what it does, and this has encouraged an "adventurous policy." India is "not remotely desirous of territory," and to have the Pakistanis base the whole survival of their country on hostility to India was irritating. "If they really had the good of Islam at heart," she said, "they would think of the 60 million Muslims in India also."[77]

During his stay in Delhi Kissinger also met India's defense minister, Jagjivan Ram, to hear him assess the Chinese military threat to India. Kissinger observed that China might intervene on behalf of

Pakistan if there were a war between India and Pakistan. He assured Ram that the United States would take a grave view of any Chinese move against India.[78] But on his return to Washington Kissinger qualified that assurance in a meeting with the Indian ambassador Lakshmi Kant Jha.

Kissinger had said that in the case of a Chinese attack that was unprovoked, the United States' interest in India would be very great; in the case of a Chinese attack provoked by an Indian attack on Pakistan, the United States would have a much harder time intervening.[79] But the media reported this conversation in a way that disturbed Indians and cheered Pakistanis. According to the media, Kissinger had conveyed the warning that if war broke out between India and Pakistan, and China became involved on Pakistan's side, "we would be unable to help you against China."[80]

The emergence of a possible coalition between the United States, China, and Pakistan did not portend well for India. The Soviets, however, had problems with both the United States and China and were not particularly interested in being evenhanded between India and Pakistan. Saunders' forecast—that US support for Pakistan as well as the opening of ties with China would drive India toward the Soviet Union—was about to come true.

Although India had championed nonalignment since its independence, it was not averse to seeking advantage from either superpower. After all, India had bought weapons from the Soviet Union for years. When the Soviets started selling military hardware to Pakistan, Indira Gandhi aspired to calibrate Soviet arms sales to India and Pakistan. She said she wanted to prevent the Soviet Union from "taking over management of the subcontinent."

Gandhi wrote to Kosygin in mid-July 1968 to protest Moscow's arms sales to Pakistan. The Soviet premier rushed to assure her that "every country in the world could envy Soviet-Indian relations," thus affirming the Soviet preference for India over Pakistan.[81]

But Gandhi entertained no illusions about the Soviet Union or any other major power, convinced that all nations "were guided only by their own interests and had no obligations to other countries which did not conform to those interests."[82] But she concluded in the summer of 1971 that it was time to accept the Soviet offer, first made by Premier Kosygin in February 1969, to sign a bilateral treaty of friendship. Gandhi had initially stalled on the proposed treaty because she did not want to risk India's ties with the United States.

Kosygin had said in Delhi soon after proposing the treaty that "if your great country is threatened at its borders, then we will be there to help you." Because Soviet relations with China had been steadily deteriorating, Brezhnev proposed a collective security system in Asia, intended to contain China, that Gandhi turned down. She agreed to a treaty of friendship without an explicit military component, which was akin to the one the Soviets had signed earlier with Egypt. But even after the draft agreement had been negotiated, for almost two years Gandhi put off signing the treaty.

But on August 9, 1971, Indian Foreign Minister Swaran Singh and his Soviet counterpart, Andrei Gromyko, signed a Treaty of Peace, Friendship and Cooperation in New Delhi. Most of the treaty's provisions comprised expressions of goodwill toward one another. India and the Soviet Union agreed to "enter into mutual consultations" in case of threat to the security of either and "to take appropriate effective measures to ensure peace and the security of their countries." Couched in diplomatic language, the two countries had effectively become security allies.

The Indo-Soviet pact sealed the fate of East Pakistan; Gandhi had completely outmaneuvered Yahya. On the ground Pakistan's forces were losing territory to the Mukti Bahini and possibly Indian regulars fighting along their side. Diplomatically Pakistan was completely isolated. Although China and the United States made sympathetic noises, neither could deny that Pakistani forces had wantonly killed Bengalis in large numbers. Now, with the Soviet Union openly standing with India, there was little chance that the United States or China would risk wider conflict by supporting Pakistan militarily.

But Yahya looked at things in a different light. When Nixon and Kissinger assured him of their interest in Pakistan's well-being, he assumed the United States would put its military muscle behind

......

Pakistan. He and his fellow generals also had an unrealistic expectation of China's willingness to save a united Pakistan. Yahya's Sandhurst training had obviously not prepared him for statecraft.

Ghulam Ishaq Khan, secretary to the cabinet who later became Pakistan's president, and M. M. Ahmad, economic adviser to the president, told US officials that Yahya was "increasingly isolated from events in East Pakistan."[83] There were also reports that the Pakistan army in East Pakistan operated autonomously and that Yahya's influence was limited to "foreign affairs affecting East Pakistan." But this influence was sufficient for Pakistan to persist with its military plans based on false assumptions.

This was the time when Nixon should have had a candid conversation with Yahya. After all, Pakistan's usefulness as a channel of communication with China had been exaggerated; the United States could have managed its quiet diplomacy with China without allowing the atrocities in East Pakistan. The US president could have told the Pakistani dictator that only direct talks with the Awami League, including Mujib, would work. Further, someone needed to illuminate Yahya about the limits of US support, given Pakistan's other drawbacks. The threat of an aid cutoff, as Bowles had proposed, could have had a sobering effect. Instead, however, Nixon stood by his friend Yahya and leaned on Gandhi, going to the extent of abusing her behind her back.

Some commentators suggest that Nixon was convinced that Gandhi "hankered for the actual dismemberment of all of Pakistan notably including West Pakistan." According to this account, the Indian prime minister had once said to Nixon that in the British division of India, "Pakistan had been most unjustly given both Balochistan and Pashtunistan."

To Nixon this meant that India questioned the inclusion in Pakistan of Balochistan and the Pashtun territories, "the entire area now forming West Pakistan's frontier with both Afghanistan and Tibet and therefore through Tibet, Pakistan's common frontier with China." He believed he had "conclusive proof" "of India's intention to crush the main body of the Pakistan army, in West Pakistan."[84]

......

Pakistani officials had also convinced Nixon and Kissinger that the Kennedy administration had given Pakistan a written promise to help protect Pakistan in case of foreign aggression. When Congress and the US media criticized the White House for its support of Pakistan during the Bangladesh crisis, Kissinger advised the new Pakistani ambassador in Washington, Major General N. A. M. Raza, to invoke the mutual security treaty and its "clarifications used in subsequent years" so as to help justify Nixon's position.[85] Kissinger wanted Pakistan to bring to light Kennedy's promise of aid in case of war, which might have silenced the administration's critics amongst Democrats. Nixon could then have claimed that Pakistan's security had been a bipartisan concern and said that he was only keeping Kennedy's commitment.

As it turned out, Pakistan and the United States had never concluded a mutual security treaty. The references to such a treaty and assurances the Kennedy administration offered to Pakistan were based on Nixon's and Kissinger's ignorance. The Pakistanis were misinterpreting the US-Pakistan Agreement of Cooperation signed on March 5, 1959, in the context of Pakistan's membership in the Baghdad Pact. The agreement obligated the United States to take appropriate action "as may be mutually agreed upon" to defend Pakistan against aggression.

The agreement, in turn, cited a March 9, 1957, Joint Resolution of the US Congress that committed the United States to assist nations against aggression by "any country controlled by international communism." It also explicitly stated that the use of force had to be consonant with the Constitution of the United States.

During India's war with China in 1962 the Kennedy administration had assured Pakistan that, if India misused US military assistance in aggression against Pakistan, the United States would take "immediately, in accordance with constitutional authority, appropriate action to thwart such aggression." Thus, the United States could not fight a war on Pakistan's behalf without congressional authorization.

By encouraging rumors that the United States was bound by treaty to fight alongside Pakistan, Nixon and Kissinger were hoping

......

to scare India. But Secretary of State Rogers explicitly told Kissinger that "The Aide Memoire of Kennedy's does not commit the U.S. to go to war in the event that Pakistan is attacked by India and we should not say that." He thought that suggesting the existence of such a commitment amounted to circumventing the US Constitution. "We certainly don't want to tell the American people that we are committed to go to war," Rogers pointed out.[86]

Kissinger's dilemma was that Yahya flatly refused to negotiate with Mujib or to accept international mediation between East and West Pakistan. Nixon refused to twist Yahya's arm, a man he considered decent but on a suicide mission. Under such circumstances Kissinger saw psychological pressure on India as the only available option for the United States when trying to prevent all-out war that might result in Pakistan's complete collapse. In their exuberant support of Pakistan Nixon and Kissinger had chosen to overlook repeated assurances from Gandhi, backed by intelligence, that India would not overrun West Pakistan.

The Indian army began military incursions into Pakistan's Eastern wing on November 21 in support of the Mukti Bahini. On December 3, 1971, Pakistan attacked India from the west in the hope of forestalling the fall of East Pakistan. India recognized Bangladesh as a sovereign country three days later and marched into East Pakistan in aid of the Bangladesh government in exile. On December 14, as the Indian forces surrounded Dhaka, the Pakistani High Command told the besieged garrison that "Yellow and White help expected from North and South shortly," a reference to their imaginary Chinese and American military support.[87]

At this point Nixon ordered the deployment of an aircraft carrier, the USS *Enterprise*, to the Bay of Bengal. The maneuver was aimed at India, but Indira Gandhi was not intimidated. In response, she directed the Indian navy, if they encountered US vessels, to invite American officers for tea aboard their ships. Further, Nixon's decision disturbed several Western allies. Canada and Britain considered it an unnecessary escalation of a local conflict.[88] Thus, the United States was almost as isolated on the issue as Pakistan. Having failed to find a face-saver for Yahya, Kissinger now sought one for his own president.

Then, a letter from Soviet leader Leonid Brezhnev provided Nixon the excuse he needed to back down. Brezhnev offered a "guarantee that there would be no attack on West Pakistan" once war had ended in the East.[89] Kissinger told Nixon that this meant "We are home." Nixon had wanted to save Pakistan, and he wanted to believe that he had done so. He did not see the irony that, in the end, a Soviet assurance—and not American arms supplied over two decades—saved only one half of Pakistan.

The United States had seen the conflict in East Pakistan as another battle in the global struggle between superpowers. An early American statement condemning Pakistani military repression in the East might have forced Yahya to reconsider his policy. Independent observers believe that the Pakistan army killed between one and two hundred thousand Bengalis in a nine-month period, whereas Bangladesh puts the figure at three million. Conversely, Pakistani forces suffered only thirteen hundred fatalities in combat operations in the Eastern wing and another fourteen hundred during war along the West Pakistan border.[90]

Pakistani forces in the Eastern wing surrendered to the Indian military and Mukti Bahini on December 16, 1971. Gandhi then declared once again that India had no territorial ambitions. "Now that the Pakistani armed forces have surrendered in Bangladesh and Bangladesh is free it is pointless in our view to continue the present conflict," she announced.[91] But Yahya vowed to continue the war with India. "We shall fight alone if we must," he said in an address to the nation. The headline of *Dawn,* Pakistan's major English newspaper, on the day of Pakistan's surrender read, "Victory on All Fronts."

In the prelude to war West Pakistanis had been fed false propaganda, and after the war's end Yahya made it clear that he did not intend to stop the hype. "No sacrifice will be too great to preserve this Islamic homeland of the 120 million people of Pakistan," he said. He then announced plans to introduce a new constitution that would provide greater autonomy to East Pakistan, as though its loss

......

was temporary. Yahya described the army's conduct as "reminiscent of the highest traditions of the soldiers of Islam." He also thanked China and the United States for their support for "the cause of peace and justice."[92]

Following Pakistan army's surrender, around ninety thousand West Pakistani soldiers and civilians were transported to India as prisoners of war. Indian troops helped the establishment of the new government of Bangladesh and then withdrew completely after three months. Four days after the surrender, on December 20, 1971, Yahya was removed from power by his own commanders. Bhutto took over as president and chief martial law administrator, the latter a temporary transitional measure. Bhutto then freed Mujib, who returned to Dhaka in triumph to become prime minister of Bangladesh.

The US "tilt" had failed to save Pakistan from a split, and it did not help Pakistan or the United States in any other way. Pakistan's army continued to promote hatred of "Hindu India" and trained its men to avenge the humiliation in Bangladesh. The Pakistani people were never fully told about America's support, and many still complain that the United States failed to save its ally from division and military defeat. As a result, although Pakistan still sought American economic and military assistance, its leaders decided neither to depend on the United States nor to trust it.

Chapter Four

Picking Up the Pieces

Four months after Pakistan's eastern half severed to become Bangladesh, Zulfikar Ali Bhutto received Sidney Sober at his elegant private home at 70 Clifton in Karachi. As president, Bhutto was still picking up the pieces of a dismembered country. West Pakistanis were slowly accepting the fact that their country had been reduced to half its former size. Parliament had been convened, an interim constitution would soon replace martial law, and work had begun on a permanent constitution. Bhutto was anxious to restructure Pakistan's economy and reconstruct its foreign policy.

Sober was a US career diplomat heading the embassy in Islamabad as charge d'affaires. Farland's tenure as ambassador was drawing to an end, and a new ambassador had not yet been named. In any case, Farland and Bhutto did not like each other. During the 1970 election campaign Bhutto had accused Farland of working for the CIA and being involved in toppling third-world governments. For his part, Farland had limited his embassy's contacts with Bhutto, accusing him of being a "U.S. Baiter."

The day he took over as president on December 20, 1971, Bhutto had met Farland to make the point, in Sober's presence, that he valued Pakistan's relations with the United States. In that meeting Bhutto had declared that "We are in one hell of a mess" before saying that "Pakistan had a real reason for coming into being" and that "this very reason justified its survival."[1] Bhutto wanted the Americans to do everything within their capacity "to assist in the monumental

......

effort which lay ahead." Farland had wished him well, expressed hopes of seeing him frequently, and then designated Sober as the "secondary" link between Bhutto and the embassy.

Since Bhutto's rise to the presidency Sober had effectively been Bhutto's principal point of contact with the US government. The two met often. During the meeting at Bhutto's Karachi home on April 3, 1972, Sober wanted to review Bhutto's persistent proposal for closer defense ties. Pakistan's defense secretary had offered the Americans a naval base along the Arabian Sea coast, and Pakistani officers had dropped "casual hints" to diplomats that it was now prepared for a US military presence. Sober informed Washington that his firm policy had been "to listen politely on such occasions and to be entirely noncommittal."[2]

Pakistan's ambassador in Washington, General N. A. M. Raza, had written a letter to the State Department providing a list of equipment Pakistan urgently needed for its armed forces. He sought "agreement in principle for release of lethal sophisticated equipment such as artillery and anti-aircraft weapons, aircraft, ground-to-ground and ground-to-air missiles, missile-carrying boats, submarines, etc. at reduced price and on deferred payment."

Attachments to Raza's letter included new requests for a hundred M-47/48 tanks, four submarines, twelve B-57 bombers, twenty-five F-5 aircraft, one thousand M-601 trucks, and some artillery and communications equipment. Pakistan also wanted the three hundred armored personnel carriers that the United States had earlier agreed to sell. It also wanted the United States to replace equipment, including seventy-four tanks, twenty-five F-86s, four B-57s, and three F-104s that had been lost in the December 1971 war with India.[3]

As he sat down with Bhutto at his Karachi home, Sober expressed concern that Pakistan had once again started asking for a substantial quantity of US arms on soft terms. This did not fit with Bhutto's emphasis on the need for normalization of relations with India. Sober referred to a visit to Washington by Pakistan's secretary general for foreign affairs, Aziz Ahmed. He noted that Ahmed had made a rather hard-line presentation on Soviet intentions in the subcontinent and, based on that, had expressed an urgent need for

American weapons. He also cited Raza's laundry list for military equipment.

Sober knew that Pakistan was not seeking weapons to defend against an impending Soviet attack. He also felt that immediate rearmament should not be the first priority for a country that had so recently suffered military humiliation. After all, Pakistan's economy was hardly back on its feet, tens of thousands of its soldiers and civilians were prisoners of war, and it had yet to recognize Bangladesh and settle issues that the Eastern wing's secession had created. Why then, Sober asked, was Pakistan requesting that the United States resume supplying military aid?

Bhutto replied that his senior military leaders were pointing to "some obvious gaps in defense structure" and wanted him to acquire some sophisticated weapons for them. He was not in a position to ignore the military, which remained powerful even after its defeat. He had forwarded the requests for defense equipment to the United States because it was the "only logical source for some types of equipment." Bhutto also voiced the hope that the United States would "loosen up soon in supply of spare parts" so as to keep operational the equipment that had been previously provided.

Discussing relations with India, Bhutto insisted that his aim remained an "honorable political settlement." He wanted to see Pakistan's military budget reduced, but whether such a cut would be possible would depend on India.[4] In a subsequent meeting with Sober Bhutto opened up further, saying that he still had "problems to contend with" in his relations with the Pakistani military. During a visit to an army officers' mess Bhutto had found officers telling him that India had not really defeated Pakistan and that Pakistanis "could give a very good account of themselves if they really had to fight."[5] Pakistan's army was apparently preparing its officers and men for another war rather than learning a lesson from repeated defeat. The army blamed foreign powers and Pakistani politicians for their poor performance and argued that they would do better if they had better equipment. Like American diplomats who served in Pakistan right after partition of India in 1947, Sober sympathized with Pakistan's leaders. Bhutto and his colleagues were trying to forge what Bhutto

· · · · ·

termed a "New Pakistan," just as Pakistan's founding generation had struggled to build their new country carved out of India. There was passion and enthusiasm in Islamabad as there had been in Karachi twenty-three years earlier.

But Sober could not understand why Pakistan was focusing on rebuilding its military before anything else. After all, the country was short of resources; poverty, disease, and illiteracy were rampant; and the loss of East Pakistan meant that it had fewer borders to protect. Still, Pakistan sought fighter jets and tanks. Sober's astonishment in this regard was similar to that of Americans who had seen Pakistanis requesting military assistance in the country's early years, ignoring other pressing problems. History was now repeating itself.

★

THE NEWS THAT Pakistani forces in the Eastern wing had surrendered had stunned Pakistanis because the West Pakistani media had been projecting imaginary victories of the Pakistan army. The religious parties had plastered the walls in major cities with posters and stickers bearing the slogan "Crush India." And only four days before the surrender, Radio Pakistan had announced that "The question of any surrender is ruled out because our troops are determined to lay down their lives."[6]

Although the military high command knew better, it did not prepare the people of West Pakistan for defeat until the very end. Only at that time did the government release sketchy reports of a grim military situation and fighting against all odds. On the afternoon of December 16, around the time the formal surrender ceremony was being held at the Race Course grounds in Dhaka, the Pakistan government put out a twenty-seven-word statement that read, "Latest reports indicate that following an arrangement between the local commanders of India and Pakistan, fighting has ceased in East Pakistan and the Indian troops have entered Dhaka."[7]

For West Pakistanis, fed on rhetoric of imminent victory in Jihad, this was a colossal anticlimax. The war had been lost and there was no way of turning the tables. Amid nationwide depression, reported the *New York Times*, "People went to mosques to pray and weep." Newspaper editorials demanded why Yahya had not told the people that defeat was so near and why he had not ordered the army to fight the Indians to death.[8]

Farland informed the State Department that he foresaw the "eventual retirement of Yahya" and the "rise to real power of Bhutto" in the aftermath of defeat. He also noted that the US government enjoyed "exceptional access" to Pakistan's government during the difficult situation and that such access to Pakistani leaders, including Bhutto, should continue for the foreseeable future. But he warned that the United States "should not confuse access with leverage with regard to what West Pakistan sees as its national interests." As things turned out, Pakistan's elite continued to see India as an existential threat and therefore defined national interest through that prism.

In an uncharacteristically realistic analysis the US ambassador observed that the Soviets would have a very limited role in West Pakistan, whereas the Chinese would retain the position of a major ally for West Pakistanis. He foresaw a period of "bitter recriminations" within the establishment and among the general public in West Pakistan. Farland said that the army was "exhausted but intact" as an institution, even though public confidence in the army had been shaken. The Pakistan army, he said, "may lean on Bhutto" to shoulder major responsibility for rebuilding national morale.[9]

As the American ambassador forecast developments within the power corridors correctly, US journalists described the national mood in their dispatches. "The Pakistanis believe that India will never rest until Pakistan ceases to exist," wrote *New York Times* reporter Malcolm Browne. "Lopsided military budgets seem certain to dominate the economy of Pakistan," he predicted. The problem, he wrote, lay in "the illusion of military parity with India." The latest war had shattered the illusion that had been "painfully maintained through two earlier wars since independence in 1947."[10] But Pakistanis preferred to live in denial, so they would soon try to re-create the illusion.

Browne pointed to "the Pakistani supposition that in the final hour of need China and the US would come to the rescue" during the East Pakistan debacle. He had seen signs in the garrison town of

Rawalpindi that read, "We love you, Mao and Nixon." Apparently, a map had been published "showing Chinese troops charging down into India." Browne noticed "a thrill of expectation" after reports that the US carrier *Enterprise* was headed for the Bay of Bengal. "There were even a few who believed up to the end that Russia would pull in her claws and return to the mediating role she assumed in ending the Indo-Pakistani war of 1965," he observed.

But there was little, if any, soul-searching among Pakistanis. Instead, the surrender in Dhaka was compared to the fall of Muslim Baghdad in 1258 to the Mongols. Like the thirteenth-century defeat, this one was also attributed to the elite's lack of piety, inadequate military preparedness, various conspiracies, and the enemy's cunning. Some Pakistanis even sought to metaphorically relocate Pakistan. "Many Pakistanis are speaking of growing closer to Central Asia and away from the Indian subcontinent," reported Browne. "New and stronger ties with Turkey, Iran and Afghanistan seem likely."

Instead of pausing to reflect on what had gone wrong, Pakistanis sought someone to blame, and over time different factions settled on their choice among Yahya, Mujib, and Bhutto as the domestic villains. There was unanimity, however, regarding the external cause of the disaster: India had caused Pakistan's breakup, and the rest of the world, including the United States, had not done enough to stop Indian aggression.

Bhutto was in New York, representing Pakistan at the United Nations, when Pakistan's army surrendered in Dhaka. He knew he would now lead Pakistan, as Yahya's position had become untenable. There were spontaneous demonstrations in several Pakistani cities against the military dictator. Junior officers had heckled a senior general close to Yahya when he tried to give a speech at army headquarters. Some senior generals were even coercing Yahya to hand over power to Bhutto. As soon as Bhutto got word of this development he sought a meeting with President Nixon and Secretary of State Rogers. The Americans then hastened to arrange the meetings at short notice.

Although Rogers had not dealt with Bhutto before, he knew that most US officials had reservations about him. Rogers had mentioned to Nixon in the Oval Office a few days earlier that Yahya might turn over Pakistan's affairs to Bhutto. Nixon had exclaimed, "The son-of-a-bitch is a total demagogue."[11] Nixon said that during his 1967 private trip to Pakistan, Ayub had given him "a rundown" on Bhutto. "He's a pretty good judge of men," Nixon said, referring to Ayub, going on to say that Bhutto was "just bad news."[12]

The US president also noted that Bhutto was "leftish." But Nixon did not quite know the real source of Bhutto's left-wing orientation. "Is he anti-India? Anti-U.S.?" the president had asked. Kissinger had explained that the Pakistani leader was "violently anti-Indian" and "pro-Chinese." But there was a silver lining for the United States in the prospect of Bhutto's rise to the helm in Pakistan: "In a way we gain a lot if he comes in," Kissinger remarked, pointing out that Nixon had less obligations to Bhutto than he did to Yahya.[13]

It is implausible that Bhutto knew of that specific exchange between Nixon, Kissinger, and Rogers; he had enough friends among Americans to know what US leaders thought of him. As such, he decided to clarify things at the outset during his meeting with Rogers. Bhutto said that he knew he was sometimes referred to as the "Yankee-baiting Former Foreign Minister," but he was nonetheless determined to open a "new chapter" in the history of Pakistan-US relations.

Bhutto's choice of words in expressing appreciation for US support for Pakistan in the ongoing crisis was interesting. He said that the US government had stood by the "basic principles of international law and civilized society as these had emerged after World War II." Pakistanis, he went on, valued American actions and statements, which, he said, "were important in demonstrating that World War II had not been fought in vain." Bhutto knew that the State Department had been less keen on Nixon's policy of tilting toward Pakistan, so he wanted to make the point that the United States had done the right thing.

The two main points Bhutto made to Rogers related to the Soviet Union and India. He said that "The whole picture of international law had been disrupted by Soviet behavior in the South Asian crisis." According to him, there were unconfirmed reports that the Soviets had "gone even to the point of providing Soviet personnel on Indian warships" and had "equipped Indian vessels and aircraft with latest missiles and technology." This was clearly meant to establish Bhutto's credentials as being anti–Soviet. On India, Bhutto said he was prepared for reconciliation with Pakistan's traditional enemy.

The Pakistani leader wanted India to "act with magnanimity" or risk becoming an "enemy of Pakistan for all time." He drew the analogy with the enmity between Carthage and Rome in ancient times, which lasted for almost a century. If India missed the present opportunity, Bhutto said, "There would be hatred for all time, utter chaos and terrible massacre." He wanted the Indians to understand that he would "need a month or more to prepare public opinion for what has taken place."

Although Pakistan had lost another war, Bhutto insisted that "India must act in humility." He added that in his view the Indians lacked vision and he could not be confident of the Indian response. Rogers observed that despite Indians' capacity to appear magnanimous publicly, they could be "very sanctimonious and self-righteous." Bhutto concurred, making the point that for that very reason a US role was necessary. "The U.S. should make clear to India that it had treaty relationship with Pakistan and that it was not going to fold up its carpets and leave," he said.

Bhutto also reminded Rogers of the ongoing dispute over Kashmir. Describing Mujib as a "good speaker" but "very blank in the head," he anticipated that the Bengali leader would not remain a central figure in Bangladesh beyond three months. Thus, he wanted an opportunity to explore the possibility of a "loose confederation" between East and West Pakistan.[14]

The meeting between Bhutto and Nixon before Bhutto's return to Pakistan was rather short because of Nixon's other prescheduled engagements. But Bhutto did tell Nixon that "Pakistan was completely in the debt of the United States for its support during the recent trying days." He repeated what he had said to Rogers about being called a "Yankee Hater" in the past and promised closer ties with the United States. Bhutto spoke of Nixon's "personal leadership and support," joked about being willing to manage his 1972 presidential campaign, and repeated the views he had shared with Rogers regarding India and the Soviet Union.

For his turn, Nixon used the opportunity to let Bhutto know that he cared about Pakistan and would work with its new leader as he had with previous ones. For Bhutto it was important to build bridges with the White House and the State Department before he assumed power in Islamabad. Pakistan would need US assistance again, especially if it were to continue confronting India.

When Nixon asked Bhutto what he thought the future held for Pakistan, the Pakistani president-in-waiting said he would take "thirty days to assess the will of the people" before establishing a series of domestic reforms. But he had already laid out his country's future foreign policy. Like before, one of its pillars would be to seek money and arms from the United States to maintain military parity with India.

On his return to Pakistan and after taking over as president, Bhutto continued his effort to charm the Americans. He had met the US president and secretary of state on Friday, December 17, and the US ambassador to Pakistan immediately after his arrival in Islamabad on Monday, December 20. On Wednesday, December 22, he visited Farland at the ambassador's residence, breaking protocol that required ambassadors to call on presidents rather than the other way around. Bhutto made it clear that he had deliberately ignored custom so as to signal strongly his "reaffirmation of a whole new period of close and effective relations with the United States."

As foreign minister, Bhutto knew how Ayub's personal connection with US leaders and diplomats worked to Pakistan's advantage. If positive personal relations worked in favor of close ties between the two countries, he worried that negative views about him might have the opposite effect. He told Farland that whatever criticism the United States may have had regarding his "past posture," he now hoped that this would be forgotten. Thus, within a period of one week he had made that point to the US president and secretary of state, and he was now repeating it to an ambassador he had lambasted not long ago during the election campaign.

......

The conversation with Farland during this unconventional visit reflected Bhutto's state of mind at the time. At age forty-three, he carried the burden of reorganizing and running a country that was only twenty-three years old. He was popular and charismatic, with education from the University of California at Berkeley as well as Oxford University. He had some experience as a cabinet minister. But the challenges Pakistan faced at the time were staggering. Pakistan had partially disintegrated, and Western scholars and journalists again expressed fears about its viability. Bhutto had taken over a militarily defeated, emotionally shattered, and economically bankrupt country. He wanted to line up America's support behind him for the monumental task ahead of him.

"Bhutto seems to have a far better chance of building a new nation than any of his predecessors," Browne wrote in the *New York Times* within a week of his assuming office. "The army is dispirited and sick of governing. The new President has a genuine popular mandate," he pointed out. "Without the dead weight of East Pakistan," the journalist calculated, "the industrial development of the west is likely to move rapidly, especially since massive aid from the US and other Western nations will probably resume soon." In his opinion Bhutto was "probably the most powerful leader Pakistan has had since the founding of the nation by Muhammad Ali Jinnah in 1947."

But Browne also foresaw Bhutto's problems. Pakistan had come into being as a homeland for the Muslims of the Indian subcontinent, and Islam was the glue that was supposed to hold everything together. He recognized that Bhutto's "interests are more secular than religious." Still, Bhutto would have to "walk a tightrope between religious fundamentalism and the needs of practical politics, between socialism and the feudal structure of Pakistan's society, between the urbane wealth of the class that produced him and the wretched poverty of the masses he now commands."[15]

Aware of these contradictions, Bhutto told Farland that Pakistan needed "a substantial influx of capital into the country" to rise out of destitution. He clarified that, by capital, he meant both private investment and government-to-government aid. He wished to assure the US government that he would make investment in Pakistan both convenient and worthwhile for foreign investors. He also spoke of wanting democracy to flourish and the need for resolving the issues among Pakistan's provinces and disparate ethnic groups. Bhutto still wanted to reach out to East Pakistan, and the idea of a confederation, which he mooted with Rogers in Washington, was still very much alive.

Farland asked Bhutto about the demand in the press that Yahya be put on trial, wondering aloud "whether this was a salutary move at a time when the climate called for reconciliation and a play-down of emotions." Apparently, Kissinger had noticed the press reports about Yahya's possible trial. He had instructed Farland to inform Bhutto the United States would have difficulty understanding the decision to do so. Bhutto said that he most certainly did not want "Yahya's head" nor was he vindictive. He added that there was a great deal of public clamor, which he found difficult to stifle. But, he noted, with the passage of time this clamor could be expected to lessen.

Having made the pitch for US investment and allaying concerns about Nixon's friend Yahya, Bhutto addressed the all-important topic of India–Pakistan relations. He said he was convinced that India had "nurtured the definite intention of liquidating West Pakistan." India, he said, had never truly recognized the 1947 partition nor, in fact, had been reconciled to it. According to Bhutto, because of India's antagonism, the future of Pakistan was closely tied to two great powers: China and the United States. He expressed the hope that his negotiations with India would provide a harmony that would allow Pakistan to exist in peace.[16]

Farland later told the State Department that "Bhutto faces difficulties in virtually every area of national activity: political, international and domestic; economic; military; and social." In foreign affairs his most pressing problem was the return to Pakistan of the ninety thousand–odd POWs and civilian internees from erstwhile East Pakistan. "India is unlikely to return them until the state of war is ended and a durable truce replaces the cease-fire," the US ambassador observed.

A settlement with India to end the state of war in the west meant negotiating territorial adjustments, he noted. This, in turn, was

•••••

linked to the problem of settling with Bangladesh the issues created by secession, including a division of assets and debts as well as a possible exchange of population between Bengalis living in West Pakistan and non-Bengalis in the East. Farland said that all these outstanding questions were related to the parallel question of third countries and, eventually, Pakistan itself recognizing Bangladesh.[17]

But before anything else Bhutto had to revive Pakistani self-confidence. A few days after his visit to Farland's residence he undertook a whirlwind tour of all parts of West Pakistan in an effort to rally a shattered nation. This was the thirty-day trip he had spoken to Nixon about. In addition to exhorting Pakistanis to claim their destiny, Bhutto also wanted to ascertain the mood of the people. He blended "the styles of shrewd diplomat, benevolent despot, and circus barker," said the *New York Times* about the tour.

"Bhutto has showered a glittering tail of oratory across Pakistan during his first month as President hoping to breathe life into a demoralized nation," the story went on. He had "succeeded in keeping so close to everyone—Pakistanis of all classes, foreign diplomats and newsmen—that it is hard to view him with detached perspective." Bhutto had targeted his "gifted rhetoric" at diplomats and foreign journalists in order to change Pakistan's "dismal image" abroad. He seemed aware that "this image is a cardinal reason for Pakistan's present financial insolvency and lack of foreign diplomatic support, affecting even the bankers of the world."

According to Browne, the newspaper's correspondent, Bhutto wanted "to mollify world criticism" by treating visitors to roast venison, folk dancing, a visit to archaeological relics, or a duck hunt. He had released Mujib, proclaimed amnesty for all political prisoners, and abolished capital and corporal punishment. He had "moved to break the power of Pakistan's financial oligarchy" and had assured his people of "rapid movement toward the establishment of democratic institutions." Thus, Bhutto took pains every day "to reassure the vast Moslem congregations that no laws repugnant to Islam will be enacted by his administration. The mullahs and tribal leaders are not at all sure about him," Browne wrote.[18]

It seemed that Bhutto was succeeding in his purpose: Pakistanis determined that he was the leader to preside over the country's revival, and world leaders, including Nixon, offered help in enabling Pakistan to get over the trauma of a second partition.

Within a couple of months of the surrender in Dhaka Pakistanis were beginning to overcome the shock of that monumental fiasco. They felt that the remainder of their country would survive and muddle through even after losing more than half its population and a large part of its territory. Just as Jinnah was once called Quaid-e-Azam (the Great Leader), Bhutto was now acclaimed as Quaid-e-Awam (the Leader of the People).

As a practical politician, Bhutto eschewed the path of national introspection. He had mustered support by appealing to the Pakistani sentiment of being victims. He spoke of "international conspiracies" while befriending individual foreigners from whom he sought help for his country. He promised that "this stigma" of defeat would be "wiped out even if it has to be done by our children's children."[19] He called upon critics to "get off our back." He did all this, but he did not encourage debate over why Pakistan broke up so soon. Pakistan's own intelligentsia likewise showed little interest in finding answers to that question.

Pakistanis were sheltered even from global reflections on their country. The international media was full of reports about the debris the Pakistan army had left behind in Bangladesh. Bodies had been discovered of Bengali intellectuals rounded up and killed the night before the end of war. There were calls for Pakistani officers to be tried for war crimes. Scholars in Europe and North America analyzed the impracticalities of the idea of Pakistan. But Pakistanis sought security in isolation from these discussions and the notion that in Bhutto they had found another savior.

Just as Americans had questioned the rationale for Pakistan's creation, they also examined in considerable detail the reasons for its breakup. For some, "the idea of Pakistan as the homeland for Muslims in South Asia no longer appeared valid."[20] After all, the majority of South Asia's Muslims no longer lived in Pakistan. Others wondered whether a nation basing its identity only on religion would ever find peace and prosperity.

In an essay titled, "A Lament for Pakistan," author James Michener wondered how people bound together by religion could descend into the orgy of violence witnessed in Bangladesh. "I cannot comprehend how the soldiers I knew in the Punjab could have behaved as they did in East Bengal," he wrote. "I cannot explain how a nation which was bound together by religion—and that alone—could have so swiftly degenerated to the point where the average Punjabi not only hated the Bengali but also wanted to kill and mutilate him. And yet I know this happened."[21]

In Michener's judgment, "Pakistan was the impossible dream that failed." It attempted to overcome differences of language, custom, economics, politics, and tradition, he wrote, pointing out the huge differences between Punjabis and Bengalis. "The Punjabi," he said, were direct and blunt but "not fond of books or philosophical discussion." Conversely, the Bengali were "the Irishman of Asia, a fiery brilliant orator given to endless disputation." The only cement that Pakistan could rely upon was religion. "And in less than 25 years religion proved unequal to the task," he affirmed.

There were many other essays and editorials that made points similar to Michener's as well as calls for Pakistanis to transform the remaining part of their country into a practical rather than an ideological state. Some argued that Pakistani militarism had failed, that the country needed to give up its cult of the warriors and focus instead on dealing with economic fundamentals. "Decisive defeat at the hands of the Indians is a bitter pill to swallow for the Pakistanis, steeped as they are in military tradition," observed one editorial in the *New York Times*. But this defeat should lead "the new leadership to abandon the myth of military invincibility." Pakistan needed "to come to terms with its Indian neighbors" and to shift the human and material resources it had "squandered on an excessive military establishment to urgent development tasks."[22]

But these ideas found little resonance in Pakistan. Instead of swallowing the "bitter pill" of military defeat, Pakistanis started preparing to avenge it. Less than eight weeks after becoming president, Bhutto sat down for an interview with foreign affairs columnist C. L. Sulzberger and proposed a renewed defense pact with the United States. Bhutto said that he was ready "to start talks tomorrow" to obtain "American arms to replace the equipment lost by Pakistan during her war with India last December."

According to Sulzberger, Bhutto praised US actions during the conflict with India, crediting them with preventing an all-out assault on West Pakistan and the Pakistan-held portion of Kashmir. He credited the US ultimatum and moving the USS *Enterprise* into the Bay of Bengal with saving West Pakistan. "The Soviet Union understood the signal and then pressed India to accept a ceasefire," he said.

But there was nothing about reconciliation with India in the interview. Sulzberger noted that Bhutto "spoke gloomily of India" and implied that "India was behaving like a virtual satellite of Moscow." He made predictions similar to those Ayub made about the Soviet Union gaining ground in the subcontinent and about India being on the verge of breaking up. "By sponsoring Bangladesh you will see that India will lose West Bengal and Assam," he declared.

"It is preposterous to think that in an association with a great power like Russia the great power's interests will not prevail," Bhutto said while commenting on Indian relations with the Soviet Union. But he did not see the paradox in his own suggestion of close defense bonds between Pakistan and the United States. If Soviet interests would prevail in that great power's ties with India, surely Pakistan could not expect that its interests would be paramount in an alliance with the United States.

Sulzberger described Bhutto's geopolitical view as foreseeing an "unending danger of Indian aggressive tendencies, fostered by Moscow." Bhutto insisted that there was a need for China and the United States to work in concert in support of Pakistan. He said that he discovered sympathy for his idea of close Pakistani ties with China during his Beijing visit but that the Chinese were against the idea of formal pacts. Bhutto then expressed confidence that Nixon's "admirable statesmanship" would succeed in fostering a new US-Chinese relationship. This in turn would help realize his vision of a US-China concert to defend Pakistan.

•••••

Bhutto also spoke at length with Sulzberger about his desire to achieve profound social and political reform in Pakistan. He denounced Yahya as "a drunken, irresponsible, man" and compared him to "Ivan the terrible." He promised to hold a national referendum on his reform program later that year and a second plebiscite on the new constitution he wanted the constituent assembly to draft. This document, he said, would put an end to any possibility that another "adventurer" could take power, because "after all we have had four dictatorships in 24 years."[23]

Once Sulzberger published his interview, Pakistan assumed that Bhutto's wishes had America's blessings. Pakistan's tendency to see everything as part of some Byzantine intrigue was widespread. Pakistanis often saw reports in major US newspapers as trial balloons or orchestrated leaks managed by an American invisible hand. If the Americans had not liked Bhutto's proposal, they reasoned, it would not have received the coverage it did in the United States. Sober warned Washington: "We are now in a somewhat euphoric stage in US-Pak relations." He voiced his conviction that "unwarranted expectations" were being built up in some quarters in Pakistan.[24]

As things turned out, the referendums Bhutto promised did not materialize. A few years later his forecast that a strong constitution would prevent another military coup also proved wrong. But after publicly stating his geopolitical views Bhutto moved energetically to try to create the US-China-Pakistan coalition to contain India. He projected India as "an enemy of Islam and Muslims" and, by extension, "an inveterate foe of Pakistan, determined to dismember it."[25]

To Pakistanis, Bhutto presented himself as "a fearless and capable thwarter of India's designs," and he described his domestic adversaries as appeasers or agents of India. Although Pakistan had just been defeated militarily, Bhutto said he would continue a policy of confrontation with India until the rights of Kashmir's people were secured and Indian Muslims' persecution ended. If Jinnah had mobilized Indian Muslims on the basis of fear of Hindu dominance, then Bhutto wanted to lead Pakistan in resisting India's domination.

But this hard-line stance against India, coupled with renewed demands for settling the Kashmir issue, rang alarm bells among the State Department's South Asia experts. Bhutto had made several suggestions to Americans in rapid succession, offering numerous facilities in return for US arms. The army and the Inter-Services Intelligence (ISI) communicated similar messages through the US military mission and the CIA station in Islamabad.

Pakistan's defense secretary, Ghiasuddin Ahmed, even identified locations along the Arabian seacoast for US naval bases. These included, from west to east, Jiwani, Gwadar, Sonmiani Bay, Karachi, and the area south and east of Karachi. He claimed that India had provided naval facilities to the Soviets at the port of Visakhapatnam and on Andaman Islands. He thought the United States might be interested in countering the expanded Soviet naval presence in that area.[26]

Pakistan officials speculated that the United States might be interested in developing a port such as at Gwadar, which could aid economic development of that region of Pakistan. In addition to new, US-developed ports, Pakistan intended to maintain and possibly enlarge the size of its prewar army. Sober, however, asked Bhutto whether doing so made sense, given the reduction in Pakistan's borders and its diminished financial capabilities.[27]

In March 1972 Rogers summarized the Pakistani plans and the American diplomats' concerns about those plans in a comprehensive memorandum for Nixon. Pakistan had offered the use of port and "tracking station" facilities for US forces along the Arabian Sea coast near Karachi, he reported. As in the case of the Badaber base near Peshawar, the Pakistani plan envisaged "access to facilities as needed," although there was still an aversion to having large numbers of US personnel in Pakistan. The new Pakistani government also welcomed US collaboration in strategic military planning.

"Bhutto's objectives in all this seem fairly clear," observed the secretary of state. "He has already taken steps to strengthen his security relationship with China. He now seeks to add a closer security association with us." Bhutto considered the prospects of US military support as fairly good because of US concerns over Soviet policy toward India and [America's] developing relations with China. What was not clear, Rogers said, was how these overtures to the United States related to "Bhutto's longer range intentions toward India."

The Americans had learned from their experience during the 1950s and 1960s that references in Pakistani military plans to dangers from Soviet expansion were only bait for the Americans; Pakistan's real military concern remained India. The State Department's outlook was that the South Asian equation had changed significantly after the December 1971 war. "We could not and should not seek to build up Pakistan as any kind of strategic counter-weight to India," Rogers cautioned.

According to him, America's basic policy objective in South Asia should be "to encourage movement toward a broad political settlement which would replace the sharp political-military confrontation that has plagued the Subcontinent for more than 20 years." The United States, he recommended, should support Pakistan's "territorial integrity and economic growth," but it should avoid Pakistan's military buildup because "it would encourage Pakistan again to postpone the difficult decisions it must make if it is to reach a basic accommodation with its stronger neighbor."[28] Rogers proposed, therefore, that the United States encourage India to be magnanimous toward Pakistan. But he was firm in saying that military supplies to Pakistan should not be resumed, as these might stimulate conflict in the subcontinent.

Nixon had given little thought to the subcontinent except in the context of the Cold War. From this view, Pakistan's willingness to line up with the United States and India's refusal to do the same made it easy for him to choose Pakistan over India. Now, however, he was being asked to decide on the basis of America's longer-term interests in South Asia. The consensus among US officials was that it was India, not Pakistan, that mattered more.

The US media also called for the need to regain India's confidence. The Indians, however, were "in no hurry to make up with a government in Washington whose unaccountable policies aroused anger and anguish even among America's best Indian friends."[29]

·····

So Nixon met with Kenneth Keating, US ambassador to India and told him to start mending fences with New Delhi. "India has a friend in the White House," Nixon asked Keating to tell the Indians. "We are going to China for reasons of our own. We took action on India because our law requires it," he added. "In reality we are India's best friend."

As if to reassure himself that his recent policy had not permanently damaged US-India relations, Nixon observed that India needed relations with all major powers and would want close ties with Washington. "The United States is the only one that has no design on her," he said. Nixon tried to justify his past decisions regarding India and Pakistan by saying, "Neither country should be a country. They are too poor, too bloodthirsty."[30]

In addition, Nixon now had to tell Pakistanis that they should no longer rely on US arms. The occasion to do that presented itself when Pakistan's secretary general for foreign affairs, Aziz Ahmed, visited Washington in March. Before the meeting, Rogers called Kissinger to warn him that the Pakistani official was going to give the president "a hard sell on renewing supply of military equipment to Pakistan." The secretary of state then alerted the national security adviser that encouragement of Pakistani expectations would be harmful. Kissinger said he doubted that Nixon, "who is very pro-Pakistan," was "even thinking about it."[31]

When Ahmed arrived in the Oval Office he played to Nixon's sympathy. Because of this, Kissinger could not sway the conversation in the direction Rogers had suggested. Ahmed had served as ambassador in Washington under Ayub and had been involved in negotiations during the heyday of Pakistan's military alliance with the United States. Thus, he knew Nixon's passions and prejudices. During the meeting Ahmed stressed that Bhutto had managed to create national unity and was about to bring martial law to an end. "Pakistan's main problems now are external," Ahmed said, pointing particularly to the difficult relationship with India.

Ahmed then repeated an argument familiar to Americans: "Pakistan is militarily very weak," he asserted somberly. "It was weak in December and is weaker now." According to him, India knew of

Pakistan's weakness and for that reason continued to hold "90,000 men that Pakistan needs for maintaining internal security and order," a reference to the prisoners of war. Ahmed told Nixon that he expected negotiations with India to be tough, as the Indians wanted to use their leverage to settle the Kashmir problem and demand Pakistan's recognition of Bangladesh.

The Pakistani diplomat went on to confide to his hosts that Bhutto intended to recognize Bangladesh; it was just a matter of time. "Bhutto had come to power with three cards to play," he said, stating that the first of these was Mujib's release, which had already been given away. The other two cards in Bhutto's hand, according to Ahmed, were the recognition of Bangladesh and "the 28,000 Bengali soldiers in West Pakistan whom Mujib wants and the 20,000 civil servants whom he also wants." Bhutto had already spoken to the Soviets about a deal involving recognition in return for an exchange of prisoners, but he had not heard back.

"India has moved three divisions to the West Pakistani border," Ahmed told Nixon. This maneuver was designed either to exert pressure on Pakistan for the negotiations or "for a more serious attack." He said that there had been some thought that the Indians would seize Pakistan-controlled parts of Kashmir and added that the Chinese did not think that such an attack would occur until after Nixon's impending visit to Moscow. Kissinger said gently that he was inclined to agree with the Chinese assessment. During this meeting both Nixon and Kissinger avoided telling Ahmed that US intelligence did not believe Pakistan's claims about Indian preparations for another attack on Pakistan.

Ahmed also complained that the Chinese capacity to give sophisticated weapons to Pakistan was very limited. France, he said, could provide some for cash, but Pakistan had no means to pay. Pakistan once again needed the United States to help equip its military. As in the past, Ahmed tried to play on potential superpower rivalry. He said he would not be surprised if the Soviet Union offered Pakistan a friendship treaty within a year. "The Soviet interest seems to be in showing that it is the USSR and not the U.S. or China who will provide security in the subcontinent," he declared.

......

As an example of the role the Soviets were playing, Ahmed mentioned that, through Ceylon, Pakistan had sent messages to the Indian prime minister, Indira Gandhi, and the answers had come back through Moscow. This showed that "the Soviets intended to keep the peacemaking process very much within their grasp." He noted that the Indians also were pushing for "greater control in South Asia. They had offered treaties of their own—similar to the one signed with Bangladesh—to Burma, Ceylon and Nepal."

Nixon heard Ahmed out and avoided saying explicitly that the United States did not want to get back into the business of supplying weapons to Pakistan. Instead, Nixon said that the United States would provide all the help it could, but "most of our help would be in the economic field." He cited difficulties with Congress and the US election in November as reasons why he could not move ahead with any military assistance. But, he said, his administration "would do all it could so that Pakistan's own resources could be free to work out its military arrangements with other friends."[32] This kept Pakistan's hopes of securing sophisticated weapons from the United States alive.

Bhutto continued to remind the Americans that Pakistan needed military materiel to deal with threats from the Soviet Union and India. Soon after Ahmed's Washington visit, he wrote a letter to Nixon claiming that the Indians were "threatening the preservation of the tenuous peace that has been achieved." He insisted that India had moved five additional divisions to the West Pakistan border, and the Indian chief of staff had recently visited Moscow to replenish military equipment. "The Soviet Union and India have stepped up their subversive activities in both Balochistan and the North-West Frontier Province," he contended.[33]

Contrary to Ahmed's evaluation of Pakistan having achieved domestic strength, a US National Intelligence Estimate contended that assessing the prospects for Pakistan was "unusually tricky." It reported that "Defeated in war, beset with unrest, its eastern province lost, ruled by new leaders, Pakistan faces a most uncertain future." It then listed several "difficult but unavoidable decisions" facing Bhutto or his successor, including making peace with India, preventing the

breakup of the country, developing a new social and economic consensus, and creating and maintaining new viable political institutions.

The intelligence forecast pointed out that "Many developments
with respect to Pakistan will be determined by decisions made outside that country and over which it will have little control." Pakistan, it said, could have a brighter future if it secured an acceptable
and amicable settlement with India and achieved a stable political
consensus.[34]

✶

THE OPPORTUNITY FOR creating a new South Asian equation came
when India and Pakistan agreed to peace talks in the summer of
1972. Bhutto then traveled to Simla, an Indian mountain resort that
served as the summer capital during the British Raj, to meet Indira
Gandhi. But this was hardly a meeting of equals. Bhutto had to negotiate the release of Pakistani POWs with someone he had publicly
derided in the past. He also had to secure the return of 5,139 square
miles of Pakistani territory that India occupied. Thus, Bhutto represented a defeated country. Gandhi, however, was the leader of a vic-
torious nation.

From India's perspective this was the moment to finally resolve the
dispute over Jammu and Kashmir. As East Pakistan had already become Bangladesh, West Pakistan could not realistically hope to maintain parity with India. Pakistani leaders had often said that Kashmir
was the core issue that poisoned India-Pakistan relations. With this in
mind, settling it once and for all when Pakistan was at its weakest
could pave the way for normal relations. The bitterness of partition
could then finally begin to erode, at least from India's perspective.

Bhutto was well prepared for the negotiation. He told Gandhi
that Pakistan's domestic political situation did not allow him to sign
a treaty settling the argument over Kashmir forever, that the Pakistani military would probably topple his fragile civilian government
if he conceded Kashmir to India or signed an explicit no-war pact.
Radical opinions would gain popularity in Pakistan, he argued, that

would accuse him of losing Kashmir in addition to East Pakistan. The Pakistani president pleaded for the middle ground. The two countries should start the process of de-escalation of tensions, he suggested. He could always return a few years later with a stronger hand at home in order to deal with the deeper sources of conflict.

Against the advice of some of her officials, Gandhi was persuaded of Bhutto's argument. Although she distrusted Bhutto, she saw him as preferable to likely alternatives. She calculated that a successor military regime would be even more hostile to India than was Bhutto. For India, domestic unrest or the balkanization of Pakistan, with its impact spreading to neighboring countries, could not be a favorable development. Gandhi concluded that it was better to postpone a final agreement on Kashmir's status than to push for Bhutto to accept India's demands immediately.

The compromise was to declare that "the two countries are resolved to settle their differences by peaceful means through bilateral negotiations." This effectively precluded war. The cease-fire line in Jammu and Kashmir was declared the Line of Control (LOC). Indian signatories interpreted this to mean that actual control was now synonymous with legal possession. Bhutto claimed later that he had saved Pakistan from the ultimate humiliation of completely giving up its claim on Kashmir.[35]

The Simla accord also facilitated the exchange of thirty-six thousand Bengalis remaining in Pakistan with ninety thousand Pakistani prisoners of war in India. Pakistan also got back the territory it had lost in the west. The *Washington Post* proclaimed that the "achievements registered at the first Indian-Pakistani summit, at Simla, surpassed all expectations." It complimented Indira Gandhi and Bhutto for building the "diplomatic foundation for a regional structure of peace such as the south Asian subcontinent has not known in the 25 years since British power retired."

Bhutto, the paper said, left Simla with something substantial—and politically necessary—to show to his countrymen. "Pakistan could not reasonably be expected to surrender its traditional claim on all of Kashmir at this time," it pointed out, adding, "Mr. Bhutto may come

· · · · ·

to that eventually but for him to come to it immediately would almost surely precipitate another military coup in Islamabad."[36]

US diplomats concurred. Sober said he saw Bhutto seeking a "new relationship with India to replace the quarter century of confrontation." But, he observed, the historical atmosphere of suspicion and distrust hampered the effort. Bhutto was willing to come to terms with the post-Bangladesh realities as long as there was no compromise on Pakistan's prestige. Thus, the future of India-Pakistan relations would be grim "if Bhutto fails in moving from confrontation to peaceful coexistence as specified in the Simla agreement."

According to Sober, in addition to a degree of normalization with India, the main planks of Bhutto's foreign policy were good ties with the United States, close relations with China, and increased participation in the "third world club."[37]

Although the Simla agreement with India was by all accounts a major success, Pakistan's religious nationalists did not perceive it as such. Anti-India hard-liners portrayed it as a sellout. As with the peace concluded at Tashkent after the 1965 war, rumors and conspiracy theories circulated about secret clauses and undisclosed side agreements. The Islamist party, Jamaat-e-Islami, orchestrated protests against the eventual recognition of Bangladesh, as its members observed the anniversary of the fall of Dhaka as the "Day of Vengeance." But by the year's end Bhutto appeared to have the levers of power firmly in his control.

★

THE UNITED STATES provided $165 million in economic assistance to Pakistan in 1972, including 600,000 tons of wheat, to be paid for in Pakistani rupees instead of foreign exchange. Bhutto asked for an additional 400,000 tons, but the United States could immediately offer only 250,000 tons. The reason behind the US hesitation in meeting Pakistan's demand in full was the Soviet Union's large-scale purchase of American grain, which left less wheat available for supply on concessional terms to other countries. But Bhutto interpreted it as a deliberate slight.

He timed the announcement of Pakistan's withdrawal from SEATO in November 1972 to coincide with conveying his anger over the US response to his wheat request. At the same time Pakistan recognized North Korea, North Vietnam, and the procommunist government in exile of Cambodia. A memo to Kissinger from Harold Saunders and John Holdridge, members of NSC staff, informed him to expect Bhutto to present a sizable shopping list for military equipment. They also sought instructions on "whether or not we want him to understand that he has taken a step which is not consistent with U.S. interests."[38] Kissinger considered it prudent not to overreact to what he saw as Bhutto's attempts to seek greater attention.

In February 1973 Pakistani commandos raided the Iraqi embassy in Islamabad to uncover a cache of arms that Pakistan claimed was intended for ethnic Baloch separatists. For any government to violate an embassy's diplomatic immunity is most unusual, but on this occasion Bhutto had a wider agenda. He used the discovery of the arms as justification for dismissing the provincial government of Balochistan, whom he accused of complicity in a conspiracy to foment armed rebellion against the Pakistan government. Members of the National Awami Party (NAP), a group that had support among Pakistan's Baloch and Pashtun ethnic groups, ran the provincial government.

Historically NAP had sought autonomy for Baloch and Pashtun ethnic groups just as Mujib's Awami League had championed autonomy for the Bengalis. As such, coming so soon after the Bangladesh war, Bhutto's allegations about designs against Pakistan's integrity appealed to the dominant Punjabis. The slogan of "Pakistan in Danger" was almost as effective for Bhutto as "Islam in Danger" had been for Jinnah before 1947.

Bhutto wrote to Nixon, describing the Iraqi arms intrigue and connecting it to the Soviets. Then he approached Sober to seek his help in working out a compromise with Baloch politicians, some of whom the US diplomat knew. Because conducting dialogue between the government and an opposition faction is not part of an embassy's normal functions, Bhutto acknowledged that he had made an extraordinary request.[39] Sober conveyed Bhutto's message to the former governor of Balochistan only to have Washington instruct him not to play a role in the domestic conflict.

Sober bowed out as political negotiator, telling Bhutto that he did not want opponents of US-Pakistan relations to misconstrue his part.[40] The unusual episode thus reflected Bhutto's bid to ascertain his standing with the Americans. Dulles and Johnson had stood by Ayub, and Nixon's tilt toward Pakistan was partly a function of his regard for Yahya. Bhutto wanted to determine whether similar goodwill existed among Americans for him. He was disappointed to learn that the United States did not consider him a friend.

Kissinger tried to explain his understanding of Bhutto's moves to Nixon after receiving the letter speaking of the "Soviet-Indian design on the integrity of Pakistan." Bhutto had said that the Soviets were behind the clandestine arms shipment uncovered at the Iraqi embassy and that it was intended for dissidents whose ultimate aim, in collusion with the Indians and Afghans, was the final dismemberment of Pakistan. Bhutto had closed his letter to Nixon by appealing "for your Government to take a clear and firm decision on your great country's attitude toward my country." Pakistan, he said, "must know where we stand with our friends."

According to Kissinger, there was no evidence of an active Soviet effort to supply arms to dissidents in Pakistani Balochistan. Kissinger had asked the CIA to review its evidence on this subject, and they had checked "thoroughly in the field and here," finding that there had been no indication of a recent increase in Soviet-supported subversive activity in Pakistan. Kissinger cited the possibility that the Iraqi arms were destined for Baloch dissidents in southeastern Iran. He then observed that "The important aspect of this letter is its general expression of concern by Bhutto rather than the specific instance itself."

Bhutto's letter, Kissinger said, showed his "growing uneasiness over the future of his relationship with the U.S." Rogers believed that Bhutto was simply trying to set the stage for the visit of a special envoy he was sending in order to push his request for American weapons. Kissinger thought that the Pakistani leader's disquiet "may have been exacerbated by the absence of a decision on military sup-

· · · · · ·

ply policy over the long term and the fact that Pakistan is still without a US ambassador after ten months."[41]

Islamabad stayed without an American ambassador until fall. At that time Henry Byroade, a career foreign service officer who had served as ambassador to Egypt almost eighteen years earlier, filled the position. As assistant secretary of state for Middle East and South Asian affairs during the Eisenhower administration, Byroade had dealt with Pakistan's earlier requests for military aid. He had served as ambassador in South Africa, Afghanistan, Burma, and the Philippines. Byroade's arrival in Islamabad was meant to reassure Bhutto. But it came only after Bhutto made an official visit to Washington in September 1973.

The United States had originally scheduled a state visit for Bhutto in July, the first such visit for Pakistan's leader after the country's bifurcation. But that summer was particularly eventful in Pakistan. Torrential monsoon rain had caused massive floods in most of Pakistan, affecting millions of people. Bhutto postponed his US trip to engage in the relief effort.

Then, on August 14, 1973—the twenty-sixth anniversary of the founding of Pakistan—the country's new constitution went into effect. Bhutto had managed to get consensus in Parliament from all parties on the new charter. The constitution was based on the Westminster model of parliamentary democracy, albeit with extraordinary powers vested in the office of prime minister. Bhutto thus vacated the ceremonial office of president for one of his loyalists and moved to the more powerful position. On the US side, a similar change occurred as Kissinger moved from the office of national security adviser to become secretary of state.

As prime minister, Bhutto was no longer head of state and, therefore, not eligible for the pomp and ceremony of a state visit. When he arrived in Washington on September 17, the State Department's Office of Protocol designated his trip as an "Official Visit." The next day Bhutto was welcomed formally with military honors at the North Portico of the White House. Then, because of rain, the president and the prime minister moved to the East Room for formal speeches.

*****

Nixon spoke of the "friendship that has bound our two countries together for over a generation." He recalled his visits to Pakistan and declared, "The independence and the integrity of Pakistan is a cornerstone of American foreign policy." Bhutto spoke about the "ease of communication and of understanding" between Pakistanis and Americans. "We share a host of common affinities despite the diversities and the distances that separate us," he affirmed.

But when private discussions began, the Nixon administration's unwillingness to provide their military with advanced weapons disappointed the Pakistanis. Kissinger said that the United States had "encouraged China to give military supplies to Pakistan" and had also had "extensive talks with the Shah" of Iran so that his own military deployment helps Pakistan. But the United States simply could not supply weapons to Pakistan itself.

Bhutto brought up the coup in Afghanistan, which had resulted in deposing the country's monarchy and replacing it with a republic under a nationalist cousin of the king. Kissinger said he had discussed the matter with the Soviet ambassador. "I told him that if the recent coup in Afghanistan remained an internal Afghan affair, that would be one matter," he said. "But if it resurrected the Pashtunistan dispute, the US would be engaged. This is the basic policy of the President."

Nixon explained that his stance against India had cost him politically at home. "We have a number of people in the US who are enthusiastic supporters of India," he remarked. He said that "At the time of the India-Pakistan war in 1971, no one could understand why we did not back India." Nixon found it ironic that "great newspapers like the *New York Times* and our columnists" argued that the United States should back India simply because it was bigger. "The world will not be safe for anybody but the very big and very strong if we adopt that as a principle of our foreign policy," he said.

Bhutto tried to make an argument similar to the one Liaquat and Ayub had made in the fifties, namely that the problems of the Middle East were interconnected with those in South Asia, and American interests were at stake in the Persian Gulf. Pakistan, rather than India, could protect those interests better. "Pakistan is situated at the mouth of the Persian Gulf," Bhutto said. "Any state that has access

. . . . . .

to the Karachi coast can dominate the Gulf. That is why the Soviet Union is so interested in that coast."

Bhutto disparaged India before proceeding to give a telescoped version of the history of US-Pakistan relations. "There are many contradictions in India and we feel sorry for the Indian people and the economic privations they suffer," he said, adding that India was disillusioned with its own lack of progress. "India has burned its fingers in the furnace of Bengal," Bhutto continued. He made the case that India was more likely to break into pieces than was Pakistan. "Over the years we have had Sikhs, Nagas, Mizos approach us for help against India," he said. "They wanted our support in their fight for autonomy within India. We did not give them our support." Implicit in the statement was the suggestion that India had played dirty in Bangladesh; if Pakistan did the same, it too could succeed in causing India's fragmentation.

According to Bhutto, Pakistan was not the only neighbor of India that had suffered at its hands; Nepal, Sikkim, Burma, and China had all suffered similarly. Pakistan, however, had been "committed to Western civilization. We have been committed to the U.S.," Bhutto declared. He recounted the relationship, almost year by year, suggesting that the Americans had let Pakistan down by helping India during its war with China in 1962. "India needs U.S. economic assistance," he said. "The U.S. does not need India. There is no reason why the euphoria toward India should continue."

Bhutto's line of reasoning echoed Jinnah's belief that the United States needed Pakistan more than Pakistan needed the United States. The generally pro-Pakistan Nixon made no attempt to question Bhutto's fundamental assumptions, stating only that "The tragedy of the early days was in not settling the Kashmir question right at the outset." But Bhutto had just demonstrated that Pakistanis considered India an existential threat. Kashmir was the manifestation, not the cause, of the conflict. The State Department had told Nixon in his talking points for the meeting that Pakistan's security problems were "primarily political/psychological and economic."[42]

The Pakistani prime minister told his US hosts that Pakistan was "going to have a problem with the Afghans" because "they lay claim

......

to two Pakistani provinces." According to him, it was not Afghanistan that wanted to revive its claim from the past. "We believe that the USSR is interested in reviving this problem. Afghanistan by itself is no problem for Pakistan," he declared.

Bhutto reported that the Soviet Union had its eyes glued to the coast. "Afghanistan alone would not fulfill Soviet ambitions; India alone would not fulfill Soviet ambitions." The Soviet objective, he said, was to get Pakistan to join the Asian Collective Security Pact that Brezhnev had proposed. Bhutto did not think that Afghanistan's new president, Mohammad Daoud, was rooted in the coup that brought him to power. "The majors and colonels under him trained in the USSR," he said. "Those young boys are difficult to predict. They will not rest until we get harpooned and lassoed."

Bhutto then asked the rhetorical question: "Is something wrong with the basic concept of Pakistan?" Then he answered it himself, saying, "I don't think this can be. Two million people have given their lives for the idea of Pakistan. But people keep calling it into question." He cited the two million dead as a reference to Muslims killed during the riots over partition, which was a consequence of the idea of Pakistan rather than preplanned sacrifice for it. Bhutto had effectively proved Nehru and Indira Gandhi's assertion that the need to justify their nationhood troubled Pakistanis most. Neither Kissinger nor Nixon knew that Bhutto's analysis was uncannily similar to the conversation Ayub had with Eisenhower in Karachi in 1959. On that occasion the Pakistani military dictator had spoken of Afghanistan with contempt and had pointed to what he described as the potential for India's disintegration. Pakistan was only twelve years old at the time, but its military ruler thought it had superior standing as a nation and a state than did neighboring countries that had existed in some form or other for much longer. Now Bhutto, an elected prime minister, was confirming that Pakistan's sense of self and its view of the "other" had not changed after democracy supplanted dictatorship. Ayub and Yahya would have said similar things, though possibly less eloquently.

Although Nixon had been very warm toward him, in the meeting Bhutto failed to get what he wanted most from the United States.

······

"In the military area, our hands are tied," the US president said. Nonetheless, he advised Bhutto to address Pakistan's "public relations problem" in the United States. In his opinion Bhutto's "credibility with the liberal establishment" would develop more support in Congress for the United States helping Pakistan. The US administration had returned to a policy limited to providing military spare parts, and Nixon wanted to wait for the right political climate before moving forward further.[43]

Bhutto had a second go at getting Nixon's support for the military supply relationship in their next meeting, which was on the second day of his official visit. He told Nixon, who was already feeling the brunt of the mounting Watergate scandal, that he felt "embarrassed to complicate a problem for a friend." He would not have raised the question at all "if Pakistan were not so badly menaced." In addition to asking for US weapons, Bhutto said, "We want a port in Baluchistan."

Apparently the Iranians were building a port at Chah Bahar, so Pakistan needed one on its coast. "The Soviets are deeply interested in this coast and they have offered to help us with oil exploration, geological survey and that kind of thing," Bhutto said to arouse Nixon's interest. "We would rather have a U.S. presence." He showed Nixon and Kissinger a map of Balochistan so they could see the location of Ormara, on the Makran coast, where the port was to be built. Bhutto promised that if the United States were interested, "there could even be a U.S. presence there."

This was a major turnabout for Bhutto. For years he had argued that maintaining equal distance and equal friendship with all major powers better served Pakistan's interests. In fact, soon after leaving Ayub's cabinet he had published a book titled *The Myth of Independence*, in which he argued for strict bilateralism. He had written that military alliance with the United States had compromised Pakistan's independence of action in relation to India, the country's main adversary. Now, however, he was offering not only bases to the Americans but also agreeing to a US military presence. But times had changed. The United States no longer saw bases in Pakistan as strategically important.

· · · · ·

Kissinger repeated the proposition of routing weapons through Iran. He wondered how Pakistan could get equipment without India not immediately learning about it. "The Indians will make a storm in a teacup whenever they learn about the slightest little bit of equipment coming into Pakistan," Bhutto quipped. "India spends some $2 billion on arms while its people are starving," he said, adding that if India were to reduce its military budget, Pakistan could do the same.

There was one problem, however, with channeling military assistance through Iran. "It is very well for Iran to say that Iran will come to Pakistan's aid," Bhutto said, but this "creates a bad reaction in Pakistan. Our people are a strong people, and they respond by asking why Pakistan needs Iran's aid." Kissinger could tell Iran's Shah that for him to talk about aiding Pakistan "suggests that Pakistan is going to disintegrate tomorrow and Iran will bail us out." The Shah should support Pakistan but not talk about it, as his pronouncements created "a feeling of inferiority" among Pakistanis.[44]

The Pakistani prime minister also asked for "500,000 tons or 600,000 tons" of wheat and 100,000 tons of edible oil under PL-480, the US law that allowed poor countries to pay for food in their own currencies. Kissinger explained that the US situation with wheat was tight but promised to look into the request. Bhutto also asked for help in attracting American private investment. Nixon remarked that "I think it is a good place to invest. If I had some money I would put it there." But he cited investors' concerns about the uncertainties of South Asia."[45]

Nixon did not comment on Bhutto's policy of nationalizing major industries, banks, and insurance companies. Although foreign investment had not been nationalized, the confidence of Pakistan's business community had been shattered, which in turn discouraged foreign investors. Americans understood the need to address economic disparities, but they did not see socialism as the solution. Treasury Secretary John Connally had discussed with Bhutto and his finance minister the potential impact of expanding the public sector on the economy soon after Pakistan's first wave of nationalization.[46] After that, American officials avoided ideological debates about economics with Bhutto or his officials.

The American media welcomed the Nixon administration's policy of engaging Pakistan without offering military assistance. The *Los Angeles Times* labeled it a policy of "Assistance without Arms." It was wise policy, the paper said, to maintain the ban on selling lethal arms to Pakistan.[47] The *Washington Post* pointed out that Nixon had been as positive about Pakistan and Bhutto as he had been during his "tilt" during the Bangladesh war, and it chided Bhutto for going about Washington "appealing publicly for more arms" and grumbling that the US government had not heeded his appeals for military supplies.

According to the *Post* there was "no region in the world where the US has come to more grief over the provision of arms" than South Asia. The paper appreciated Bhutto for doing "a superb job in restoring his country's spirit and sense of progress" and admired his great skill in starting dialogue with India and Bangladesh. However, it called upon the administration to formulate US policy toward the subcontinent "guided by the new realities of the subcontinent."[48] These new realities had made India more powerful in the region than it was before.

The US decision to withhold military supplies from both Pakistan and India was based on past experience. Both countries had previously obtained US weapons to defend themselves against communist aggression. Both had used them only to fight each other. In Pakistan's case American military assistance had been expected to create a greater sense of security; instead, it had enhanced Pakistan's willingness to start military confrontation. The United States had also discovered the limits of its leverage in getting Pakistan and India to settle their issues over Kashmir.

At the time Bhutto asked for military equipment in return for bases, US policy makers prioritized avoiding conflict in the subcontinent. The United States had entered a phase of détente with the Soviet Union, and US intelligence on Soviet moves was generally good. The United States knew that Pakistanis felt threatened by India, but they did not agree that the Soviets threatened Pakistan.

The United States was also aware that Bhutto felt exposed to Pakistan's military establishment—a menace that could increase if he failed to get the generals what they wanted. But the Americans calculated that the chances of avoiding war in South Asia would increase if the United States refused to induct more arms into the region than otherwise.

The US refusal to resume military supplies was intended to force a policy reappraisal in Islamabad; instead, it invigorated Pakistan's search for economic and military assistance from other sources. The rise in oil prices immediately after the 1973 Arab-Israeli war had enriched Iran and Arab oil producers' coffers. The sheikhdoms in the Gulf region had thus emerged as fully independent countries, with cash on hand and little infrastructure. Their militaries and police forces had yet to get off the ground. On his return from the United States, Bhutto started working on schemes for Pakistan to benefit from the Middle East oil boom.

During his meeting in Washington, Bhutto had proudly told Nixon and Kissinger that he had accomplished the difficult feat of simultaneously maintaining good ties with Iran and the Arabs. Pakistan, he had said, maintained good relations with the Arab states "even with the new messiah in Libya," a reference to Muammar Qaddafi. "Pakistan has had some pilots in Libya until they were asked to take off against the Sixth Fleet and we told them nothing doing," Bhutto confided.[49] He wanted to make sure the Americans did not interpret negatively his links with anti-American Arab governments.

Then, in 1974, Pakistan hosted the second summit meeting of Muslim heads of state at Lahore. Amid much fanfare, kings and presidents of thirty-five Islamic countries and the head of the Palestine Liberation Organization (PLO) assembled to give life to the Organization of Islamic Cooperation (OIC), originally formed five years earlier. For many Pakistanis it was the realization of their long-held dream of Pan-Islamic leadership.

Bhutto used the occasion to recognize Bangladesh, as Islamic countries' support for this decision helped him overcome opposition from domestic ultranationalists. He also benefited from being at the side of every Muslim king and potentate, and he developed close ties with most of them. One of the special relationships forged as a result of the Islamic Summit was with Saudi Arabia. Within a year that country provided Pakistan with an interest-free loan of $100 million.

The Saudis made generous contributions toward charities and the building of mosques. When Pakistan faced a balance of payments crisis in 1975, Arab countries and Iran chipped in $770 million for Pakistan and pledged another $391 million in support of specific projects.[50] The Saudis also gave a grant of $30 million in addition to a soft loan of the same amount from the Saudi Development Fund.[51]

In return Pakistan flattered the Saudi royal family by naming towns, roads, schools, and mosques after them. During a six-day state visit, King Khalid of Saudi Arabia referred to Islam as the "indissoluble bond of unfailing strength and indestructible solidarity" between the two countries.[52]

Pakistan also started exporting skilled and unskilled workers to Middle Eastern countries. These workers earned wages much higher than they could in Pakistan. Their hard currency earnings, when converted into Pakistani rupees, enabled their families to live better than others could. The government then added a few sweeteners to the prospect of a tough life in the desert: overseas workers were allowed tax-free import of consumer goods that were otherwise exorbitantly taxed.

Manpower export had the potential to reduce Pakistan's dependence on foreign aid and provided Pakistan with a new source of foreign exchange. It was also a bonanza for the families of those working in the Gulf. However, it also powered consumption and some construction instead of becoming the source of investment in Pakistan's industrialization.

Further, Pakistan's bloated government and ever-expanding military needs did not allow dependence on external assistance to end. By the time Bhutto was removed from power in 1977, remittances had risen to nearly half a billion dollars. In subsequent years worker remittances continued to rise, reaching $14 billion in 2012. But even with increasing remittances, Pakistan has continued to seek aid not only from the United States and Western industrialized nations but also from the Arab countries that Bhutto had wooed.

* * * * *

The availability of petro-dollars helped Pakistan, at least in the short-term, to deal with its military supplies problem. Pakistan signed agreements with Saudi Arabia, Libya, Jordan, Iraq, Oman, United Arab Emirates, and Kuwait to open Pakistani military training institutions to their country's officers. In exchange for cash or arrangements to pay for military equipment, Pakistan also offered military advisers and trainers for several countries. As a result, within the first year there were 893 Pakistani advisers and 914 military trainers in the Middle East.[53]

The military manpower deals were sometimes transformed into barter arrangements to buy hardware Pakistan needed. Libya gave Pakistan $200 million to purchase arms in return for Pakistani pilots for the Libyan air force. Abu Dhabi funded Pakistan's purchase of thirty-two Mirage V fighter aircraft from France at a cost of $330 million and contracted Pakistani crews to fly twenty-four for its own air force.

But the potentially largest Arab-backed military purchase never came to fruition. Saudi Arabia offered to fund Pakistan's purchase of 110 American A-7 fighter bombers, which would have cost $200 million. But by that time the United States had become concerned about Pakistan's covert nuclear weapons program. The United States demanded that Pakistan withdraw its decision to purchase a $150 million nuclear waste reprocessing plant from France before it would consider selling the A-7s to Pakistan.

★

WHEN INDIA ANNOUNCED on May 18, 1974, that it had tested a "peaceful nuclear device," Americans were preoccupied with controversies related to the Watergate scandal. Although the timing of the test may have been a shock, the United States had been tracking India's nuclear program for a while. Soon after the Bangladesh war, in February 1972, the State Department's Bureau of Intelligence and Research (INR) had sought the CIA's opinion on the possibility of an Indian nuclear test.

The INR director, Ray Cline, had written in a report forwarded to CIA Director Richard Helms that "India probably has undertaken research directly related to the development of nuclear weapons, and may well have fabricated one or more nuclear devices."[54] India apparently had fifty to sixty kilograms of plutonium at the time, produced in its Canadian-Indian Reactor, US (CIRUS) facility at Trombay. This would serve as fissionable material for devices, which the Indian government wanted to test as peaceful nuclear explosives (PNEs).

The United States and Canada had assisted India in building the CIRUS reactor, and India's agreements with both countries restricted it to peaceful purposes. But the agreements did not provide for inspection or verification procedures to determine the uses for CIRUS-produced plutonium. Moreover, Cline pointed out, the language of the agreements did not specifically preclude "peaceful" nuclear explosions. India had not accepted US and Canadian interpretations of these agreements as precluding all nuclear explosions on the grounds. In the North American reading, any such explosion would be identical to a nuclear weapons test.

"Regarding the prospects of an Indian decision to proceed with a nuclear test," Cline had stated that in his judgment, "such a decision is unlikely during the next few months and may well be deferred for several years. The political and economic restraints would appear—in the near term—to outweigh the international political or military benefits which could flow from becoming the world's sixth nuclear power."[55]

His assessment was based on the fact that India still lacked a viable delivery system for nuclear weapons. A nuclear test conducted several years before having the means to deliver an atomic bomb would be of "very limited military value." Although the tests might confer a new status on India and "the immediate reaction of the Indian populace could be quite favorable," Cline observed, the long-term costs could be very high. India would have to divert resources from critical domestic programs and could lose foreign technical assistance.

The US intelligence community had precise information on India's capabilities in producing plutonium as well as about the facilities where it was produced. It also knew that several aircraft in the Indian Air Force could be adapted to deliver nuclear weapons. According to Cline, these included Canberra light jet bombers as well as Mystere IV, Hunter, SU-7 FITTER, and MIG-21 FISHBED fighters. But he anticipated that "the Indians would have some difficulty developing a nuclear weapon suitable for delivery by the fighter aircraft."

The B-57 Canberra, for example, had a four thousand–pound payload. It could carry a nuclear bomb, but it did not possess "sufficient range capabilities to constitute a strategic threat to China." India would require a longer range bomber, which it was unable to produce immediately. The United States and other producers would probably impose restrictions on exporting long-range bombers to India right after nuclear tests. The Indians would most likely try to acquire a strategic missile system. Cline's conclusion in 1972 was that although India could conduct a nuclear test, it most likely would not do so. He inferred that the prospect of international sanctions would outweigh the increased status and the political and military gains of demonstrating a nuclear weapons capability with no delivery system in sight. The only overriding factor in this evaluation could be if Chinese-Indian tensions resumed, coupled with a thaw in Sino-Soviet relations. Interestingly, there was no mention of Pakistan as even being a factor in India's pursuit of nuclear weapons capability. For example, the B-57 Canberra bombers, which Cline cited as a possible delivery vehicle, could reach Pakistan even if they could not strike China. But the Americans saw India's nuclear program only in the context of China and did not take likely Pakistani reaction into account when they initially discovered India's plans.

Two years later, when India conducted its tests, Pakistan protested the loudest. The American media also found India's explanation for the test—that it was solely for peaceful purposes—"galling." In an editorial titled, "India Joins the Club," the *Los Angeles Times* said, "The world cannot easily forget New Delhi's waspish comments on the uses and abuses of power by other nations, the sanctimonious protests of international virtue."[56]

The US embassy in Delhi attributed the timing of the test to India's need for a psychological boost. "India has exploded a nuclear device at a time when India is in deep economic difficulty," it reported. The government was contending with "a rising tide of disillusionment and discontent, corruption, mismanagement, labor indiscipline, rampant inflation." Food shortages and the impact of the high cost of crude oil had led to "dismal economic performance and severe political unrest."

Indian leaders sought to re-create the "atmosphere of exhilaration and nationalism that swept the country after 1971." They had just wrapped up an agreement with Pakistan and Bangladesh on residual issues from the Bangladesh war. A nuclear test was therefore the next step to make Indians feel that they were citizens of a stronger nation.

Any international backlash, condemnation, and retribution to the test would help Indira Gandhi's government appeal to "chauvinist feeling" at home. "The picture of a government embattled and standing up to foreign abuse could be quite useful to the Indian leadership today," US diplomats in India concluded.[57]

For Pakistanis, the Indian nuclear tests were a near catastrophe. Since independence they had sought parity with India, only to learn over the course of three wars that they could not militarily defeat their larger neighbor. After each defeat Pakistan's leaders had generated an explanation for failure, thereby keeping the rivalry alive at least at a psychological level. In the eyes of Pakistanis, theirs was a special country destined to compete with India's Hindu imperialism. Pakistan's military was even more special, being the inheritor of proud Muslim warrior traditions.

As such, Pakistan had never accepted its reverses. It had bounced back with excuses. Failure in the 1965 war was the result of the American aid cutoff. The more recent rout in East Pakistan was attributed to the treachery of the Bengalis, who had been influenced by Hindus. The whole world had lined up against Pakistan, and the Americans and the Chinese just didn't do enough to save their ally.

Finally, the Arab and other Muslim nations just did not have enough religious fervor to stand by Islamic Pakistan.

So the Indian nuclear test shocked Pakistan at many levels. It put India in a league different from Pakistan, and this contradicted everything every Pakistani leader since Jinnah had told the Pakistani people. The Americans—and almost everyone else in the world—saw India's nuclear ambitions as directed against China. For Pakistanis, however, it was aimed squarely at Pakistan. With nuclear weapons India could now try to dominate the subcontinent and undo Pakistan once and for all.

Ambassador Byroade informed the US government that the Indian nuclear test had greatly exacerbated Pakistan's "chronic feeling of insecurity." The government had initiated efforts "to seek urgent security guarantees and arms aid from major powers." For Pakistanis, India's decision, in defiance of world opinion, served as proof of "Indian intransigence and South Asian hegemonic ambitions." Islamabad wanted nonproliferation advocates to "deal firmly with India," Byroade said, so that Pakistan and other non-nuclear nations may feel more secure. In Byroade's view, Pakistan's sense of alarm and urgency was "undoubtedly genuine."

The Pakistanis were under no illusion, the US ambassador continued, that additional conventional equipment would in any way provide comparability to Indian military might. But the Indian nuclear test had further sharpened the already "painful awareness" of Pakistan's capabilities, as most of Pakistan's military hardware was "worn and obsolete in terms of what not only India but Pakistan's other neighbors possess."[58] Byroade's reference was to Iran, where the Shah was using oil money to buy sophisticated weapons on the international market. But Iran had never threatened Pakistan's security, so the US ambassador was repeating Bhutto's point that Iran's possession of better arms generated a sense of inadequacy among Pakistanis.

According to Byroade, Bhutto had rejected opposition demands that Pakistan embark on its own nuclear weapons program. He wanted Washington to know that there would now be intense pressure for "qualitative improvement in the armed forces to create credible deterrent against at least conventional Indian military threat." In other words, Pakistan would need superior conventional weapons to feel secure, and this might prevent the country from trying to build nuclear weapons of its own.

As it turned out, Bhutto had already initiated a covert nuclear weapons program. In an interview with the *Guardian* in 1965 he had said that if India built the bomb, "we will eat grass, even go hungry, but we will get one of our own. We have no other choice."[59] The Pakistan Atomic Energy Commission (PAEC) was following India's route of using plutonium produced at a Canadian-supplied nuclear reactor. Pakistan was in the process of acquiring a reprocessing plant from France that would enable it to extract fissionable material.

A Pakistani metallurgist, Dr. Abdul Qadeer Khan, who worked at a Dutch uranium enrichment plant, wrote to Bhutto right after the Indian tests. Khan said that he could help Pakistan take the shorter route to making an atom bomb—through uranium enrichment. Bhutto then set up two parallel teams to help Pakistan acquire nuclear weapons capability more quickly.

PAEC continued to seek fissile material from plutonium while Khan returned to Pakistan from the Netherlands with stolen designs for a uranium enrichment facility. But the covert nuclear program did not preclude that Pakistan would seek the resumption of military supplies from the United States. Because the US embassy in Islamabad was initially ignorant of Pakistan's nuclear plans, Byroade had become quite sympathetic to Pakistan's request for conventional weapons. He therefore advised the US government to lift the ban on military supplies to Pakistan.

Meanwhile, in the denouement of the Watergate scandal, Gerald Ford became America's president after Nixon resigned from the presidency on August 9, 1974. Ford retained Kissinger as secretary of state. Unlike Nixon, Ford did not have strong views on Pakistan or South Asia, so US policy on Pakistan moved completely into the hands of the State Department. Thus, Kissinger's and diplomats' opinions carried even more weight than they did before. Kissinger found the embassy in New Delhi seeking greater attention for India, following their nuclear test, just as Byroade had recommended that the United States open military supplies to Pakistan in order to provide Pakistan reassurance.

Rumors that the United States might expand relations with India in order to contain nuclear proliferation caused disquiet in Islamabad. Ahmed, who now carried the title of minister of state for foreign affairs, asked Kissinger during a meeting in Washington whether there had been a "dramatic improvement in relations between the United States and India." Kissinger assured him that any improvement in ties with India would not be at Pakistan's expense. The United States simply wanted to wean India away from the Soviets, he said.

Kissinger explained that some of the "Embassy people" in Delhi felt the United States had to prove itself to the Indians. "It is an American masochistic sense of guilt that we must perform a national duty by giving aid to India," he retorted. "We have no illusions about Indian policy," he went on, "but their and our purposes may be served by the illusion of better relations. There are also domestic advantages in this. Internationally there is no significance, no real change." Ahmed replied that the better way of proving to the Indians "the futility of arming themselves" would be to supply "sophisticated arms" to Pakistan.

The secretary of state brought up the subject of India's nuclear ambitions. "I am less outraged by the Indian bomb than some," he said. "I see it as a trap for India. They will never be able to use it in practice. And if the bomb spreads, it will equalize India's military superiority." Ahmed did not agree, arguing instead that "If the Indian army were in difficulty they would use the nuclear bomb in desperation as a last resort."

Kissinger said that India would have to lose a war "very badly" before using a nuclear weapon. "Will you beat them?" he added sarcastically. The Pakistani diplomat instinctively said, "We can if we have arms," before checking himself—"But we're not planning to do that." He insisted that Pakistan just wanted enough weapons to defend itself against India and Afghanistan, who were being supported by the Soviet Union. But for the last three years the United States had not supported Pakistan militarily. Kissinger promised that he would push for cash sales first, but the matter would have to be handled delicately.

Ahmed moaned once again about the difficulty of buying arms on the open market. Pakistan preferred its old relationship with the United States when planes and tanks as well as money to raise army divisions were provided through the budget of the US Department of Defense. "The French are slick businessmen," he added. Pakistan had bought three Breguet-Atlantique Long-Range surveillance aircraft from the French. "The French gave us half-price on the aircraft—38 million francs—but with the service and modifications the total price was 220 million francs."

"They are not only fleecing us, but also skinning us," Ahmed said of the French. "The Croatale missiles increased from 200 to 350 million francs by the time we reached agreement. They know we have nowhere else to go and they exploit us." Further, although the Iranians had helped convert Pakistan's US-supplied tanks to be powered by diesel fuel, they were reluctant to cross-train Pakistani crews on their equipment.

When Kissinger offered to raise the matter with the Iranian Shah, Ahmed said that he didn't want the Shah to know he had complained. "He has been very good to us," Ahmed said about the Shah. But he did seek US help in nudging Saudi Arabia and Iran to increase balance-of-payments support. They were already providing $200 million between them, but Pakistan needed more. There were also the by-now routine requests for wheat and edible oil.[60] If Kissinger found it comical that Pakistani officials privately asked for so much support but publicly insisted on decrying their benefactor, he kept that to himself.

When Kissinger visited Islamabad a month later Bhutto voiced Pakistan's concern about the United States growing close to India once again. Kissinger, who had just been to India, jokingly remarked, "After seeing India, I am thinking about supplying nuclear weapons, not only conventional arms, to Pakistan and even Bangladesh!" He tried to reassure Bhutto by telling him that he had told the Indians that the United States was committed to Pakistan's independence and integrity.

......

Kissinger told Bhutto that he had pointed out to the Indians Pakistan's apprehensions about Afghanistan and Balochistan. The Indians "swore they were exercising a moderating influence," he reported. The Indian assertion had been so strong that Kissinger felt he would be in a good position to go back to them. "If you can get evidence that I can produce," he said in relation to Pakistani charges that India supported secession in Balochistan, "I would make a case with them." If Bhutto had any evidence, he did not offer it.

The Pakistani prime minister then explained his motivation for continuously seeking sophisticated weapons. "We would like to be able to strip our army of its power and put it in its place," he averred. "But we must protect our borders. If we are stronger, it will enable us to do more in negotiating." In Bhutto's opinion the Indians were "so stupid and arrogant, they cannot negotiate. They are getting so uppity." He alleged that India had a history of "trying to thrust out" a new formulation for the old view that India sought hegemony over its neighbors. Bhutto then told Kissinger: "If Pakistan's existence is not important to the United States then say so." He said that because of Pakistan's ties with Iran, China, and the Gulf, "we can be useful to you."[61]

During this meeting Bhutto had expressed optimism about resolving Pakistan's concerns about Afghanistan. He asked Kissinger to tell the Afghans that Pakistan was ready to negotiate but "not barter away" its territory—a reference to the notion of Pashtunistan. From Bhutto's perspective, this was an important meeting, as Kissinger had agreed with his critique of India. The secretary of state might have been simply making conversation, but it nonetheless emboldened Pakistani officials. They believed they had made some headway in convincing the United States that India was a security threat by virtue of its "hegemonic" core.

On February 4, 1975, Bhutto arrived in Washington for his second official visit. By now Kissinger was able to commit that the United States would rescind the ban on transferring military equipment to Pakistan. This would open the way for Pakistan to buy weapons for cash, as the secretary of state had suggested earlier. Kissinger told Bhutto to stay quiet on the matter, however, until he had informed

• • • • •

the Indians and Congress about the decision. He asked for only one assurance in return: Pakistan had to declare that "there will be no nuclear development outside of safeguards."

This was because the US Congress was voicing concern about nuclear proliferation. Pakistan, like India, had not signed the Nuclear Non-Proliferation Treaty (NPT). Because of this, the House Foreign Affairs Committee had questioned Kissinger in closed session about the wisdom of reopening the sale of advanced weaponry to Pakistan. The committee's chairman, Lee Hamilton, a Democrat from Indiana, had requested that lifting the ban on arms supply to Pakistan should be linked to guarantees in the nuclear field. Pakistan must observe safeguards that would allow it to use nuclear technology for peaceful purposes, such as power generation, but not to develop an atomic bomb.

Pakistan, Bhutto recalled, objected to the nonproliferation treaty "on a moral basis." India refused to sign the treaty because, it said, the agreement was discriminatory because it allowed five countries to retain nuclear weapons but denied the right to others, thus creating what Indian diplomats described as "nuclear apartheid." But Pakistan did not have a similar universal objection. "India has not signed," Bhutto said. "Of course we will sign if India signs." Kissinger reiterated that Pakistan's nuclear program should remain "under safeguards you couldn't divert your efforts to a nuclear explosion."[62]

A few days after meeting Bhutto Ford lifted "the embargo on U.S. sales of lethal military equipment to Pakistan and India." He laid out guidelines that would ensure that the "sale of defense articles and services" would "meet the legitimate security needs for modern and effective forces in Pakistan and India." The most important of these was that all military sales to the subcontinent were to be on cash basis. The presidential statement on the occasion also said that the United States did not want to "stimulate an arms race in that region or restore the pre-1965 situation in which the US was a major regional arms supplier."[63] Pakistan immediately rushed to line up funding from its Arab friends for its purchases.

The prospect of resuming military supplies from the United States heartened Pakistanis. Bhutto wrote a letter to Ford, thanking him for the decision. Among other things, the letter made reference to a conversation between Ahmed and Kissinger, stating, "Dr. Kissinger informed Mr. Ahmed that he had spoken to Gromyko in very strong terms to the effect that an Indian attack on Pakistan with Soviet equipment would invite a response from the United States." This attracted Kissinger's attention. He asked Byroade to clarify "some important nuances which if not precisely grasped, could lead to misunderstandings."

According to the American account, Kissinger had only informed the Pakistani diplomat of a conversation with the Soviets in general terms, during which the United States told Soviets that they would hold the USSR responsible for "the use made of their equipment anywhere, and especially in Pakistan." Similarly Kissinger had asked Ahmed if it would be acceptable for the United States to ask the Chinese what their response might be if Pakistan was attacked. He had also remarked that a general war involving the Soviets and the Chinese would have "the gravest implications for the whole of Asia and for U.S. policy in the area."

But the Pakistanis had interpreted Kissinger's conversation with Ahmed as an assurance of US involvement on Pakistan's behalf.[64] Kissinger, however, did not want Pakistan to misconstrue his queries as commitments. Obviously his banter, aimed at making the Pakistani leaders feel at ease, had once again led to exaggerated expectations in Islamabad.

Even this incident involving potential misunderstandings did not inhibit Kissinger's sense of humor during his subsequent meeting with Ahmed. The Pakistani official arrived with two lists of weapons that Pakistan sought. Kissinger joked, "I hope the nuclear weapons are on the second list." A chastened Ahmed laughed along. "The 1960 models are in surplus now so we should be able to give you some," Kissinger shot back. Then he added seriously: "I had better watch what I say since there is no telling what you might report back to Bhutto."

Kissinger asked Ahmed if Pakistan had the money to buy the equipment it was seeking. Ahmed said, "We will find it from Saudi Arabia." But he first wanted to know what was available and at what price. Pakistan wanted the A-7 aircraft and other weapons in a hurry, he said. "India might well attack us the 2nd or 3rd week of November in Kashmir." By now Kissinger had become accustomed to Ahmed's warnings of an impending Indian attack. He said, half in jest, "If you narrow the gap with India to 1 to 10 you will be in good shape." He then added, "Seriously, we want you strong enough so that India will be afraid to attack."

According to Ahmed, the Afghans would join an Indian war effort if Pakistan seemed to be in trouble, but Pakistan had failed to secure Chinese assurances of support. "That is why we need weapons off the shelf," he said. After a wide-ranging conversation on US-China relations and how the Soviets were menacing Pakistan, Ahmed ended on the same note on which he almost always ended: he asked for one million tons of American wheat under PL-480, the Food for Peace program.[65]

The perennial shortage of wheat did not distract Pakistan from its nuclear ambitions, however. Pakistan persisted with the $150 million deal for the plutonium reprocessing plant from France. Thus, the two countries submitted a safeguards agreement to the International Atomic Energy Agency (IAEA), and its approval would clear the way for the sale. But the United States had obtained intelligence that raised alarm bells about Pakistan's intentions.

Initially the United States had wondered whether Pakistan would be able to pursue a nuclear weapons program given its economic limitations, and Kissinger had hoped to dissuade Bhutto from seeking an atomic bomb by offering advanced conventional weapons. But now it was apparent that Pakistan was putting together elements of a weapons program. The country had only one nuclear reactor, it had made no plans for expanding nuclear power generation, and the reprocessing plant purchase pointed toward a scheme to produce fissile material.

Nonproliferation advocates demanded that the Ford administration put pressure on Pakistan and France to cancel their reprocessing plant deal. "A nuclear arms race on the subcontinent is not in the interest of Pakistan or of the world," said a *New York Times* editorial. "Suspension of the Pakistan deal would improve chances to discourage India from going any further with the nuclear weapons development which New Delhi insists it still does not plan," it argued.[66]

Ford decided to write directly to Bhutto. His letter began by welcoming the "forthright assurances that Pakistan will not divert its civil nuclear development efforts into an explosives program." He listed uranium enrichment, heavy water production, and chemical reprocessing as potential routes to nuclear proliferation. South Korea had recently agreed to forego acquiring a national reprocessing plant. Ford asked that Pakistan do the same.[67]

Ford's request was the administration's first attempt to convey to Pakistan the difficulty it faced at home over the proliferation question. Congress had passed the Symington Amendment to the 1961 Foreign Assistance Act that governed foreign aid. Named after Senator Stuart Symington, a Missouri Democrat, the amendment barred all US economic and military assistance to countries that acquired or transferred nuclear technology without full safeguards and international inspections.

Kissinger tried to persuade Bhutto with a simple explanation of political realities. He told the Pakistani ambassador, Sahibzada Yaqub Khan, that the reprocessing plant had become a domestic issue in US politics. "You know what the American domestic situation is," he said. Kissinger then explained the US political scene. "You know that if the Democrats win, they would like nothing better than to make a horrible example of somebody," he observed—a statement, which taken out of context, later fed Pakistani hatred toward the United States.

Kissinger was summing up the Democrats' political options in order to point out why they might target Pakistan over nonproliferation. "They would love to take on the French, but they can't," he said. "They cannot be accused of being anti-European integration and anti-NATO, let alone anti-Atlantic. If the Democrats win, you will face an assault and they will attack you." In a sympathetic tone Kissinger told Yaqub that credit and arms sales would become "much more difficult, even impossible" if the Democrats won the US election. "You know that the last thing I want to do is to be responsible for this."[68]

But, as Kissinger feared, the Democrats won the election. The new president, Jimmy Carter, did not have any affection for Pakistan nor did the leading members of the incoming National Security team. As he left office, Kissinger remembered to put Pakistan's request for military aid on the list of issues he considered a priority for his successor as secretary of state, Cyrus Vance. He requested that Vance help get congressional approval for the sale of A-7 planes for Pakistan. Kissinger also hoped that a solution would be found for the "nuclear matters."[69]

★

WHILE BHUTTO NEGOTIATED with the United States for military aid and over the nuclear reprocessing plant, he also made two critical decisions with grave implications for his political survival. He appointed General Muhammad Zia-ul-Haq, a lackluster officer, as the army chief in March 1976. He also scheduled parliamentary elections for March 1977. In both decisions the head of Inter-Services Intelligence (ISI), Lieutenant General Ghulam Jilani Khan, advised Bhutto closely.[70]

Zia was personally religious and was closely connected to several Islamists by virtue of his social and family origins. Jilani advised Bhutto that a mild-mannered, religiously inclined army chief could not be a threat to civilian authority. This was critical because, based on Pakistan's history, Bhutto had good reason to worry about military coups. He had once told Kissinger that he retained the defense minister's portfolio because "one has to maintain tight control in order to avoid a coup."[71]

A later US Defense Intelligence Agency (DIA) rundown of Zia said, "Bhutto reportedly appointed Zia to the top Army post over the heads of generals with more seniority, because of his reputation as a professional 'soldier of Islam' with only mediocre ability and little political ambition." According to the DIA, Bhutto thought Zia would "place no obstacles in the way of Bhutto's popular rule."

The profile further stated, "Zia has been described as 'dumb like a fox' and it has been suggested that 'he may have deliberately cultivated his image as inexperienced and indecisive in order to lull potential opponents into underestimating him'."[72] Zia's cunning, ambition, and ruthlessness later proved to be a death sentence for Bhutto.

Soon after Bhutto scheduled elections his opponents united under the banner of the Pakistan National Alliance (PNA). This energized the disparate opposition, which put up a good show, with massive anti-Bhutto rallies in large cities. The ISI had told Bhutto that he would win 70 to 80 percent support in the country's key regions.[73] Once the campaign began, however, the race seemed tighter.

Bhutto had ruled with a firm hand, and the election unleashed sentiment against his authoritarianism, middle-class anger over his nationalization, and the deeper ideological opposition to his secular tendencies. Although the PNA ran an animated campaign, when the votes were counted Bhutto's PPP won overwhelmingly. The PNA then accused Bhutto of massive voter fraud.

The PPP had won 155 seats in the lower house of Parliament, the National Assembly, with 58.1 percent of the total votes cast. The PNA secured only 36 seats, with 35.4 percent of the votes. The opposition had won in the Pashtun province and in all the major cities where they held large rallies, with the exception of Lahore. The PNA's poor showing in the Punjab province, only 8 seats out of 116, created the impression in the minds of almost everyone, including Bhutto himself, that the election results may have been altered.

Bhutto offered the PNA a compromise. He proposed reelection on the thirty-five to forty seats that observers said had been stolen. But the PNA was by now in the hands of virulently anti-Bhutto Islamists. They rejected any compromise and started violent street protests. The protests continued for several months, paralyzing the major cities and leading to curfews and martial law in some places.

While Pakistan convulsed domestically, the Carter administration considered ways of dissuading Pakistan from going nuclear. Deputy Secretary of State Warren Christopher drew up a list of "significant benefits" that might induce Bhutto to change his mind. "Bhutto's overriding consideration," Christopher stated, "remains his determination to stay in power." In Christopher's final analysis, Bhutto's decision on how to deal with the nuclear processing question would be determined by his judgment of the effect it would have on his domestic position.

Christopher's list of incentives included cash sales of F-5E and A-7 aircraft as well as air defense radar, general utility helicopters, and C-130 transport planes. He also proposed $100–135 million in economic assistance over two to three fiscal years as well as "generous" food aid under PL 480. But Carter wrote, "No" in his own handwriting on virtually all the items on Christopher's list. He also scribbled, "Don't favor Pakistan buying nuclear processing plant from France."[74]

Meanwhile, the PNA's demonstrations became more violent when its leaders switched from calling for new elections to demanding an Islamic government. Barred from rallying in open spaces, protestors now gathered in mosques and offered themselves for arrest or death in the name of Islam.

Bhutto tried to stem the religious tide by introducing prohibition and shutting down nightclubs. The weekly holiday was moved from Sunday to Friday. But the religious fervor of fanatical protestors did not subside. Clashes between police and protesters continued, and in some towns the army was called in to shoot demonstrators.

During the US presidential election campaign Carter had spoken of human rights as an important concern for US foreign policy. With this in mind, his administration felt compelled to deal with reports of the street violence in Pakistan. The State Department blocked a $68,000 shipment of tear gas, enraging Bhutto and boosting the opposition supporters.

Since the days of Iskander Mirza and Ayub Khan, Pakistanis had an overstated sense of US involvement in their domestic affairs. Meetings between diplomats and local politicians, deemed routine in most countries, were seen as signals of what the superpower might want locally. The Americans, for their part, had not understood Pakistani national narcissism. The State Department's decision regarding tear gas might have been part of the global policy on human rights, but in Pakistan it was seen as specifically targeting the country's embattled leader.

Bhutto's supporters soon began spreading allegations that the United States, particularly the CIA, had funded the opposition. Payments of as much as $25 million were mentioned. In a speech to Parliament, Bhutto mocked the Carter administration's concern with human rights, stating that if his party had been given $25 million, "I could afford to be worried about human rights, too."

In some demonstrations members of Bhutto's Pakistan People's Party (PPP) marched as they shouted, "Down with Jimmy Carter." A senior government figure was quoted in the *Washington Post* as saying, "With the advent of a new right wing government replacing Mrs. Gandhi in India, it is entirely possible that the US is making some sort of deals in New Delhi at our expense."[75]

Interestingly, a similar suspension of military contracts did not accompany the ban on tear gas. Shipments of wire-guided TOW anti-tank missiles, bombs, machine gun ammunition, communications equipment, vehicles, and two World War II vintage naval destroyers were under way. This materiel, worth $150 million, was delivered on schedule.

Finally, Bhutto himself went public with allegations that the violent PNA protests against him were part of a "vast, colossal, huge international conspiracy" financed by the United States. The reason for the alleged conspiracy, Bhutto told a joint session of Pakistan's Parliament, was that the United States could not forgive him for failing to support the US role in Vietnam and for supporting the Arab cause against Israel.

The *Post* reported on the "rambling, one hour and 45 minute speech delivered without notes" as "marked by outbursts of fist-shaking rage against the United States"—which he termed "an elephant which does not forget or forgive." Bhutto claimed that a US diplomat in a telephone conversation with one of his colleagues on April 12 allegedly said of Bhutto: "The party's over, the party's over. He's gone," evidently meaning that the opposition would succeed in ousting the premier. "Well gentlemen," the premier said, to cheers, "the party is not over."[76]

Bhutto did not explain how he knew of the telephone conversation. Pakistani intelligence, which often conducts wiretapping widely in the country, most likely provided him the nugget. One of the diplomats in the conversation, Howard Schaffer, told me years later that he was talking about an actual dinner party in Karachi that Bhutto attended. He had asked his colleague in Karachi if the party was over, and his colleague replied, "The party is over. He's gone."

The prime minister's intelligence service could have misled him, or he could also have been playing to Pakistanis' emotions. "People like to believe in conspiracy theories on the subcontinent," the *New York Times* quoted a Pakistani political observer soon after Bhutto's allegations.[77] In some ways Bhutto was simply maneuvering for political space by externalizing a domestic problem. The US embassy in Islamabad referred to this as "the reemergence of the anti-American theme in Pakistan."[78]

By now the polarization within Pakistan had reached its peak. The Islamist parties had whipped up hysteria about Bhutto being a bad Muslim and the need to Islamize Pakistan's laws. American missionary Clifford Manshardt, who had experience in South Asia, tried to explain what was going on to Americans. He recognized Bhutto's mistakes and excesses, but "What puts Bhutto in such jeopardy," he wrote, "is the determination by orthodox religious leaders to frame their opposition as a Holy war."[79]

As summer approached, Pakistan's political standoff continued. Saudi Arabia persuaded Bhutto and PNA leaders to negotiate over new elections. Then, just as the negotiations were on the verge of concluding successfully, Zia imposed martial law. Most American observers blamed "the quarrelsome blundering of the politicians" rather than generals' ambition for the return to military rule.

The military was said to have taken over "after six years of initially promising but eventually inept and unstable democratic government." The *Los Angeles Times* described Bhutto as "a talented but volatile politician" who had invited his own downfall by coming to rely increasingly on the military.[80] Initially Zia detained all politicians including Bhutto, announced that fresh elections would be held within ninety days, and promised that the army would return to the barracks after holding elections. But he soon reneged on his promise.

......

Zia ruled Pakistan for eleven years, longer than any other military dictator and with far greater brutality. He executed the still-popular Bhutto after a show trial, ostensibly on charges of plotting the murder of a political opponent. Bhutto refused to seek clemency from Zia, and his death by execution made him a folk hero as well as a symbol of civilian resistance to military dictatorship; his political weaknesses and flaws were forgotten by even his opponents, with the exception of hardcore Islamists, who continued to hate him in death as they did when he was alive. Zia went on to change many aspects of life in Pakistan as part of "Islamization" of the country. The country's educational system was revamped to ensure that future generations of Pakistanis would be more Islamic and xenophobic than were previous ones. From an early age anti-Semitism as well as fear and hatred of India were instilled in Pakistan's fast-growing populace.

Pakistan had received almost $1 billion in US economic assistance from 1972 to 1977, the years that Bhutto governed the country. But military aid during this period stood at a meager $1.87 million, most of it in the form of training for officers and spare parts for US-made equipment. Bhutto was, however, able to secure considerable military assistance from China and was also able to purchase weapons from European countries.

But Pakistan's generals attributed Bhutto's failure in reopening the American pipeline to his socialist leanings and past anti-American rhetoric. Although he remained suspicious of India and saw it as an existential threat to Pakistan, Bhutto did not initiate any adventures against India either. Zia attempted to rectify those "mistakes."

Chapter Five

A Most Superb and Patriotic Liar

On July 4, 1982, Pakistan's military dictator, General Muhammad Zia-ul-Haq, served coffee to General Vernon Walters at Army House, the British-era bungalow in Rawalpindi that served as the official residence of Pakistan's army chief. Although Zia had declared himself president of Pakistan, he had chosen not to move to the official Presidential Palace. The modest military bungalow went well with Zia's cultivated image of humility, as it also signaled that the real source of his power was not the office of president but rather his status as army commander.

Walters had come as a special envoy representing US President Ronald Reagan. He had served as deputy director of the CIA, spoke at least seven languages, and was widely respected in the United States as an intermediary with foreigners. Walters had served as interpreter for Eisenhower and Nixon in their foreign visits, but he was sent to Zia on what was the American Independence Day holiday to deliver a tough message. For this, he needed diplomatic, not linguistic, skills.

US intelligence had obtained evidence that Pakistan was clandestinely purchasing sensitive technology to develop nuclear weapons. There were indications that the Chinese had provided Pakistan assistance in the form of designs of key components for an atom bomb.

......

At this time the Reagan administration was providing large amounts of economic and military aid to Pakistan. This aid was conditional on Pakistan foregoing the nuclear option. Walters had brought a letter from Reagan that shared US information about Pakistan's violation of its explicit stipulation. He was also given the task of asking Zia to stop the nuclear program or risk facing an aid cutoff.

During their meeting on July 4 Walters presented to Zia the US government's conclusions based on what he described as "incontrovertible intelligence." Pakistani representatives had "transferred designs and specifications for nuclear weapons components to purchasing agents in several countries." These agents were arranging the fabrication of nuclear weapons components. "I described to Zia our information, the problem it created for both our countries and what was needed if we were to salvage our relationship," Walters reported to Washington after the meeting. The special envoy had emphasized that debating the evidence he had come to discuss would not be useful. Nonetheless, Zia denied any knowledge of Pakistani efforts to acquire components for a nuclear explosive device.

When Walters had finished, Zia said with a straight face that Pakistan did not have a nuclear weapons development program. "He did not doubt that President Reagan had evidence he considered incontrovertible," Walters wrote in the cable about their meeting. Zia insisted that he would not develop a nuclear weapon and would not explore a nuclear device.

Zia then said that he could not believe that designs for a nuclear device could have been submitted to foreign purchasing or manufacturing agents without his knowing, and he had "no knowledge of any such weapons development programs." He added dramatically: "Pakistan might not be a large or important country but it was an honorable one." He could give his word of honor as a soldier that Pakistan would not develop, much less explode, a nuclear weapon or explosive device.

While recording Zia's response, Walter added his own comment: "Either he really does not know," the American general said, "or he is the most superb and patriotic liar I have ever met."

......

Walters and Zia met again the next day, which, coincidentally, was the fifth anniversary of Zia's military coup. This time the Pakistani ruler spoke earnestly about President Reagan. "The president must be right," he said, adding, "Your information must be right. I accept its authenticity." But he wanted to see the details of the evidence, knowing well that in the field of intelligence, details can give away sources and methods through which a conclusion was reached.

"It is not Pakistan's fault," Zia pleaded. "It is a plot. I'd like you to be cautious." Walters replied that the United States had reviewed its information very clearly and given it a second look. "We are confident of it," he said. He would not put the flat denial in writing and in a formal response to Reagan's letter, but Zia argued that the US information was a "total fabrication." Walters interpreted this as a matter of keeping face. In his opinion Zia was saying that "it did not happen but you can be sure it won't happen again."

Walters, who had been inducted in the US Military Intelligence Hall of Fame, proceeded to make a famously erroneous conclusion. "I believe that he now knows that we have the ability to watch Pakistani activities in this field that he had not suspected previously," he said. This would "certainly have an inhibiting effect on what they do." He recommended that the United States "must continue to watch their activities closely and give careful consideration to the awkward and difficult problems of perhaps making available to President Zia some sanitized parts of our evidence."[1]

In October Walters returned to meet Zia because US intelligence continued to detect Pakistani efforts to procure sensitive technology and materials. He had to warn Zia that US aid was in "grave jeopardy." Pakistan was about to receive the first batch of F-16 aircraft that it had wanted for a long time, but revelations about the nuclear program could put that transfer on hold. Walter showed drawings of Chinese-influenced nuclear weapons designs that US intelligence had obtained.

Zia went on the offensive. He insisted he was an "honorable man"—a phrase he used several times—and asked to be treated as such. He had conveyed his firm assurances on the subject to the US president in writing, and he stood by them. What else did the United

......

States expect him to do? Bhutto had once confronted Kissinger with the statement: "If Pakistan's existence is not important to the US, then say so." Zia was now using a similar tack; he complained about signs that the United States was pulling away from Pakistan.

The Pakistani dictator noted that there was a press campaign "questioning Pakistan's nuclear intentions," rumors about Indian and Israeli collusion against Pakistan's nuclear facilities, and "nonsensical speculations about 'Islamic bombs'." He brought up the name of *New York Times* reporter Judith Miller, who had written some of the stories about Pakistan's nuclear program. He implied that America's Jewish lobby was trying to punish Pakistan, "perhaps because of Pakistan's support for its Islamic partners on the Arab-Israeli issue." Zia demanded to see the US intelligence information to decide if it was authentic or just an extension of the hostile propaganda by Israel's and India's supporters.

Zia ended his conversation with the words: "General Walters! I am an honorable man. We are an honorable people. I ask you to tell your President that I give him my word of honor as President of Pakistan and as a soldier that I am not and will not develop a nuclear device or weapon." Walters said there was no way he could reject this assurance. He remarked, "I hope no further blips would show on our radars"[2] The retired American three-star general could not imagine that the serving four-star Pakistani would lie to him, especially after invoking his honor with his hand on his heart.

The blips on the radar that Walters had spoken of continued to show up. Because the United States refused to share the evidence, the Pakistanis could not figure out how the Americans kept on finding out what they were doing. Zia was due to visit Washington on a state visit that December, so Secretary of State George Shultz decided to brief Reagan about the possibility that he may have to address the matter directly when the two presidents met at the White House.

"Pakistan is in the advanced stage of a nuclear weapons program," Shultz's briefing paper highlighted. The United States had tried to block Pakistan's nuclear program by building a new security relationship, including a significant aid package, hoping this would reduce the "underlying incentive for acquisition of nuclear weapons." But Pakistan's nuclear program was motivated in large part by fear of India, and the United States was unwilling to provide a security guarantee against India.

Shultz told Reagan that there was "overwhelming evidence that Zia has been breaking his assurances to us. We are absolutely confident that our intelligence is genuine and accurate." He also shared the intelligence community's belief that, if forced to choose between US aid and a nuclear weapons capability, Zia would opt for the latter. "Zia could well believe that we will never pose that choice for him," Shultz observed.[3]

When they met on December 7, 1982, Reagan mentioned the nuclear question to Zia but did not give it a higher priority than Pakistan's role as a frontline state in confronting the Soviet Union. After meeting Zia, Reagan wrote in his diary for that Tuesday: "The weather turned out fine for the official greeting ceremony for Pres. Zia of Pakistan. We got along fine. He's a good man (cavalry). Gave me his word they were not building an atomic or nuclear bomb. He's dedicated to helping the Afghans & stopping the Soviets."[4]

★

PAKISTAN'S NUCLEAR AMBITIONS were already an issue in relations with the United States when Zia toppled Bhutto in July 1977. The deal to buy 110 A-7 fighter bombers was its first casualty. After the Ford administration allowed cash sales of US weapons, the Pakistanis scrambled to get funding from the Saudis for the A-7s. But within a few months of coming to office—and at the height of anti-Bhutto protests—the Carter administration suspended the deal. The decision was linked to Pakistan's contract for the purchase of a nuclear reprocessing plant from France.[5]

Carter was also uncomfortable with Zia's status as a military ruler. To establish a firm grip on power, Zia had introduced public lashings, calling them an Islamic practice. Dissident journalists were among those lashed in public stadiums, and the lashings were shown on television. As Bhutto's trial dragged on, Zia arrested thousands of his supporters in order to prevent a backlash to the former prime minister's eventual execution. Carter, with his concern for human rights, could not ignore Zia's conduct at home. When he visited India in January 1978 he refused to add even a stopover in Pakistan.

Just two days before Zia's coup Arthur Hummel had presented his credentials as the new US ambassador to Pakistan. Hummel was a career diplomat who knew Chinese, having been born to missionary parents in China. His posting in Pakistan was probably linked to the country's role in the evolving US-Chinese entente. He had served as ambassador to Burma, but this was hardly enough to prepare him for the issues he faced in Pakistan. After four years in Islamabad Hummel then served as ambassador in Beijing.

Hummel's arrival in Pakistan had coincided with Bhutto's removal from power and Zia's military takeover. For Pakistani conspiracy theorists, the new ambassador was the hatchet man sent to enforce Washington's writ on an out-of-control ally. But the Carter administration had set a different mission for Hummel: he was to ensure that Pakistan did not go forward with obtaining the nuclear reprocessing plant. The French had informed the Americans that if they backed out of the deal, Pakistan would simply go ahead with building a plant on its own, or Pakistan could also look for some other collaborator. So Hummel spent the entire first year as ambassador building ties with Zia and his close advisers.

Almost nine months later he told the secretary of state about his efforts to dissuade Pakistan from pursuing nuclear weapons. "We are not simply trying to make nuclear weapons production more difficult for Pakistan," he wrote. "We are attempting to deny them the option." He said he wanted to forestall the Zia regime from announcing that it would "go it alone" because that would tie everyone's hands. Hummel also wanted to avoid "promising, even implicitly, more than we know we can deliver" and did not want assistance and aid to be treated as more valuable bargaining chips than they really were.[6] It was a tall order, but Hummel felt he had an obligation to give it a try.

Hummel soon found out that getting a public commitment from Pakistan that it would abandon nuclear ambitions was not easy. Pakistan's establishment had embraced the belief that nuclear weapons were "the only guarantee of Pakistan's national survival in the face of both an inveterately hostile India that cannot be deterred conventionally and unreliable external allies that fail to deliver in extremis."[7] Any public avowal by a Pakistani administration that it would forego the nuclear option would invite charges that it was selling out national interest.

Agha Shahi, the new foreign minister, explained the situation to Hummel, stating, "No government of Pakistan could give even private assurance not to engage in reprocessing and still survive in face of public opinion."[8] Bhutto had claimed that the CIA destabilized his government for trying to secure Pakistan's nuclear future. Thus, giving up reprocessing so soon after the coup would paint the new government as an American lackey. Shahi characterized American requests for private assurance as "impinging on the sovereignty of Pakistan."

While Zia and his officials avoided making commitments on the subject, they engaged with Hummel in a manner that raised his hopes. Because of this, he advised Washington to keep the discussion of the nuclear question quiet. But Zia broke the silence himself. In an interview he told a Saudi newspaper that no Muslim country had nuclear arms. "If Pakistan possesses such a weapon it would reinforce the power of the Muslim world," Zia was quoted as saying.

Hummel had been convinced that Zia wanted good relations with the United States and was willing to settle disagreements outside of the public view. As such, he conveyed to the State Department that he saw Zia's interview as a "gaffe" and requested that the US government not "publicize Zia's gaffe at this point. To do so could measurably complicate Zia's already difficult domestic position."[9]

Contrary to the ambassador's assertion, however, Zia's statement was not a gaffe. Soon Zia made a similar statement in an interview with Bernard Nossiter of the *Washington Post*. "The West has got it," Zia said about nuclear technology. "In the East, Russians have got it. The Chinese have got it. The Indians have got it. The Jews have got it. Then, why should Pakistan, which is considered part of the

· · · · ·

Muslim world, be deprived of this technology particularly when we are a developing country and are very short of energy resources."[10] Although he avoided using the term "weapons," it was clear what he meant.

Hummel also bought into Zia's version of events when media reports suggested that Pakistan was supporting opposition groups from Afghanistan. After the BBC reported that an eight-party joint front had been created in Pakistan's northwest city of Peshawar in order to oppose the leftist government that had taken power in Afghanistan, Hummel told Washington that he did not see the Pakistan government's hand in "sponsoring such a group at this time or even permitting it to operate on Pakistan soil."[11]

The US ambassador saw Pakistan's policy toward the Afghan regime as similar to America's—"one of watchful waiting." In his view "Pakistan would have nothing to gain from such a provocation." But later events would prove that the BBC report was accurate. Pakistan had indeed been supporting the Afghan opposition, in effect provoking the Soviet Union. Once the Soviets got directly involved, the United States would have no choice but to synchronize Afghan policy with Pakistan. By buying into Zia's story, Hummel and his team failed to anticipate the emerging sequence of events in Afghanistan.

By the end of August 1978 US pressure had resulted in France halting the Pakistani reprocessing plant project. Once Zia announced that France had backed out of the agreement, the United States announced that it would resume aid. The administration had already asked Congress to approve $69 million in development aid to Pakistan for the 1979 fiscal year in addition to $53.4 million in food aid.[12]

Around this same time Zia accelerated Pakistan's role in Afghanistan. The Afghan president, Mohammad Daoud, had been an ardent supporter of the demand for Pashtunistan. Although India publicly did not support the Afghan claim, Pakistan had always voiced fear of an Afghan-Indian "pincer movement" intended to undo Pakistan.[13] Pashtun nationalist leaders were periodically cast as traitors, most recently after Bhutto dismissed the elected government of Balochistan.

......

Daoud's overthrow of the king had come within months of Bhutto's action to consolidate central Pakistani rule over the "Pashtunistan" territories.

Although Daoud was a member of the erstwhile royal family and had conservative instincts, he had ended up in alliance with the relatively small Afghan communist party, the Peoples Democratic Party of Afghanistan (PDPA). Pakistan's alliance with the United States had resulted in only limited American aid making its way to Afghanistan. As prime minister under the king from 1953 to 1964, Daoud had sought more resources to modernize Afghanistan and develop its infrastructure. When the United States held back, he turned to the Soviet Union. By the time Daoud seized complete power, Soviet aid amounted to more than three times that of the United States. By 1978 several thousand Soviet engineers, machinery operators, and other technical specialists worked at different levels in Afghanistan, along with some military advisers.[14]

But the search for economic benefits was only one factor in Daoud's foreign policy. He also hoped to become actively engaged on behalf of Pakistan's Baloch and Pashtun in an effort to force Pakistan's hand in reopening discussion about the Durand Line, the British-drawn border between Pakistan and Afghanistan. Bhutto had wanted to settle the matter. Talks were initiated with Daoud through the Shah of Iran, but Bhutto's removal from power brought that process to an end.

Pakistan's concerns about India had always overshadowed its worries over Afghanistan. But ensuring loyalty of its Baloch and Pashtun citizens and fending off any questions about the Durand Line had also been important. After discovering arms in the Iraqi embassy, Bhutto had started a small war in Balochistan that lasted four years and was aimed at rooting out Baloch secessionism. That counterinsurgency operation along the Afghan border had resulted in the death of thirty-three hundred Pakistan soldiers and fifty-three hundred Baloch.[15] After taking power Zia expanded the insurgency Pakistan had prepared against Afghanistan during Bhutto's rule. The Soviets also started preparations for the power struggle that many expected would follow the elderly Daoud's death.[16]

·····

Pakistan's allies or instruments of influence in this game of intrigue were Afghan Islamists. Religious sentiment had always been strong in Afghanistan. Once Afghanistan introduced an elected Parliament in the 1960s, small Islamist factions emerged, seeking the creation of an Islamic state based on Sharia law. These factions coalesced into Jamiat-e-Islami Afghanistan (Islamic Society of Afghanistan) by 1972, led by Burhanuddin Rabbani, a professor of theology at Kabul University. Pakistan gave refuge to Rabbani the next year.

Soon after Rabbani's arrival in Peshawar in 1973, the ISI provided him support. Some of his associates, such as Gulbeddin Hekmatyar and Ahmed Shah Massoud, were given military training. Pakistan was already running a low-level insurgency to expand its influence in Afghanistan when, on April 28, 1978, the PDPA's military cadres killed Daoud and, in a military coup, took power. Pakistan recognized the new regime and maintained diplomatic relations as it also accelerated the Islamist insurgency and started seeking US support for its Afghan project.

In Zia's calculation it was only a matter of time before Pakistan's Islamist protégés became more than a mere nuisance in Afghanistan. As the PDPA regime implemented radical social and economic policies, resentment against the new order in Kabul spread through the Afghan countryside. When land reform limited land holding to five acres, a large number of Afghan landowners became enemies of the regime. The PDPA also tried to change by decree conservative social norms, such as those relating to the treatment of women. It was also less respectful toward clerics and traditional tribal leaders.

These policies created a larger pool of disgruntled Afghans from which the Islamists could now recruit insurgents. In addition to the Jamiat-e-Islami and Hizb-e-Islami (Islamic Party founded by Hekmatyar in 1976), which were already active, several new Afghan groups began to organize. These anticommunist parties were led by conservative politicians and tribal leaders who had been excluded from or persecuted under the new political order in Afghanistan. Meanwhile, Zia ensured that the ISI exercised overall control over the insurgency across the border.

......

Pakistani officials started ringing alarm bells about the spread of communism in the region. But the Carter administration was unmoved. Then Zia made what Hummel saw as an "uncharacteristically sarcastic" remark. "Although US-Pakistan relations are now at the lowest ebb," he said, "it is not good that they should be seen publicly as being at the lowest ebb." Pakistan's Foreign Secretary Sardar Shahnawaz, who was present in Zia's meeting with Hummel, insisted that Pakistan needed international support against Afghanistan because of "the highly aggressive and ominous statements from Kabul" about Pashtunistan.[17]

In February 1979 the American ambassador in Kabul, Adolph Dubs, was killed in a botched rescue attempt after an extremist leftist faction had kidnapped him to demand the release of their leader from prison, whom the Afghan government denied holding. Security forces attempted to rescue Dubs, against the advice of the US government, and the ambassador was killed in the ensuing gunfight.

The event was, however, eclipsed by the fall of the Shah in Iran and the return to Tehran of Ayatollah Khomeini. Pakistani officials complained about Washington's lack of interest in developments in Afghanistan. The State Department responded by talking to members of the US Congress and their staff about the need to "reknit" ties with Pakistan. The briefing material prepared for winning over Congress cited Pakistan's importance to US foreign policy and the danger of a "disintegrating or radicalized" Pakistan as reasons for restoring economic and military aid.[18] With hindsight, it appears that the State Department expressed the fear of Pakistan's disintegration and radicalization at regular intervals and asked Congress to approve aid, as though that were the only cure available for a recurring ailment.

But the nuclear proliferation problem had not yet been solved. A CIA study found that Pakistan had a strong motivation to "develop at least a potential nuclear capability, in part for prestige purposes but more strongly because it genuinely believes its national security could ultimately be threatened by India." It also spoke of the possibility of Chinese cooperation with Pakistan in the nuclear field. But the CIA misread Zia, who it thought gave "relatively lower priority" to the pursuit of a nuclear option than did Bhutto.[19]

The State Department downplayed the prospects of Pakistan actually making an atom bomb, saying the country "lacked the technical skills and industrial capacity to complete the French project in the near future." Intelligence about Pakistanis "shopping around" to acquire technology for a gas centrifuge was accompanied by comments about the "enormous" problems in developing such technology.

According to the State Department the United States could "restrict Pakistani purchases of items which might be used in a centrifuge" program. Pakistan, it asserted, would hesitate to proceed with developing nuclear weapons if Washington made it clear that Pakistan's US aid would be at risk. "Pakistan feels troubled both from within and without," said the Department's brief for members of Congress. Reviving substantial US aid would help Pakistan overcome its difficulties and would provide the United States "some influence."[20]

Just as the State Department started making the case for reopening aid for Pakistan, the US ambassador in Paris, Arthur Hartman, reported a conversation he had with his Pakistani counterpart, Iqbal Akhund. "Akhund told me the other day that Pakistan has every intention of finishing the reprocessing plant on its own," he wrote. According to Hartman, Akhund "virtually admitted that the purpose of the plant was military—to give the Pakistani people, Indians and others a perception of a Pakistani military capability."

Akhund had vigorously justified Pakistan's nuclear program on other grounds as well. He had insisted that Pakistan was not breaking US laws on nonproliferation. The Pakistani ambassador had apparently told Hartman that "the Indian and Afghan situations" mandated the need for a nuclear weapons capability. "This did not mean that Pakistan would explode a device," the US diplomat summed up Pakistani thinking as conveyed by Akhund. "It meant simply that Pakistan should have the capability to do so."[21]

The Pakistani diplomat had confirmed CIA suspicions that Pakistan planned to acquire nuclear weapons capability at all costs. John Despres, the national intelligence officer for nuclear proliferation, had informed his superiors at the beginning of 1979 that Pakistan's nuclear acquisition network was growing and that it would soon have all it needed for a bomb. Despres forecast that Pakistan would be able to produce highly enriched uranium possibly by 1982 and had "probably already acquired the technology—designs, plans and technical expertise" that was needed for this purpose.[22] As it turned out, he was right.

Hummel met Zia twice after the CIA report, and both times Zia denied Pakistan's nuclear program. The ambassador showed satellite photographs of a top-secret facility at Kahuta, near Islamabad, where Abdul Qadeer Khan (often referred to as A. Q. Khan), the Pakistani metallurgist who had brought stolen designs for a uranium enrichment plant from the Netherlands during Bhutto's tenure, had set up shop to eventually enrich uranium. With a straight face Zia said, "That's absolutely ridiculous. Your information is incorrect."

Then he insisted that "We have to clear this up. Tell me any place in Pakistan you want to send your experts and I will let them come and see." But Hummel's efforts to follow up on the offer proved futile. The Foreign Ministry denied permission for US inspectors to visit Pakistani nuclear installations, stating that India had also refused inspections.[23]

US officials considered their options to get Pakistan to give up the nuclear program. Hummel thought that because Pakistan's greatest concern related to India, the United States should consider negotiating "reciprocal India-Pakistani guarantees" or "multilateral security guarantees for Pakistan." The United States could also "buy time" by seeking control over nuclear supplies without imposing sanctions until security guarantees against India "were all that was left to get Pakistan out of the nuclear business."[24]

Officials at the National Security Council also proposed an "audacious buy off" involving a "security and stability package" totaling $290 million for the first year in military and economic aid to help allay Pakistan's fears of India. The United States would then propose a "no weapons building, no weapons use" understanding between the two South Asian states. But this proposal was difficult to get through Congress. Because there was also no guarantee that Pakistan

.....

would accept the buyoff, it could as easily take the aid and still go ahead with its own plans.[25]

So Deputy Secretary of State Warren Christopher traveled to Rawalpindi to meet Zia and Shahi. According to Hummel's account of the meeting, neither Zia nor Shahi denied Pakistan's effort to build the bomb, and both refused to halt it. Christopher warned them that Pakistani nuclear activities could lead Washington to impose sanctions as specified by the Symington Amendment. In response, Shahi spoke of America's "double standard" in its treatment of India and Pakistan. According to him, the United States never pushed India as hard as it was pushing Pakistan.[26]

By now Senator John Glenn, a Democrat from Ohio, had added a further amendment to the Foreign Aid Act dealing with nuclear proliferation. This amendment called for sanctions against countries that acquired or transferred nuclear reprocessing technology or exploded or transferred a nuclear device. Zia's "virtual confirmation" of the uranium enrichment program had made action under the Symington and Glenn Amendments inescapable.[27] After examining all possible courses available to it under US law, the Carter administration announced that aid to Pakistan would be terminated.

Pakistan reacted with calculated anger. As before, it denied that it was trying to develop nuclear weapons and denounced Washington's decision to terminate aid. But it then went a step further. A senior official of the Ministry of Foreign Affairs attributed the US policy to the influence of "Zionist circles." He said the Zionists "feared that an atomic bomb developed in this Islamic country would be used by 'the Moslem world' to menace Israel."[28]

Ironically, at this stage no one in the US or Israeli government had even hinted at the possibility of a Pakistani bomb being a threat to Israel, nor had there been much mention thus far of an Islamic bomb in the media. In fact, Zia was the only one who had spoken in some interviews about Pakistan's nuclear program being an asset for the Muslim world.

The aid cutoff had coincided with Bhutto's execution on April 4, 1979. Pakistan was, as the *Washington Post* noted in an editorial, "in convulsions" over Zia's decision to eliminate the popular leader. This

......

was not a moment when Pakistan could be expected to "respond positively to pressure on the sensitive nuclear question."[29] But for Zia, who had no intention of stopping the nuclear program anyway, the US decision offered a way of dealing with the negative sentiment that his virtual assassination of Bhutto generated.

By blaming "Zionists" for the US decision on aid, Zia was trying to stem the tide of criticism in the Muslim world over his decision regarding Bhutto. He was also trying to secure the interest of oil-rich Arab rulers in Pakistan's nuclear program. The termination of US aid meant that Pakistan would need an alternative source of funding both for its economy and its rising military expenditures. Thus, labeling Pakistan's nuclear program a shared asset for all Muslims could open the door for more petro-dollars.

Officials within the US administration were sharply divided over the best way to stop Pakistan from conducting a nuclear test and to prevent the transfer of nuclear technology to other countries. Approaches were made to create consensus among Western nations for a "no-test, no-transfer" approach to Pakistan. There was little support in Europe for applying pressure, and administration officials disagreed over what "carrots" could be offered. No one knew if a sale of F-16 fighter aircraft jets would be enough to convince the Pakistani military to scale back the nuclear program.

Secretary of State Cyrus Vance and Carter's special representative on nonproliferation, Gerard C. Smith, met with Shahi in Islamabad, warning him that a nuclear test would harm US-Pakistan relations. Smith said that Pakistan was "entering the valley of death" because India "can utterly destroy you." Shahi responded that "the value of a nuclear capability lies in its possession, not in its use."[30] Realizing that the Americans were desperate to get Pakistan to comply with US laws on nonproliferation, Pakistan ratcheted up its demands for military assistance, making it harder for those who wanted to buy Pakistan out of its nuclear ambitions.

The Americans were equally frustrated when they tried to get the Indians to agree to a joint India-Pakistan agreement on the nonuse and nondevelopment of nuclear weapons. Indian Prime Minister Morarji Desai told the US ambassador to India, Robert Goheen,

......

that he had already made a pledge to that effect. If the United States could get Pakistan to do the same, "the two pledges would be as good as a joint agreement," he argued. Desai also said that if he discovered that Pakistan was ready to test a bomb or if it exploded one, India would act "to smash it."[31]

Zia had two messages for two audiences. In pursuit of American aid he told the *New York Times* that "Pakistan is not making a bomb." He also insisted that "Pakistan is not in a position to make a bomb and has no intention of making a bomb." But in order not to disappoint Pakistanis and others in the Muslim world who wanted Pakistan to go nuclear, he confirmed reports that Pakistan had embarked on a program to produce enriched uranium, saying, "Pakistan is close to it, if we have not already acquired the technology of making enriched uranium."[32]

The game of hide-and-seek over Pakistan's nuclear weapons program continued for almost two decades. Pakistan's leaders, notably Zia, defined Pakistan's nuclear capability as a shared asset for all Muslims. But in later years Pakistanis expressed indignation over the Western media describing the Pakistani bomb as the "Islamic Bomb."

★

THE CARTER ADMINISTRATION initially paid little attention to Pakistan's Jihad in Afghanistan, as it was preoccupied with the fast-moving events in Iran; Pakistan's nuclear program was also a major irritant. But Zia did not give up. He sought American attention for Pakistan through a series of interviews with the US media.

"The Soviet Union is now sitting on our borders," Zia told Sig Gissler of the *Milwaukee Journal* soon after Carter's inauguration. He recalled Pakistan's role in bridging the relations between China and the United States. "Has the free world any interest left in Pakistan?" he asked, insisting that the country could still be "a bastion" of US policy.[33] "The USA has never been able to stand by its allies," he said in another interview with CBS. "They have always let them down."[34]

......

Zia's solicitations led the CIA to decide that it could use Pakistan's services in dealing with the operational fallout of the Iranian revolution. Tehran had been the center of a huge network of American spies in the Middle East and Central Asia, but many of the CIA's human intelligence assets had to be moved out of Iran to safety. The CIA had also lost its listening posts in Iran. When US officials contacted Zia for "collaboration in the collection of communications intelligence," he readily agreed.[35] But he sought a greater role for the ISI in all operations.

Many Iranians with American connections moved out of their country through Pakistani Balochistan and onward through Karachi. The CIA also worked with Pakistani intelligence to "improve Pakistan's electronic intercept capabilities."[36] Zia insisted that, to cover Pakistan's tracks, the number of American intelligence specialists in the country be kept to a minimum. The CIA had to deal extensively with the ISI to access data that American intercept installations had collected.

The Iranian connection formed a closer bond between the CIA and ISI than before. Zia then made a strong pitch for US involvement in Pakistan's Afghan project. Together, he argued, the United States and Pakistan could help roll back communism in Afghanistan and diminish Soviet prestige. American journalists were invited to report on the training program for anticommunist Afghan guerrillas even though Islamabad officially denied the program's existence. The *Washington Post* reported that at least two thousand Afghans were being trained at Pakistani bases, guarded by Pakistani troops.[37]

Anticommunist hard-liners were Zia's target audience in Washington. Pakistan had recruited Afghan Islamist warriors in its effort to finally end the notion of Pashtunistan, but Zia wanted the Americans to believe that this was part of their ideological struggle against global communism. A breakthrough for Zia came when, in July 1979, Carter approved a modest program of CIA assistance to the Afghan Islamist resistance, routed through Pakistan.

Zia had already convinced the Saudis to join his project. Saudi intelligence officials raised with their US counterparts the prospect of defeating the communists in Afghanistan. The CIA's directorate of operations reported that the Saudis could be expected to fund and encourage the Pakistanis. Other governments could also be expected to join in. At one meeting of US officials dealing with national security, Defense Department official Walter Slocombe asked if there was value in keeping the Afghan insurgency going, "sucking the Soviets into a Vietnamese quagmire?"[38]

The Americans also weighed the risk of provoking the Soviets before initiating covert support for the Pakistani project. For years the conventional narrative about the war in Afghanistan has revolved around the Soviet invasion in December 1979. But Carter signed the first authorization "to help the Mujahideen covertly" on July 3, 1979, "almost six months before the Soviets invaded Afghanistan."[39] And Pakistan had been recruiting and training the Mujahideen for years before that.

Americans like to believe that the war in Afghanistan was "Charlie Wilson's War."[40] In fact, however, it was Zia-ul-Haq's war, which the Americans expanded with their money and sophisticated weapons. Carter's first authorization only covered "support for insurgent propaganda and other psychological operations in Afghanistan; establishment of radio access to the Afghan population through third-country facilities; and the provision either unilaterally or through third countries of support to the Afghan insurgents, in the form of either cash or nonmilitary supplies." A little over half a million dollars was allocated. All of it was drawn within six weeks.[41]

The US embassy in Kabul made a feeble attempt to alert Washington about the retrograde beliefs of its new Afghan allies. "The available manifesto issued by some opposition groups calls for a social and economic system based on the 'fundamentalist' tenets of Islam," an embassy cable stated. "An opposition-led regime would probably not have social and economic reforms (so necessary for this backward country) high on its priority list." It also warned that, if successful, the Mujahideen would probably carry out "thousands of personal vendettas" against officials serving in the communist regime.[42]

The Americans got another warning about the perils of partnership with Pakistan when Islamist students burned down the embassy in Islamabad on November 21, 1979. The students were reacting to rumors that the United States was responsible for the seizure of Islam's holiest shrine, the Grand Mosque in Makkah. Several embassy officials were trapped in the burning building, resulting in the death of four people, including two Americans. The Pakistan military took four hours to arrive at the site and several more to restore order.

"Some Americans and some Western diplomats maintained that the police here stood by for several hours without challenging the irate crowd," the New York Times reported the next day. "Among the Americans who lived through the violence there was not much gratitude" for the police or the Pakistan army, the paper said. Its reporter also did not find "much contrition among Pakistanis."[43] A group of fifty students marched in Rawalpindi the next day to honor one of the demonstrators who had been killed.

Zia's cabinet "expressed its understanding for the enraged sentiments of the Moslems in Pakistan," even though it regretted its "inappropriate and irresponsible" expression. Hummel, for his part, avoided direct comment on the government's inadequate and delayed response in protecting the embassy. He said that the judgment of whether Pakistan bore some responsibility for the US embassy's destruction would have to be made in Washington.[44]

This reflected the Islamists' potential for anti-American violence and the government's sympathy with their sentiment. US diplomats wondered why the Pakistan army took so long to come to the embassy's rescue. In subsequent coups troops were able to move between their quarters in Rawalpindi to the general area where the US embassy was located in less than thirty-five minutes. Some American officials felt that the Pakistanis wanted the Americans to "sweat a bit," whereas others believed that Pakistani intelligence instigated demonstrations in several cities, but the one in Islamabad got out of hand.[45]

Zia privately cited the incident as evidence of why the United States needed a military strongman like him to control an emotional and volatile Pakistani nation. Only a dictator like him could channel the religious fervor of Pakistanis against the Soviets instead of allowing it to run against the United States, he averred.[46] In the context of developments in Iran, this argument found some favor among Americans. Eventually Zia agreed that Pakistan would compensate the United States for its totally gutted embassy building. But he was already working on ensuring that Pakistan received enough American assistance to cover much more than the building's cost.

Almost a month after the attack on the US embassy in Islamabad Soviet troops marched into Afghanistan in support of the country's embattled communist government. The Soviet intervention was a response to the complex infighting between Afghan communist factions. With access to Soviet archives, several scholars have concluded that there was no grand design in the Soviet military's move. Opinion in Washington had so far been divided between those who saw the Afghan communist regime as a Soviet cat's paw and those who considered developments in Afghanistan independent of superpower rivalry.[47] The direct induction of Soviet troops settled that argument: the Soviets had been sucked into their "Vietnam quagmire."

The Carter administration was already looking weak to Americans as a result of the Iranian hostage crisis, in which revolutionary students had taken fifty-two Americans from the US embassy in Iran. The crisis was ongoing when Soviet tanks crossed into Afghanistan. So Carter could not afford to respond weakly to this new challenge. For the American public both events symbolized a decline in US power. There was little Carter could do at this stage about the hostages, but he could certainly flex some muscle over Afghanistan to project strong leadership.

In February 1979 Carter had played down the importance of Afghanistan during a speech at the Foreign Policy Conference for Editors and Broadcasters. He had said that the regime in Afghanistan, a nation under Soviet influence, was replaced by a regime more closely aligned with the Soviet Union.[48] But after the Soviet invasion he said that Afghanistan "was a sovereign nation, a nonaligned nation, a deeply religious nation, and the Soviets invaded it, brutally."[49] Carter described "the Soviet invasion of Afghanistan and the installation of a puppet government" as a serious threat to peace.[50]

The day after the Soviet troops marched into Afghanistan, National Security Adviser Zbigniew Brzezinski wrote a memo to

•••••

Carter in which he said that although Afghanistan "could become a Soviet Vietnam," it posed a grave challenge for the United States in the short term. The Carter administration, he feared, would come under pressure to be as decisive militarily in Iran as the Soviets had been in Afghanistan. But the United States had to be careful to avoid direct confrontation with the Soviet Union.

Brzezinski argued that Iran and Afghanistan were now both "in turmoil," while Pakistan was "both unstable internally and extremely apprehensive externally." Soviet success in Afghanistan, he argued, "could produce Soviet presence right down on the edge of the Arabian and Oman Gulfs." In his analysis it was essential that the Afghan resistance continued. "This means more money as well as arms shipments to the rebels, and some technical advice," he wrote.

Consequently, the national security adviser proposed a review of US policy toward Pakistan to include "more guarantees" and "more aid." He stated that the United States "should encourage the Chinese to help the rebels also" and "should concert with Islamic countries both in a propaganda campaign and in a covert action campaign to help the rebels."

In Brzezinski's view the Afghan guerrillas were "badly organized and poorly led." They had limited foreign support and "*no* sanctuary, no organized army, and no central government—all of which North Vietnam had." Instead of being "sanguine about Afghanistan becoming a Soviet Vietnam," the United States would have to create circumstances for that to happen. "The Soviets are likely to act decisively," he warned, adding that "in world politics nothing succeeds like success, whatever the moral aspects."[51]

Carter initiated discussion within his administration over the appropriate American response to the new Afghan situation. At a meeting of the National Security Council, chaired by Carter, the question of the Soviet invasion's impact on Pakistan came up. CIA Deputy Director Frank Carlucci, Secretary of Defense Harold Brown, and Brzezinski agreed that the United States needed to bolster Pakistan through greater economic and military assistance.

White House Counsel Lloyd Cutler reminded everyone present of the legal problem of providing aid to Pakistan. Secretary of State

Vance explained that the Symington Amendment precluded the US government from providing military credits to Pakistan. After reading the law from his brief, he concluded that money could not be provided to Pakistan under the foreign assistance act as long as Pakistan persisted with its nuclear program.

Carter said he thought Zia had given an assurance that he would not test nuclear weapons but that he could not bind his successor. Vance replied that the Pakistanis had pulled back from that commitment; Zia was now saying only that "they would not test a nuclear weapon in the next six months." That was inadequate to provide the US president room to waive the restrictions under the Symington Amendment.

Vance pointed out that the United States could try to change the provisions of the Symington Amendment, but "if we take this approach we also confront the whole non-proliferation issue head on." Another way, in his view, would be to have a "special provision" that simply said that, notwithstanding any other provision of law, the United States would go ahead with assistance to Pakistan. Brzezinski suggested that if the administration offered one-time emergency support to Pakistan, Congress might support the idea of the "notwithstanding any other provision of law" approach.[52]

While the Americans worried about a Soviet military presence in Afghanistan threatening Pakistan, Zia looked upon it as an opportunity. Fifty thousand Soviet troops were now in a country that shared a long mountainous border with his own. If Pakistan was able to elicit so much interest from the United States based on its relative proximity to the Soviet Union, it could do much better now.

Zia somberly spoke to a string of American visitors, including journalists, of the danger the Red Army's presence next door posed. But he did not move any troops from Pakistan's border with India to its border with Afghanistan. No one asked him why the Pakistan army was not immediately reconfigured. Without moving the troops, Zia could not confront the Soviets, whom he accused of planning to cross the Khyber Pass and reach the Arabian Sea through Pakistan. There would have to be at least some Pakistani resistance before American and other Western troops came to Pakistan's defense.

*****

For Zia the Soviet intervention in Afghanistan brought an international recognition that had eluded him since his ascent to power. The Americans initiated discussions about augmenting Pakistan's defenses with several countries. Brzezinski and Christopher traveled to Saudi Arabia and got the kingdom's concurrence for a unique arrangement. The Saudis would match dollar for dollar anything the United States spent on arming the Mujahideen. They would also provide cash for military equipment that could be provided to Pakistan only on the basis of cash sales. In return Pakistan would provide "military input to Saudi security."[53]

Defense Secretary Brown told China's vice premier, Geng Biao, in Beijing that the United States planned to resume economic and military assistance to Pakistan despite the nuclear problem. The United States will continue to object to the nuclear program, Brown said, but "We will now set that aside for the time being and concentrate on strengthening Pakistan against potential Soviet action."[54] Given Pakistan's close ties with China, Brown's message was bound to reach Islamabad even before the defense secretary had returned to base.

The US policy that emerged immediately after Soviet troops moved into Afghanistan revolved around Pakistan. As Vance wrote in his memoir, Carter was willing to seek congressional approval to waive the legal prohibition on military aid to Pakistan. At the same time the United States would reaffirm its nuclear nonproliferation policy and press Pakistan to provide acceptable guarantees that it would not develop a nuclear weapon. But the first step was to reach agreement with Pakistan on the terms of an assistance package.[55]

The relationship between the United States and Pakistan had flipped. The *New York Times* headline "Pakistan Is No Longer the Ardent Suitor, but the Prize to Be Courted" captured it exactly.[56] Zia handled the new situation with panache. He was eager to partner with the United States, but he made it seem like a difficult decision. He emphasized Pakistan's "strategic position" and its being the "backdoor to the Gulf" and praised the United States as the champions of the free world.[57] But he also spoke of the vulnerability of Pakistan to Soviet and Indian pressures.

......

Zia wanted to bargain for the maximum support from the United States while accepting the minimum of conditions. He told a group of newspaper editors that he was reluctant to accept US arms because "We have had bitter experiences" with US aid in the past. He said he wanted to know from Washington just what kind of military aid it was considering sending to Pakistan and on what terms. "Zia has told associates that a limited amount of U.S. aid is meaningless," reported the *Washington Post*.

Pakistan's wish list for military equipment included advanced fighter-bomber aircraft, artillery, communications equipment, and "either more and better tanks or sophisticated antitank weapons to allow it to defend itself against a tank attack." On the list were planes that would "not be fully supplied to the U.S. Air Force until the mid-1980s." Pakistan, as before, could not afford to buy the sophisticated weapons it required. It wanted the United States "to either give it the weapons or to arrange for favorable credit terms. Pakistan feels the US owes it this."[58]

These weapons were ostensibly being sought in view of the threat posed by the Soviet presence in Afghanistan. But items such as tanks could not conceivably be used along Pakistan's mountainous border with Afghanistan; they were clearly intended for the plains of the Punjab and Sindh, along the border with India. In fact, Pakistan had been asking for American tanks since it lost many in the 1965 war, long before any Soviet soldier had crossed into Afghanistan. No sooner had Zia asked for US weapons than Indian Prime Minister Indira Gandhi voiced her fears that these might eventually be used against India.

Zia was finally getting his wish of US involvement in the Jihad Pakistan had initiated in Afghanistan. Pakistan's interest in the project had been to force Afghanistan into settling its claims on Pakistan's Pashtun territories. But now that the Soviet military move had shocked the Americans into paying attention, Zia played hard to get. He was aware that at least some people in the US government would not mind paying a higher price for Pakistan's cooperation in bleeding the Soviets.

⋅⋅⋅⋅⋅

The Pakistani dictator added assurances against a possible threat of attack from India to the list of his demands from the United States before accepting aid against the Soviets. Brzezinski publicly reassured Pakistan "that the United States stands behind them" and reiterated the terms of the 1959 US-Pakistan mutual defense treaty, which committed the United States to come to Pakistan's aid in case of communist attack.[59]

Brzezinski wrote later that "the Pakistanis were rather concerned that they might be the next target of Soviet military aggression."[60] But he still stated plainly that the United States could not guarantee support in the event of an Indian attack. Zia realized that the Americans were interested primarily in the covert war that would bleed the Soviets. He bargained hard for favors for Pakistan without shutting off the clandestine program of assistance to the Mujahideen. This won him the support of anticommunist hard-liners in the United States.

The covert program expanded dramatically to include new weapons and advanced training for the Mujahideen. Thus, the insurgents were totally dependent on Pakistan. Arms deliveries had stepped up as a result of funding from Saudi Arabia and the CIA.[61] Zia wanted to convince the United States of the value of supporting the Afghan Mujahideen while he also wanted to send the message that the hopes of creating a Vietnam-like quagmire would remain unfulfilled without meeting Pakistan's demands.

Zia then went on an offensive in the US media. He said he would not risk the wrath of the Soviet Union without "a good treaty of friendship and in conjunction with others, economic and military assurance in that order of priority." He also rejected as "peanuts" the offer of a $400 million two-year economic and military aid package that the Carter administration was cobbling together. "If this is true," he said, "it is terribly disappointing. Pakistan will not buy its security with $400 million. It will buy greater animosity from the Soviet Union, which is now more influential in this region than the U.S."[62] Shahi, the Pakistan foreign minister, separately said that Pakistan expected "several billion dollars" in US military aid to "build up its defense along its western border with Afghanistan." Playing the bad cop, Shahi also said, "We are sick of depending on the political whims of the U.S. and U.S. public opinion which from time to time puts Pakistan in the doghouse."[63]

The Pakistani message was designed for maximum effect in Washington. "All that we are trying to do is enable us to stand on our own feet and fight for ourselves," Zia said, appealing to the American respect for self-sufficiency. He claimed that he was only seeking "moral help," a sort of "hand on my back" so that "I can really put my chest out and say 'No I am not alone. We have friends in this world'."

In response, skeptics pointed out that Pakistan had received significant amounts of US aid in the past. Zia replied that it had not been enough, "otherwise we wouldn't have been in bad economic trouble." He reflected Pakistan's overall attitude toward US assistance, that it was somehow owed to Pakistan. When a reporter reminded him that economic aid since 1948 totaled $5 billion, Zia looked surprised. "Unfortunately it hasn't been effective, partially due to our own fault. Our own economic policies haven't been that effective," he said.

Zia insisted that Pakistan was the only country where the West still had influence in a broad crescent stretching "right from Turkey down to Vietnam."[64] If the United States wanted to help Pakistan, it needed to give an assurance about Pakistan's security and integrity, he told *ABC News*. "If any country like Soviet Union attacks Pakistan it will be war with the free world or with the United States and the United Kingdom." Zia argued that if United States could give security guarantees to South Korea, Israel, Taiwan, and Egypt, why could it not provide one for Pakistan?[65]

Few Americans, including many considered experts on South Asia, remembered that Liaquat had sought a similar guarantee in 1950 when there were no Soviet troops in Afghanistan—little had changed in Pakistan's security thinking in thirty years. The Pakistanis had either not understood or did not want to understand the reasons for US unwillingness to go to war for Pakistan, especially against its principal foe, India.

· · · · ·

The Americans were willing to ignore the fact that Pakistan's primary security concern was still a country with which the United States had no major conflict. It was only a matter of time before Pakistan's usefulness against the Soviets would subside and the old argument—about the United States deserting Pakistan in dealing with India—would resurface. Zia's message was targeted at those Americans who did not bother with details about other countries' history or with their long-term strategic thinking.

In one interview Zia insisted that "connivance" of the Soviet Union and India in 1971 had bifurcated Pakistan, glossing over Pakistan's domestic circumstances that led to Bangladesh's secession. He also insisted that he could prove that "there is a great conspiracy against Pakistan" to "strangulate Pakistan."[66]

Zia also voiced the belief that Israel and "their friend India" were involved in an "organized conspiracy against Pakistan" at a time when India and Israel did not even have full diplomatic relations.[67] But US policy makers did not pay attention to these manifestations of a conspiracy-theory mindset. There were a few voices, some echoed in the columns of major American newspapers, that warned that close military ties with Pakistan would lead to entanglements that the United States could do without. But within the administration there was consensus that fueling Jihad in Afghanistan could be useful for US interests, and for that reason Pakistan had to be armed and funded.

From Zia's perspective, getting American attention was just the first step; the next was getting enough support. He was looking for a latter-day Dulles, not the cautious officials of a reluctant superpower, which was how he saw Carter's administration. Americans knew a little more about Pakistan now than they did in the era of Dulles. But Pakistan also had more friends in the United States than it did earlier, Zia thought. The head of Saudi intelligence, Prince Turki bin Faisal Al-Saud, was also guiding the Pakistani military regime in handling the Americans. Zia wanted to negotiate a deal that would get American backing not only for the immediate needs for the Mujahideen in Afghanistan but also for Pakistan's longer-term requirements.

......

Bombarded with the pros and cons of aiding Zia and Pakistan, the US media reflected the debates among American policy makers. The *Washington Post* said that the United States had to accept Zia for what he was: "the man running Pakistan now." It supported giving Zia's regime "the kind and amount of help that will make plain that the U.S. understands its larger stake in the security of Pakistan, and then—eyes open—to try to limit the collateral damage."[68]

Conversely, the *New York Times* reminded the administration that "the understandable desire to discourage further Soviet advance in Asia" should not be at the expense of nonproliferation goals. "Preventing the spread of nuclear arms in Asia is no less important to world security than containing the Soviet Union," the paper said in an editorial. "Pakistan should not be misled about the depth of the American commitment to non-proliferation," it insisted.

The *Times* also questioned the wisdom of seeking India's "tolerance for aid to Pakistan" by way of opening "shipments of nuclear fuel for its American-built reactor."[69] Meanwhile, India said that the "induction of arms into Pakistan" would convert South Asia into "a theatre of Great Power confrontation and conflict." The Indian government felt that once Pakistan again started receiving sophisticated US weapons, it would "de-accelerate" the process of normalization with India.[70]

Zia made no effort to address India's concerns; instead, he repeated the Pakistani mantra: Pakistan wanted "equality to be the determining factor" in India-Pakistan relations.[71] For Indians, this was code for an aggressive posture toward them, as it had been in the past. They protested vehemently that the United States was about to make a mistake. Pakistan's military preparedness, the Indians argued, would only exacerbate Pakistani jingoism against India. Carter sent former Defense Secretary Clark Clifford to India in an effort to placate Indian leaders.

As an elder statesman who had also advised Truman, Kennedy, and Johnson, Clifford was much admired in India. In Delhi he offered India cutting-edge military equipment to offset the impact of US supplies to Pakistan. But the wisdom of this attempt to win over both Pakistan and India with inducements comprising military

......

hardware was questionable. All it did was reinforce Pakistan's belief that it could militarily beat India with the right weapons as it also offered India some equipment to match the weapons provided to Pakistan.

"It is hard to watch Zbigniew Brzezinski and Clark Clifford tracking over South Asia," observed the *Washington Post*, "the one sewing up the details of a substantial military and economic package to Pakistan, the other offering a new arms package including sophisticated guidance systems and smart bombs to India—without feeling a little warning buzz of unease."[72] This article thus voiced fears that the United States would be repeating the mistake of military supplies policy that led to both Pakistan and India using American weapons in their earlier wars.

The problem for the United States was that it wanted to get involved in Afghanistan, but there was no way of bypassing Pakistan to do so. In a brief for members of Congress, the Congressional Research Service summarized the American dilemma. "U.S. options for influencing events in Afghanistan," it said, "are limited to providing direct or indirect assistance to the Afghan guerrilla forces and refugees and to support the regime of President Zia-ul-Haq in neighboring Pakistan." In both cases the options required working through the Pakistani government "since that country is the only haven of the Afghan insurgents to which U.S. has access."[73]

The Carter administration also tried hard to balance concerns over nonproliferation with the opening for calibrated confrontation that the Soviet invasion of Afghanistan presented. "The administration plans to seek urgent congressional approval for a substantial amount of economic and security assistance to Pakistan over the next 18 months," the State Department informed American embassies in several European capitals. But it emphasized that US global nonproliferation policy remained unchanged.

The Symington and Glenn Amendments would remain in place, and the United States would "continue to press the Pakistanis" on the issue of nuclear proliferation. But instead of coercive measures, the United States would focus on persuasion. The United States thought that it was "in Pakistan's own best interest to abandon its nuclear enrichment and processing programs and other sensitive nuclear activities."[74] If someone in the US government had a blue-print of how they would convince Pakistanis to give up on what they considered their national interest, they did not put it in writing.

Brzezinski led an American team to Pakistan to persuade Zia that he should accept the US offer, which could increase once Carter had won reelection in November 1980. The *New York Times* quipped that Brzezinski told Zia that "$400 million in aid was hardly 'peanuts'—and that a certain Georgia farmer would always know how to raise more."

However, the White House had not yet considered where China came in and had ignored the possibility of a fourth war between In-dia and Pakistan. With or without a Soviet involvement, would Americans have to defend Pakistan? "What if Pakistani bungling and Soviet meddling stir rebellion in Baluchistan, near the Persian Gulf?" the *New York Times* queried. "Can Gen Zia hold the loyalty of his peoples? Could Americans help him? Should they?" Pronounce-ments about arming Afghan insurgents and building Pakistan's mili-tary reflected a mood, the *Times* editorial declared, but until these questions were answered, it was not yet a policy.[75]

Zia announced at a press conference that the US offer of aid was inadequate and Pakistan would not be able to accept it unless its quantum was increased significantly. In separate editorials the *Wash-ington Post* and the *New York Times* both suggested that Pakistan's re-fusal of the American offer of aid might have been a good thing. The *Post* argued that Pakistan was not the place where the United States should "draw a line" against further Soviet adventures. In its view the "Zia regime would have taken fresh American arms and used them first against the very non-Punjabi minorities that it needs to conciliate in order to strengthen and legitimize its rule." The pa-per hoped that Zia's rejection of the quantum of aid would prevent "unwise and irreversible policy choices" being made.[76]

The *Times* pointed out that $400 million could not be described as "peanuts." Pakistan, it said, was using the Soviet invasion of Af-ghanistan to advance "more grandiose ambitions." The country was "seeking instant, massive and unconditional military help on a scale

· · · · ·

that would have served no American interest." In the paper's opinion, "no amount of American military assistance (remember Iran)
could really have secured the Zia regime from the internal insurgencies of disaffected ethnic minorities."[77]

The Carter administration and the US media were both unaware
that Zia had turned down the aid package based on a careful forecast
of the American election's outcome. Carter was facing a primary
challenge from Senator Edward Kennedy, the US economy was tor-
pid, and the hostage crisis in Iran was dragging on, with no end in
sight—Carter would probably not win reelection. Zia's friends in
Saudi Arabia as well as in the United States advised him that the
likely Republican candidate, Ronald Reagan, would be more likely
to support Pakistan's plans in Afghanistan than would the embattled
Carter administration.

Historically, Pakistan had never turned down American aid, even
when it was meager compared with the country's request. The Pakistani pattern had been to accept what was offered while continuing
to ask for more. Zia was now treading new ground. In the hope of a
better deal down the line, Pakistani officials told reporters that they
were waiting to find out what Saudi Arabia would offer them before
accepting the US offer. The Pakistanis had in mind a military and
economic package from Washington of $2 billion annually over a
five-year period—a total amount of $10 billion.[78]

Amidst the haggling over the size of an aid package for Pakistan,
the CIA director received warning that the Pakistanis were interpreting US willingness to resume aid as acceptance of their nuclear
program. The CIA's Nuclear Proliferation Intelligence section observed that the "Pakistani resolve to move ahead with its nuclear
program" had been reinforced.[79]

By the time the US presidential primaries concluded, Zia had
made up his mind: he would wait until after the US elections before
concluding an aid deal with the United States. The likelihood of
Ronald Reagan becoming president appeared much greater, so instead of negotiating with a lame-duck administration, Zia would
spend the rest of the year approaching conservative anticommunists
in the United States.

Zia's plan was to portray the Afghan Mujahideen as a primitive, tribal David challenging the Soviet Goliath in a remote part of Central Asia. By the time the new American president was in office, he reasoned, there would be sufficient momentum for the idea of supporting a Holy War in Afghanistan. In addition to inviting almost every American and British journalist known for his anticommunist credentials, Zia also reached out to retired military officers, businessmen, and socialites with political connections.

Among the people Zia invited to visit Pakistan and meet the Mujahideen was Texas socialite Joanne Herring, whose second husband, Robert Herring, was chairman of the Houston Natural Gas (HNG) Company. HNG, which later emerged as Enron, had business interests in the greater Middle East, and Robert was offered the position of Pakistan's honorary consul in Houston. He, in turn, proposed that Joanne simultaneously hold the title of honorary consul for Morocco and Pakistan.

The Herrings were politically well connected, though Joanne was known more for glamour than for political wisdom. In her memoir, written years later, she spoke of Pakistan as an Arab nation, demonstrating that she knew little about the country she represented as honorary consul. But she was devoutly anticommunist and knew many influential people who shared her beliefs. Zia knew that, and so he showered her with hospitality in order to use her connections.

Zia wanted the Afghan Mujahideen to become heroes to American anticommunists. On his suggestion, Joanne brought along her photographer son, Robin King, and adventurer and moviemaker Charles Fawcett to Pakistan. Their joint effort, facilitated by Pakistan's information ministry and army public relations, resulted in a documentary film about the Soviet occupation of Afghanistan and the brave men resisting it.[80]

Herring showed the film *Courage Is Our Weapon* at parties and in salons upon her return to the United States. Those who viewed it included donors to conservative causes, Republican public officials, and several individuals who could be expected to hold senior appointed positions in a Republican administration.

By the time of the US presidential election in November 1980, Zia had succeeded in creating the image of the Mujahideen as simple, honorable peasant soldiers resisting communist occupation of their homeland. The obscurantism of Afghan resistance leaders remained well hidden, as did the regional political motives of their Pakistani sponsors. For example, long before the Soviet invasion Mujahideen leader Gulbeddin Hekmatyar was known in Kabul for throwing acid on women who did not cover their faces. Now Americans such as Herring viewed him with the romance that Western leftists once felt for Ho Chi Minh or Che Guevara.

★

WITH RONALD REAGAN'S inauguration as the fortieth president of the United States, Zia came close to fulfilling his desire to secure Pakistan's interests in Afghanistan with American help. The new administration was eager to implement Brzezinski's advice that the United States would have to take several actions to convert Afghanistan into a quagmire for the Soviets similar to the one the Americans were sucked into in Vietnam.

"From the outset," explained Robert Gates, who was then the CIA's deputy director, "the Reagan administration targeted covert action, foreign assistance, diplomacy and even direct military intervention on Third World battlegrounds in opposition to the Soviets, Cubans, Libyans—and anyone else perceived to be a surrogate of the Soviet Union."[81] Afghanistan was a particularly attractive battleground because the Soviets—and not their surrogates—were directly in the battlefield.

Understanding the US objective, Zia realized his position of strength in bargaining with the Americans. Some US assistance was already trickling in for the Mujahideen, but Zia said that Pakistan was "not ready to serve as a conduit for the supply of arms to the Afghan freedom fighters."[82] In doing so he wanted to make sure that the terms of engagement as well as full operational control of the Jihad stayed in Pakistan's hands.

Some Americans outside the administration could see what he was doing. Zia, said a *Washington Post* editorial, was "plainly ready to trade on the country's strategic utility" for the United States so as "to acquire the aid and arms necessary to protect his country and to keep himself in power." It advised caution "in broadening American commitment to a regime that is at once uncertain and necessarily fixed on its own agenda."[83] But the new US secretary of state, Alexander Haig, dismissed these concerns. He underscored the Reagan administration's "determination to stop Soviet expansionism" and told a Pakistani delegation of the administration's commitment "to being supportive of Pakistan."[84]

In Haig the Pakistanis had found their new Dulles. In a message to all US embassies titled "U.S. Policy towards Pakistan," Haig declared that "Pakistan's security is inextricably linked to our own security and to that of industrialized democracies, primarily because of Western and Japanese dependence on Persian Gulf oil." The United States, he said, had "concluded that a stronger, more self-confident Pakistan" was "essential for the enhanced deterrence to Soviet expansionism which we seek."[85]

Like Dulles, Haig also expressed admiration for Pakistan's "large well-trained armed forces and its good Islamic credentials."[86] He also reasoned subsequently that Pakistan's sense of insecurity motivated its quest for nuclear weapons. If the United States helped Pakistan feel secure, there would be no reason for Pakistan to continue seeking a nuclear deterrent, he argued.

The new administration also changed the US objective from stopping Pakistan's nuclear program altogether to building a "closer security relationship," which would make the Pakistanis develop the sense of being "more secure." Such a relationship would "provide Pakistan with incentives to forego, or at least delay, a nuclear test" and would work better than alternative approaches, argued a new CIA paper on nonproliferation.[87] But Zia repeatedly made it clear that making Pakistan feel secure, especially in relation to India, was not going to be easy.

The Pakistani dictator continued his media offensive even after the contours of an aid program had been agreed on by the spring of

1981. He told *Newsweek* that India had been building its military strength "not for China or any smaller neighbor but Pakistan." The Jaguar aircraft and tanks from the Soviet Union, he said, could not be used against China "because of the mountainous terrain."[88]

According to Zia, Pakistan could not pose a threat to India, so the only plausible reason for its military buildup had to be its desire for Pakistan "to remain a weak state" that "accepts Indian hegemony."[89] He told the BBC that Pakistan wanted "Indians to realize that they must accept the existence of Pakistan; that they must reconcile themselves to Pakistan being a reality."[90]

In June the State Department announced that the United States and Pakistan had agreed on a $3.2 billion military and economic aid program to strengthen Pakistani defenses against a serious threat from Soviet troops in Afghanistan. The statement made no reference to the nuclear weapons issue.[91] Included in the package were advanced F-16 fighter jets that Pakistan had sought for many years.

Zia saw this as a major success. He would now receive US money to maintain domestic government spending as well as to equip his military. American assistance would consolidate his dictatorship, just as it had enabled Ayub to rule for a decade. The military would get much-needed equipment, and Pakistani Islamists could be trained alongside the Afghans to become a secondary militia for both regional and domestic purposes. Pakistanis also assumed that they could continue their nuclear program as long as they did not conduct a nuclear test.

In an effort to ensure that the US commitment remained long term, Zia also revived the idea of US bases in Pakistan that had earlier been mooted by Ayub in the 1950s and by Bhutto immediately after the Pakistani defeat in the 1971 war with India. Zia raised the matter with State Department Counselor Robert "Bud" McFarlane during a meeting in Islamabad. "Why don't you ask us to grant bases?" asked Zia. McFarlane was unprepared for the question. He responded that it would be "inconceivable" for the United States to seek military bases in Pakistan.[92] But the offer reinforced Pakistan's willingness to be a close American ally.

· · · · ·

The US Congress, however, challenged the Reagan administration's new Pakistan policy. Hearings on Capitol Hill focused on the nuclear issue, forcing the administration to cite Pakistan's "absolute assurances" that it was neither developing nor planning to develop nuclear weapons. Under Secretary of State James Buckley, who had visited Islamabad to conclude the aid agreement, told the Senate Government Affairs subcommittee: "I was assured by the ministers and by the President himself that it was not the intention of the Pakistan Government to develop nuclear weapons." He insisted on the distinction "between the nuclear option and a nuclear weapon."[93]

Although there was widespread support in Washington for the Afghan Mujahideen and the idea of undermining the Soviet Union, aid to Pakistan remained unpopular. The *Washington Post* advised against visibly embracing Zia, whose position it deemed unpredictable. Pakistan should only be given arms that show "clearly which Pakistani purpose the U.S. supports—not competition with India but defense of its Afghan border against Soviet incursions."[94] The *New York Times* demanded that legal restrictions be imposed that force Pakistan "to choose between usable weapons and a costly nuclear badge."[95]

One of the most prescient warnings appeared in a letter to the editor in the *Times* by Jeremiah Novak, a former corporate executive who wrote occasional columns about Asian affairs, captioned, "How Pakistan Can Get U.S. Jets and Build the Islamic Bomb." It pointed out that the Reagan administration's willingness to believe Pakistani assurances on the nuclear issue had failed to analyze "the divergence between U.S. and Pakistani goals." Novak highlighted reports about Saudi Arabia providing Pakistan with nearly $2 billion of aid, an additional economic package in return for the stationing of Pakistani troops in Saudi Arabia, and the money for Pakistan's purchase of American F-16s. "This second package is linked to the Islamic bomb Pakistan is alleged to be building," Novak wrote, adding that "the bomb may be ready for a test explosion in October 1982, when the Saudi-financed F-16's are to be delivered." He argued that an American withdrawal of aid would be too late to stop Pakistan from going nuclear. He cited Shahi's statements about the "Israeli menace" and his support for the Islamic revolution of Iran so as to suggest that Pakistan expected broad backing of the Islamic countries in its nuclear endeavors.

According to Novak, Shahi had said that the United States had to defend Pakistan because of its confrontation with the Soviet Union, not "for altruistic reasons but because the whole balance of power in the gulf region will come under danger." Assisting Pakistan while compromising on US policy goals, he argued, could "give the Arabs access to the bomb, entangle Pakistan in Middle East politics and endanger India."[96] The Reagan White House, however, most likely paid no attention to a letter in a newspaper, as it was also ignoring more official correspondence on the same issue.

Around the same time the US embassy in London informed Washington that West German national Heinz Mebus "may attempt to circumvent French export control regulations concerning calcium metal." According to the embassy's report, Mebus had previously "supplied a large amount of equipment to Pakistan's uranium enrichment program." His attempts to buy calcium metal would advance Pakistan's nuclear program. The State Department understood that Pakistan was procuring the calcium metal not for use in an energy program but instead "for use in a nuclear explosive device."[97] But for the Reagan administration, fighting the Soviet Union through proxies in Afghanistan was more important.

Soon after taking office Reagan had appointed his presidential election campaign manager, William Casey, as director of the Central Intelligence Agency. Casey enjoyed the president's confidence and was the first CIA head to attend meetings as a fully participating cabinet member. According to Gates, "Bill Casey came to the CIA primarily to wage war against the Soviet Union."[98] He faced the task of building up the CIA's capability for military and political action outside the United States at a time when the agency was recovering from criticism of its past illegal and inappropriate activities.

Casey hoped to enhance support for anticommunist insurgent organizations around the world. Under his leadership the CIA helped more than a quarter of a million people take up arms against communism. The CIA extended support to rebels in Nicaragua, Angola,

Cambodia, and Ethiopia as well as Afghanistan. But in all of these theaters of war CIA personnel were directly involved in the planning, training, and conduct of operations. For Afghanistan, however, Zia offered a different model. Pakistan's ISI would run the show for the CIA as long as it received funding and weapons.

Since June 1979 the ISI was headed by General Akhtar Abdul Rahman, an infantry officer loyal to Zia who shared his ideological vision based on Islamic nationalism. As a junior officer, Rahman had aided the tribal militias raised in 1947 to fight in Kashmir. Thus, he was not new to managing religiously motivated irregular fighters. Soon after taking command of the ISI he crafted a detailed plan for expanding the insurgency in Afghanistan. Once Casey became chief of the CIA, Rahman built a close relationship with him and other CIA officials.

Pakistan's interest was not only to help the Americans drive the Soviets out of Afghanistan but also to ensure that the next government in Kabul was totally beholden to Pakistan. Strengthening Afghan Islamists would create a counterweight to Pashtun nationalism. Pakistan could always divert covert funds from the Afghan insurgency toward fomenting insurgencies against the source of its perceived principal threat, India. Support from all over the Muslim world was expected to fulfill Pakistan's pan-Islamist aspirations. Zia also hoped to rally Pakistanis around the banner of Islam and Jihad.

There was some concern that the Soviets might use India to wage direct war against Pakistan in case the war in Afghanistan became unbearable for Moscow. For that reason, Zia told Casey that the US-Pakistan objective in Afghanistan should be "to keep the pot boiling, but not boil over."[99] Casey did not see any problem with the more local aspects of Zia's ambitions; for him Afghanistan was just one battlefield in a global war. Letting the ISI take the lead role saved Casey the headache of operational details of a covert war as it also protected him from blame if anything went wrong.

The ISI recruited and trained Mujahideen from among the three million Afghan refugees in Pakistan. Peshawar and Quetta became the major centers for the Afghan Jihad. Although many secular and liberal Afghans also joined the fight against Soviet occupation, the

ISI showed preference for radical Islamist factions. The CIA provided money and arms and was content with taking credit in the United States for the successes of the Afghan "freedom fighters." From 1981 to 1983 the CIA's covert program was funded at the same level as Carter proposed—around $60 million a year from the United States, with a matching amount from Saudi Arabia.[100] But beginning in 1984 funding levels increased dramatically.

A colorful Texan congressman, Charlie Wilson, adopted the cause of the Afghan Mujahideen, partly under the influence of Joanne Herring, the Texas socialite. Wilson was the senior Democrat on the Defense Appropriations Subcommittee of the House Appropriations Committee. He pushed a $40 million increase in funding through Congress just as Casey persuaded the Saudis to raise their contribution to $75 million for 1984 and to $100 million in 1985. Increased Saudi commitment required the United States to increase its contribution because of the matching funds agreement already in place.

There was another big increase in the fall of 1984. On October 11, 1984, Casey proposed to the Saudis that each country provide $250 million for the next year to handle larger Soviet offensives expected in the spring and to bring increasing pressure on the Soviets. This was a huge jump. Two weeks later Casey sent word to the Pakistanis and the Saudis that the United States was planning to spend $250 million in 1985. By the end of the year Wilson was urging that the US commitment go up to $300 million.[101]

These vast amounts were almost entirely funneled through the ISI, which by the mid-1980s had become several times larger than its original size. Not surprisingly, then, the ISI really liked Casey. Brigadier Mohammad Yousaf, who ran the Afghan operation, appreciated the autonomy Casey allowed his agency. "Whatever his personal motivations," he wrote of Casey: "the result for us was always positive. He would often turn to his staff who were perhaps disputing some request of ours with the words: No, the General knows what he wants"—a reference to ISI's General Rahman.[102]

According to Yousaf, the CIA supported the Mujahideen by buying arms, ammunition, and equipment. "It was their secret arms procurement branch that was kept busy," he wrote. But "a cardinal rule

. . . . .

of Pakistan's policy" barred the Americans from being "involved with the distribution of funds or arms once they arrived in the country. No Americans ever trained or had direct contact with the Mujahideen, and no American official ever went inside Afghanistan."[103]

The Pakistanis justified operational control not by acknowledging their separate agenda but by claiming that the CIA was not competent to deal with the ground realities of Afghanistan. "I stress that the CIA's strength was in their access to sophisticated technology," explained Yousaf. "If it was possible to solve a problem by technical means they would get the answer, but if military decisions had to be made on the basis of experience, military knowledge, or even applied military common sense, then in my view few CIA officers could come up with workable solutions," he observed.[104]

The CIA and other American supporters of the Pakistan-based insurgency focused solely on Soviet losses. The Red Army lost more men and equipment than they had in any military engagement since World War II. Once the Mujahideen had been provided shoulder-borne Stinger surface-to-air missiles, the Soviet ability to keep the insurgents at bay diminished further.

Meanwhile, Pakistan took advantage of its operational autonomy to pursue its own agenda. Barely a year after the United States resumed large-scale aid to Pakistan and got deeply involved in the Afghan war, the State Department's Bureau of Intelligence and Research noted concern about Pakistan's nuclear program. The Pakistanis, it said, "have not slowed their efforts to get the bomb," and it reported that there was "new evidence of significant Peoples Republic of China assistance on at least the weapons-design side."[105]

This intelligence resulted in the two visits to Pakistan from US Presidential Envoy Vernon Walters, during which Zia assured him of being "honorable" and promising not to build a nuclear weapon. George Shultz, who had replaced Haig as secretary of state, pressed Reagan to raise the matter with Zia during his state visit in December 1982. But the US president was still content to accept Zia's word of honor and continued to maintain close relations with him because of Pakistan's centrality to the war against the Soviets in Afghanistan.

......

The nuclear program was not Pakistan's only clandestine activity to which the United States chose to turn a blind eye. Washington also ignored Indian accusations about Pakistan's role in fomenting rebellion among Sikhs in India's Punjab state. Soon after the beginning of America's augmented assistance program to Pakistan, a group of religious Sikhs started demanding a separate homeland, to be called Khalistan. Graffiti appeared in Delhi with the message, "The Sikhs Are a Nation." India asserted that Pakistan's ISI was funding the Khalistan campaign.

US media reports cited Sikh separatists speaking of establishing close ties with the Jamaat-e-Islami, a Pakistani fundamentalist organization active in supporting the Afghan Mujahideen. A branch of the Jamaat was also active in Kashmir. "One day the people of Kashmir will turn to Pakistan and we will benefit," Sikh activist Gajendra Singh was quoted as saying. "One thing is certain: the next war with Pakistan will result in a Pakistani Kashmir and a sovereign Khalistan."[106]

The Sikh insurgents resorted to terrorist tactics, resulting in harsh measures from the Indian government. An official Indian report spoke of "the encouragement, connivance and assistance of certain foreign powers" in the plans to create an independent Sikh state. "In time the militant movement would have developed into a full-scale insurgency which would have crippled the armed forces in any future confrontation across the borders," the report said. The border referred to was obviously Pakistan, the only country that shares the Punjab border with India.[107]

India asserted that the Sikh militants were well trained and well disciplined militarily. Their training was allegedly carried out in what were ostensibly religious camps in the Pakistani-controlled portion of Kashmir, in the Indian state of Jammu and Kashmir, and in Sikh temples across India. The report quoted a number of Sikh exiles as having said that Pakistan was a natural ally and that it had promised aid. But Pakistan denied involvement although Zia said that gunrunners could have smuggled arms into Punjab without the government's knowledge.[108]

The United States decided to ignore allegations of Pakistani involvement in the Sikh uprising. When Prime Minister Indira

Gandhi was killed in October 1984 by an enraged Sikh bodyguard, Washington tried to calm the ensuing India-Pakistan tensions without publicly acknowledging Pakistan's ties to Sikh militants. The Khalistan militancy would end years later, only after India initiated retaliatory terrorist strikes in Pakistani Punjab. By then twenty thousand people had been killed in India along with dozens in Pakistan. The collateral damage of the war to bleed the Soviets had spread out of Afghanistan. A Pakistan-backed insurgency in Kashmir was soon to follow.

Another casualty of the focus on Afghanistan was the human rights situation inside Pakistan. Thousands of political prisoners languished in jail, and after anti-Zia demonstrations in Sindh in 1983, more than one hundred people were sentenced to flogging in a single application of "Islamic law." Dozens of demonstrators were killed.[109] US Defense Secretary Caspar Weinberger arrived in Pakistan amidst the riots, describing them an "internal problem they seem to be dealing with." Weinberger said Pakistan occupied a "critical strategic position" against the Soviet Union. "They have a strong military," he declared, "and we are trying to strengthen it all the more."[110]

Zia had modeled the now-expanded ISI on the Soviet KGB or the East German Stasi, which tried to control their citizens as part of their effort to maintain national security. The ISI had become the arbiter of Pakistani patriotism. The intelligence apparatus spied widely on Pakistani citizens, imprisoning those who disagreed with the government's policies. The media was fully controlled and was often used to build a specific national narrative. Benazir Bhutto, the daughter of the elected prime minister Zia had toppled and executed, became an internationally celebrated political prisoner before being forced into exile in London in January 1984.

In 1985 the United States completed its disbursement of the $3.2 billion aid package for Pakistan. At this point Pakistan and the administration were forced to address Congress's nuclear proliferation concerns before approving additional aid. Pakistani diplomats as well as officials in the Reagan White House supported an amendment to the Foreign Aid Bill that would help get around the restrictions of the Symington and Glenn Amendments that forbade aid to countries with unsafeguarded nuclear programs.

Named after Senator Larry Pressler, a Republican from South Dakota, the Pressler Amendment allowed aid to flow to Pakistan as long as the US president certified on an annual basis that Pakistan did not possess a nuclear explosive device. In a letter to Zia that praised his contribution to the war against the Soviets, Reagan warned of "serious consequences" if Pakistan enriched uranium beyond 5 percent.[111] The hopes expressed by Haig that US-provided advanced conventional weapons would keep Pakistan from continuing with a nuclear program had, by now, proved futile.

Within months of the Pressler Amendment's adoption the US Defense Intelligence Agency reported that Pakistan had produced an atomic weapon in October 1985 "with on sight technical assistance" from China. The US intelligence community believed that Pakistan was producing enough highly enriched uranium for at least one atomic weapon.[112] But still the administration committed itself to providing $4.02 billion in aid to Pakistan over the next six years, including additional F-16 aircraft.

The White House presumed that Pakistan would hold uranium enrichment levels below 5 percent to continue qualifying for US assistance. This gave Pakistan the capability for going nuclear later but enabled the US president to certify that Pakistan did not, as of yet, possess nuclear weapons. Each year, from 1986 to 1988, Reagan signed the certificate required under the Pressler Amendment to keep the aid flowing. His successor, George H.W. Bush, did the same in 1989.

By the end of Reagan's term the CIA had spent $2 billion in aiding Afghan resistance fighters through Pakistan's ISI. The Saudis had officially matched the amount and had also provided additional support of an undisclosed amount. As the idea of an Islamic Holy War became popular, volunteers from several Arab and Muslim countries flocked to Pakistan to fight alongside the Afghans. These warriors, most of whom constituted Al-Qaeda and its associated terrorist groups after the collapse of the Soviet Union, brought in extra funding from private Saudi contributors. At one point some estimated that these private donations to the Afghan Jihad contributed $25 million per month.[113]

The United States had succeeded in bleeding the Soviet Union in Afghanistan. The United States had hoped to roll back what had been expanding Soviet influence in the third world, and so Afghanistan, for the United States, was just the larger of a series of covert wars—the others being fought in Nicaragua, Cambodia, Ethiopia, and Angola—that were meant to punish the Soviet Union and inflict a heavy cost in men, money, and prestige. The CIA estimated that Soviet costs between 1981 and 1986 in Afghanistan, Angola, and Nicaragua amounted to about $13 billion.[114] Soviet casualties in Afghanistan included 13,310 dead and 35,478 wounded.[115]

By contrast, the United States lost no soldiers in its proxy engagements. By 1987–1988 the Americans had achieved their objective in Afghanistan. The Soviets, now led by the reformer Mikhail Gorbachev, were willing to negotiate a way out of their Afghan quagmire. But Pakistan's more expansive plans for permanent influence in Afghanistan and for extended Jihad to Kashmir were still incomplete. Under US direction Zia agreed to indirect talks in Geneva with the Soviet-installed Afghan government. But he dragged the talks so as to strengthen the hands of Mujahideen groups he wanted to see in control of Kabul later.

Zia had organized controlled parliamentary elections in 1985 and appointed a civilian prime minister whom he expected to be weak and compliant. The new prime minister, Muhammad Khan Junejo, was a conservative provincial politician who slowly extended press freedom and demanded the removal of martial law. Although Zia kept Junejo from being briefed about Afghanistan for almost a year, the prime minister insisted on reexamining Zia's assumptions about the Afghan war.[116]

Like many Pakistani civilians, Junejo recognized that the country could not afford the burden of three million permanent Afghan refugees; the presence of a large number of trained militants on its soil undermined the writ of the Pakistani state. Further, arms intended for the Mujahideen had seeped into Pakistani cities and towns, producing a culture of violence. Drug trafficking had exponentially increased, as areas bordering Afghanistan were allowed to descend into lawlessness. From Junejo's perspective, Pakistan needed an international agreement leading to a Soviet withdrawal and the repatriation of Afghan refugees and militants.

Junejo also allowed Benazir Bhutto to return from exile to a rapturous welcome from millions of supporters. During her exile she had made a favorable impression on Western journalists, diplomats, and some US congressmen. Although she was careful not to criticize the United States upon her return to Pakistan, Bhutto joined Junejo in questioning the wisdom of Pakistan's Afghan policy.

Despite Zia's reservations and the ISI's objections, in April 1988 Pakistan and Afghanistan's communist government signed an agreement, with the United States and the Soviet Union as guarantors. The Geneva Accord set a timetable for the complete withdrawal of Soviet troops from Afghanistan between May 15, 1988 and February 15, 1989. The Americans cheered what was clearly a Soviet defeat, but for Pakistan, war was far from over.

The Pakistanis had given more than two-thirds of the resources the CIA provided to Islamist groups.[117] As the Soviets began to withdraw, the ISI worked in tandem with these groups to exert control over Afghanistan. "We have earned the right to have [in Kabul] a power which is very friendly toward us," Zia told American scholar Selig Harrison. "We have taken risks as a frontline state and we will not permit a return to the prewar situation, marked by a large Indian and Soviet influence and Afghan claims on our own territory."[118]

Zia predicted that "The new power will be really Islamic, a part of the Islamic renaissance which, you will see, will someday extend itself to the Soviet Muslims." But he did not live to lead Pakistan as it attempted to realize this dream. On August 17, 1988, he was killed in a mysterious plane crash along with General Rahman; the US ambassador to Pakistan, Arnold Raphel; and the chief of the US military mission to Pakistan, Brigadier General Herbert Wassom. Several other Pakistan army generals and officers were also killed.

Conspiracy theorists, later joined by one of Zia's daughters, accused the United States of eliminating Zia to preempt the Islamic renaissance he had spoken about. Once again the United States had

·····

supported a Pakistani military dictator by providing several billion dollars in economic aid and upgrading Pakistan's military hardware. American leaders had chosen to trust Zia's word against hard intelligence about Pakistan's nuclear program. However, not only had the United States failed to influence Pakistani policies, even the followers of the dictator it supported were not willing to see America positively. Pakistan's state ideology and its perceived national interest were simply not congruent with those of the United States.

But not all American officials had been blind to the divergence in US and Pakistani interests, especially toward the end of the anticommunist Jihad in Afghanistan. After traveling through Afghanistan and Pakistan, Edmund McWilliams, a Foreign Service officer, had alerted the US government of the rising peril, noting that "Gulbeddin Hekmatyar—backed by officers in ISI's Afghan bureau, operatives from the Muslim brotherhood's Jamaat e Islami, officers from Saudi intelligence, and Arab volunteers from a dozen countries—was moving systematically to wipe out his rivals in Afghanistan" ahead of the Soviet withdrawal.[119]

Like Archer Blood, whose telegram documenting Pakistan army atrocities in Bangladesh had no effect on Nixon, McWilliams was ignored. The Reagan administration wanted to celebrate its triumph against the Soviets, not worry about what Pakistan might do next. McWilliams was sent back to Washington a few months later, as Afghanistan descended into civil war soon after the Soviet withdrawal.

US assistance to Pakistan was suspended in 1990 after George H. W. Bush failed to certify, as required by the Pressler Amendment, that Pakistan did not possess nuclear weapons. The collapse of the Soviet Union by 1991 significantly decreased US interest in both Afghanistan and Pakistan until the terrorist attacks in New York and Washington, DC, on September 11, 2001. Ironically, the origins of those terrorist attacks could be traced to the radical Islamist groups that had been raised and trained in Pakistan with covert US funds.

Chapter Six

Denial and Double Game

On May 14, 1992, I received a phone call from a diplomat serving at the US embassy in Islamabad. He was requesting an urgent meeting at my office in the prime minister's secretariat. US Ambassador Nicholas Platt had met Prime Minister Nawaz Sharif earlier in the day and delivered an important letter from Secretary of State James Baker. "Sharif did not read the letter in the ambassador's presence and seemed uninterested in its contents," said the caller.

He wanted to brief me on the letter's contents in my capacity as special assistant to the prime minister. I would then be able to draw attention to the US message so that it was fully understood within the Pakistani government.

Within an hour of the telephone conversation the diplomat arrived with copies of Baker's letter to Sharif and a summary of Platt's conversation with Sharif. The George H. W. Bush administration had been conveying their concerns about Pakistan's support for terrorism in Indian-controlled parts of Kashmir. Baker was now threatening that unless that support discontinued, the United States might declare Pakistan a state sponsor of terrorism.

"We have information indicating that ISI and others intend to continue to provide material support to groups that have engaged in terrorism," read the letter dated May 10. "I must take that information very seriously," Baker noted but discounted Pakistani claims that support for the Kashmiri militants came from private groups and Islamist parties and not from the government or its agencies. He appreciated Sharif's earlier promises that "Pakistan will take steps to distance itself from terrorist activities against India."

According to Baker, US law required applying "an onerous package of sanctions" against "states found to be supporting acts of international terrorism and I have the responsibility of carrying out that legislation."[1] When he delivered the letter, Platt made it clear that the United States did not believe official Pakistani claims that the Islamists were acting on their own. His talking points, handed to the prime minister in writing for effect, said that the United States was "very confident" of its information. "Your intelligence service, the Inter-Services Intelligence Directorate, and elements of the Army, are supporting Kashmiri and Sikh militants who carry out acts of terrorism," Platt affirmed. This support, he continued, comprised "providing weapons, training, and assistance in infiltration." To remove all ambiguity, he insisted that "We're talking about direct, covert Government of Pakistan support."

Platt went through a list of earlier Pakistani explanations and clarified that none of them applied. "This is not a case of Pakistani political parties, such as Jamaat-e-Islami, doing something independently but of organs of the Pakistani government controlled by the President, the Prime Minister and the Chief of Army Staff." He anticipated the assertion that the United States' information may have come from the Indians and said that it was based exclusively on US intelligence and not on Indian sources. "Please consider the serious consequences to our relationship if this support continues," the ambassador had pleaded, apparently to an uninterested Pakistani prime minister. The US did not want to take such a drastic step as to place Pakistan on the American government's state sponsors of terrorism list but could not ignore the requirements of the law. "You must take concrete steps," Platt exhorted Sharif, "to curtail assistance to militants and not allow their training camps to operate in Pakistan" or in Pakistani-controlled parts of Kashmir.[2]

The scope of sanctions Pakistan would face as a state sponsor of terrorism was far wider than the ones that had been imposed over its nuclear program. US law forbade the slightest indirect assistance to terrorist states. This meant shutting down funding from the IMF, the World Bank, and other international financial institutions as well as barriers to bilateral trade. Being designated as a state sponsor of terrorism would also have meant the end of export-import bank financing for projects in Pakistan.

After being briefed about the US warning, I went to Sharif and explained that he should not take it lightly. He retrieved Baker's letter, still unopened, from his drawer and asked me to coordinate a meeting of senior officials from his secretariat, the foreign office, and the armed forces. The original letter was immediately passed on to the foreign secretary, Shehryar Khan, who arranged for all concerned to assemble at the prime minister's house a few days later.

Sharif opened the meeting by asking me to read the letter out loud and to summarize its implications. Everyone, including the army chief, General Asif Nawaz, listened carefully. No one spoke while Sharif gave instructions to his staff regarding snacks he wanted served to all of us—Sharif often asked for specific food items during meetings, as if it helped him concentrate his mind. As plates of food were passed around, he asked if anyone had comments or suggestions. The ISI director-general, Lieutenant General Javed Nasir, was the first to speak.

Nasir, a tall man with a flowing beard, often flaunted his religious piety. He began by blaming the "Indo-Zionist lobby" in Washington for America's changed attitude toward Pakistan. Platt, he said, was a Jew and could not be trusted. He insisted that Pakistan demand evidence from the United States of its allegations. I gently pointed out that Platt came from a well-known New York Protestant family. Undeterred, Nasir continued with his argument that the Jihad in Kashmir was at a critical stage and could not be disrupted. "We have been covering our tracks so far and will cover them even better in the future," Nasir said, "These are empty threats." The United States could not declare Pakistan a terrorist state because of "our strategic importance." The Saudis and Pakistan were America's only allies in the greater Middle East, he averred, so the United States needed Pakistan to deal with the changing situation in Muslim Central Asia after the Soviet Union collapsed. "All we need to do is to buy more time and

......

improve our diplomatic effort," Nasir emphasized. "The focus should be on Indian atrocities in Kashmir, not on our support for the Kashmiri resistance."[3]

Sharif agreed with Nasir's assessment, which reflected the consensus of the meeting. Shehryar and I were the only ones who argued that Pakistan needed to reconsider Pakistani support for Kashmiri militants. It would undermine Pakistani diplomacy, get Pakistan labeled a terrorism sponsor, and was unlikely to result in a settlement of the Kashmir dispute. Shehryar said that Pakistan would "probably be more successful by focusing on diplomacy and political action" in favor of the Kashmiris instead of "setting off bombs." Nasir's response was that "the Hindus do not understand any language other than force."

Nasir and others dismissed these concerns and focused on the need for "better management of relations with the U.S." Sharif said that as long as Pakistan could be useful to the United States, the United States would remain favorably disposed toward Pakistan. The subsequent discussion shed some light on the views of various participants and institutions about dealing with the United States.

The ISI chief said the CIA needed the ISI. According to him the US intelligence community did not want to disrupt the relationship built during the Afghan Jihad. "We know how to take care of the CIA," he said, adding, "We know what they need and we give it to them in bits and pieces to keep them happy." Sharif said that it was important to talk to Americans nicely while "doing whatever you have to." There were always enough disagreements among American policy makers that "anyone can find someone who supports them," he contended.

According to Sharif, Pakistan could deal with allegations of sponsoring terrorism by reaching out to the American media and Congress. He would allocate $2 million "as the first step" for that purpose and announced at the meeting that I would be in charge of this expanded lobbying effort. He did not allow me to speak, and I had to wait until the next day to turn down the assignment.

The final word came from the army chief. Nawaz said that it was not in Pakistan's interest to get into a confrontation with the United

States, but "We cannot shut down military operations against India either." The army chief suggested that Pakistan get off the hook with the United States by making some changes in its pattern of support for Kashmiri militancy without shutting down the entire clandestine operation—and that is precisely the policy Pakistan adopted over the next few years.

The following day I informed the prime minister's principal secretary that the response to the American demarche alarmed me and that I wanted to resign. Sharif came back with the suggestion that instead of resigning and, thus, creating a negative political story, I should go as Pakistan's ambassador to Sri Lanka. This provided a decent interval for both of us without causing embarrassment or speculation. By the time I returned from Sri Lanka in May 1993, General Nawaz had died from a heart attack and Sharif was on the verge of being removed from office in a palace coup.

On November 1992 Americans had elected Bill Clinton as their new president. The new US administration did not follow up on its predecessor's threat of declaring Pakistan a state sponsor of terrorism. Then, the election of a new government in Pakistan after Sharif's removal from office further wiped the slate clean. Pakistan's clandestine support for Kashmiri militants increased, and within a couple of years the ISI helped create and bring to power the Taliban in Afghanistan.

Within the Pakistani government the ISI's belief was reinforced that Pakistan did not need to fear crippling sanctions from the United States, even after intimidating warnings. Now, in addition to having nuclear weapons, Pakistan was home to groups that Americans considered terrorists.

★

ALTHOUGH THE DEATH of General Zia-ul-Haq in August 1988 changed Pakistan's politics, the army and ISI made sure that the country's policies remained the same. Instead of imposing martial law, the new army chief, General Aslam Beg, allowed the civilian chairman of the Senate, Ghulam Ishaq Khan, to ascend to the presidency as provided in the constitution. As a career civil servant, Ishaq had served in senior positions with all of Pakistan's military rulers and was especially close to Zia. The army trusted him to carry on with Pakistan's secret nuclear program in addition to promoting Islamist rule in Afghanistan and confrontation with India.

Ishaq and Beg scheduled parliamentary elections for November, knowing that these would most likely be won by the Pakistan People's Party (PPP), led by Benazir Bhutto. After executing Bhutto's father, Zia had violently repressed the party. For eleven years Pakistan's soldiers had been told to view the party as "the enemy." Because of this, Beg viewed the thirty-five-year-old Benazir as eager to reduce the army's influence, develop ties with India, and end the war in Afghanistan without insisting on installing there a government of Pakistan's choice.

Beg also considered Bhutto too close to the Americans for comfort. Like all Pakistanis, she was unlikely to bring Pakistan's nuclear program to an end. But Beg thought she might accept international inspections that could preempt his own plans for leveraging nuclear capability.

Beg had told me while Zia was alive that "Pakistan needs to show its spine" to the United States. He believed that a nuclear Pakistan could tie up with Iran and China in order to create a third pole in a multipolar world.

The head of the ISI, Lieutenant General Hamid Gul, shared Beg's vision of Pakistan as a major power and his paranoia about American influence. He had grand designs for projecting Pakistan's power into Afghanistan and onward into Central Asia as well as for breaking up India after liberating Kashmir. According to Gul, the ISI could wage covert wars throughout the region and change Pakistan's fortunes. He shared these views openly with Pakistanis and created a massive network of local politicians and journalists to build national consensus around these beliefs.

Gul's dream had one fatal weakness, however. Pakistan's Afghan operation had benefited from vast inputs of American and Saudi money. The United States would not likely continue funding the ISI in projects that did not advance American interests. But like all

*****

dreamers, Gul was undeterred. Instead of realizing that a great power cannot be built through other nations' money, he determined that his grandiose plans could be implemented if the ISI controlled an elected civilian government. Elected civilians would somehow raise the money for the ISI to spend on its inflated covert operations.

The Americans were unaware of Gul's ideological predilections and fantasies. A Defense Intelligence Agency (DIA) profile described Gul as "a powerful mediator" who had organized "the unruly Afghan Alliance Leaders into a viable institution." He was characterized as "a sincere and caring individual who is attempting to do what is best for the Afghan Alliance as well as for Pakistan." In what turned out to be a massive miscalculation, the DIA believed that Gul was "a strong supporter of Pakistan's ties to the U.S; is generally friendly towards the U.S. and the West and very comfortable with foreigners." The US intelligence community thought that Gul did not "have any particular political contacts of any significance within Pakistan."[4] They were wrong on all counts.

As soon as parliamentary elections were announced, Gul and the ISI initiated efforts to create an anti-Bhutto alliance of conservative politicians and Islamists. Gul and his deputy, Brigadier Imtiaz Ahmed told journalists that the ISI had intelligence about Bhutto promising the Americans to "roll back" the nuclear program. They claimed that she would prevent a Mujahideen victory in Afghanistan and stop plans for Jihad in Kashmir in its tracks, though they offered no evidence for their allegations. Although Jihad had not yet started in Kashmir, the ISI was apparently preparing for it. The domestic political struggle had become intertwined with the army's ideological national security agenda.

The PPP won the election, and Benazir Bhutto became the first elected woman leader of an Islamic country. But the ISI-backed Islamic Democratic Alliance (IJI) secured control of Punjab, Pakistan's largest province and home to most of its soldiers and civil servants. Nawaz Sharif, scion of a rich Kashmiri family from Lahore and a protégé of Zia, rose to national prominence as chief minister of the province. His campaign had been based on nationalist rhetoric against India and the United States. He had also called for declaring

* * * * *

Pakistan a nuclear weapons power and for openly supporting the Mujahideen in Kashmir.[5]

Sharif's election campaign had unleashed a xenophobic Pakistani nationalism tinged with more Islamism than had previously been the norm in Pakistani politics. Ideas nurtured under Zia's authoritarian rule now had a democratic manifestation. Beg and Gul could keep Bhutto in check by pitting the Punjab provincial government against the prime minister. The ISI-manipulated Pakistani media portrayed Bhutto as an American "agent of influence." Sharif described her publicly as "a security risk."

Bhutto began her stint in office by releasing political prisoners and removing restrictions on the media. But most members of her government had spent the preceding decade either in prison or in forced exile, neither of which were good training grounds for government. As a result, they fumbled as they took office, and the ISI-backed opposition gave Bhutto little room to maneuver. But she was widely admired in the United States. Although she approached foreign relations carefully, making great effort not to upset the military, her calls for "a new era in relations" with India did not sit well with the army's hawks.[6]

Soon after Bhutto's inauguration as prime minister, the Soviets completed their withdrawal from Afghanistan in February 1989. The ISI had predicted that once the Soviets withdrew, the Mujahideen would displace the Soviet-backed government within two to three months. The Americans had deferred to the ISI's judgment. But the Afghan communist government, led by Najibullah, proved more resilient. Efforts by the Mujahideen to gain control of Jalalabad, a major Afghan city close to the border with Pakistan, failed miserably. Bickering among the Mujahideen became public, as did complaints from moderate Afghans against the ISI's support for Islamist factions.

Bhutto proposed a political solution that would enable the creation of a transition government in Kabul. But the ISI, led by Gul, persisted with their plan to use force to install their favorite Islamist groups in power. Bhutto's civilian Intelligence Bureau obtained evidence of Gul's clandestine political activities against the government, and she then removed Gul from the ISI, though Beg immediately reassigned him to a major military command.[7] Gul was able to direct Sharif and his domestic opposition as well as interact with Afghan Mujahideen commanders even though he was no longer formally the head of ISI.

During her state visit to Washington in June 1989 Bhutto received a warm welcome at the White House. At the state dinner President George H. W. Bush spoke about a relationship that went back to 1971, "when she attended Harvard and came with her dad to the United Nations." Bhutto described Washington as "one of the great citadels of democracy" and spoke of the prospects of close ties between Pakistan and the United States based not on geopolitical considerations but instead on shared values.[8]

She also became the only Pakistani prime minister to be invited to address a joint session of Congress. The US media recognized Bhutto's "claim on American backing" on the ground of her adherence to democracy and moderation in the Islamic world.[9] But in private talks with US officials she realized that the Americans did not think she was fully in control, and they could not offer her any help in asserting authority.

The United States had also learned that Pakistan was enriching uranium in violation of Zia's promise of capping enrichment at 5 percent, and Bhutto was unable to promise that enrichment would be capped. Bush agreed to certify one last time that Pakistan did not possess nuclear weapons in return for Bhutto's commitment that Pakistan would not produce an atomic bomb, but while the tough opposition that Sharif put up at home distracted her, Pakistan violated that commitment without her full knowledge. She asserted later that she was told about Pakistan's nuclear enrichment program but not informed of the exact level of enrichment.

By the end of the year spontaneous protests against tainted elections in Kashmir grew into a violent anti-Indian insurgency. Pakistan's religious parties competed with one another to raise funds in support of various insurgent groups. The United States then started receiving intelligence of the ISI's complicity in the Kashmir insurgency. Deputy National Security Adviser Robert Gates traveled to South Asia in May 1990 to prevent the situation in Kashmir from degenerating into a full-blown war between India and Pakistan.

Gates cautioned Indian leaders against using force against Pakistan and proposed a series of confidence-building measures. In Islamabad he stressed the American view that "India would soundly defeat Pakistan in any military clash." He described Pakistani support for the insurgency in Kashmir as "an extremely dangerous activity." But Pakistani officials flatly denied that they were helping the Kashmiri resistance. Ishaq was stiff during the discussions, and Beg was at times "accusatory and confrontational." Gates also shared American concerns about Pakistan pressing ahead with its nuclear program contrary to its promises.

CIA analysts had concluded that Pakistan had taken the final step toward "possession" of a nuclear weapon by machining uranium metal into bomb cores. Washington was certain that "Pakistan had crossed the line." But Ishaq and Beg told Gates that Pakistan's nuclear capability had not advanced. Unless Pakistan melted down the bomb cores that it had produced, Gates warned, "Bush would not be able to issue the Pressler amendment certification needed to permit the continued flow of military and economic aid." When the Pakistanis denied that they had "crossed the line," Gates commented, "If it waddles like a duck, if it quacks like a duck, then maybe it is a duck."[10]

The Pakistanis had lied to Gates on both issues he raised in Islamabad. Although Bhutto was the best disposed toward the United States among Pakistan's major power players, she did not control the levers of power. The State Department and the CIA did not see any advantage in trying to secure the Pakistan military's subordination to an elected civilian; instead, they effectively leaned in the military's favor by directly discussing major issues with Beg and other generals, assuming that the military could deliver on key issues of US interest —Afghanistan, nuclear weapons, and security in South Asia.

This view was based on the camaraderie that had evolved between the American and Pakistani militaries and intelligence agencies during the war against the Soviets. However, US diplomats and spies had failed to grasp the ideological undercurrents reflected in the conduct of Beg and Gul. Robert Oakley, who served as US ambassador in Islamabad from 1988 to 1991, admitted years later that "the United States made a mistake in continuing to support the largely ISI-driven Pakistan policy on Afghanistan."[11] Richard Armitage, assistant secretary of defense for international security affairs at the time, said, "We drifted too long in 1989 and failed to understand the independent role that the ISI was playing."[12]

The mistake proved costly. The ISI orchestrated public sentiment in favor of its actions in Afghanistan and Kashmir as well as in the nuclear sphere, making rational debate on Pakistan's policy choices impossible. Anyone disagreeing with any element of these policies faced attacks from the agency's allies in domestic politics and the media. The frenzy of Islamist mobs in Pakistan's major cities now reinforced denial in meetings with foreign officials.

In August 1990 Ishaq dissolved Parliament and dismissed Bhutto's government under presidential powers that Zia had written into the constitution. The decision to remove Bhutto was carefully timed to minimize the possibility that Washington might speak up in her favor.[13] The dismissal was announced four days after the Iraqi invasion of Kuwait and had been engineered by the army leadership. The *Washington Post* reported that "Some Pakistani generals are said to be eager to step up a proxy war with India."[14] But the prospect of war in the Persian Gulf distracted the United States. Although the *New York Times* saw Bhutto's ouster as "the defeat of democracy in Pakistan," the US government let it slide, seeing it as an internal Pakistan affair.[15]

The military supported Sharif even more directly in the 1990 election. Beg solicited funds from bankers and businessmen, ostensibly for ISI covert national security operations, and then funneled them to Sharif and several parliamentary candidates from his party. With this help, Sharif was elected prime minister with a thumping majority. Bhutto alleged that the ISI had stolen the election for Sharif and the Islamic Alliance.[16] Years later Beg and the ISI director-general, Lieutenant General Asad Durrani, admitted before the Supreme Court of Pakistan about the ISI's role in that election, claiming they had acted in the national interest.[17]

Sharif had run an even more intensely nationalist campaign than he had two years earlier. A "Hindu-Jewish alliance" in the United States was targeting Pakistan, his party claimed. Newspaper advertisements averred that the United States wanted to prevent Pakistan

.....

from becoming a nuclear power, which was its right and destiny. There was much bombast about resisting Indian hegemony that the United States sought to impose on Pakistan.

Beg and Gul had set the anti-American tone of the campaign with a purpose. The White House was due to make a decision on the annual certification about Pakistan's nuclear program as required by Congress. Both the ISI and the Pakistan Foreign Office had assumed that the United States still needed Pakistan because of its interest in Afghanistan and Central Asia. Thus, the fear of a rising tide of anti-Americanism was meant to scare Washington that it might lose Pakistan. The Pakistanis thought their noise would nudge Bush into certifying again that Pakistan did not possess nuclear weapons, and this would keep aid flowing, notwithstanding US concerns about uranium enrichment and building weapons cores.

The assessment in Islamabad proved wrong. Just days before the Pakistani election Bush refused certification, triggering sanctions on US aid under the Pressler Amendment. Bush and his advisers saw their decision as a legal matter: Pakistan had crossed the threshold beyond which verbal assurances could no longer be the basis of a presidential determination of the country's nuclear program. Bush felt he could not lie to Congress in the presence of the overwhelming evidence US intelligence had collected.

Likewise, the United States had failed to recognize that no Pakistani government could curtail the nuclear program. Having acquired the bomb, expecting Pakistan to give it up was unrealistic; instead, this was the time for the United States to accept Pakistan's nuclear status as a fait accompli. If nuclear weapons were Pakistan's ultimate guarantee against its psychological fears against India, that purpose had been achieved. Rather than limiting itself to implementing Pressler sanctions while Pakistan persisted with denial and bluster, the United States could have asked Pakistan to be honest about the nukes and then negotiated safeguards against further proliferation.

The Pakistani government continued to lie to the United States as well as to the Pakistani people. To the Americans, Pakistani officials insisted that there had been no change in Pakistan's nuclear status, whereas the Pakistani public was told that the Americans were discriminating against Pakistan by preventing access to technology available to India. The allegation of discrimination, however, was not really true. The Symington and Glenn Amendments had imposed the same restrictions on India as they had on Pakistan.

In fact, the Pressler Amendment had been written to help Pakistan get around the provisions of the Symington and Glenn Amendments. It had allowed Pakistan to continue to receive aid as long as the US president could certify that Pakistan had not crossed the red line. Thus, Pakistan was not being victimized so the United States could help India. The issue was Pakistan's dependence on US aid: India had pursued nuclear weapons without making specific commitments to the United States because it did not accept conditional aid as Pakistan had done.

Americans had repeatedly told Pakistani leaders that Pakistan could not make the bomb and get aid at the same time, and Pakistan made and broke several promises about its nuclear program so as to keep the aid flowing. Bush had been "genuinely sad" when he could no longer certify that Pakistan did not possess a nuclear device.[18]

The administration had even tried to delay sanctions "to give the government the Pakistanis would elect in October 1990 a chance to deal with the nuclear problem."[19] But congressional opposition had prevailed, arguing that lowering standards for Pakistan would lead to an erosion of nuclear proliferation standards for all nations.

When the Pressler sanctions were imposed, Pakistan was the third-largest beneficiary of US aid. Despite Pakistan's protests that the sanctions amounted to an American abandonment of Pakistan, the United States softened the blow by continuing to disburse $1 billion in economic assistance for ongoing projects. Nonetheless, Pakistan lost approximately $300 million in annual arms and military supplies, although it did receive the remaining portion of the economic aid package for another three years after the sanctions went into effect. Pakistan was also allowed commercial purchases of military equipment until 1992.[20]

But after 1990 all that the Pakistani government told its citizens through the mass media was how the United States turned away from Pakistan and victimized it after Pakistan had helped America

.....

defeat the Soviet Union in Afghanistan. The United States made no serious effort to explain its perspective to Pakistanis. Over time even Americans started believing that the Pressler sanctions were somehow an American mistake that created a breach in an otherwise functional alliance.

Washington and Islamabad were still deadlocked over the nuclear program when the ISI escalated the Kashmir insurgency soon after Sharif's inauguration as prime minister. Afghanistan also continued to simmer, with the ISI continuing to push for an Islamist government in Kabul. US hopes of winning back Pakistan were raised somewhat when Sharif clashed with Beg over Pakistan's response to Iraq's occupation of Kuwait.

Beg wanted Pakistan to tilt in Iraq's favor and told an audience of Pakistani military officers that the Gulf War was part of "Zionist" strategy.[21] He spoke of the need for "strategic defiance" by medium-sized powers such as Iraq, Iran, and Pakistan, with the help of China, against the dictates of the United States. Such defiance, he argued, would protect the sovereignty of smaller nations. Islamists marched in Pakistani cities protesting against the United States, supporting Beg's point of view.

Sharif's associates suspected that Beg wanted to take over in a military coup after massive anti-American protests. But the Gulf War involved Saudi Arabia's interests, so for economic reasons, Sharif did not want to rupture relations with the kingdom. With the backing of the Pakistani president and several generals, Sharif named a successor to Beg two months ahead of his scheduled retirement date. American officials considered the new army chief, General Asif Nawaz, friendly toward the United States.

Seeing an opening, Sharif tried after the Gulf War to break the stalemate over the nuclear question. Foreign Secretary Shehryar Khan and I traveled to Washington to bridge the credibility gap in Pakistan's previous claims on the subject. Shehryar admitted on the record in an interview with the *Washington Post* that "Pakistan had the capability to make a nuclear bomb."[22] We expected that the United States and Pakistan could now discuss Pakistan's nuclear ambitions honestly instead of being bogged down in incredible denials.

· · · · ·

However, the United States did not see the official Pakistani admission as an opportunity to negotiate. This worked to the advantage of the covert operatives in Islamabad; the ISI argued that coming clean with the Americans was a mistake. Sharif was accused of going behind the backs of the army and the ISI to cut a deal with the United States. As had been the case with Benazir Bhutto, the national security establishment was unwilling to trust a civilian prime minister's conduct of foreign relations without the ISI scrutinizing him. By then Pakistan had became mired in what American journalist Steve Coll described as a "political culture of shadow games," in which the acronyms of intelligence agencies, such as MI (Military Intelligence), ISI (Inter-Services Intelligence) and IB (Intelligence Bureau) became part of everyday vocabulary. According to Coll, "Unproven reports" of secret wiretappings, video tapings, and sexual blackmail schemes were ubiquitous. "And nearly everyone of prominence believes his or her telephone is bugged," he added.[23]

The intelligence services had become Pakistan's kingmakers in addition to controlling insurgencies in Afghanistan and Kashmir. Developments in the former communist bloc in Europe, which culminated in the breakup of the Soviet Union, distracted the Bush administration. Pakistanis felt that their country and Afghanistan had fallen off the US radar. Sharif's ambassador to Washington, Abida Hussain, observed that at this stage US interest in Pakistan was no more compelling than the Pakistani interest in the Maldives.

Like several other judgments in Islamabad, this was also not an accurate reading of American policy. However, Pakistan dodged sanctions when Bill Clinton was elected US president in November 1992.

✦

CLINTON HAD "a fascination with India," according to Strobe Talbott, who served as his deputy secretary of state.[24] India had adjusted to the collapse of the Soviet Union more effectively than had Pakistan. It had backed away from socialism, opened its markets, and recognized the new status of the United States as the world's sole superpower. Clinton saw India's "resilient democracy, its vibrant

· · · · ·

high-tech sector, its liberal reforms that had begun to revitalize a statist and sclerotic economy, and its huge consumer market—as a natural beneficiary of globalization." He considered India "potentially a much more important partner for the United States than was then the case."[25]

Meanwhile, Pakistan's Foreign Office completely missed the emerging US-India entente. The army and the ISI insisted on demanding American engagement on the basis of Pakistan's "services" during the Cold War, and several US diplomats and generals still had good memories of their past interaction with Pakistanis. But they could not move relations forward solely on the basis of nostalgia for Kissinger's China trip or even the war that bled the Soviets in Afghanistan.

Benazir Bhutto's election for a second term as prime minister in 1993 provided an opportunity for a more realistic Pakistani foreign policy. Bhutto had little affection for Islamists who hated her and questioned her right to lead the country as a woman, though she had been dismissed from office previously for disagreeing with Pakistan's military. This time she wanted to exercise greater caution.

Sharif had put Bhutto's husband, Asif Zardari, in prison on myriad corruption charges that were withdrawn once Sharif's government was removed. Zardari had been targeted because jailing him was easier than arresting the more popular and charismatic Bhutto. But now he was seen as a political figure in his own right. He joined the government, first as minister for environment and then as minister for investment. Although he was portrayed and perceived as a venal figure, Zardari played an important role in defining economic growth as the Bhutto government's top priority.

The first spouse traveled around the world, soliciting investment. He proposed numerous changes in Pakistan's economic policies, making the country attractive for international business. Bhutto declared publicly that instead of soliciting aid, Pakistan would try to become more competitive in the global economic arena. But both Bhutto and Zardari had to contend first with Pakistan's stigma of terrorism. They soon discovered that opening up Pakistan for business was not going to be easy: the Pakistan military wanted to settle the Afghan and Kashmir issues before allowing the civilians of Pakistan to be part of globalization.

While India expanded its high-tech sector and allowed multinational corporations to set up shop, Pakistan focused on acquiring weapons from various sources. The Pentagon discovered Pakistan purchasing air-to-air missiles and their components from China in addition to extended-range antiship and antitank missiles.[26] The CIA reported nuclear cooperation between Pakistan and North Korea. An expensive submarines deal with France and a tanks purchase from Ukraine followed.

Bhutto struggled to rebuild the frayed relations with the United States. She handed over Ramzi Ahmed Yusuf, the key figure in the 1993 bombing of the New York World Trade Center, who was arrested in Pakistan on a tip from US intelligence.[27] Although this step earned praise from the US government, it was not enough to secure the removal of Pressler sanctions. But Bhutto managed to settle another Pakistani complaint with the Americans.

At the time of the aid cutoff in 1990 Pakistan had paid $658 million for seventy-one F-16 aircraft that could not be delivered once the sanctions were imposed. Assuming that the sanctions would end soon, the Pakistan military had not asked for the money back. Pakistan ended up paying for storage of twenty-eight planes at an American air base for over three years.

During a meeting with Clinton Bhutto secured an agreement to reimburse Pakistan in full with a combined package of military aid and cash. The military aid, worth $358 million, would be in the form of P-3 surveillance aircraft and TOW antitank missiles. The twenty-eight F-16s in storage would be sold to a third country, thus enabling Pakistan to use the cash to buy fighter jets from France.

Then, relations with the United States came to at a standstill when the ISI decided to end the Afghan civil war by supporting the Taliban. The Mujahideen groups had fought amongst themselves since 1992, when the collapse of the Soviet Union resulted in the end of the Najibullah regime in Afghanistan. Although Pakistan had extensively supplied weapons and advice to its protégés in the civil war, Mujahideen groups favored by Pakistan had failed to prevail. It was time for Pakistan to change tack. Instead, the ISI put its weight behind a group of religious students (Taliban is Pashtu for "students") who had challenged the warlords in the southeastern province of Kandahar.

The constructed narrative at the time presented the Taliban as pious, naïve, and well-meaning villagers who were reacting to the excesses of the warlords. But soon after their rise the US government received reports about "Pakistan's deep involvement in Afghan politics and Pakistan's evident role in the Taliban's recent military successes." US intelligence learned that the government of Pakistan and the ISI were "deeply involved in the Taliban take over in Kandahar and Qalat." Pakistan's efforts were meant to sabotage UN peace efforts by Mahmoud Mesteri, special envoy of the UN secretary general for Afghanistan.[28]

The ISI briefed Bhutto about the Taliban's rise as a local phenomenon. She worried about their reported misogyny and their propensity for violence. She asked me for my views on the ISI's analysis that they could bring peace to Afghanistan and secure Pakistan's interests. I said that the ISI had previously said the same thing about Pashtun warlord Gulbeddin Hekmatyar. Bhutto agreed but laughed, saying that we civilians could not stop the ISI even if we wanted to.

Another Bhutto adviser, Ijlal Zaidi, voiced concern about the Taliban's core beliefs. Zaidi had served among Pashtuns as a civil servant. He wondered whether madrasa students with a narrow worldview and no modern education were equipped to run a country. "They will ruin whatever is left of Afghanistan. They will kill Shias and then they will come after Pakistan," he said. The ISI's major-general, Aziz Khan, said he could not understand why so many people in the Bhutto government were so averse to the spread of Islam.

The Taliban took control of most of Afghanistan's territory and eventually marched into Kabul. Bhutto's interior minister, Nasirullah Babar, became the public face of Pakistani support for them. Initially the United States was also unperturbed by a strong Pashtun force unifying Afghanistan. American oil company Unocal started negotiating a gas pipeline from Turkmenistan to Pakistan through Afghanistan.[29] But by 1996 the Taliban's human rights violations and their

· · · · ·

hosting of Osama bin Laden and his Al-Qaeda network made the United States and the Taliban implacable foes.

In March 1996 the *New York Times* reported that Bhutto's government was having second thoughts about supporting the Taliban even though Babar continued to support them in public.[30] The ISI had moved its training facilities for Kashmiri Mujahideen into Afghanistan, where anti-American terrorists and Kashmiri Jihadists trained together.[31] The US State Department found that Harakat-ul-Ansar, a group active in Kashmir, was composed of "Afghan war veterans from Algeria, Tunisia, Sudan, Egypt, and other countries" and included between six to sixteen Americans.[32]

But the United States went along with Pakistan's insistence on distinguishing Kashmiri freedom fighters from global terrorists. While noting the ties between Harakat and Afghan war veteran Jalaluddin Haqqani, a US official observed that there was no indication that Harakat posed any threat to the United States "at this stage" or that it had "any plans to target the U.S. or any U.S. interests."[33]

Later, however, the CIA expressed concern over Harakat's "recent increase in its use of terrorist tactics against western targets and civilians and its efforts to reach out to sponsors of international terrorism such as Osama bin Laden and Muammar Qadhafi." The agency also cautioned that "they might undertake terrorist actions against civilian airliners."[34] According to the CIA's estimate, the ISI provided "at least $30,000—and possibly as much as $60,000—per month" to Harakat. At the US government's urging, the Bhutto government banned Harakat-ul-Ansar, but within days its leaders resurfaced at the head of a new organization called Harkat-ul-Mujahideen.

As America's interest in India grew, Pakistan's national security apparatus, particularly the ISI, became more hostile and defiant toward Washington. Conspiracy theories flourished. Media outlets closely linked to the ISI blamed even ethnic and sectarian violence in Pakistan on the CIA. In March 1995 two Americans working in the US consulate were killed as they drove from home to work.[35] In an editorial the *Wall Street Journal* blamed the attack on a minority in Pakistan that wanted "to build an isolationist wall against a world that still needs American leadership and friendship."[36]

. . . . .

The decision to sponsor Islamist groups for Jihad in Afghanistan and Kashmir made it impossible to prevent the Jihadis from using Pakistan as a base of operations for coordinating Jihad against other countries. Americans learned of at least four thousand militants—including Pakistanis, Indians, Arabs from several countries, and a small number of Americans—being trained by just one Jihadi group in making bombs, throwing hand grenades, and shooting assault weapons. A different militant organization group proudly boasted that its members killed in Tajikistan, the Philippines, Bosnia, and Kashmir. "We'll fight in any part of the world where Muslims are being victimized whether by Hindus, Christians, Jews or communists," declared the spokesman of yet another group.[37]

In response, a Western diplomat in Islamabad said, "The government at the highest levels is sufficiently frightened of these people, but its ability to crack down on them is very limited."[38] The Philippines government protested during Bhutto's visit to Manila that "Pakistanis were fighting alongside Muslim extremists battling for autonomy" in Mindanao, and Russia alleged that Pakistanis had been among Islamists fighting in Chechnya. Arab governments in Egypt, Algeria, and Jordan also identified their foes among those living in Pakistan since the anti-Soviet Afghan Jihad. But when the issue was raised in government meetings ISI and Interior Ministry officials dismissed the reports as "western propaganda."

Then, in November 1996, Bhutto was dismissed from office once again and Zardari was put behind bars. Parliamentary elections three months later brought Sharif back as prime minister, this time as head of the Pakistan Muslim League. Now, instead of being seen only as the political successor of Zia, he sought to claim the mantle of Jinnah.

Soon after coming to office for a second time Sharif launched what he described as a campaign to free Pakistan of dependence on the United States and international financial institutions. He asked Pakistanis working overseas to contribute to a fund in hard currency that would enable Pakistan to pay off its foreign debt. "Pakistan must break the begging bowl," he declared. Once Pakistan was free of debt, Sharif claimed, it could pursue its policies without fear of superpower pressure.

· · · · ·

The "improve the nation by paying off its debt" campaign was launched amid great fanfare and patriotic zeal. National television showed women taking off their gold bangles and other jewelry to help Pakistan regain its independence. Parallels were drawn between the debt repayment campaign and the sacrifices of early Muslims who gave up worldly possessions to support Prophet Muhammad in the early seventh century. But in the end the government raised only $178.3 million against a national debt of $35 billion. Sharif learned that appealing to individual patriotism was no substitute for sound economic policies or pragmatic international relations.

Even in the face of this debacle, hard-liners continued to push for minimal ties with the United States and confrontation with India. At the ISI's urging, Pakistan recognized the Taliban regime in Kabul soon after Sharif's election as prime minister in March 1997 as the legal government of Afghanistan and allowed them to open an embassy in Islamabad. A few months earlier, in July 1996, Osama bin Laden had moved to Afghanistan under Taliban protection and was organizing Al-Qaeda as a global network of Islamist terrorists. The United States wanted Pakistan to exercise its influence over the Taliban to seek bin Laden's extradition for several acts of terrorism, especially the 1998 attacks on US embassies in Africa and the 2000 attack on the USS *Cole*.

Over time Pakistan's relationship with the Taliban became a persistent irritant to US-Pakistan diplomacy. Pakistan was the only country with a Taliban embassy, although Saudi Arabia and the United Arab Emirates had also recognized their regime. At the United Nations the United States participated in efforts by several nations to isolate and sanction the Taliban. But Pakistan provided oil, subsidized by Saudi Arabia, and wheat to the Taliban.[39] Furthermore, the ISI engaged extensively with the Taliban, facilitating travel of their Jihadi allies from around the world through Pakistani airports.

US officials worried about Pakistan as the transit point for global terrorists. Liberal Pakistanis warned against blowback from Pakistan's continuing Afghan adventure. Taking the cue from Afghanistan, religious extremists in parts of Pakistan pushed for Sharia rule in their regions. As a result, violence spread in various parts of the country, especially in the port city of Karachi. When a Pakistani was convicted in a US court for terrorist killings outside CIA headquarters, in Karachi four Americans working for the Union Texas Oil Company were shot to death in retaliation.[40]

In March 1998 the US embassy's deputy chief of mission, Alan Eastham, met with senior Pakistani diplomat Iftikhar Murshed to express concern over Osama bin Laden's fatwā declaring war on the United States. Among the fatwā's signatories was Fazlur Rahman Khalil, a leader of Harakat-ul-Ansar, which had close ties to the ISI. Murshed insisted that although Pakistan provided support to the Taliban, it had little if any control over their actions. "If Pakistan held up wheat consignments to the Taliban," said the Pakistani diplomat, "the Taliban would say 'what the hell! We can smuggle enough wheat into Afghanistan to feed ourselves'."[41]

Murshed was effectively saying that Pakistan was no longer in control of its border with Afghanistan. In reality, however, it had made a conscious decision to keep the border open. Although the Durand Line ran through 1,640 miles of difficult mountainous terrain, there were only forty or so points where heavy vehicles could cross over. If Pakistan wanted to get serious, it could monitor these major routes, thereby making large-scale movement of arms, oil, or foodstuff impossible.

The Pakistani military had openly embraced the concept of "Strategic Depth," the notion that Pakistan's security against India lay in virtual control over Afghanistan. The Taliban could be obscurantist supporters of global terrorism who posed a threat to Pakistan, but as long as they refused an Indian presence, they helped assure Pakistan's national security. The United States, however, did not agree with Pakistan's reasons or actions in relation to Afghanistan; but Washington was not willing to apply more direct pressure on Pakistan to effectively blockade the Taliban.

In April 1998 Pakistan tested its nuclear-capable Ghauri missile. In response, the United States mulled over sanctions under US laws relating to proliferation of missile technology. Acquisition of the missile and related equipment and technology from foreign sources would trigger the sanctions.[42] Once again Pakistan was offered insufficient carrots and no sticks to induce it to cap its nuclear program.

......

An offer of thirty-eight F-16 fighter bombers that had been with-
held in the past convinced Pakistani officials that they, not the Americans, held the stronger cards in the game. "If great quantities of arms
did not dissuade Pakistan from developing nuclear arms despite its
assurance that it would refrain," asked Harvard academic Nathan
Glazer writing in the *New York Times*, "why would anyone believe
that lesser quantities—delivered when we have less leverage over
all—would have a different effect?"[43]

The nuclear issue took an entirely different turn when India
tested its nuclear weapons on May 11 and 13, 1998, thereby declaring
itself a nuclear power. Pakistani public opinion overwhelmingly favored Pakistan conducting its own tests.[44] Clinton then made an attempt to forestall Pakistan's tests by promising "economic, political
and security benefits" if Pakistan showed restraint.[45] He telephoned
and offered "planes, huge amounts of financial aid, and a prize certain to appeal to Sharif—an invitation for him to make an official
visit to Washington."

But, as Talbott later noted, the lure of money, praise, and gratitude
from around the world was far less powerful than Pakistan's fear of
India, having been instilled in Pakistanis for five decades. India had
"ratcheted up its fifty-year-old campaign to humiliate, intimidate, and
perhaps even eradicate" Pakistan, Talbott observed. It would have been
impossible for any Pakistani leader to refuse to test at this point.[46]
Sharif could not pass up the chance to become a national hero. Nuclear weapons would bring Pakistan—and Sharif—enormous prestige, as Pakistani public opinion overwhelmingly supported the tests.

On May 13 the State Department informed the White House that
Pakistan was ready to conduct its own tests. "Islamabad which has
accused Washington of 'complicity' in allowing the Indian nuclear
tests is increasingly less likely to heed US calls for restraint," Secretary of State Madeleine Albright told National Security Adviser
Sandy Berger.[47] No one in United States even considered the alternative of talking to both India and Pakistan and welcoming them in
the nuclear club.

Pakistanis also lacked imagination. They did not link their tests
with an offer to sign the Comprehensive Test Ban Treaty (CTBT)

......

and to act more responsibly as a nation by shutting down terrorism; instead in their meetings with the Americans, Pakistani officials railed against India. When Talbott traveled to Islamabad with the US Central Command (CENTCOM) commander, General Anthony Zinni, he found his meetings "a bracing experience." According to Talbott, Foreign Minister Gohar Ayub (son of Ayub Khan, the military dictator) "fidgeted" during his opening courtesies and then "unleashed a broadside that went on for nearly half an hour."

Pakistan was on the verge of becoming a declared nuclear weapons power, but its leaders were demonstrating that they were only a frenzied mob. Ayub gave Talbott "a history lesson featuring the perfidy of India going back to 1947." He called India a "habitual aggressor and hegemon" and described the United States as "a fair-weather friend." When Talbott spoke, Ayub and Foreign Secretary Shamshad Ahmad "rolled their eyes, mumbled imprecations under their breath, and constantly interrupted."[48]

Ayub accused the Clinton administration of being "more enamored than ever" with India and told the Americans that "you don't understand the Indian psyche." When Talbott tried to speak, Ahmad cut him off and said that "the NPT was dead. So was the CTBT. Those treaties had been sick before—now India had 'murdered' them." Ayub, therefore, rejected the offer of carrots. "Those rotting and virtually obsolete airplanes," he said, were "shoddy rugs you've tried to sell us before." The Pakistani people, he added, "would mock us if we accepted your offer. They will take to the streets in protest." Talbott calmly replied that Pakistanis were more likely to protest if they didn't have jobs.

"Mark my words," said Gohar Ayub, his lips pursed and his fists clenched, "now that India has barged its way into becoming the world's sixth nuclear power, it will not stop there. It will force itself into permanent membership of the UN Security Council." The Pakistani officials said that the international outrage over Indian nuclear tests would soon subside, implying that they expected Pakistan to be quickly forgiven as well, after its tests.

Ayub contemptuously rejected Talbott's claim that Pakistan already had the ability to deter its enemies without testing because the Indians knew it had nuclear bombs. "As any military man knows," he said, "before a weapon can be inducted into military service—even a water bottle—it must be tested." According to Talbott: "He meant the comment to carry particular weight, since he was the son of Mohammad Ayub Khan, the first in a series of generals to rule the country."[49]

Talbott and Zinni then had a much calmer exchange with the army chief, General Jehangir Karamat. In him, they detected "a subtle but discernible undertone of long-suffering patience bordering on scorn" for Pakistan's political leadership. But Karamat avoided hyperbole. He asked for "a new, more solid relationship" with the United States, in which there was no "arm twisting" or "forcing us into corners."

Further, the American arguments against testing did not impress the army chief, as he was also concerned about India's desire to "cut Pakistan down to size." In his view the ruling party in India sought to use nuclear intimidation to "solve the Kashmir problem once and for all" by forcing Pakistan to give up all claims to the disputed territory. The US officials understood that they had "gotten the same answer to our entreaties in both our meetings: a bombastic 'no' from the foreign ministry and a polite one from the cool customer in Rawalpindi."[50]

Talbott then described his conversation with Sharif as "a Hamlet act" that he found "convincing in its own way" but "rather pathetic." The prime minister said his own political survival was at stake. If he did what the Americans wanted—not test—Sharif claimed that Talbott would find himself dealing "not with a clean-shaven moderate like himself" but instead with an Islamic fundamentalist "who has a long beard."[51]

On the evening of May 28 Sharif announced in a televised speech that Pakistan had successfully exploded five nuclear devices earlier in the day. The US ambassador in Islamabad, Tom Simons, noted that Sharif blamed the international community for failing to restrain India, which in turn had forced Pakistan to go nuclear. He spoke of "tough times ahead" and called for "an era of austerity and simplicity" in anticipation of harsh international sanctions.

······

To show his solidarity with his people, Sharif said he would give up "the newly-opened and palatial Prime Minister's Secretariat building," which he proposed could be converted into a hospital, women's university, or some other charity use. Reporting on the speech to Washington, Simons quipped, "It remains to be seen how long Pakistanis will rally around the flag once international sanctions kick in, further challenging this already vulnerable economy." He described Sharif's notion that "Pakistanis will 'sacrifice' by giving up long cherished 'rights' such as stealing natural gas and electricity and avoiding taxes" as unrealistic. "Pakistanis have always preferred talking about eating grass (in pursuit of national security) rather than actually having to eat it," Simons observed.[52] He was proven right. The day after the nuclear tests the government froze all foreign currency accounts in Pakistani banks, offering to pay them back in Pakistani currency. Although the measure was designed to bolster the country's foreign exchange reserves, the account holders did not like this forced sacrifice. What's more, the prime minister's secretariat was never converted into a hospital or university and to this day continues to house the government's offices.

The United States imposed economic sanctions on both India and Pakistan in the aftermath of their nuclear tests. Private lending and US government credits as well as guarantees to the two governments were shut down as were all military sales. But agricultural credits continued as did lending to the private sector. As expected, the restrictions affected Pakistan more than they did India. This led to increased anti-Americanism and greater pro-Taliban sentiment in Pakistan. The ISI argued that the nuclear tests had exacerbated tension with India, which in turn increased "Pakistan's need for a pro-Pakistan, anti-India regime in Kabul."[53]

If the rationale for Pakistan's acquisition of nuclear weapons was to feel secure, it did not entirely succeed; nuclear tests should have bolstered Pakistan's national self-confidence, and the government should have focused on ending external military adventures involving irregular forces. But instead the government told Pakistanis by way of media propaganda that the country's "nuclear assets" were now under threat from the United States, India, and Israel.

......

There was no substance to this fear. Even at the height of the Cold War, the United States had not "taken out" Russia's nuclear weapons; India could not risk the fallout of radiation from Pakistani nuclear facilities by sabotaging them; and Israel was too far away. The contrived fear of the nuclear weapons being taken away or destroyed served only one purpose: to maintain Pakistan as a national security state. Instead of nuclear weapons being seen as a source of ultimate security for Pakistan, Pakistanis were now scared about the security of their nuclear weapons.

The possession of nuclear weapons also encouraged impunity in the ISI's clandestine operations in Afghanistan and Kashmir. Members of the Northern Alliance that was fighting the Taliban claimed that regular Pakistani troops were now fighting alongside the Taliban, although Americans were unable to find evidence to support these claims. Nonetheless, the United States recognized the possibility that "Pakistani military advisors were involved in training Taliban fighters."[54]

Pakistani nationals constantly bolstered the ranks of Afghan Taliban. At one point the US embassy in Islamabad estimated that 20 to 40 percent of Taliban soldiers were Pakistani. US diplomats acknowledged that the presence of Pakistani volunteers in Afghanistan "solidifies Pakistan-Taliban relations." But the United States still adopted the formal position that "this does not indicate outward or official Pakistani government support." Osama bin Laden was reported as "supporting pro-Taliban Arab fighters from an office in Herat"—an Afghan city bordering Iran and away from the Taliban stronghold of Kandahar.[55] This was apparently misinformation from Taliban and Pakistani officials who wanted to hide from the Americans the closeness between the Taliban and bin Laden.

Pakistani critics of the Taliban—like me—found America's traipsing around the question of ISI backing for the Taliban distressing. We could see evidence of official tolerance and support for the Taliban in our cities. Posters of Osama bin Laden, taped speeches by Jihadi clerics, and Taliban publications inserted in Pakistani newspapers were distributed or sold openly outside mosques. Pakistani journalists traveled to Kandahar and Kabul with ISI facilitators and returned to tell their stories. But both Pakistani and US officials kept up appearances, saying that there was insufficient proof of Taliban activity in Pakistan.

In August 1998 Clinton authorized cruise missile strikes on an Al-Qaeda camp in Afghanistan. In his memoir he said that he had responded to CIA intelligence about a meeting between bin Laden and his top staff. Al-Qaeda had only recently attacked the US embassies in Kenya and Tanzania and attempted to hit a US naval vessel. "The meeting would provide an opportunity to retaliate and perhaps wipe out much of the al Qaeda leadership," Clinton explained. "We had to pick targets, move the necessary military assets into place, and figure out how to handle Pakistan."[56]

If the United States launched air strikes inside Afghanistan, its planes would have to pass through Pakistan's airspace. Clinton realized that "Pakistan supported the Taliban and, by extension, al Qaeda." He also knew that "the Pakistani intelligence service used some of the same camps that bin Laden and al Qaeda did to train the Taliban and insurgents who fought in Kashmir." The US president worried that if Pakistan found out about the planned attacks in advance, "it was likely that Pakistani intelligence would warn the Taliban or even al Qaeda."[57]

After the Indian and Pakistani nuclear tests, Strobe Talbott had started talks with Pakistan's Foreign Secretary Ahmad and India's Foreign Minister Jaswant Singh so as to reduce chances of military conflict in South Asia. He worried that if the US missiles passed through Pakistani airspace, Pakistan might assume that India had launched them. Pakistan could retaliate, "conceivably even with nuclear weapons."

Clinton decided to send the vice chairman of the joint chiefs of staff, General Joe Ralston, to have dinner with the top Pakistani military commander at the time the attacks were scheduled. Ralston would tell him what was happening a few minutes before the US missiles entered Pakistani airspace, "too late to alert the Taliban or al Qaeda, but in time to avoid having them shot down or sparking a counterattack on India."[58]

When the attack occurred, however, bin Laden and his deputies were not in the Zhawar Kili camp. The US strikes killed several members of a Pakistani Jihadi group and, according to Clinton, "some Pakistani officers who were reported to be there to train Kashmiri terrorists."[59] Taliban leader Mullah Omar publicly declared that the Taliban "will never hand over bin Laden to anyone and [will] protect him with our blood at all costs."[60]

The United States thus established that there was a Pakistani connection with bin Laden because of the presence of Pakistanis at the Al-Qaeda camp.[61] But instead of pressing Pakistan on this issue, US officials became defensive when Islamabad "decided to take a hard line against the strikes." The Pakistani Foreign Ministry called US officials to "protest the illegality of the U.S. action." Assistant secretary of state for South Asia, Karl Inderfurth, did "not expect the negative Pakistani reaction to subside."[62]

"The most sincere reaction of the government of Pakistan to the Bin Laden strikes," wrote Inderfurth, "is exasperation at the unneeded difficulties this event has created for them in dealing with their domestic political situation, and in particular, in keeping the religious parties happy and relatively off the street."[63] When the Americans pressed him to do something about Al-Qaeda, Sharif asked them to train an ISI team secretly in order to hunt down bin Laden—a plan that did not materialize.

Howard and Teresita Schaffer, in their book, *How Pakistan Negotiates with the United States*, highlighted Pakistani leaders' tendency to consistently invoke negative domestic public opinion as a negotiating tactic. The Schaffers are both veteran American diplomats with extensive experience in South Asia. They have noted, with hindsight, what US officials ignore while dealing with Pakistanis. "Pakistan has often used its weakness as a strategic asset in its negotiations with the United States," they point out.[64] Sharif employed this "having the lower hand" tactic once again when Pakistan's military precipitated the "Kargil crisis" in the summer of 1999, creating the specter of nuclear war.

★

*****

In December 1998, at Clinton's invitation, Sharif visited Washington. He sought the end of the sanctions imposed after Pakistan's nuclear tests. For his part, Clinton urged Pakistani action on terrorism and nudged Sharif toward India-Pakistan rapprochement. Soon after the visit the US embassy in Islamabad complained that the Pakistani government was "not disposed to be especially helpful on the matter of terrorist Osama bin Laden." Pakistani officials apparently "all took the line that the issue of bin Laden is a problem the U.S. has with the Taliban, not with Pakistan."

In an effort to persuade Pakistanis to change their policy on Afghanistan, US Ambassador William Milam met with Foreign Minister Sartaj Aziz. He urged the Pakistani government to "get active in trying to convince the Taliban to expel terrorist Osama bin Laden" and to change its pro-Taliban policies. "Have four years of all-out support for the Taliban improved Pakistan's position?" Milam asked Aziz. He insisted that Pakistan needed to use its influence with the Taliban to convince them to expel bin Laden to a place where he could be brought to justice.

The ambassador found that "Aziz listened carefully, but his response contained little that was new."[65] Meanwhile, the Pakistanis began their dialogue with India. The two countries agreed to open the passenger bus service between Delhi and Lahore. On February 20, 1999, Indian Prime Minister Atal Bihari Vajpayee traveled to Lahore on the inaugural bus trip. Vajpayee's bus diplomacy led to "a summit filled with symbolism and hope of warmer relations" between the two nuclear-armed adversaries.[66] Clinton then publicly commended the two prime ministers "for demonstrating courage and leadership by coming together and addressing difficult issues that have long divided their countries."[67]

Except for Pakistani Islamists, who organized violent demonstrations, most Indians and Pakistanis supported Vajpayee's "Bus Diplomacy." The Indian leader belonged to the Hindu nationalist Bharatiya Janata Party (BJP), which was seen in Pakistan as virulently anti-Pakistan. On Pakistani soil he affirmed India's respect for Pakistan as a neighbor; this was meant to reassure Pakistanis who still believed in an existential threat from India. Finally, a Hindu nationalist

......

stood under the Pakistani flag at the site where the demand for partition of India was first made. The dispute over Pakistan's right to exist had ended.

Sharif, as head of the Muslim League, represented the hard-line anti–India position. His willingness to negotiate with India symbolized Pakistan's desire for finally moving beyond the arguments of the partition in 1947. He reiterated Jinnah's desire for Pakistan and India to live as neighbors like Canada and the United States. The two leaders agreed on an elaborate peace process: there would be a "composite dialogue" on all differences between the two countries, including the Kashmir issue. But they would not wait to ease travel restrictions and do business with one another until all issues were resolved.

The détente had just begun when, in spring of 1999, the Indians discovered a Pakistani force occupying mountains on their side of Kashmir. Initially Pakistan denied that it had crossed the Line of Control in Kashmir. Those occupying the mountains in Kargil, said Islamabad, were Kashmiri Mujahideen. The Indians, however, saw the occupation as a major escalation. The new Pakistani positions put India's major highway in Kashmir within shelling range. In response, India deployed its army as well as air force to evict the intruders.

The architect of the military operation in Kargil was General Pervez Musharraf, a flamboyant officer who had replaced the mild-mannered Karamat as Pakistan's army chief a few months earlier. Musharraf had sent in troops drawn from Pakistan's Northern Light Infantry Division to occupy difficult mountainous terrain, hoping to force the Indians to negotiate a Kashmir settlement more quickly than the civilian peace process could achieve. However, he did not anticipate India's resolve to recover fifty-one square miles of barren, snow-capped territory.

By June the Indian forces had fought to recover most of the territory. India released a tape-recorded conversation between Musharraf and his deputy, Lieutenant General Aziz Khan, which left no doubt about Pakistan's actions in Kargil. Aziz was the same officer who, while serving at the ISI, had supported the Taliban and expressed disappointment at Bhutto's lack of fervor for Islam. The conversation between Musharraf and Aziz Khan took place while Musharraf was in Beijing and Aziz Khan at army headquarters in Rawalpindi.

The international community, including China and the United States, unanimously demanded Pakistan's withdrawal from Kargil. Thus, Musharraf and his fellow generals had managed to unite the international community against Pakistan. How the Indians got hold of the Musharraf–Aziz tape recording remains a mystery to this day. General Ehsan-ul-Haq, who served as head of military intelligence at the time, later told me what Pakistani generals suspected: the Americans had taped the conversation. It had been given to the Indians to embarrass Pakistan and force its withdrawal from the Kargil heights. The tape was just the first of a series of embarrassments that eventually forced Pakistan's retreat.

Musharraf's blunder had created a South Asian version of the Cuban Missile Crisis. Vajpayee felt betrayed, whereas Sharif worried about a full-blown war. The Americans were concerned about reports that Pakistan's generals might use nuclear weapons to reverse defeat in conventional fighting. Sharif wanted to end the crisis, but he wanted to do so with a face-saver. He called Clinton on July 2 and "appealed for American intervention immediately to stop the fighting and to resolve the Kashmir issue."[68]

A more desperate call followed the next day. Clinton felt that Sharif "had gotten himself into a bind with no easy way out." The US president agreed to see him in Washington, but Sharif had to know that Clinton "would not agree to intervene in the Kashmir dispute, especially under circumstances that appeared to reward Pakistan's wrongful incursion."[69]

When they met at Blair House on American Independence Day, Sharif told Clinton that he wanted desperately to find a solution that would allow Pakistan to withdraw "with some cover." He found himself in a position similar to that of Ayub before Lyndon Johnson right after the 1965 India–Pakistan war. Pakistan could not win the war, but it would not accept defeat. Sharif told Clinton that the fundamentalists in Pakistan would move against him if he did not portray at least some success in moving Pakistan's case for Kashmir forward. Clinton spoke angrily about Pakistan's irresponsible behavior as it moved to the brink of nuclear war. He then took up the subject of terrorism.[70]

Bruce Riedel, who was present at the meeting, quoted Clinton as saying that "the ISI worked with bin Laden and the Taliban to foment terrorism." Clinton said he had a draft statement that would also mention Pakistan's role in supporting terrorists in Afghanistan and India. Was that what Sharif wanted? Clinton asked. "You've put me in the middle today, set the U.S. up to fail and I won't let it happen," he said. "Pakistan is messing with nuclear war."

Clinton's own account of the meeting says that he told Sharif: "I would have to announce that Pakistan was in effect supporting terrorism in Afghanistan" unless Pakistan did more to help find bin Laden. On the day he met with Sharif, Clinton also signed an executive order placing economic sanctions on the Taliban—freezing its assets and prohibiting commercial exchanges. Clinton realized that "the Pakistani military was full of Taliban and al Qaeda sympathizers" and that Sharif did not have full control. "But I thought we had nothing to lose by exploring every option," Clinton observed.[71]

At the end of that meeting Sharif agreed to announce a Pakistani withdrawal from Kargil. Pakistan would restore "the sanctity of the Line of Control." Clinton promised to take a personal interest in resuming the India-Pakistan dialogue. On returning to Pakistan, Sharif asked the army to proceed against those responsible for the military fiasco. Musharraf knew that his would be the first head to roll, so he went on a tour of Pakistan's garrisons to galvanize support for his position as their commander.

In October, when Sharif tried to remove Musharraf from his position as army chief, Musharraf loyalists in the army, led by Aziz and Lieutenant General Mahmud Ahmed, overthrew the civilian government in a military coup. Sharif was arrested, and Musharraf assumed power first as chief executive and later as president. Most Americans saw the coup as "cause for alarm in South Asia and the rest of the world," but there were some voices advocating the Pakistan army's case.[72]

. . . . .

An editorial in the *Wall Street Journal* summed up the concerns of US officials about the direction Pakistan was taking. "The first order of business for Washington should be to demand Islamabad's full cooperation in the anti-terror campaign," it said. The paper cautioned, "Pakistan's generals may assume that having nukes will let them, like Russia, get away with murder. Any wobbling in Washington that confirms that impression makes murder almost guaranteed."[73]

Steven Weisman, who had spent years in South Asia as a reporter asked, "If Pakistanis are not capable of governing themselves, why would Pakistanis wearing uniforms be any different?" Michael Krepon, a scholar, pointed to a different problem. "The Pakistani army generals are trying to convince themselves that defeat in Kashmir was snatched from the jaw of victory by Sharif and his stupid diplomats," he said. "This theory recurs in Pakistani history and it is very dangerous."[74]

American conservatives embraced an alternative view. The front-runner for the Republican nomination for the presidency, Texas governor George W. Bush, could not name Musharraf in an interview for a Boston television station, but he nonetheless spoke positively of "The new Pakistani general." Bush said, "It appears this guy is going to bring stability to the country and I think that's good news for the subcontinent."[75] In an article titled "Pakistan: Democracy Is Not Everything," Richard N. Haass, who had served as a member of the national security council and special assistant when Bush's father was president, made the same argument in greater detail.[76]

Robert "Bud" McFarlane, who, as a Reagan adviser, had worked closely with Zia during the war against the Soviets, also publicly defended the coup. He described Pakistani democracy as "a feudal cabal" and Pakistan's periods of military rule as "more stable and prosperous." McFarlane claimed that "military control is inevitable and in Pakistan's interest" in the short term. But Pakistan's long-term stability would be possible only if the superpowers helped Pakistan secure a settlement of the Kashmir dispute as the Pakistan army demanded.[77]

This reflected the opinion of Pakistan's generals who had for years put much else on hold in pursuit of an elusive victory over India.

Musharraf, who was apprehensive about international isolation, was heartened by the support of those in the United States who cherished memories of Pakistan's Cold War alliance with the United States. He appointed Maleeha Lodhi, who had served as ambassador to the United States before, as his representative in Washington. Pakistan's policies on nuclear proliferation and terrorism, however, had not changed. But by changing faces, Pakistan hoped to win over the Americans once again.

★

The Clinton administration did not trust Musharraf's new military regime. Musharraf spoke about changing Pakistan as it also continued to support the Taliban and Pakistani terrorist groups. Within a couple of months into his coup an Indian Airlines passenger jet traveling from Kathmandu, Nepal, to Delhi was hijacked to Kandahar, Afghanistan. India released three prominent Kashmiri terrorists to secure the release of 155 hostages. Although there was no direct evidence of official Pakistani involvement, the released terrorists returned to heroes' welcomes in Pakistan.

In January 2000 Clinton sent Inderfurth to Islamabad to seek Musharraf's help in capturing Abu Zubaida, one of Osama bin Laden's key lieutenants who was believed to be living in Peshawar. The United States also demanded that Pakistan stop supporting terrorism in India and Kashmir. The Americans saw Musharraf's response as partially conceding the ISI's role in aiding the Kashmiri militants: he attached conditions to his agreement that they would stop. Pakistan, he said, would use its "influence" in Kashmir to calm the situation there if India reduced its own buildup of troops along the border.[78]

Musharraf promised that he "would not stay in power any longer than required." Clinton was scheduled to visit the subcontinent in the spring of 2000, but Inderfurth conveyed that it would be difficult for Clinton to visit Pakistan if the country remained a dictatorship and there was no progress on the issues that mattered to the United States. Musharraf warned that a presidential snub would "strengthen the hand of the extremists," which was essentially what Sharif had said to Talbott "in seeking American leniency before and after the Pakistani nuclear test."[79]

Clinton arrived in Bangladesh on March 18, 2000, for a weeklong visit to the subcontinent. There was considerable debate within his national security team over whether to visit Pakistan. In the end Clinton decided on a five-hour stopover in Islamabad. "I'm going to try to keep us in the play there," he remarked, "both for what happens inside that country and for getting them to cut out the bad stuff they're doing in the region." The US Secret Service appealed to Clinton not to go to Pakistan because of the danger of assassination.[80]

The US president was effectively snubbing Musharraf by stopping in Islamabad for only a few hours. He spent one full day in Bangladesh and five days in five cities of India. Clinton explained in his memoirs that he decided to go to Pakistan "to encourage an early return to civilian rule and a lessening of tensions over Kashmir; to urge General Musharraf not to execute the deposed prime minister, Nawaz Sharif, who was on trial for his life; and to press Musharraf to cooperate with us on bin Laden and al Qaeda."[81]

Musharraf had agreed to somewhat humiliating conditions to be able to host Clinton, however briefly. For example, no one in military uniform could receive the president at the airport, and the two presidents would not be photographed shaking hands. Musharraf felt he needed the imprimatur of American engagement, if not US support, for his political longevity. He hoped that he would be able to convince Clinton of his worth—and that of Pakistan—as a US ally.

As one of the conditions of his visit, Clinton had insisted that he be allowed to make a televised address to the people of Pakistan. In that speech he tried to rebut the Pakistani narrative of America's relationship with their country. Clinton appealed to the Pakistani people to turn away from terror and nuclear weapons and turn toward a dialogue with India on Kashmir, to embrace the test ban treaty, and to invest in education, health, and development rather than arms.

Clinton described himself "as a friend of Pakistan and the Muslim world," quoted Jinnah, and spoke of the "real obstacles" that were "holding Pakistan back from achieving its full potential." He asked

......

difficult questions, such as: "Are you really more secure today than you were before you tested nuclear weapons? Will these weapons make war with India less likely or simply more deadly? Will a costly arms race help you to achieve any economic development? Will it bring you closer to your friends around the world, closer to the partnerships you need to build your dreams?"

He said he understood Pakistani concerns about Kashmir but highlighted the "stark truth" that "there is no military solution to Kashmir." Clinton posed other questions to Pakistanis: "Will endless, costly struggle build good schools for your children? Will it make your cities safer? Will it bring clean water and better health care? Will it narrow the gaps between those who have and those who have nothing? Will it hasten the day when Pakistan's energy and wealth are invested in building its future?"

The speech was an attempt to deprive Pakistani leaders and diplomats of their constant argument that public opinion restrained them. Clinton was demonstrating that putting forward different arguments can change public opinion. He warned of the danger that Pakistan may grow even more isolated. He laid out an alternative vision for Pakistan "rooted in tomorrow's promise, not yesterday's pain, rooted in dialog, not destruction." Then he concluded by saying, "If you choose that future, the United States will walk with you. I hope you will make that choice."[82]

In their private meeting Musharraf stuck to the traditional Pakistani script, nor did the Pakistani media follow Clinton's public appeal with similar messages aimed at altering the Pakistani narrative. As soon as Clinton left the country, Pakistan's media reverted to its usual pattern. The United States was accused of siding with India, ignoring the just Kashmir cause, and acting as an imperial power. Moreover, Pakistani officials continued to flatly deny allegations of Pakistani support for the Taliban and the Kashmiri Mujahideen.

Clinton did succeed, however, in saving Sharif's life. Under a deal guaranteed by Saudi Arabia, Musharraf allowed the former prime minister to move to the kingdom with his family. Sharif promised to stay out of Pakistani politics for ten years in return for a full pardon in the cases that had been initiated against him.

······

In September 2000 the State Department noted an increase in direct Pakistani involvement in Taliban military operations. "While Pakistani support for the Taliban has been long-standing," said a cable from Washington sharing intelligence with the US embassy in Islamabad, "the magnitude of recent support is unprecedented." Pakistan was apparently providing the Taliban with materiel, fuel, funding, technical assistance, and military advisers. Large numbers of Pakistani nationals had moved into Afghanistan "to fight for the Taliban," ostensibly with the tacit acquiescence of the Pakistani government.[83]

Secretary of State Madeleine Albright advised the US ambassador to Pakistan to remind the Pakistanis that "We will not accept a Taliban victory and do not believe others will either." She was still appealing to reason, not realizing that passion dictated decisions in Islamabad. Albright pointed out that Taliban victory would bring not peace and stability but rather further unrest. The only mildly threatening remark she made referred to "further measures in the Security Council" that would "not serve Pakistan's interest."[84]

Under-Secretary of State Thomas Pickering followed up on Albright's warning. He told a Pakistani official in November of US disappointment with Pakistan's failure to help with capturing or killing Osama bin Laden. He warned of an arms embargo on the Taliban and asked for Pakistan's help. The United States, he said, "would always act to protect U.S. interests at a time and place of its own choice."[85] Pakistan's generals had heard threats before, however, and this was not particularly menacing. In any case, the United States was mired in controversy over its presidential election, and, as in the past, Pakistan's leaders were willing to take their chances with the new administration.

✦

ISLAMABAD WELCOMED the inauguration of George W. Bush as president of the United States. After all, during his campaign, Bush had spoken little about South Asia. Although in one speech he spoke of "the arrival of India, the world's largest democracy, as a power of global significance,"[86] on other occasions he had expressed confidence that military rule might stabilize Pakistan. From Musharraf's point of view that was a positive sign.

The incoming national security adviser, Condoleezza Rice, believed that the United States needed Pakistan's cooperation in order to succeed in replacing the Taliban with a broad-based government in Afghanistan. But like the Clinton administration, the Bush team just did not know how to get Pakistan to shift from supporting the Taliban. Afghan-born academic Zalmay Khalilzad, who had dealt with Pakistan during the Reagan administration, was brought in to lead that effort.[87] Vice President Dick Cheney worried about Musharraf's tenuous hold on power.[88] Others were also concerned about Islamist radicals seizing power in Pakistan and gaining access to its nuclear arsenal.

There was clearly a huge gap in the Bush administration's knowledge about Pakistan. Rice was surprised when Russian President Vladimir Putin brought up the subject of Pakistan during his meeting with Bush at the G-8 Summit meeting in Genoa in July 2001. "He excoriated the Pervez Musharraf regime for its support of extremists and for the connections of the Pakistani army and intelligence services to the Taliban and al Qaeda," she wrote in her memoir. Putin said that the extremists "were all being funded by Saudi Arabia" and that it was only a matter of time until it resulted in a major catastrophe.

"We, of course, knew of the connections between Pakistan and the Taliban and had been hammering Islamabad," observed Rice. "But I was taken aback by Putin's alarm and vehemence and chalked it up to Russian bitterness toward Pakistan for supporting the Afghan Mujahideen, who had defeated the Soviet Union in the 1980s." Only later did Rice realize that Putin was right. "Pakistan's relationship with the extremists would become one of our gravest problems," she noted. "Putin never let us forget it, recalling that conversation time and time again."[89]

Pakistani officials lied with impunity to visiting US officials. On August 30 Foreign Office officials in Islamabad told a team of congressional staffers that Pakistan did not support the Taliban; it only interacted with them. They denied that "the ISI or any part of the government," armed or otherwise, assisted the Taliban militarily. Pakistan was "a conscientious member of the U.N.," committed to support the UN sanctions against the Taliban, they claimed.

The Pakistani officials said they found "many Taliban policies against women personally distasteful" but insisted that they reflected "more a medieval Afghan mentality prevalent in Afghan society than mainstream Islam." The officials advised that the United States engage with the Taliban, with one Pakistani diplomat stating, "Change comes slowly. Doing business with people promotes change; corrupt the Taliban with aid and a reborn economy," he suggested.[90]

The Bush administration's ambivalence toward Pakistan ended on September 11, 2001, with the Al-Qaeda attacks on the Pentagon and on New York's World Trade Center, in which more than three thousand people were killed. The United States reacted strongly against what most onlookers saw as an act of war on US homeland. American intelligence immediately identified the terrorists who had hijacked the planes before ramming them into symbols of American power. Given Al-Qaeda's involvement, US military action against Afghanistan was inevitable.

The head of the ISI, Lieutenant General Mahmud Ahmed, was in Washington at the time. He was summoned to the State Department the next morning for a short meeting with Deputy Secretary Richard Armitage, who delivered a terse message: "Pakistan must either stand with the U.S. in its fight against terrorism or stand against us. There was no maneuvering room." Armitage said that "the right choice by Pakistan" could lead to lifting of sanctions and a positive relationship with the United States. Mahmud assured him of Pakistan's "unqualified support" and said that he spoke on Musharraf's behalf.[91]

Two days after the 9/11 attacks, Wendy Chamberlin presented her credentials to Musharraf as the new US ambassador to Pakistan. In a forty-minute meeting following the presentation of credentials, Musharraf told the ambassador that Pakistan was "with you in an action plan for Afghanistan." He emphasized repeatedly that Pakistan "had been a frontline state in the past and would be a frontline state again." Chamberlin said bluntly that the September 11 attacks had changed the fundamentals of the debate. Pakistan needed to "act with the US—not to urge dialog but to act." Musharraf declared that "we are together in this."[92]

Musharraf later received a phone call from Secretary of State Colin Powell. According to Musharraf's account of Mahmud's conversation with Armitage and his own with Powell, the two US officials had threatened Pakistan. The Pakistani dictator understood their message as: "we should be prepared to be bombed back to the Stone Age" if they did not comply with American demands. He wrote later that he "war-gamed the United States as an adversary" and decided to switch alliance from the Taliban to the United States.[93]

The list of nonnegotiable demands that Powell presented to Musharraf included unequivocal condemnation of the 9/11 attacks, denying Al-Qaeda safe haven in Pakistan, sharing intelligence, granting over-flight rights, and breaking diplomatic relations with the Taliban.[94] There were also several specific requests for logistical support. Although Musharraf had agreed to submit to the US demands, the ISI was not willing to give up on its decades-long investment in Afghanistan. There was considerable debate within the Pakistan military about the extent to which Pakistan should support the United States.

Musharraf announced his decision in an address to the Pakistani people. He alluded to the US threat and suggested that India would benefit if Pakistan did not cooperate with the Americans. "Our critical concerns, our important concerns can come under threat," he said. "When I say critical concerns, I mean our strategic assets and the cause of Kashmir. If these come under threat it would be a worse situation for us."[95]

He was implying that he was making a sacrifice on the Afghan front so that the Kashmir front could remain alive. The obligatory anti-American demonstrations and media hype soon followed the speech. Although the Americans thought they had won Musharraf over, Musharraf had made a tactical choice, not a strategic one.

Mahmud made two trips to Kandahar to meet Taliban leader Mullah Omar. He told Chamberlin that Omar wanted to pursue "a negotiated solution" and advised the Americans "not to act in anger," saying that "real victory will come in negotiations." According to the ISI chief, America's strategic objectives of getting Osama bin Laden and Al-Qaeda would best be accomplished by coercing the Taliban to do it themselves. "If the Taliban are eliminated," he said, "Afghanistan will revert to warlordism."[96]

The ISI did not want the Taliban defeated militarily. Mahmud said he wanted Pakistan to avoid the "fallout" from a US attack on its neighbor.[97] But the United States had already aligned itself with the Taliban's foes, the Northern Alliance, whereas the ISI had always seen the Northern Alliance as closer to India, Iran, and Russia. Musharraf replaced Mahmud with Lieutenant General Ehsan-ul-Haq so as to convince Americans that the ISI would not impede their military operations in Afghanistan. As the United States commenced bombing Afghanistan, hundreds of Pakistani military advisers and ISI operatives assisting the Taliban were evacuated.

Although this could have been an opportunity to make a clean break with terrorist groups, Musharraf did not force the Jihadi groups out of business. Pakistan was "warehousing some extremists and leaving others untouched." Some Pakistani officials, reported Paul Watson of the *Los Angeles Times*, argued that action against Pakistani Jihadis would alienate Pakistan's religious groups.[98] Militant groups were banned amid fanfare, and sometimes their leaders were detained. But then the groups reemerged under new names, and courts freed the detained leaders, claiming lack of evidence.[99]

Over the next few years the United States and Pakistan lapsed into a now-familiar pattern. The United States provided large amounts of economic and military aid, including a fresh batch of F-16 aircraft, some frigates for the navy, and updated equipment for the army. Pakistan handed over several Al-Qaeda figures that the CIA and FBI had located in Pakistani cities, particularly in the first two years after 9/11. In a unique arrangement Pakistan also received reimbursement for what it spent to fight terrorism. Total aid and reimbursement between 2002 and 2012 amounted to $25 billion.

However, Pakistan made no fundamental shift in attitude toward Afghanistan or India. An attack by Kashmiri militants on the Indian Parliament soon after December 2001 resulted in the threat of an-

......

other India–Pakistan war. Although both sides mobilized along the border, US diplomacy was able to defuse the crisis. Musharraf also agreed to go through the motions of a peace process with India, which yielded no substantive result.

By 2005 the Taliban had resurfaced in Afghanistan. American intelligence discovered, once again, that the Taliban's activities were being directed from Pakistan while, as before, Pakistan denied its involvement. Further, terrorists involved in attacks on trains in Spain and on London's subway were found to have trained in Pakistan. Several countries' intelligence services stressed Pakistan's position as "a principal recruiting ground and logistical center for global terrorists."[100]

What's more, Pakistan's halfhearted participation in the war against terrorism made it a major victim of terrorism. Some Jihadi groups determined that they would wage war on the Pakistan army and the ISI in addition to fighting the West and India. Junior military men from secret cells linked to Al-Qaeda twice targeted Musharraf for assassination. Thus, Pakistan's tolerance of extremism allowed new, more virulent offshoots of old groups. Terrorist attacks in Pakistani cities claimed thousands of lives. Instead of rallying the people against these extremists, however, Pakistan's establishment termed it the price Pakistan paid for supporting the United States. Officials demanded even greater monetary compensation from the United States for the losses Pakistan suffered on account of allying itself with the US-led war on terror. Clerics, politicians, and journalists blamed America rather than the Taliban for terrorist attacks in Pakistan. Once again, anti-Americanism had provided refuge against honestly facing Pakistan's own problems.

Bush acknowledged that Musharraf either "would not or could not" fulfill all his promises. According to Bush, "Part of the problem was Pakistan's obsession with India. In almost every conversation we had, Musharraf accused India of wrongdoing." Four days after 9/11 the Pakistani ruler had told Bush that the Indians were "trying to equate us with terrorists and trying to influence your mind."

Although Bush had invested heavily in securing Pakistani cooperation against Al-Qaeda and the Taliban, he found that "the Pakistani military spent most of its resources preparing for war with

India. Its troops were trained to wage a conventional battle with its neighbor, not counterterrorism operations in the tribal areas. The fight against the extremists came second."[101]

When Bush visited the subcontinent in 2006 he signed a civil nuclear deal with India, which was tantamount to accepting the legitimacy of India's status as a nuclear power. Pakistan, however, could not get such a deal because it was unwilling to submit to any international discipline. Pakistani nuclear scientist Dr. A. Q. Khan had been found running an illicit network that traded in designs and material for uranium enrichment to Libya, North Korea, and Iran. Instead of coming clean, Pakistani officials had fulminated against Indian and Zionist plots. This precluded any possibility of bringing Pakistan's nuclear program out of the shadows.

The highlight of Bush's trip to India included the civil nuclear deal and agreements on US investment. In Pakistan the US president arrived to the news that a US consular officer had been killed in a terrorist attack on the consulate in Karachi, but this did not prevent Bush from staying at the American ambassador's residence or continuing with his trip as planned.[102] During his discussions he focused on the fight against extremists and the full civilianization of Musharraf's regime. Bush pushed Musharraf "to shed his military affiliation and govern as a civilian. He promised to do it. But he wasn't in much of a hurry."[103]

By 2007 the Bush administration's view of Musharraf and Pakistan had changed significantly. On February 26 Cheney and CIA Deputy Director Steve Kappes warned Musharraf during an unannounced visit to Islamabad that the tribal areas along the border with Afghanistan had become a safe haven for both the Taliban and Al-Qaeda. After realizing that Musharraf and the Pakistan army were unable or unwilling to deal with the problem, the United States ramped up the use of armed drones—unmanned aerial vehicles—in the region.[104]

The US tone was becoming tougher. Pakistan's media characterized the American message as "Do More." But both officials and leaders of public opinion rejected the suggestion that Pakistan had become the epicenter of global terrorism. "Pakistan does not accept dictation from any side or any source," an indignant official said in response to reports of Cheney's demands. When members of Congress talked about cutting aid, Pakistani officials responded by condemning "discriminatory legislation."[105]

During the summer of 2007 Musharraf faced his strongest domestic challenge. Opposition parties joined lawyers protesting the sacking of the Pakistan chief justice, who had until then been a Musharraf ally. Religious parties and retired servicemen supported the protests more out of their distaste for Musharraf than concern for full democracy. For the first time there was a chink in Musharraf's armor, and it seemed that he might not be able to retain complete authority. He had already ruled for eight years—no Pakistani dictator had lasted more than a decade in power.

The Bush administration recognized the need to look beyond Musharraf. US diplomats reached out to Bhutto and Sharif, both of whom were in exile. Sharif still had to overcome his agreement with Musharraf involving the Saudis. But Benazir Bhutto was ready to return to Pakistan. She and her husband had faced legal proceedings in corruption cases that had dragged on, all with no result; Zardari had spent more than eleven years of his life in prison without being convicted of a single crime. Bhutto asked the Americans to demand that Musharraf provide her party a level field by ending prosecution that amounted to persecution.

From exile Bhutto had spoken out against extremism. She had also castigated Pakistan's inadequate response to the terrorist challenge, promising a more robust policy if she came to power. Her argument that a democratic leader could fight terrorism more effectively appealed to Washington. The US ambassador, Anne Patterson, reported from Islamabad that "her party has more political legitimacy than any other party in Pakistan."

On Bhutto's return to Pakistan on October 18, hundreds of thousands of supporters in Karachi received her. The US embassy estimated the crowd to be between five hundred thousand to two million. "She will have to fight for the right to again become Pakistan's Prime Minister," observed Patterson. "But for today, she is basking in the applause of hundreds of thousands of fans."[106] A suicide bomber attacked her rally, killing 136 people and injuring more than 450. Bhutto survived and continued her campaign.

Bhutto's return paved the way for Sharif to break his ten-year exile deal and come back to Pakistan. On November 28 Musharraf retired as chief of army staff and handed the baton to General Ashfaq Pervez Kayani, who had previously served as the head of the ISI. Kayani was the first spy chief to lead the army. As a young officer he had studied at the US Army Command and General Staff College at Fort Leavenworth, Kansas. Reflecting the American tradition of optimism about personnel changes, Pentagon officials now pinned their hopes on Kayani. In background briefings he was described as pro-American and anti-extremism.

Then, on December 27, 2007, in a second suicide attack, Bhutto was assassinated. In conversations with several people, including me, she had expressed concern over Musharraf's refusal to provide her adequate security. Nonetheless, she refused to stop campaigning in what she said was a final battle to save Pakistan from obscurantism. Her death was mourned across the board in Pakistan, even by erstwhile opponents; her followers saw her as a martyr. When elections were held in February 2008 Bhutto's PPP—now led by her widower, Zardari—won the most seats in Parliament.

Zardari named party loyalist Yusuf Raza Gilani as prime minister. I was named Pakistan's ambassador to Washington and presented my credentials to Bush in May 2008. Zardari replaced Musharraf as president of Pakistan in September 2008, after Musharraf resigned when faced with impeachment. The Americans now had a new set of interlocutors. We were eager to fight terrorism for Pakistan's sake and to redefine Pakistan's relationship with the United States.

Chapter Seven

Parallel Universes

O n May 11, 2011, I sat down for what turned out to be a grim conversation with the US special representative for Afghanistan and Pakistan, Marc Grossman. The well-reputed diplomat had succeeded Richard Holbrooke as the Obama administration's point man for the two troubled countries. Ten days earlier US Special Forces had killed Al-Qaeda leader Osama bin Laden in Abbottabad, a Pakistani garrison town that was home to the Pakistan Military Academy. In response, a wave of anger directed at the Americans swept over Pakistan. The view in Islamabad was that the United States had violated Pakistani sovereignty. As an ally, Pakistanis thought, the United States should have conducted the Abbottabad raid jointly with Pakistani troops.

Grossman spoke softly, as he always did, but his message was unmistakably tough. He was in Islamabad soon after the bin Laden raid and found the atmosphere there "surrealistic." He said that explaining to Americans how the world's most wanted terrorist could be hiding in as important a city as Abbottabad was difficult. According to Grossman, "Some forces in Pakistan" were still not willing to confront the fact that bin Laden was hiding in Pakistan.

He explained that if Secretary of State Hillary Clinton were to visit Pakistan later in the year, as planned, she would "raise some critical questions to the Pakistani leadership." The two countries needed to discuss "the essence and direction" of future relations "if this relationship is to be salvaged." The United States wanted access to the family

· · · · ·

of bin Laden. It wanted an investigation into how he and his family were residing in Abbottabad. Above all, Pakistan needed to stop blaming the United States and start facing the fact that "somebody, somewhere" in Pakistan was responsible for protecting an international terrorist mastermind.

The next day I was asked to come to the White House for a meeting with Lieutenant General Douglas Lute, the National Security Council's coordinator for Afghanistan and Pakistan. Lute had dealt with issues relating to the war in Afghanistan as well as relations with Pakistan for several years. He had served under President Bush and had continued under Obama. As a soldier, he was always more frank than the diplomats. But this time he seemed to choose his words carefully.

Lute said that the United States and Pakistan had come to "forks in their relationship" in the past, where one path led to isolation and the other to continued partnership. In many of these cases the two countries had chosen the path of partnership. "This is one such moment," he insisted. Lute objected to the tone in Pakistan over the bin Laden incident. He said the government of Pakistan took too long to educate its people about the event in Abbottabad. For Americans, Prime Minister Gilani's address to the nation was "disappointing," as it did not address the key question regarding bin Laden's presence in Pakistan.

A CIA official present at the meeting said that Pakistan would gain nothing by stepping up anti-American rhetoric. "The poison thus spread will last longer and much beyond the time when the two militaries and intelligence agencies have made up," he said. He was basing his statement on past experience. By now the Americans obviously understood that whipping up public sentiment was often the Pakistani military's modus operandi for seeking a new deal for aid and arms.

Then Lute made a veiled threat: "Countries have been designated state sponsors of terrorism on less evidence than that available on Pakistan," he said. US Navy SEALS had found "a whole treasure trove of material" at the compound where bin Laden was killed. There were many unanswered questions. Instead of responding to these questions quietly, however, Pakistan was "raising the level of noise." If the noise did not stop, Lute said, the United States could reveal its findings publicly. Once the role of Pakistan was revealed, the US public and Congress would demand "measures that may go well beyond the past pattern of only cutting off aid."

For several months, then, the killing of bin Laden cast a shadow over US-Pakistan relations. Pakistan demanded that the United States vacate the Shamsi Air Base in the Balochistan desert that it had used for operating drones over Pakistan's tribal areas. The United States agreed because Pakistan had the legal right to terminate the base and Americans had alternative staging sites for the drones anyway. Islamabad then asked for a comprehensive treaty between the two countries "to regulate" all aspects of the relationship. Washington said that would take time. The United States then slowed the flow of aid but did not cut it off. Pakistanis thought the worst was over.

On September 13, 2011, terrorists attacked the American embassy in Kabul. Grossman called me in to the State Department for what I knew would be another difficult meeting. As I sat down in his ground-floor office, he exclaimed, "We had a terrible day yesterday." The Afghan Haqqani network, which was based in Pakistan's tribal areas, had apparently perpetrated the embassy attacks. For years the United States had asked Pakistan to act against them, but the ISI considered them allies since the days of the anti-Soviet Jihad. A truck bomb a few days earlier, which injured seventy-seven Americans, was also traced to the same terrorist group.

Grossman said that the latest attack in Kabul would now be the main topic of discussion for the meeting between Clinton and Pakistan's foreign minister, Hina Rabbani Khar, which was to take place in a few days. Pakistan wanted to discuss a memorandum of understanding as a first step toward a full-fledged treaty. Grossman said it seemed that the two sides were in "parallel universes." Pakistanis spoke about everything but terrorism, pretending it was not happening. What we need, he said, is "a conversation among adults trying to solve a problem." It was time to "put it all out there."

The US diplomat shared with me his frustrations in dealing with Pakistan. Soon after he came to office in January CIA contractor Raymond Davis had killed two Pakistanis in Lahore on suspicion of trying to rob him. The United States had claimed diplomatic immunity. Davis had been in Pakistan for three years, but the US embassy had never notified the Pakistan government that he was a diplomat. The ISI then fueled protests over American efforts to spy on Pakistan through men like Davis.

Davis was released when a judge allowed him to pay blood money to the victims' relatives; Islamic law had provided a face-saver. The ISI also managed to seek more details about CIA personnel in Pakistan after helping Davis win his freedom. But Grossman recalled that the incident marked a downward spiral in the US-Pakistan relationship that had hit rock bottom after the United States discovered bin Laden in Abbottabad. The best way to strengthen relation between nations was to "civilianize and privatize" them, he said. At that time 90 percent of Pakistan's relations with the United States were government related. They involved military-to-military, intelligence-to-intelligence and State Department-to-Foreign Office interaction. Business, investment, travel, tourism, education, and everything else represented only 10 percent of ties.

According to Grossman, healthy bilateral relations were usually 60 percent private and 40 percent government. He went on to say that the US geological survey had conducted flights in Afghanistan and revealed a wealth of rare earth metals. The logical conclusion was that something like that was also present on the Pakistani side, "since geology does not follow the Durand Line." But, he argued, there was something wrong in a relationship when Pakistan would not even allow a flight of the geological survey because of the fear that "you want our nukes," he said wistfully.

As Pakistan's ambassador, I could not tell my American counterpart that in my heart I agreed with his analysis.

Clinton met Khar at the Waldorf-Astoria Hotel in New York a few days later. She had been a friend to Pakistan as first lady, senator, and, now, as secretary of state. During this meeting, which I attended, she also voiced her exasperation over Pakistan's policies. According to Clinton, there was significant evidence that the Haqqani network based in Miranshah, in Pakistan's North Waziristan province, organized and executed the attacks on the US embassy and ISAF headquarters in Kabul.

· · · · · ·

There had been communication between the Haqqani network and elements within the Pakistan government prior to the attack.

"We know the relationship between the Haqqani network and the Pakistan Army and ISI," Clinton said. The United States believed that Pakistani officials shared intelligence with the network and facilitated movement of its operatives. The Haqqani network moved men and materials across the border, and some of its operatives who moved in just prior to the recent attacks were still in Afghanistan awaiting orders. "This was not intelligence provided by Afghans or Indians but gathered from many sources," Clinton explained.

The United States wanted Pakistan to act against the Haqqani network or to let the United States punish them by ending ISI facilitation for the terrorists. It also wanted decisive action against Lashkar-e-Taiba, a Pakistani group that had links to Al-Qaeda and was involved in the November 2008 terrorist attacks in Mumbai. Clinton also shared what she described as US concern about "governance issues." She supported democracy in Pakistan but found the civilian government adrift. "One can't pretend that the military and ISI are not following a different agenda" from the civilian leaders, she observed.

Clinton also complained that there was an effort to paint everything the United States did for Pakistan negatively. "This effort is led by the ISI," she said meaningfully. The Pakistani media environment was "toxic" with anti–United States stories that had no basis. There were concerted efforts to shape a negative public opinion of the United States. "Pakistan can better inform its public," the top US diplomat asserted. When the United States criticized Pakistan, she noted, it did so openly and officially. But anti–United States statements and stories in Pakistan were unattributed, and the hidden hand behind these needed to be curbed. "Pakistan," Clinton said, "has entire machinery devoted to sowing hatred against the United States."

In an effort to address all possible issues Clinton then took up the nuclear question. "The US has said many times that it has no intention to denuclearize Pakistan," she pointed out. If Pakistan wanted to be accepted as a nuclear state and be considered for a civil nuclear option in the future, then there was no reason for it to oppose proliferation of fissile material. The United States had invited Israel and India—the other countries outside the Non-Proliferation Treaty—to work with the major powers on fissile cutoff. Pakistan, then, was the only intransigent one. She made clear that the United States' interest was solely about fissile material falling into terrorist hands.

"It was one thing to invest in a nuclear program for your own security," Clinton went on. "This was a sovereign decision Pakistan took, as did India and Israel. But Pakistan went ahead and proliferated to Libya and North Korea." Pakistan's leaders should not act as if there were no difference between Pakistan's behavior and that of Israel and India in nuclear matters, she stated. "If Pakistan wants parity with these countries, it should act like them," she concluded. Pakistan had to "overcome the mistrust engendered by onward proliferation."

Khar's response only proved Clinton's points. Instead of addressing the specific issues, she insisted that "the U.S. should not humiliate Pakistan and its institutions publicly." Pakistan needed "rock-solid evidence" on ISI's alleged ties to terrorists, she said. "Our sacrifices and contribution to the counter-terrorism effort must also be fully appreciated." The American representatives shook their heads as Khar stated that Pakistan was being made "a scapegoat."

After Clinton had left the room Khar told other Pakistani participants that in her opinion the meeting had gone well. I told her frankly that her bland statements had cut no ice with the Americans. Pakistan needed to address the substantive issues, I said, or we risked far more than our relations with the United States.

★

DURING HER YEARS in exile from 1997 to 2007, Benazir Bhutto had given great thought to dealing with Pakistan's myriad problems. She realized that her previous stints as prime minister had not lived up to her promises. On both occasions the elected government was not allowed to complete its term. Although the army and ISI had made it difficult to alter Pakistan's national security policies, civilian leaders' inexperience and lack of preparation had also impeded their success, as had their reputation for corruption. Bhutto wanted to be better prepared if she got a third chance to lead the country.

A few months after 9/11 I had opted for exile in the United States. In 1999, after irritating the Sharif government, I spent a few months under arrest. As is often the case in Pakistan, Pakistan Federal Investigating Agency (FIA) had initiated false criminal cases against me to cover up political motivations. As a vocal critic of Musharraf, I could not expect to be spared under military rule. Thus, the prospects of teaching at a US university and researching at an American think tank were far preferable to the possibility of another spell in prison.

Bhutto and I met regularly during her visits to the United States, where she was well liked on the lecture circuit. We discussed Pakistan's future. I often shared the findings of my research, which shed a very different light on the country's history from what most Pakistanis have been led to believe. In 2005 Zardari arrived in the United States for medical treatment after eight and a half years in prison. My wife, Farahnaz Ispahani, and I continued our discussions about Pakistan with Bhutto and Zardari.

On most occasions Bhutto identified terrorism and military rule as Pakistan's greatest problems. She argued that Pakistan could not make any progress without tackling the terrorist menace. The country also had to turn away from militarism and invest in its people. Education, health care, and infrastructure should take priority over spending endlessly in the name of national security. Pakistan, she felt, had become less secure as a result of neglecting human development. The policy of using nonstate actors to bolster national security had backfired, and Jihadi terrorists now posed a major risk to Pakistan.

In *Pakistan: Between Mosque and Military*, published in 2005, I documented the longstanding ties between Pakistan's Islamists and the state-security apparatus. I argued that US aid for military regimes in Pakistan had not only undermined Pakistani democracy; it had also inadvertently helped foster religious extremism. In a comment that offended Pakistan's military, I said that Pakistan had become a rentier state: it lived off payments from a superpower for its strategic location and intelligence cooperation rather than on the strength of the productivity of its economy.

Bhutto asked me to write a paper for her on how the foreign policy of a future democratic government should differ from that of the previous military regimes. In my paper I pointed out that Pakistan had made a mistake when it attempted to become a regional power while also being dependent on assistance from other countries. A better option for Pakistan would be to normalize relations with India and Afghanistan. Chinese President Jiang Zemin had also suggested just that in his address to the Pakistani Parliament in December 1996.

"We should look at the differences or disputes [with neighbors] from a long perspective," Zemin had said, suggesting, "If certain issues cannot be resolved for the time being, they may be shelved temporarily so that they will not affect the normal state-to-state relations."[1] His message to Pakistanis, whom he called China's "friends in need and brothers bound by common fate," had been unmistakable: Pakistan should not allow disputes with its neighbors to hold its foreign relations hostage. It should set aside the unresolved issues and pursue normal relations for its longer-term stability.

I argued in my paper for Bhutto that just as China did not give up its rights over Taiwan, Pakistan need not give up its claim on Kashmir. But it should start trade with India, which would enhance Pakistan's economic growth. It would also ensure peace, which is a precondition for development. In the case of Afghanistan, Pakistan should befriend the government in Kabul instead of trying to impose one of its choosing. Pakistan would need to put all terrorist groups out of action, come clean on its nuclear program, and admit that its resentment of the United States was because we were dependent on it.

Since 1947 dependence, deception, and defiance have characterized US-Pakistan relations. We sought US aid in return for promises we did not keep. Although even strong allies do not have 100 percent congruence of interests, in the case of Pakistan and the United States, the divergence far exceeded the similarities. Pakistan wanted to be able to act like Hafez Assad's Syria while demanding that the United States treat us like Israel.

In dealing with terrorism Pakistan could follow Colombia's model. There, with American backing, President Álvaro Uribe and his political allies confronted the lawlessness the drug cartels created. Pakistan could likewise shed the tag of a failing state by dealing with the problem and restoring the writ of the state. Instead of using public opinion as an ex-

· · · · ·

cuse to refuse action, Pakistan's leaders could build public opinion in favor of their new national agenda.

Bhutto and Zardari were intrigued by the idea of a new relationship with the United States that would be strategic rather than tactical, based, as it had been in the past, on asking for aid. They agreed with the concept of a self-confident Pakistan, free of the burdens of past blunders. Eliminating terrorism would be a future civilian government's first priority. Pakistan would work closely with the United States for this purpose. In return we would seek US assistance, but it would be directed toward standing on our own rather than being dependent on another. Within a few years Pakistan would be pursuing trade instead of depending on aid.

After Bhutto's assassination and the subsequent elections the PPP-led coalition government proceeded to implement this vision. But without Bhutto, mobilizing public opinion for a major shift in Pakistan's orientation proved difficult. Within weeks of taking office the government became mired in domestic controversies, gaining a reputation for ineptitude and corruption. The military and the ISI refused to fully subordinate themselves to the civilians. On issues that mattered to the Americans, the civilians were simply unable to deliver.

Gilani and Zardari asked for American patience, often citing their domestic compulsions. They believed that their responsibility for Pakistani policies relating to terrorism and nuclear proliferation started after they came to power, and thus, they should not be blamed for difficulties they had inherited. They often blamed the United States for its past support for Zia and Musharraf, to whom they attributed many of Pakistan's current troubles. Consequently, the United States often found civilian officials repeating explanations and excuses they had heard before instead of discussing solutions for long-standing problems.

When the civilian government first came into office the Bush administration offered it full US support. Soon after his election as prime minister, Gilani met Bush on the sidelines of a conference at the Egyptian resort town of Sharm-el-Shaikh. Gilani emphasized his commitment to fighting terrorism because "I have lost my own great leader, Benazir Bhutto" to extremists. Bush was visibly moved. Gilani was invited to Washington, where Bush reiterated his support.

$\cdots\cdots$

Within days of Zardari's election as president Bush met him in New York on the occasion of the UN General Assembly session. Zardari was concerned about Pakistan's economy, which had been jolted by the year of anti-Musharraf protests. Foreign exchange reserves had dipped to precarious levels. But the US economy was going through its own crisis. In a meeting with the editors of the *Wall Street Journal*, Zardari had proposed that the United States infuse $100 billion into the Pakistan economy as aid, investments, and bank deposits; instead, officials in the Bush administration helped Pakistan secure $7.6 billion from the IMF.

In the final few months of the Bush administration most of its officials felt obligated toward Pakistan. They had supported Musharraf and had been disappointed. They now wanted civilian rule to succeed. National Security Adviser Stephen Hadley created a regular monitoring system so that both sides could review their specific commitments. Zardari had asked my predecessor, Major General Mahmud Durrani, to serve in the newly created post of national security adviser on the Pakistani side. Durrani and Hadley conferred regularly to translate promises into actions.

At one point soon after the formation of the Gilani government Pakistan found itself unable to meet the payment schedule for upgrading the F-16 fighter jets from the Reagan-Zia era. The Bush administration helped out by shifting $230 million in aid to Pakistan from counterterrorism programs to upgrading the aging F-16 fleet. Our air force claimed that it would use the planes to bomb terrorists. One congressional critic derided the argument, however, stating, "Using F-16s this way is like hitting a fly with a sledgehammer."[2]

Everyone knew that the F-16s were part of Pakistan's arsenal against India. Representative Nita Lowey, a New York Democrat who headed the House appropriations subcommittee on foreign operations, demanded a demonstration of "how these F-16s would be used to fight Al Qaeda and the Taliban in order to get Congressional support."[3] But the mood in Washington was to help the new civilian government, which did not want to delay upgrading Pakistan's old F-16s. As the request for reallocating funds from counterterrorism programs to pay for the F-16s came through the newly elected civilians, as a favor to Pakistan's newly elected leaders, Congress did not press its objections.

The United States had been flying drones over the tribal areas bordering Afghanistan for several years, and during Musharraf's last year the US drone campaign had been presented in Pakistan as a violation of Pakistani sovereignty. Still, the CIA and ISI communicated regularly on the subject of drones. The ISI did not like Pakistani civilian officials finding out anything about their dealings with the United States about armed Predator drones, but the US government wanted the civilian leadership to remain in the picture.

At one point CIA Deputy Director Steve Kappes complained that the "coordination process with Pakistan" in the use of drones was getting lengthier. "Sometimes we do not get the decision up to four days," he said, implying that the ISI had signed off on drone strikes much faster in the past. Kappes also lamented that Pakistanis had a different threat perception than did the United States and did not consider the war against terrorism as their war. "But Al-Qaeda is equally focused on Pakistan," he insisted. Zardari and Gilani initially asked that the United States should provide Pakistan its own drones so that the program could be described to sovereignty-conscious Pakistanis as a joint program, but the ISI and the army leadership preferred things the way they were. The generals only wanted more say in who the US drones targeted. Under Musharraf Pakistan had distinguished between "good" and "bad" Taliban; those with ties to the ISI enjoyed protection, whereas the ones trying to operate independently or attacking Pakistan's security forces were targeted for elimination. By protesting against the drones publicly while privately negotiating over whom the drones might target, the ISI sought to manipulate a delicate balance among various Taliban factions.

In the summer of 2008 Chairman Joint Chiefs Admiral Michael Mullen traveled to Pakistan with Kappes to demand action against several specific groups, including the Haqqani network, responsible for killing US troops in Afghanistan. Pakistan agreed to act sequentially against the various groups the Americans identified, beginning with the easier targets first. But Durrani conveyed the ISI's denial of the existence of the Taliban's main decision-making body, the Quetta Shura. The United States was certain about its intelligence and was not impressed by Pakistani denials.

· · · · ·

Pakistan did promise to close down a Madrassa run by the Afghan Haqqanis, but it cited "limitations of capacity" in response to all other requests for action, asking for more equipment and assistance before its forces could act in the tribal areas along the Afghan border. Moreover, the Pakistan army put in its own request for US drones to target Baitullah Mehsud, whose Pakistani Taliban group threatened the Pakistan military directly. At this point the United States had a list of "High Value Targets" marked for assassination by drones, primarily consisting of Al-Qaeda leaders and Afghan Taliban commanders. Conspiracy theorists claimed that the United States did not eliminate Mehsud because eliminating threats to Pakistan were not a US priority. However, US officials added Pakistani Taliban to their list of targets after the ISI's request, and a Hellfire missile fired from an American Predator subsequently killed Mehsud. But his death silenced the conspiracy theories only temporarily; soon other stories of alleged American perfidy were in circulation in Islamabad.

Pakistan's security establishment's unwillingness to speak openly about allowing drone operations was matched by America's own secrecy about the entire program. But the CIA-ISI cooperation in the matter was an open secret in Washington, and US media reported on the arrangement in some detail.[4] Over the years the drones became a major issue in the rhetoric surrounding the relationship. The United States insisted that their strikes only targeted terrorists with precision. Meanwhile, the ISI kept quiet about some strikes, possibly the ones they approved, while encouraging protests about others that killed some of their Jihadi allies. The civilians were seldom briefed in detail about the ISI-CIA relationship and had little say in its conduct, though reports in the Pakistani media continually accused the elected leaders of bending over backward to fulfill an American agenda. Thus, the army and the ISI retained control over the relationship with the United States while also keeping anti-Americanism alive as a means of fending off US demands that they considered against their regional policies.

In October Lieutenant General Ahmed Shuja Pasha became director-general of the ISI. Pasha was short in physical stature, pleasant in demeanor, and had a tendency to wear his patriotic fervor on his sleeve. He was close to Kayani, the army chief, who had assured Mullen about

Pasha's professionalism and his commitment to eliminate terrorists. But Pasha's tenure as head of the controversial organization began with a bang. On November 26, the American Thanksgiving Day holiday, twelve coordinated terrorist attacks in the Indian financial capital, Mumbai, killed 166 people and left more than 300 injured.

The terrorists took over several hotels and a Jewish Community Center. They used firearms and hand grenades, took hostages, and did not stop until all but one of them had died three days later. Communications between the terrorists and their handlers were recorded. Indian commandos arrested the last remaining gunman, Ajmal Kasab. Americans were among the dead.

The Pakistan-based Lashkar-e-Taiba (LeT), a group with close ties to the ISI, had executed the attack. Pakistan, however, initially denied any connection to the attack. Instead of trying to identify and punish terrorists, Pakistan focused on refuting reports of Pakistani complicity. When Kasab revealed during interrogation that he was from Pakistan, the ISI's media wing swung into action to deny journalists access to his village.

The Mumbai attacks lost Pakistan the Bush administration's sympathy for good. Deputy Secretary of State John Negroponte excluded all officials from a meeting with Durrani to address the national security adviser and me in private. Although Negroponte was known as a friend of Pakistan, on this occasion his language reflected a degree of agitation, whih was something unusual for a diplomat of Negroponte's experience. "Why do we sense a degree of guilt in Pakistan's conduct?" he asked deliberately.

Negroponte wondered why Pakistan refused access to the LeT planners it had arrested. Was it concerned that they might speak of their relations with the ISI? "It is time for Pakistan to come clean," he said. "The past can go away only by moving forward." Durrani said that Pakistan's courts would determine the legality of requests for access, drawing a sharp rebuke from Negroponte. "We know about Pakistan's courts," he said, adding, "They order the hanging of elected prime ministers when the army asks them and don't look at legal niceties." Durrani spoke of the Pakistani government's "political compulsions." The United States, he said, must give elected leaders "time and space" to

· · · · ·

fulfill their promises. Over the next three and a half years as ambassador I heard visiting Pakistani officials make the same request repeatedly.

If Negroponte's tone in his meeting with Durrani was agitated, the tone of Secretary of State Condoleezza Rice on this occasion was downright angry. She began with the words: "I will not sugarcoat anything I say to you today," and then went on to prove that right. She addressed Durrani and me to say, "We have no doubt about the commitment of President Zardari, Prime Minister Gilani, or the two of you to opposing terrorism, but there is a serious problem with Pakistan."

She said that there was "clear evidence" in relation to the Mumbai attacks. She acknowledged that there was no direct link between the attackers and the Pakistan government, but "when people have been trained and intelligence operatives have relations with people who have been trained for such attacks then there is a connection." She suggested that Pakistan stop asking for proof and stop claiming that there is no proof. "This does not serve you," Rice emphasized. "What you think and what the whole world thinks are two different things."

According to Rice, Pakistan had all the information it needed to shut terrorist operations down forever. After all, ISI knew who it had trained and equipped for terrorism. "I realize that there could be instability if you go after the Jihadis groups," she observed, "but you will be consumed if you do not." It seemed that she felt the need to convey her strongly held views before she ended her tenure. She had been diplomatic with Pakistani officials for eight years, but now she wanted to get it out.

Rice said that "Focusing your energies on an Indian threat that does not exist is a colossal mistake." Pakistan had to "make a strategic decision that association with terrorists has to come to an end." According to her, Pakistan could not "keep these people as an option" because "keeping contacts with various Jihadi groups is not acceptable." She said the United States and Britain would help if Pakistan lacked the capacity to take on the terrorists.

Durrani responded to Rice's angry tone with some heated remarks of his own. He said that the ISI was involved in training LeT, "just as we were all involved together in dealing with Afghanistan during the 1980s." He insisted that Pakistan's "point of view on Jammu and Kashmir was right, and that allowed us to use" the option of supporting militants. But he claimed that the ISI's links with LeT were broken in 2002. "To the best of my knowledge," Durrani stated, "there is no operational correction between ISI and LeT." He said that Pakistan had changed the ISI leadership four times and had changed three layers of personnel. "Pakistan is not keeping the Jihadis as an option," he emphasized. But Rice did not relent. Without raising her voice but remaining extremely curt, like a schoolteacher reprimanding her favored pupil, she proceeded again: "You are truthful as far as you know but not right."

According to Rice, there were continued contacts between LeT and ISI. "There is material support to LeT and the LeT has just recently killed six Americans," she added. I sent a detailed account of the Rice-Durrani conversation to Islamabad. "As I have said in many telegrams since becoming ambassador," I remarked, "the view from Washington is very different from the way issues and matters are being perceived in Islamabad."[5]

Soon after Durrani's trip the United States shared intelligence with Pakistan that proved the LeT's culpability. Individuals involved in planning the attacks were arrested after it became obvious that lack of action could again bring India and Pakistan to blows. ISI Chief Pasha then visited the United States for a meeting with CIA Director Michael Hayden. He admitted that the planners of the Mumbai attacks included some "retired Pakistani army officers." According to Pasha, the attackers had ISI links, but this had not been an authorized ISI operation.

Pasha came for tea to the embassy before returning to Pakistan. He spoke of the "difference between having links and exercising authority, direction and control." According to Pasha, it was important to put the Mumbai incident behind us and move on. There was clearly no intention to act against LeT. I took the opportunity to share with Pasha the names of ISI officers who had been egging on journalists back home to attack me as an American agent. He promised to "take care of the problem" just as he had promised Hayden to deal with the fallout of the Mumbai attacks.

• • • • •

Subsequently the CIA received "reliable intelligence" that the ISI was directly involved in the training for Mumbai.[6] The trial of the LeT masterminds arrested in Pakistan for the attacks dragged on. On several occasions Americans detected the terrorist prisoners using cell phones to direct further terrorist attacks.

In January 2009 Gilani fired Durrani, possibly at the behest of some ISI officers, for publicly acknowledging Kasab's Pakistani citizenship.[7] Thus, the government had lost one of its main interlocutors with the Americans. The position of national security adviser was never filled again. This left discussion with the United States of counterterrorism issues solely in the hands of the ISI. Later Kasab's Pakistan connection could not be kept a secret anyway. He gave detailed testimony to an Indian court about his life in Pakistan and his training for terrorism. Pakistani journalists were able to trace his family, some of whom expressed pride in his contribution to Jihad. Officially, however, Pakistan maintained the fiction that it had no knowledge of Kasab. When he was executed in India three years later, Pakistan did not allow his family to claim his body for burial in his hometown.

✦

RIGHT BEFORE Barack Obama's inauguration Vice President–elect Joe Biden arrived in Islamabad on a one-day trip. As a senator, Biden had strongly supported the restoration of democracy in Pakistan. He had been persuaded by Bhutto's argument that elected civilians could fight terrorism more effectively than could dictators such as Musharraf. Zardari conferred one of Pakistan's highest civilian awards, Nishan-e-Pakistan, on Biden.

Biden shared Obama's position with Zardari. Obama would make a concerted effort to win the war in Afghanistan and to defeat Al-Qaeda, he said. Pakistan could help the United States in fixing Afghanistan, and in return the United States would help Pakistan address its fundamental problems. If the ISI broke its ties with the Taliban, the United States could prevail in Afghanistan with a lot less bloodshed. America's next vice president was speaking of a "grand bargain" that would strengthen a democratic Pakistan, benefit its people, and rid the region of terrorism.

Zardari said that he could help only if he were sufficiently strong at home. He did not want to be hated "for being an American stooge." He said that Pakistan needed "economic resources so that I can show the people that there's something in it for them." Biden said he understood Zardari's political needs. As vice president, he would help get a significant aid package through Congress for Pakistan.

But, Biden added, "If you do not show spine then all bets are off." Senator Lindsey Graham, a Republican from South Carolina who was accompanying Biden, asked Zardari to end "the indecision that plagues your country." Pakistan had to figure out its enemies and its allies, Graham said. "We're your allies," he emphasized; "We're not your enemies." When Zardari brought up the subject of India, Biden said that the change Americans sought included a fundamental transformation in Pakistan's attitude toward India and vice versa.

Soon after his inauguration Obama appointed Richard Holbrooke as his special representative for Afghanistan and Pakistan. Holbrooke had brokered the Dayton Peace Accords in Bosnia-Herzegovina, among other diplomatic achievements. He knew how to coax and bully recalcitrant foreign leaders. However, he abhorred war and conveyed genuine caring for the people of other nations. Although many Americans commented on his ego and his penchant for publicity, among Pakistanis he was seen as a master negotiator who made even the weakest leaders feel good.

Holbrooke and I met the day his appointment was announced. He told me that his objective was "to ensure a successful end to the war in Afghanistan and a stable Pakistan and a stable Afghanistan." He said that contrary to views expressed in some circles, the United States had no ulterior motives regarding Pakistan. "The US will never ask Pakistan to do anything that harms Pakistan's national interest," he remarked. But as a friend, the United States wanted to have "candid discussions about what Pakistan's national interests and priorities might be."

Regarding India, Holbrooke said, "I will deal with India by pretending not to deal with India." Then he added that India also came within the purview of his brief to the extent that it impinged on Pakistan and

......

Afghanistan's security. He asked me rhetorically if the United States could be "friends with both India and Pakistan at the same time." He wondered if Hamid Karzai was the best man to lead Afghanistan under the circumstances and whether alternatives were available.

Holbrooke said that Pakistan had become the focus of the policy community in Washington, and he did not envy my job. "Increased focus and scrutiny," he commented, "raise questions to which there were no easy answers." From that day Holbrooke and I became good friends. He assembled a huge staff drawn from various agencies within the US government as well as nongovernment advisers. He traveled frequently to Pakistan and around the world to drum up support for a comprehensive strategy to end the Afghan war.

On the eve of Holbrooke's first visit to Pakistan as special representative, a Pakistani court ordered the removal of all restrictions on nuclear proliferator A. Q. Khan. The timing of the decision was meant to convey to the United States that Pakistan's fundamental attitudes would not change anytime soon. The chairman of the House Foreign Affairs Committee, Howard Berman, cautioned that Khan's release "could lead to reduction of U.S aid to Pakistan."[8] But Holbrooke chose to ignore the event. His sights were on the broader strategic picture.

Over the next two years Holbrooke developed close ties with Zardari, Kayani, and a host of Pakistani politicians and public figures. Along with National Security Adviser James Jones and with the full support of Secretary of State Clinton, Holbrooke organized a multilayered "Strategic Dialog" between Pakistan and the United States. The Dialog covered many tracks, from agriculture to security. Holbrooke's team became involved with schemes for conserving water and managing Pakistan's energy crisis. They sought to win the trust of Pakistani officials by handling issues such as opening the US market for Pakistani mangoes.

But the Pakistani military and ISI mistrusted Holbrooke from the start. Kayani preferred to deal with Mullen, assuming that a man in uniform would be prove to be the more effective interlocutor. When the US Congress approved what came to be known as the Kerry-Lugar-Berman Bill, which authorized $1.5 billion annually for five years (a total of $7.5 billion), the Pakistani military reacted negatively to the bill's conditions against military intervention in politics. The aid package was the largest the United States had ever offered Pakistan for civilian purposes such as education, health care, poverty alleviation, and infrastructure.

All US foreign aid legislation included reporting requirements for the executive branch, and this bill was no exception. But hard-liners in the Pakistan army had convinced themselves that Holbrooke and I had connived to insert "humiliating" conditions about civilian control over the military. Pakistan's religious nationalists termed it a conspiracy to put Pakistan's army under American control. Holbrooke worked with Mullen and Senator John Kerry, a Democrat from Massachusetts, to defuse the situation. I offered to resign, but Zardari laughed off the affair as a routine effort to derail civilian rule.

In an attempt at humor I sent a copy of Samuel Huntington's book *The Soldier and the State: The Theory and Politics of Civil-Military Relations* to Kayani along with a four-page summary. The book deals with the role of a professional military in a democracy. Kayani acknowledged receiving the book and appreciated the summary. But I have no reason to believe that it affected his thinking or decisions in any significant way. Kayani was personally always agreeable with civilians. The Pakistan army, as an institution, still remained a long way from accepting the right of civilians to debate, let alone define, national interest.

Holbrooke's efforts at finding a comprehensive solution for the Afghan problem, including an end to terrorist safe havens, received little support from Pakistan's generals. They sensed that he did not have the full backing of all parts of the US government. Media reports and some books spoke of Holbrooke lacking Obama's full support, and Holbrooke's critics suggested that he was "all over the place" and lacked pointed aims. But in Islamabad the sense was that the ISI could still deal separately with the CIA, and Mullen remained Kayani's principal conversational partner.

Pasha and the ISI continued to propel hypernationalist sentiment. Pasha once told me that this was one of the few tools Pakistan had for leveraging itself in an asymmetric relationship. Americans often ignored the rumors and misinformation routinely circulated through Pakistan's media, though sometimes they reacted to point out the absurdity of

. . . . .

the tactic. Holbrooke once mentioned a story in which Pasha had snubbed Mullen, "the highest ranking U.S. military officer" and "the Special Representative of the U.S." He said he realized that it may have something to do with "perceived domestic needs in Pakistan," but it should not be forgotten that "there were domestic political compulsions on the US side as well." He asked, "Now why would your side lie about something like that?"

Parallel to the US–Pakistan Strategic Dialog, Holbrooke also initiated tripartite talks between Afghanistan, Pakistan, and the United States. After the first round of the tripartite talks Pasha complained that this format amounted to boxing Pakistan in. The civilians were able to keep the dialogue going. But more often than not, discussions about Afghanistan always ended up being about the ISI's role there. One of Holbrooke's deputies remarked that the frequency of interaction had only one advantage: it had inadvertently made Pakistan's generals incrementally less deceitful.

US media and members of Congress criticized Pakistan for its appeasement of terrorists when, on several occasions, it showed a preference for talking to Taliban instead of fighting them. Although several agreements were signed in different parts of the country, the Taliban broke all of them. Americans could not understand why Pakistani leaders had difficulty making a clear choice, but Zardari and Gilani did not find sufficient support at home for a bold decision. They thought US economic support was insufficient and anti-Americanism in Pakistan was too strong to sign up as closer US allies than they already were.

During the first year of the Obama administration some US officials had already reached the conclusion that the United States could not achieve its goals in Afghanistan as long as Pakistan continued to support the Taliban with "weapons and logistical support." There were calls for cutting off military aid and reimbursements under the Coalition Support Funds program as a substitute for trying "to buy off Islamabad with more economic aid."[9]

Clinton and Holbrooke were largely responsible for preventing that from happening. Congress approved $828 million for aid to Pakistan in 2009. That same year an international conference in Tokyo pledged $5.5

billion to be provided by various international donors. But for Pakistanis, the money was never enough. Every now and then Pakistani officials showed up with charts to illustrate the presumed economic loss the country suffered because of terrorism and the war against it. They asked the United States to compensate Pakistan for lost investment, lost revenue, and lost economic opportunities. Americans considered the aid they were already giving to be a huge amount of money and did not accept that US taxpayers should bear even greater cost for Pakistan's sake. No one in Washington believed that Pakistan's problems were America's responsibility and that they were caused exclusively by the country's role in the anti-Soviet Jihad and the war after 9/11 against terrorism. US officials were often too polite to say so directly, but in their view, successive Pakistani leaders had made a series of wrong choices, and blaming the United States was just a way of refusing to take responsibility for those Pakistani decisions.

In May Zardari and Obama had their first meeting as presidents. Obama had hosted a trilateral meeting that also included Karzai. Likewise, he invited Zardari to the White House for a direct conversation. Obama said that "the average U.S. Congressman" wanted to help Pakistan in beating back terrorism, but US aid was being used "to bolster conventional arms against India." "We do not begrudge your concerns about India," he stated. "But we do not want to be part of arming you against India."

Obama also said that the United States did not believe that India wanted to attack or threaten Pakistan any longer. He said he knew history and realized that at some point Pakistan may have been justified in its fears of India. "But I want you to hear it from me," he went on, "that they are focused on economic development." Zardari summed up his talking points about why Pakistan still viewed India as a threat, and then added, "We are trying to change our worldview. But it's not going to happen overnight."

That summer Pakistani troops moved against the Taliban in the Swat Valley after they had come relatively close to the Pakistani capital. The pretext of a lack of national consensus vanished as cable news stations "suddenly" discovered videos of Taliban atrocities. TV commentators and newspaper editorialists changed their stance; instead of describing the war against terrorists as an American war, as they had done so far, they finally spoke of the threat to Pakistan from terrorism.

"Finally, the mind-set has changed," the *Washington Post* quoted a retired security official as saying. The paper described him as someone "who often reflects military thinking." His next quote was: "There is a realization that the threat to Pakistan in modern times is not Indian divisions and tanks, it is a teenaged boy wearing a jacket full of explosives."[10] The prospect of Pakistani seriousness in counterterrorist and counterinsurgency operations heartened US officials.

In response, the United States mobilized a sizeable relief effort for those displaced by the fighting. Once the fighting was over, the Pakistan army received favorable press in the United States. Soon, requests for military equipment followed, and a few months later the momentum dissipated when domestic politics and a long-drawn battle with Pakistan's Supreme Court distracted the civilian government. The army returned to its previous debate about whether terrorism had replaced India as the new existential threat to Pakistan.

In the fall Clinton arrived in Pakistan for a three-day visit. Her well-choreographed visit included many public events, including town hall meetings with students, civil society leaders, women, and Pashtun elders. She answered tough questions from Pakistani journalists and asked some difficult ones herself.[11] Clinton's visit was the second effort from a senior US official to confront the myths and conspiracy theories that had fed anti-Americanism in the country; her husband, Bill, had made the first through his televised address to the Pakistani people during his five-hour visit in 2000. She expressed surprise that no one in Pakistan knew Osama bin Laden's whereabouts.

Clinton described the Kerry-Lugar-Berman aid as a demonstration of American "goodwill towards the people of Pakistan," noting that "it does not help when we do something like this, and people question our motives."[12] She asked the government to "do more to shut down Al Qaeda," but she also spoke of the need to broaden the relationship.

Soon after Clinton's visit Jones, the national security adviser, brought a letter from Obama to Zardari, offering that Pakistan and the United States become "long-term strategic partners." The letter laid out elements of the "grand bargain" that Biden had spoken of a few days before Obama's presidential term began. The letter even hinted at addressing Pakistan's oft-stated desire for a settlement of the Kashmir dispute.

Obama wrote that the United States would tell countries of the region that "the old ways of doing business are no longer acceptable." He acknowledged that "some countries"—a reference to India—had used "unresolved disputes to leave open bilateral wounds for years or decades. They must find ways to come together." But in an allusion to Pakistan he said, "Some countries have turned to proxy groups to do their fighting instead of choosing a path of peace and security. The tolerance or support of such proxies cannot continue."

"I am committed to working with your government," said the US president, "to ensure the security of the Pakistani state and to address threats to your security in a constructive way." He asked for cooperation in "defeating Al Qaeda, Tehrik-e-Taliban Pakistan, Lashkar e Taiba, the Haqqani network, the Afghan Taliban and the assorted other militant groups that threaten security." Obama then wrote of his "vision for South Asia," which involved "new patterns of cooperation between and among India, Afghanistan and Pakistan to counter those who seek to create permanent tension and conflict on the subcontinent."[13]

My interpretation of Obama's letter was that it presented an opportunity for Pakistan to overcome past misgivings and build a real alliance with the United States. Since the 1950s Pakistan had wanted an American role in South Asia. Now it was being offered one. In the end Pakistan would have to negotiate the Kashmir issue directly with India. But at least now the American president was saying that he would nudge the Indians toward those negotiations. Pakistan could finally be a strategic US ally rather than an occasional transactional partner.

But the view from Islamabad was different. In his meetings in Islamabad Jones had remarked that "US strategic interests lay East of Afghanistan." He meant to assure his hosts of Pakistan's centrality to US policy. The Obama administration was in the middle of its review of US policy in Afghanistan. Jones had hinted that Pakistan was the epicenter of that review and had also stated that the main issues relating to Al-Qaeda, extremism and terrorism, were in Pakistan. The Foreign Office asked me to convey Pakistan's concern that it was being treated "as the problem."

......

In a meeting with me after his visit, Jones stressed that he had wanted to reassure Pakistanis that any perception that the United States was leaving the region was simply wrong. "Pakistan's success is fundamental to America's success in the region," he told me. "The US is, therefore, counting on Pakistan in its efforts to eliminate the terrorist threat." Jones said that if Pakistan was ready to make "a strategic commitment to common objectives," the United States was ready to be "a partner for the twenty-first century."

The Obama administration had asked for "fundamental readjustments" before the two countries could be "partners for a long time to come." But Islamabad was not ready for them. When Zardari's reply arrived, it had clearly been drafted by a committee of Foreign Office and ISI bureaucrats, repeating old clichés about Afghanistan and the threat to Pakistan from India.

Kayani had given Jones his own more-than-fifty-page-long thesis on Pakistan's strategic threats and interests. I was allowed to read it in Islamabad, but no Pakistani civilian was provided a copy to keep. As I read it, it felt familiar; I wondered where I had read it before. Then I realized that its contents were remarkably similar to the paper President Ayub Khan had given President Eisenhower in 1959. Obviously, for Pakistan's permanent institutions of state, nothing had changed in half a century. Pakistan had missed the opening for defining its partnership with the world's sole superpower on more favorable terms than ever before.

According to Bob Woodward, Obama told his confidante Tom Donilon in November that he saw the "cancer" of terrorism as being in Pakistan. "The reason we are doing the target, train and transfer in Afghanistan is so the cancer doesn't spread there," the US president reportedly said. "We also need to excise the cancer in Pakistan."[14] The New York Times reported Obama's view that "it did not matter how many troops were sent to Afghanistan if Pakistan remained a haven."[15] Other reports cited Biden as describing Pakistan as the "greater danger" over Taliban control of the Afghan countryside.[16]

In 2010 Obama deployed several thousand more troops into Afghanistan in what was described as a "troop surge," committing the United States to spending an additional $30 billion annually on enhancing its

......

military presence there. The United States would thus make a serious effort to defeat the Taliban insurgency. Efforts for "a lasting partnership with Pakistan" would continue. Obama wanted to go down in history as a strong US president who did not hesitate to hunt terrorists in farther lands in pursuit of US national interests.

After the surge was announced Holbrooke persisted with his diplomatic efforts to find an Afghan endgame. The Strategic Dialog also continued, as did the flow of US economic assistance and Coalition Support funds. Terrorist attacks inside Pakistan or involving Pakistanis abroad also remained a constant. The most significant of these was the attempt to set off a truck bomb in New York's Times Square on May 1, 2010. Although the bomb did not go off, if it had, it could have killed a large number of people.

For Americans this was a reminder of their vulnerability to attacks resembling 9/11. The FBI identified Faisal Shahzad, a thirty-year-old Pakistani-American as the man responsible for the plot. Shahzad told the FBI that he had trained in bomb making in Pakistan's Waziristan region.[17] For Americans already wary of Pakistan, this was further proof that Pakistan's failure to deal with terrorists was a direct threat to US security.

During a meeting at the White House Jones told me that the Americans considered the Times Square attempted bombing as "a successful plot." It was foiled by luck, not intelligence or law enforcement activity. "Neither American nor Pakistani intelligence could intercept it," he remarked. US intelligence had reported that other similar plots were underway "involving several overlapping and interconnected groups." Pakistan had been helpful in investigating Shahzad and his connections, but the United States wanted Pakistan to help preempt attacks, not just investigate them after the fact.

Jones also visited Islamabad, where he conveyed a message from Obama to Zardari and Kayani. "The President wanted everyone in Pakistan to understand," he declared, "that in case of a successful attack in the US, there are some things even he would not be able to stop." Jones turned the Pakistani refrain about political compulsions on his hosts: "Just as there are political realities in Pakistan, there are political realities in the US," he said.

The national security adviser wanted Pakistanis to "understand clearly the message" that if a plot succeeds and its origins were traced to Pakistan, "no one will be able to stop the response and consequences." In a matter-of-fact tone he also added that what he had said was not a threat—it was "just a statement of political fact."

Jones listed four specific actions the United States sought from Pakistan. First, the ISI needed to share "all intelligence with us and we will share intelligence with you." Second, there should be immediate sharing of passenger data of flights originating from Pakistan. Third, counterterrorism cooperation should be enhanced. Fourth and finally, there should be an end to holding up visas for American intelligence and law enforcement personnel, "which is holding up our ability to protect against the terrorists."

The ISI claimed that it was already sharing all possible intelligence. Pakistan's Ministry of Defense refused to share flights' passenger data, offering only to examine the data itself, which it was presumably doing anyway. The rationale for not allowing Americans to process the data directly was a familiar one: "The Americans might monitor the movements of Pakistan's nuclear scientists," Defense Secretary Lieutenant General Athar Ali told me. When US officials offered to let Pakistanis withhold some of the data while sharing the rest, the answer was still "No."

In the case of visas for US officials, Pakistan's military was averse to the presence of large numbers of Americans in Pakistan. The CIA usually notified the ISI of its operatives working in Pakistan, but the ISI suspected that some of the others, coming as aid workers or diplomatic staff, were also spying on Pakistan. They had no answer to the US assertion that they routinely followed and monitored US officials' activities and did not need to deny visas for officials of an allied country. As a result, hundreds of visa applications were kept pending for months. After Clinton raised the matter with Gilani, the embassy in Washington was allowed discretion in expediting the issuance of visas. But soon reports surfaced in Pakistan that I was issuing visas to CIA operatives to spy on Pakistan.

Although we had streamlined the visas process, no visa was issued without following all procedures. The embassy's defense attaché, who reported to the ISI, handled visa requests from the Pentagon and the CIA. Finally, Pasha personally got involved in clearing CIA visas. He claimed that he only wanted to make sure that the ISI knew each CIA operative in Pakistan so they could protect them. But the noise about American spies and the unfounded allegations against me were just meant to keep down the number of Americans in Pakistan; this was hardly the way allies behaved with one another.

Then, in the middle of 2010, Pakistan suffered the worst floods in its history. Several million people were affected; a vast number lost their homes. Even though the United States sent several helicopters to assist in the relief effort, Holbrooke ensured that the Americans made the largest contribution to the $1.7 billion flood relief effort, and Kerry traveled to the flood-affected areas to show American support, opinion polls conducted after the floods showed little change in Pakistani anti-Americanism.

In October Kayani arrived in Washington as part of Pakistan's delegation for another round of the Strategic Dialog. Jones, who was stepping down as national security adviser, proposed that I bring the foreign minister, Shah Mahmood Qureshi, and Kayani to meet him on his last day at work. This would be an opportunity for Jones's successor, Tom Donilon, to meet the Pakistani team and could also be an occasion for Obama to drop in and deliver in person some key messages to Pakistan's army chief.

The meeting took place on October 20 in the Roosevelt Room of the White House. Fifteen minutes into the meeting Obama dropped in and stayed for almost half an hour. He began with polite remarks about US interest in "a strong, stable Pakistan" and economic support for Pakistani democracy. But then he repeated what Jones had said a few months earlier, and it sounded more ominous coming directly from the president of United States.

Obama said that his greatest concern related to extremists in Pakistan who target the United States—in Afghanistan and the US homeland. "If a successful attack is launched by people or groups traced to Pakistan," he said, "my hands would be tied." He repeated his invitation to Pakistan to work together in preventing that scenario. "I want to deal with this in a way that is respectful for Pakistan's sovereignty," Obama

· · · · ·

continued. "We are mindful of your concerns in your neighborhood and your strategic objectives."

In a firm tone Obama then delivered his core message: "The US is not interested in Pakistan being vulnerable," he declared. "It cannot, however, accept that your strategic concerns should include support for murderous groups." If Pakistan could build trust around this issue, it would "make my job easier in relation to helping Pakistan." He said that if Pakistan and the United States failed to build trust, "we will be on collision course." As long as Al-Qaeda and its affiliates operated in Pakistan, this would restrain Pakistan's relations with the United States.

Obama addressed Kayani and said that "your intelligence is wrong" that he should fear the United States. Obama decided to address Pakistani conspiracy theories directly. "You are hearing from the President of the United States that the US wants a strong, stable Pakistan," he said. "It is not in our interest to have a debilitated Pakistan."

Qureshi made a long-winded request that Obama should visit Pakistan and that it should equal the length of time he spends visiting India. Kayani voiced agreement with everything that Obama had said. But he then handed Obama a twelve-page paper to explain Pakistan's strategic perspective. Obama went to India in November, skipping Pakistan.

Holbrooke died on December 13 from complications of a torn aorta. I had met him for breakfast at the Four Seasons Hotel in Georgetown the day before he fell ill. He expressed frustration with Pakistan's unwillingness to change. "Everyone around the world wonders 'What does Pakistan's army want?' I wonder if they know themselves," he remarked. Holbrooke said that he intended to continue working for "as long as I can to make a difference" and advised me to do the same.

Zardari attended the Washington memorial service for Holbrooke. Obama then invited him, accompanied only by me, for a meeting in the Oval Office. During the meeting Obama and Clinton asked Zardari familiar questions about Pakistan's lack of leadership in the war against terror. They also expressed surprise that he had said nothing when a religious fanatic killed his friend Salmaan Taseer, the governor of Punjab. Zardari tried to explain Pakistan's domestic politics. Clinton continued the conversation, but Obama became quiet. As we left the

White House Zardari asked me if I had noticed that Obama had "switched off."

A few days later US–Pakistan relations began their nosedive with the Raymond Davis affair, in which the US contractor had killed two Pakistanis in Lahore when he thought they were trying to rob him, followed by the American raid in Abbottabad.

✱

I WAS ON MY WAY to Islamabad from Washington via London and Dubai on the evening of May 1, 2011, when US Navy SEALS conducted their clandestine operation to kill Osama bin Laden in his fortified compound in Abbottabad. The Americans had kept their plans secret from Pakistan, and no one in our government had any clue about the commando mission. I first learned about bin Laden's death when I turned on my cell phone upon landing at Heathrow Airport in the early morning of May 2. Among the many messages waiting for me was one from the foreign minister, instructing me to turn around immediately and return to Washington.

While I had slept on my flight to London, Mullen had called Kayani and Obama had spoken to Zardari. Although the United States had conducted the operation in complete secrecy and in violation of Pakistani sovereignty, Obama had mentioned Pakistan positively in his speech announcing bin Laden's elimination.

The United Nations had declared the Al-Qaeda leader an international terrorist, and any evidence that Pakistan offered him sanctuary would have been a violation of UN Security Council resolution 1267 and 1373. Mindful of that, Pakistan's initial official response to the event was a statement issued by the Foreign Office describing bin Laden's death as "a major setback to terrorist organizations around the world." The statement was issued after a meeting among Zardari, Gilani, and Kayani. It also said the US operation "illustrates the resolve of the international community including Pakistan to fight and eliminate terrorism."

"Al-Qaeda had declared war on Pakistan," the statement continued. It added that "Scores of Al-Qaeda sponsored terrorist attacks resulted in deaths of thousands of innocent Pakistani men, women and children" and claimed that "Pakistan has played a significant role in efforts to eliminate terrorism." Bin Laden's presence in Pakistan and the US ability to penetrate Pakistan's air space without our military finding out had embarrassed Pakistan's security. But the Pakistan government, backed by the military, preferred to look upon the incident positively so as to avoid being accused of complicity in protecting the world's most wanted terrorist.

Within a couple of days, however, the position in Islamabad began to shift. The ISI and the military faced criticism within and outside the country for their inability to track down bin Laden in a compound close to the Pakistan Military Academy. Some Pakistani critics wondered aloud whether the United States could repeat the success of their undetected commando operation against Pakistan's nuclear installations or other terrorists, such as Taliban leader Mullah Omar, who were believed to be under Pakistani protection. Opposition politicians called for the dismissal of ISI Chief Pasha, resulting in the ISI turning the tables by focusing on how civilian leaders' collaboration had enabled Americans to violate Pakistan's sovereignty.

On May 3 Pakistan's Foreign Office issued a second statement expressing, "deep concerns and reservations on the manner in which the Government of the United States carried out this operation without prior information or authorization from the Government of Pakistan." But this statement still recognized "the death of Osama bin Laden" as "an important milestone in the fight against terrorism" and insisted that "the Government of Pakistan and its state institutions have been making serious efforts to bring him to justice."

However, by then Islamists and hard-liners in the military, who described the operation against bin Laden as a US aggression on Pakistani soil, were swaying Pakistani public opinion. Instead of blaming the military for failing to detect bin Laden's presence as well as the US operation to kill him, the ISI diverted the Pakistani media's attention to fabrications that the elected civilians had helped the CIA create a massive intelligence-gathering network within Pakistan.

Parallel Gallup polls in Pakistan and the United States soon after bin Laden's killing showed the wide gap between the two nations' views. Two-thirds of Pakistanis polled condemned the US military action, contrasting with Americans' nearly universal approval.[18] A Pew Poll a month later showed that a majority of Pakistanis thought it was a bad thing that Osama bin Laden had been killed at all.[19] The Pakistani public was responding to what Pakistan's media told them; the airwaves were clogged with sentiments about how the United States had violated Pakistan's borders and should, therefore, be deemed its enemy. Some media persons spoke of bin Laden as a Muslim hero, and others claimed that he had not been killed in the US operation but rather had died of natural causes earlier. According to this last bizarre theory, the Americans had frozen bin Laden's body, only to use it later to proclaim success at a time that suited the US government.

The Obama administration felt the Pakistan government was doing little to inform Pakistan's people of the importance of bin Laden's elimination. Some US officials saw the ISI's hand behind the orchestration of anti-American protests and hinted that it wanted to avoid scrutiny of its complicity or incompetence in bin Laden's presence in Pakistan. The most benign theory about bin Laden hiding in Pakistan suggested that the ISI had failed to look for him, while ISI-protected Pakistani Jihadi groups offered him sanctuary without telling their contacts within the government.

Soon after the Abbottabad raid, Grossman and CIA Deputy Director Michael Morrell traveled to Islamabad to propose actions that Pakistan could take to build confidence in its commitment to fight terrorism. They shared intelligence about a bomb-making factory run by the Haqqani network in North Waziristan. According to the CIA, Al-Qaeda as well as the Taliban and Pakistani Jihadi groups used improvised explosive devices (IEDs) made at this factory. Kayani and Pasha promised that the Pakistan army would send in troops to shut down the illicit factory that was manufacturing the IEDs. A few days later the CIA sent time-stamped photographs showing the facility being dismantled hours before the army's arrival. The dismantling began after a man on a motorcycle went into the factory, thus leading to speculation that he had come to tip off the terrorists about the impending army operation.

The Americans concluded that Pakistan's failure to combat terrorism went beyond its law enforcement agencies' and armed forces' incompetence. They saw the ISI as deeply penetrated by Jihadist sympathizers

......

and the civilian government as unable to make firm decisions because of fear of public opinion, which was manipulated to prevent closer US-Pakistan cooperation against terrorism.

★

IN THE AFTERMATH of the US operation against bin Laden I made several attempts to bridge the gulf between the American and Pakistani understanding of each other's positions. But there was little willingness in Islamabad to accept that there was anything wrong on our end that needed to be fixed. The Abbottabad raid had caused Americans to see Pakistan negatively, and the average American now saw it as Osama bin Laden's sanctuary. I reported to the Pakistan government testy conversations with congressmen in which they said that voting for aid for Pakistan was becoming difficult because their constituents were not willing to support a country they saw as an "enemy." Senator Mark Kirk, a Republican from Illinois, told me frankly that he and many of his colleagues saw Pasha as a "bold-faced liar." But Pakistani officials rejected every US criticism or suggestion as manifesting "American arrogance."

Then in September, Admiral Mullen decided to publicly voice his vexation with the Pakistan army's unwillingness to be honest in its dealings with America. He had spent four years cultivating a friendship with Kayani, meeting the Pakistani general twenty-six times.

In congressional testimony Mullen described the Afghan Haqqani terrorist network as "a veritable arm of Pakistan's Inter-Services Intelligence agency." He said support for extremist groups, including the Haqqani network and anti-Indian terror organization Lashkar-e-Taiba, was part of the Pakistani government's policy and served Islamabad's interests. "The support of terrorism is part of their national strategy," Mullen observed.[20] For Kayani and other Pakistani generals, Mullen's statement should have served as a warning that anger toward Pakistan was not limited to US politicians; the US military, which had traditionally cultivated close ties with Pakistan, was also now losing patience. But there was no change in the generals' attitude either, probably because of their belief that the United States needed Pakistan for its disengagement from Afghanistan and would, therefore, continue to tolerate its support for some militant groups.

By November 2011 I myself had become a victim of the mistrust and misunderstanding between the two nations. A US businessman of Pakistani origin, now residing in Monaco, claimed in an article that I had asked him to deliver a secret memo to Mullen, seeking US help in thwarting a military coup right after the US operation that killed bin Laden. Kayani and Pasha claimed that their inquiries supported my accuser's claim. The Pakistani media dubbed the affair "Memogate." To prove my fidelity to Pakistan, I returned to Islamabad and resigned from my position as ambassador.

Pakistan's Supreme Court, without regard to legal or constitutional niceties, intervened directly. Without any trial, it created a Commission of Inquiry and barred me from leaving Pakistan. For two months I remained holed up, first in the Presidential Palace and later in the prime minister's house. I had not been charged with any crime but was nonetheless being portrayed as a traitor who sought foreign help against my own country's army. I feared that a terrorist would kill me if I went out. Eventually the court relented and allowed me to leave Pakistan.

Several months later the Commission of Inquiry alleged that I had acted against Pakistan's interests and had authorized the controversial memo. Pakistani hard-liners claimed I was an American agent of influence, with access in Washington's power corridors. Were that true, there would have been no reason for me to seek help—certainly not from a disreputable businessman—to deliver a message to the US government. To date, more than a year later, I have not been charged or tried. However, the Commission's report could lead to charges of treason, a conviction that carries the death penalty.

My sincere efforts to transcend the parallel narratives that have shaped US-Pakistani relations were not always appreciated in Pakistan, where conspiracy theories and hatred for the United States have become a daily staple of the national discourse. My detractors in Pakistan's security services and among pro-Jihadi groups have long accused me of being pro-American; they failed to see that advocating a different vision for my troubled nation was actually pro-Pakistan.

......

The expectation that Washington should simply do whatever the Pakistani hypernationalists desired remains unrealistic, as it has since 1947. My countrymen will someday have to come to terms with global realities. Pakistan cannot become a regional leader in South Asia while it supports terrorism. To think that the United States would indefinitely provide economic and military assistance in return for partial support of US objectives is delusional.

Americans must also overcome their fantasy that aid always translates into leverage and that personal relations with foreign officials can change what those officials consider to be their national priorities. If the Pakistanis have been reticent in their cooperation, Americans have resorted only to halfhearted sanctions. Successive administrations have waited until their last few months in office to deliver the toughest messages. By then, however, it is usually too late for threats to be effective. The history of constant misunderstandings confirms that Pakistan and the United States have few shared interests and very different political needs. Just because they don't get along does not mean they must be antagonists, however; they should just lower their expectations of one another, inject a cautious wariness in their future plans, and recognize that their electorates are fatigued by the other. Pakistan cannot pursue its dreams of being India's military equal by seeking American aid. If $40 billion in US aid has not won Pakistani hearts and minds, billions more will not do the trick. Unless Pakistanis define their national interest differently from how their leaders have for over six decades, the US-Pakistan alliance is only a mirage. The relationship needs redefinition, based on a recognition of divergent interests and an acknowledgement of mutual mistrust. Only then will Pakistan and the United States share the same reality.

Notes

Chapter One: False Start

1. "Pakistan:'Better Off in a Home'," *Time*, August 25, 1947, 33.

2. Margaret Bourke-White, *Halfway to Freedom: A Report on the New India in the Words and Photographs of Margaret Bourke-White* (New York: Simon & Schuster, 1949), 91–93.

3. Secret Telegram from George R. Merrell, Charge de Áffaires US Embassy New Delhi to Secretary of State George C. Marshall, May 2, 1947, *Foreign Relations of the United States* (hereafter *FRUS*) 3 (1947): 154–155.

4. Bourke-White, *Halfway to Freedom,* 91–93,

5. William Phillips, *Ventures in Diplomacy* (Boston: Beacon Press, 1952), 359.

6. Tom Treanor, "The Home Front," *Los Angeles Times*, March 23, 1943.

7. Abdul Sattar, *Pakistan's Foreign Policy, 1947–2005* (Karachi, Pakistan: Oxford University Press, 2007), 11.

8. Sartaj Aziz, *Between Dreams and Realities: Some Milestones in Pakistan's History* (Karachi, Pakistan: Oxford University Press, 2009), 28.

9. Stanley Wolpert, *Jinnah of Pakistan* (Delhi, India: Oxford University Press, 1984), vii.

10. Telegram from Consul General [India] Macdonald to the Secretary of State, March 8, 1947, *FRUS* 3 (1947): 149–150.

11. Fortnightly Report to the Viceroy by Sir Evan Jenkins, Governor of Punjab, February 1947, British India Library, Records of the Political and Secret Department, L/P & J/5/250, 3/79.

12. Entries in Mr. Casey's Diary, dated September 1 and September 11, 1945, documents 84 and 103 in *The Transfer of Power 1942–7*, vol. VI, ed. Nicholas Mansergh (London: Her Majesty's Stationery Office, 1976), 194–195, 246–247.

*****

13. Letter from Sir B. Glancy to Viceroy Field Marshal Viscount Wavell, August 16, 1946, L/P & J/5/248: ff 50–1, document 29, in Mansergh, *The Transfer of Power*, 71–72.

14. Dennis Kux, *The United States and Pakistan, 1947–2000: Disenchanted Allies* (Washington, DC: Woodrow Wilson Center Press, 2001), 7. See also Ayesha Jalal, *The Sole Spokesman: Jinnah, the Muslim League and the Demand for Pakistan* (Cambridge: Cambridge University Press, 1985).

15. Speech at a Lunch Given by Dr. Ziauddin Ahmed, Aligarh, India, March 8, 1944, cited in *Sayings of Quaid e Azam M. A. Jinnah*, ed. Rizwan Ahmed (Karachi, Pakistan: Pakistan Movement Research Center, 1970), 14.

16. Interview with the Associated Press, July 1942, cited in Ahmed, *Sayings,* 28.

17. M. Rafique Afzal, *Pakistan: History and Politics, 1947–1971* (Karachi, Pakistan: Oxford University Press, 2001), 99.

18. Aslam Siddiqui, *Pakistan Seeks Security* (Karachi, Pakistan: Longmans Green, 1960), 89.

19. "Emergency in Pakistan," editorial, *New York Times,* August 29, 1948.

20. "Reuters Report of Jinnah's Meeting in Cairo," in *Quaid e Azam and the Muslim World: Selected Documents*, ed. Atique Z. Sheikh and M. R. Malik (Karachi, Pakistan: Royal Book Co., 1978), 168.

21. The Parliamentary Debates [Hansard], fifth Series, vol. CL, July 10, 1947, col. 2445 (London: His Majesty's Stationery Office, 1947).

22. Ibid., July 16, 1947, col. 809.

23. "Reuters Report of Jinnah's Meeting in Cairo."

24. Bourke-White, *Halfway to Freedom*, 93–94.

25. Ibid.

26. *Quaid-e-Azam Mohammed Ali Jinnah's Speeches as Governor-general of Pakistan, 1947–48* (Karachi: Government of Pakistan, 1964).

27. "That Man," *Time,* September 20, 1948, 38.

28. Liaquat Ali Khan, *Pakistan: The Heart of Asia* (Cambridge, MA: Harvard University Press, 1950), 16.

29. "Mr. Nehru Again," editorial, *Dawn,* June 1 1949.

30. Sri Prakasa, *Pakistan: Birth and Early Days* (Meerut, India: Meenakshi Prakashan, 1965), 83.

31. Vazira Zamindar, *The Long Partition and the Making of Modern South Asia: Refugees, Boundaries, Histories* (New York: Columbia University Press, 2007), 176–177.

32. Abdus Sattar, "Fifty Years of the Kashmir Dispute: The Diplomatic As-

pect," in *Fifty Years of the Kashmir Dispute*, ed. Suroosh Irfani (Muzaffarabad, Pakistan: University of Azad Jammu and Kashmir, 1997), 11–12.

33. "Mr. Nehru Again."

34. Jawaharlal Nehru, "Speech at Aligarh University in March 1948," in *Jawaharlal Nehru Speeches, Volume 1: September 1946–May 1949* (New Delhi: The Publications Division, Ministry of Information and Broadcasting, Government of India, undated), 337–338.

35. Memorandum of Conversation between Assistant Chief of the Division of South Asian Affairs and Others with Sir Girija Shankar Bajpai, Secretary General Ministry of External Affairs, Government of India, April 2, 1948, *FRUS* 5 (1948): 501–506.

36. Nehru, *Speeches, vol. 1*, 338.

37. "Liaquat Asks Army for Social Service and Sacrifices," *Dawn*, April 10, 1948.

38. Record of the Interview between Lord Ismay and Jinnah, India Office Records, Mountbatten papers, Miscellaneous Manuscripts Section, Eur F.200/191, April 9, 1947.

39. Telegram from John Winant, Ambassador to the United Kingdom, to Secretary of State on Discussion with Sir Paul J. Patrick, Assistant Under Secretary of State, India Office, February 21, 1946, *FRUS* 5 (1946): 79–80.

40. Z. H. Zaidi, ed., *M. A. Jinnah-Ispahani Correspondence, 1936–48* (Karachi, Pakistan: Forward Publications Trust, 1975), 503.

41. Memo from US Ambassador to India Grady to the Secretary of State, July 2, 1947, *FRUS* 3 (1947): 158.

42. Memo of Conversation by Joseph S. Sparks of the Division of South Asian Affairs, December 26, 1947, *FRUS* 3 (1947): 175–179.

43. US Embassy New Delhi Cable to State Department, July 11, 1947, *FRUS* 3 (1947): 161–162.

44. Memo of Conversation by Joseph S. Sparks of the Division of South Asian Affairs, December 26, 1947, *FRUS* 3 (1947): 175–179.

45. George McGhee, *Envoy to the Middle World: Adventures in Diplomacy* (New York: Harper & Row, 1983), 91.

46. US Consulate Karachi Cable to State Department, June 21, 1947, 845.000/6–2147, Department of State Records, National Archives.

47. Minutes of Cabinet Meeting, September 9, 1947, 67/CF/47, National Documentation Center, Islamabad.

48. US Embassy Karachi Cable to State Department, September 2, 1947, 845F.00/9–247, Department of State Records, National Archives.

49. Memorandum from Ambassador Alling to Secretary of State Marshall, the Ambassador in Karachi [Paul Alling] to the Secretary of State [Marshall], March 22, 1948, 845F.00/3–2248, Department of State Records, National Archives.

50. Letter from Acting Secretary of State to Ambassador of Pakistan, dated December 17, 1947, *FRUS* 3 (1947): 172–174.

51. Report, dated April 19, 1949, by the State-Army-Navy Air Force Co-ordinating Committee (hereafter SANACC) Sub-Committee for the Near and Middle East, *FRUS* 6 (1949): 8–31.

52. Memo from Secretary of State Marshall to President Truman, March 11, 1948, *FRUS* 5 (1948): 496–497.

53. Report, dated April 19, 1949, by the SANACC Sub-Committee for the Near and Middle East, 8–31.

54. "Ispahani Wants More Aid for Small Nations," *Dawn*, November 28, 1947.

55. "American Aid," editorial, *Pakistan Times*, July 3, 1948.

56. Ameen K. Tareen, "Pakistan and the Marshall Plan," *Dawn*, September 5, 1949.

57. "American Aid."

58. US Embassy Karachi Cable to State Department, January 2, 1948, 845F.001/1–248, Department of State Records, National Archives.

59. "Mob Protest at Embassy in Pakistan," *San Francisco Chronicle*, May 22, 1948.

60. "To the Americans," editorial, *Dawn*, September 13, 1948.

61. "From the Americans," editorial, *Dawn*, September 14, 1948.

62. "That Man," 38.

63. *Nawai Waqt*, editorial, October 6, 1948.

64. Ghulam Moinuddin, "Spotlight on American Gutter Press: Lies and Slanders of Time," *Dawn*, October 11, 1948.

65. Kux, *The United States and Pakistan*, 26.

66. Ibid., 31–33.

67. McGhee, *Envoy*, 91.

68. Shuja Nawaz, *Crossed Swords: Pakistan, Its Army and the Wars Within* (Karachi, Pakistan: Oxford University Press, 2009), 96.

69. State Department Background Memorandum on the Visit to the US of Liaquat Ali Khan, April 14, 1949, President's Secretary's File, Harry S. Truman Library, cited in Kux, *The United States and Pakistan*, 33–34.

70. McGhee, *Envoy*, 97, 93.

71. Ibid., 93.

72. Ibid., 97.

73. S. M. Burke, *Mainsprings of Indian and Pakistani Foreign Policies* (Minneapolis: University of Minnesota Press, 1974), 127.

74. British Commonwealth Relations Office, Note on the Liaquat Visit, June 30, 1950, Prime Minister's Office 1216, Public Records Office, United Kingdom.

75. S. M. Burke and Lawrence Ziring, *Pakistan's Foreign Policy: An Historical Analysis* (Karachi, Pakistan: Oxford University Press, 1990), 123–124.

76. Ibid.

77. British Embassy Washington Letter to Foreign Office, June 1, 1950, UK National Archives, Documents Online 35/2981, cited in Kux, *The United States and Pakistan*, 36.

78. Burke and Ziring, *Pakistan's Foreign Policy*, 123–124.

79. Khan, *Pakistan*, 27–33.

80. Joseph Loftus, "Liaquat Ali Seeks Arms for Pakistan," *New York Times*, May 5, 1950.

81. Khan, *Pakistan*, 139.

82. Kux, *The United States and Pakistan*, 38.

83. Nawaz, *Crossed Swords*, 97.

84. Ibid.

85. Memorandum from Ambassador Avra Warren to Secretary of State Acheson, dated May 15, 1951, *FRUS* 6 (1951): 2204–2205.

86. Telegram from Secretary Acheson to Ambassador Warren, May 24, 1951, *FRUS* 6 (1951): 2205–2206.

87. "Policy of the United States with Respect to Pakistan," Department of State Policy Statement, April 3, 1950, *FRUS* 5 (1950): 1490–1498.

88. Dean Acheson, *Present at the Creation: My Years in the State Department* (New York: W. W. Norton & Co., 1987), 336.

Chapter Two: Aid, Arms, and Bases

1. "Aid to Pakistan," editorial, *New York Times*, June 28, 1953.

2. "A Noble Gesture," editorial, *Dawn*, June 26, 1953.

3. Department of State Bulletin, May 18, 1953, 723 890D.2311/5–1953, Department of State Records, National Archives, *FRUS* 11 (1952–1954): 1827, note.

4. Memorandum of Conversation by Secretary of State, June 12, 1952, *FRUS* 11 (1952–1954): 1819–1820.

5. Latif Ahmed Sherwani, *Pakistan, China and America* (Karachi, Pakistan: Council for Pakistan Studies, 1980), 50.

6. Ibid.

7. Memo from the Secretary of State to the Embassy in India, January 22, 1947 *FRUS* 3 (1947): 139–140.

8. C. L. Sulzberger, "Asia's Complex Issues Spread Before Dulles," *New York Times*, May 24, 1953.

9. Jawaharlal Nehru, "Broadcast Speech, September 7, 1946," in *India's Foreign Policy: Selected Speeches September 1946–April 1961* (New Delhi: Publications Division, Government of India, 1961), 2.

10. Telegram from Ambassador to the Soviet Union to Secretary of State, March 20, 1948, *FRUS* 5 (1948): 499.

11. "Mr. Dulles' First Report," *New York Times*, May 31, 1953.

12. Shirin Tahir-Kheli, *The United States and Pakistan—The Evolution of an Influence Relationship* (New York: Praeger, 1982), 3.

13. Ibid.

14. Dennis Kux, *The United States and Pakistan, 1947–2000: Disenchanted Allies* (Washington, DC: Woodrow Wilson Center Press, 2001), 57.

15. National Intelligence Estimate, June 30, 1953, *FRUS* 11, pt. 2 (1952–1954): 1083–1089.

16. Eisenhower Note to Dulles and Dulles reply, November 16, 1953, John Foster Dulles Chronological Files, Dulles papers, Dwight D. Eisenhower Library.

17. "Pakistan: A Second Turkey," editorial, *Pakistan Times*, November 9, 1953.

18. "Pakistan-US Military Pact," *Pakistan Times*, November 24, 1953.

19. "Nixon Ends Tour of World," Associated Press, December 14, 1953.

20. Telegram from the Acting Secretary of State to the Embassy in Pakistan, December 4, 1953, *FRUS* 11, pt. 2 (1952–1954): 1831.

21. Richard M. Nixon, *The Memoirs of Richard Nixon* (New York: Grosset and Dunlap, 1978), 132.

22. Minutes of NSC Meeting, December 24, 1953, National Security Council Series, *FRUS* 11, pt. 2 (1952–1954): 1835–1836.

23. Ibid.

24. Memo of Conversation between Vice President Nixon, Governor-General Ghulam Muhammad, and Ambassador Horace Hildreth, December 7, 1953, *FRUS* 11, pt. 2 (1952–1954): 1831–1832.

25. Ibid.

26. Memorandum of Conversation between Anthony Eden and Secretary Dulles, Bermuda, December 7, 1953, Foreign Office 371/106937, UK Public Records Office.

27. "Text of Agreement," *Dawn*, May 20, 1954.

28. "Mutual Defense Agreement," editorial, *Times of Karachi*, February 26, 1954.

29. Memo by Acting Secretary of State to Executive Secretary of NSC, August 19, 1952. *FRUS* 11, pt. 2 (1952–1954): 1059.

30. "Bases in Pakistan," editorial, *Washington Post*, December 11, 1953.

31. Ronald Steel, *Walter Lippmann and the American Century* (New York: Random House, 1981), 503–504.

32. Minutes of Meetings, March 25 and 27, 1954, of the Committee to Conduct Negotiations with the American Survey Team, Prepared by Maj Gen Musa, Pakistan Army GHQ Archives, in *Crossed Swords: Pakistan, Its Army and the Wars Within*, Shuja Nawaz (Karachi, Pakistan: Oxford University Press, 2009), 108–110.

33. The Ambassador in Pakistan [Hildreth] to the Department of State, Karachi, Pakistan, August 17, 1954, *FRUS* 11, pt. 2 (1952–1954): 1864–1865.

34. The Secretary of State to the Embassy in Pakistan, Washington, DC, August 20, 1954, *FRUS* 11, pt. 2 (1952–1954): 1865–1867.

35. Memorandum of conversation between Secretary of State and Prime Minister Mohammad Ali Bogra, Washington, October 18, 1954, *FRUS* 11, pt. 2 (1952–1954): 1868–1869.

36. Memorandum for the Record by C. C. Kirkpatrick of the Office of the Assistant Secretary of Defense for International Security Affairs, Washington, DC, January 18, 1955, *FRUS* 8 (1955–1957): 413–417.

37. Memorandum by the Assistant Secretary of Defense for International Security Affairs [Hensel], Karachi, Pakistan, February 17, 1955, *FRUS* 8 (1955–1957): 413–417.

38. Telegram from the Embassy in Pakistan to the Department of State, Karachi, Pakistan, December 13, 1955, *FRUS* 8 (1955–1957): 452–453.

39. Nawaz, *Crossed Swords*, 134.

40. Walter Lippmann, "Dulles Attempting to Escape Reality," *Los Angeles Times*, April 4, 1958.

41. Hans J. Morgenthau, "Military Illusions," *The New Republic*, March 19, 1956, 14–16.

42. "Pakistan and the West," editorial, *Pakistan Times*, February 16, 1956.

......

43. Memorandum of Conversation, Department of State, April 29, 1958, *FRUS* 15 (1958–1960): 635–637.

44. Herbert Feldman, *Revolution in Pakistan: A Study of the Martial Law Administration* (Karachi, Pakistan: Oxford University Press, 1965), 209.

45. Ibid.

46. Muhammad Ayub Khan, "Pakistan Perspective," *Foreign Affairs*, July 1960, 548.

47. Memorandum for the Record of a Meeting, Karachi, Pakistan, January 26, 1959, *FRUS* 15 (1958–1960): 697–699.

48. Memorandum of Conversation, July 17, 1959, *FRUS* 15 (1958–1960): 741–744.

49. Memorandum of Discussion at the 308th Meeting of the National Security Council, Washington, DC, January 3, 1957, *FRUS* 8 (1955–1957): 18–29.

50. Letter from the Ambassador in Pakistan to the Assistant Secretary of State for Near Eastern, South Asian, and African Affairs, December 27, 1957, *FRUS* 8 (1955–1957): 487–489.

51. Editorial Note, *FRUS* 15 (1958–1960): 615.

52. Kux, *The United States and Pakistan*, 113.

53. Memorandum of Conversation between Pakistan Ambassador Aziz Ahmed and Department of State, May 8, 1959, *FRUS* 15 (1958–1960): 726–729.

54. Ulysses S. Grant, United States' eighteenth president, had visited India after he relinquished office in 1877.

55. Russell Baker and Paul Grimes, "Eisenhower Gets a Warm Welcome from Pakistanis," *New York Times*, December 8, 1959.

56. Memorandum of a Conversation, Karachi, Pakistan, December 8, 1959, *FRUS* 15 (1958–1960): 781–792.

57. Ibid.

58. Ibid.

59. Ibid.

60. Ibid.

61. Memorandum of a Conversation between President Eisenhower and Prime Minister Nehru, New Delhi, India, December 13, 1959, *FRUS* 14 (1958–1960): 524–525.

62. Memorandum of Conversation, New Delhi, India, December 10, 1959, *FRUS* 15 (1958–1960): 521–522.

63. Ibid.

· · · · · ·

64. Memorandum of Conversation, Department of State, Conference Files: Lot 64 D 560, CF 1521, *Editorial Note, FRUS* 15 (1958–1960): 794–796.

65. Memorandum from the Assistant Secretary of State for Near Eastern and South Asian Affairs to the Deputy Under Secretary of State for Political Affairs, December 2, 1960, *FRUS* 15 (1958–1960): 819–821.

66. John F. Kennedy, "A Democrat Looks at Foreign Policy," *Foreign Affairs*, October 1957, 44–59.

67. "Mr. Kennedy and India," editorial, *Morning News* (Karachi, Pakistan), June 8, 1961.

68. Herbert Feldman, *Revolution in Pakistan* (Karachi, Pakistan: Oxford University Press, 1965), 205, note.

69. "Relations with Pakistan," editorial, *New York Times*, March 7, 1961.

70. Memorandum of Conversation between Vice President Johnson and President Ayub Khan, Karachi, Pakistan, May 20, 1961, *FRUS* 19 (1961–1963): 45–50.

71. Ibid.

72. Memorandum of Conversation between President Kennedy and President Ayub, Washington, DC, July 11, 1961, *FRUS* 19 (1961–1963: 66–74.

73. Ibid.

74. "Government Secret," *Chicago Daily Tribune*, July 17, 1961.

75. Memorandum from Robert W. Komer of the National Security Council Staff to the President's Special Assistant for National Security Affairs [Bundy], Washington, DC, January 6, 1962, *FRUS* 19 (1961–1963): 179–181.

76. Ibid.

77. Memorandum for the Record, Washington, DC, June 19, 1962, *FRUS* 19 (1961–1963): 278–279.

78. Memorandum from the President's Deputy Special Assistant for National Security Affairs to President Kennedy, Washington, DC, November 3, 1962, *FRUS* 19 (1961–1963): 363–368.

79. "Betrayal of Asia," editorial, *Dawn*, October 20, 1962.

80. Mujahed, "Nehru in Hitler's Footsteps," *Dawn*, November 26, 1962.

81. Memorandum from Robert W. Komer of the National Security Council Staff to President Kennedy, Washington, DC, November 12, 1962, *FRUS* 19 (1961–1963): 375.

82. Memorandum of Conversation among Ayub, Harriman, and Sandys, Rawalpindi, Pakistan, November 28, 1962, *FRUS* 14 (1961–1963): 409–412.

83. Notes by Secretary of State Rusk, Washington, DC, May 5, 1963, *FRUS* 19 (1961–1963): 575–577.

84. Ibid.

85. Central Intelligence Agency, Job 80 B 01285A, Box 6, McCone Files, DCI Meetings with President Johnson, November 23–December 31, 1963, *FRUS* 19 (1961–1963): 693.

86. Sherwani, *Pakistan, China and America*, 130.

87. "Pakistan Pops a Bubble," editorial, *Chicago Tribune*, September 3, 1963.

88. Memorandum of Conversation, Karachi, Pakistan, December 20, 1963, *FRUS* 19 (1961–1963): 712–717.

89. Letter from President Ayub to President Johnson, Rawalpindi, Pakistan, July 1, 1964, *FRUS* 25 (1964–1968): 129–130.

90. Memorandum of Conversation between Johnson and Amb. Ghulam Ahmed, Washington, DC, July 7, 1964, *FRUS* 25 (1964–1968): 132–134.

91. Memorandum of Conversation between Johnson and Ambassador Mc-Conaughy, Washington, DC, July 15, 1964, *FRUS* 25 (1964–1968): 136–138.

92. Telegram from the Embassy in Pakistan to the Department of State, Karachi, Pakistan, August 11, 1964, *FRUS* 25 (1964–1968): 143–146.

93. Telegram from the Department of State to the Embassy in Pakistan, Washington, DC, August 16, 1964, *FRUS* 25 (1964–1968): 147–148.

94. Nawaz, *Crossed Swords*, 200–201.

95. Aslam Siddiqui, *Pakistan Seeks Security* (Karachi, Pakistan: Longmans Green, 1960), 65–67.

96. Memorandum from Robert Komer of the National Security Council Staff to President Johnson, Washington, DC, August 28, 1965, *FRUS* 25 (1964–1968): 341–342.

97. Ibid.

98. Memorandum for the Record, Washington, DC, September 2, 1965, *FRUS* 25 (1964–1968): 345–346.

99. Ibid.

100. Telegram from the Embassy in Pakistan to the Department of State, Karachi, Pakistan, September 9, 1965, *FRUS* 25 (1964–1968): 379–383.

101. Ibid.

102. Telegram from the Office in Pakistan to the Department of State, Rawalpindi, Pakistan, September 6, 1965, *FRUS* 25 (1964–1968): 360–364.

103. Ibid., 365–366.

104. Telegram from the Embassy Office in Pakistan to the Department of State, Rawalpindi, Pakistan, September 10, 1965 *FRUS* 25 (1964–1968): 385–388.

105. Ibid.

106. Telegram from the Embassy in Pakistan to the Department of State, September 18, 1965, *FRUS* 25 (1964–1968): 406–407.

107. Ibid., 409–411.

108. A. R. Siddiqui, *The Military in Pakistan—Image and Reality* (Lahore, Pakistan:Vanguard Books, 1996), 107.

109. Memorandum from the President's Deputy Special Assistant for National Security Affairs [Komer] to the President's Special Assistant for National Security Affairs [Bundy], Washington, DC, October 7, 1965, *FRUS* 25 (1964–1968): 448–449.

110. Ibid.

111. Ibid.

112. Record of Meeting, Washington, DC, December 15, 1965, Johnson's Comments to Advisers Concerning Meeting with Ayub, *FRUS* 25 (1964–1968): 511–513.

113. Memorandum from the President's Special Assistant to President Johnson, April 26, 1966, *FRUS* 25 (1964–1968): 624–625.

114. Telegram from the Embassy in Pakistan to the Department of State, Rawalpindi, Pakistan, October 13, 1967, *FRUS* 25 (1964–1968): 903–905.

115. Telegram from the Department of State to the Embassy in Pakistan, Washington, DC, October 30, 1967, *FRUS* 25 (1964–1968): 914–917.

116. Memorandum of Conversation between President Johnson and President Ayub, December 23, 1967, *FRUS* 25 (1964–1968): 934.

117. Telegram from the Embassy in Pakistan to the Department of State, Rawalpindi, Pakistan, April 6, 1968, *FRUS* 25 (1964–1968): 961–964.

118. Telegram from the Department of State to the Embassy in Pakistan, Washington, DC, July 14, 1968, *FRUS* 25 (1964–1968): 994–995.

119. Selig Harrison, "India, Pakistan and the United States," *The New Republic*, September 7, 1959, 17.

120. Chester Bowles, typescript "New Delhi Diary" entry for August 9, 1963, Bowles papers, Sterling Memorial Library, Yale University, box 392, folder 159.

Chapter Three: A Split and a Tilt

1. Conversation among President Nixon, the President's Assistant for National Security Affairs [Kissinger], and the President's Assistant, November 5, 1971, *FRUS* E-7 (1969–1976).

2. Ibid.

·····

3. Conversation between President Nixon and his Assistant for National Security Affairs [Kissinger], Washington, DC, December 8, 1971, *FRUS* E-7 (1969–1976).

4. Conversation between President Nixon and his Assistant for National Security Affairs [Kissinger], Washington, DC, December 9, 1971, *FRUS* E-7 (1971).

5. The term "tilt" is used in international diplomacy to describe a country's support for another that stops short of open alliance or publicly declared support. International relations commentators described US support for Pakistan in the 1971 crisis as a "tilt."

6. Intelligence Memorandum No. 612/69, Prepared in the Office of Current Intelligence, Directorate of Intelligence, Central Intelligence Agency, Washington, February 6, 1969, *FRUS* E-7 (1969–1976): 1–10.

7. Intelligence Note No. 117, from the Director of the Bureau of Intelligence and Research to Secretary of State Rogers, Washington, DC, February 20, 1969, *FRUS* E-7 (1969–1976): 1–3.

8. Ibid.

9. Herbert Feldman, *The End and the Beginning: Pakistan 1969–1971* (Karachi, Pakistan: Oxford University Press, 1975), 13.

10. "Tweedle Khan Takes Over," *Economist*, March 29, 1969.

11. Letter from British High Commission in Rawalpindi to South Asia Department of the Foreign and Commonwealth Office London, dated May 13, 1969, in *The British Papers: Secret and Confidential, India, Pakistan, Bangladesh Documents 1958–1969*, ed. Roedad Khan (Karachi, Pakistan: Oxford University Press, 2002), 915.

12. Memorandum from the President's Assistant for National Security Affairs [Kissinger] to President Nixon, Washington, DC, March 25, 1969, *FRUS* E-7 (1969–1976): 1–2.

13. Telegram 50241, from the Department of State to the Embassy in Pakistan, April 2, 1969, *FRUS* E-7 (1969–1976): 1–2.

14. Telegram 4169, from the Embassy in Pakistan to the Department of State, April 25, 1969, *FRUS* E-7 (1969–1976): 1–10.

15. Telegram from Secretary of State Rogers to the Department of State, May 26, 1969, *FRUS* E-7 (1969–1976): 1–5.

16. Memorandum of Conversation between Kissinger and Amb. Agha Hilaly, May 16, 1969, *FRUS* E-7 (1969–1976): 1–2.

17. Memorandum of Conversation among Nixon, Yahya, Kissinger, Foreign Secretary S. M. Yusuf, and Ambassador Hilaly, Lahore, Pakistan, August 1, 1969, *FRUS* E-7 (1969–1976): 1–10.

• • • • •

18. National Archives, Nixon Presidential Materials, NSC Files, Box 1320, NSC Unfiled Material, 1969, 9 of 19, China, 1969–1972, Document 26, *FRUS* 17 (1969–1976).

19. National Archives, Nixon Presidential Materials, NSC Files, Box 1032, Files for the President—China Material, Cookies II, Chronology of Exchange with the PRC, February 1969–April 1971. Note drafted by Saunders on August 29, 1969, China, 1969–1972, Document 28, *FRUS* 17 (1969–1976).

20. Ibid.

21. Analytical Summary Prepared for the National Security Council Review Group, Washington, DC, November 22, 1969, *FRUS* E-7 (1969–1976): 1–10.

22. Ibid., NSC Files, Box 1244, Saunders Subject Files, Pakistan Military and Intelligence, January 20, 1969–December 31, 1969.

23. Memorandum from Acting Secretary of State Richardson to President Nixon, Washington, DC, February 10, 1970, *FRUS* E-7 (1969–1976): 1–3.

24. Transcript of Telephone Conversation between the President's Assistant for National Security Affairs [Kissinger] and the Assistant Secretary of State for Near Eastern and South Asian Affairs [Sisco], Washington, DC, June 12, 1970, *FRUS* E-7 (1969–1976): 1.

25. Memorandum of Conversation between Kissinger and Air Marshal Nur Khan, Lahore, Pakistan, August 1, 1969, *FRUS* E-7 (1969–1976): 1–3.

26. Memorandum of Conversation between Hilaly and Kissinger, Washington, DC, June 17, 1970, *FRUS* E-7 (1969–1976): 1–2.

27. Telegram 5012, from the Embassy in Pakistan to the Department of State, June 21, 1970, *FRUS* E-7 (1969–1976): 1–2.

28. Telegram 7805, from the Embassy in Pakistan to the Department of State, October 5, 1970 *FRUS* E-7 (1969–1976): 1.

29. Memorandum of Conversation between Nixon and Yahya, Washington, DC, October 25, 1970, *FRUS* E-7 (1969–1976): 1–3.

30. Ibid.

31. Ibid.

32. Ibid.

33. Airgram A-109 Memorandum of Conversation with Yusuf Haroon, from U.S. Consulate Karachi to State Department, in *The American Papers: Secret and Confidential India-Pakistan-Bangladesh Documents, 1965–1973*, ed. Roedad Khan (Karachi, Pakistan: Oxford University Press, 1999), 373.

34. Herbert Feldman, *The End and the Beginning: Pakistan 1969–1971* (Karachi, Pakistan: Oxford University Press, 1975), 46–47.

35. See, for example, Political Assessment from the U.S. Embassy Rawalpindi to the Department of State, dated February 13, 1970, in Khan, *The American Papers*, 327–346.

36. Memorandum from the President's Assistant for National Security Affairs [Kissinger] to President Nixon, Washington, DC, November 20, 1970, *FRUS* E-7 (1969–1976): 1–2

37. All figures from Election Commission of Pakistan, Report on the General Elections Pakistan 1970–1971, vol. 1 (Karachi, Pakistan: Election Commission of Pakistan, 1972).

38. Intelligence Brief from the Director of Intelligence and Research to Secretary of State Rogers, "Pakistan: Election Results Suggest Fresh Problems," December 8, 1970, *FRUS* E-7 (1969–1976): E-7.

39. Ibid.

40. For an account of Bhutto and the military leaders coordinating strategy toward Mujib and the Awami League, see Hasan Zaheer, *The Separation of East Pakistan: The Rise and Realization of Bengali Muslim Nationalism* (Karachi, Pakistan: Oxford University Press, 1994), 136–140.

41. Memorandum from the President's Assistant for National Security Affairs [Kissinger] to President Nixon, Washington, DC, February 22, 1971, *FRUS* E-7 (1969–1976): 1–2.

42. Ibid.

43. Telegram 540, from the Consulate General in Dacca to the Department of State, February 28, 1971, *FRUS* E-7 (1969–1976): 1–2.

44. Kamal Matinuddin, *Tragedy of Errors: East Pakistan Crisis 1968–1971* (Lahore, Pakistan: Wajidalis, 1994), 75–76.

45. Sherbaz Khan Mazari, *The Journey to Disillusionment* (Karachi, Pakistan: Oxford University Press, 1999), 136.

46. Robert Victor Jackson, *South Asian Crisis: India, Pakistan, and Bangla Desh: A Political and Historical Analysis of the 1971 War* (New York: Praeger, 1975), 20.

47. Sydney H. Schanberg, "Bengalis and Punjabis: Nation Split by Geography, Hate," *New York Times*, December 1, 1970.

48. Siddiq Salik, *Witness to Surrender* (Karachi, Pakistan: Oxford University Press, 1978), 29. At the time Salik was the military's public relations officer in East Pakistan. Others attribute the quote to Major General Muhammad Akbar, head of Inter-Services Intelligence (ISI), but say it was specifically aimed at Mujib. See Matinuddin, *Tragedy of Errors*, 156.

. . . . .

49. Schanberg, "Bengalis and Punjabis."

50. Talukder Maniruzzaman, *The Bangladesh Revolution and Its Aftermath* (Dacca: Bangladesh Books, 1980), 79–80.

51. Fazal Muqeem Khan, *Pakistan's Crisis in Leadership* (Islamabad, Pakistan: National Book Foundation, 1973), 51.

52. Salik, *Witness to Surrender*, 53.

53. Transcript of Telephone Conversation between President Nixon and His Assistant for National Security Affairs [Kissinger], San Clemente, California, March 29, 1971, *FRUS* 11 (1969–1976): 35–37.

54. Ibid.

55. Telegram 165, from American Embassy Islamabad to State Department, "Admiral Ahsan on Events in East Pakistan," dated August 17, 1971, in Khan, *The American Papers*, 643.

56. Transcript of Telephone Conversation between President Nixon and His Assistant for National Security Affairs [Kissinger], San Clemente, California, March 30, 1971, *FRUS* 11 (1969–1976): 37–38.

57. Telegram 959, from the Consulate General in Dacca to the Department of State, March 28, 1971, *FRUS* E-7 (1969–1976): 1–2.

58. Telegram 978, from the Consulate General in Dacca to the Department of State, March 29, 1971, *FRUS* E-7 (1969–1976): 1–3.

59. Telegram 986, from the Consulate General in Dacca to the Department of State, March 30, 1971, *FRUS* E-7 (1969–1976): 1–2.

60. Telegram 2954, from the Embassy in Pakistan to the Department of State, March 31, 1971, *FRUS* E-7 (1969–1976): 1–2.

61. Telegram from the Consulate General in Dacca to the Department of State, Dacca, Bangladesh, April 6, 1971, *FRUS* 11 (1969–1976): 45–47.

62. Sydney Schanberg, "An Alien Army Imposes Its Will: East Pakistan," *New York Times*, July 4, 1971.

63. Chester Bowles, "Pakistan's Made-in-USA Arms," *New York Times*, April 18, 1971.

64. Henry Kissinger, *The White House Years* (New York: Little Brown, 1979), 854.

65. Telegram from the Embassy in Pakistan to Department of State, April 8, 1971, *FRUS* 11 (1969–1976): 52–56.

66. Memorandum from Harold Saunders of the National Security Council Staff to the President's Assistant for National Security Affairs [Kissinger], Washington, DC, April 19, 1971, *FRUS* 11 (1969–1976): 85–87.

67. Memorandum from the President's Assistant for National Security Affairs [Kissinger] to President Nixon, Washington, DC, April 28, 1971, *FRUS* 11 (1969–1976): 91–99.

68. Airgram A-118, dated July 2, 1971, in Khan, *The American Papers*, 614–615.

69. Michael Hornsby, "President Yahya Dashes Hopes of Reconciliation," *The Times* (London), July 3, 1971.

70. Tad Szulc, "Diplomatic Striptease in Foggy Bottom: US and Pakistan," *New York Times*, June 11, 1972.

71. Zaheer, *The Separation of East Pakistan*, 296.

72. Letter from Indian Prime Minister Gandhi to President Nixon, New Delhi, India, May 13, 1971, *FRUS* 11 (1969–1976): 117–119.

73. "Pakistan Condemned," editorial, *New York Times*, July 14, 1971.

74. Conversation among President Nixon, his Assistant for National Security Affairs [Kissinger], and the Ambassador to Pakistan [Farland], Washington, DC, July 28, 1971, *FRUS* E-7 (1969–1976).

75. Kissinger, *The White House Years*, 861.

76. Conversation among President Nixon, the President's Assistant for National Security Affairs [Kissinger], British Foreign Secretary Douglas-Home, and the British Ambassador to the United States [Cromer], Washington, DC, September 30, 1971, *FRUS* E-7 (1969–1976).

77. Memorandum of Conversation between Henry Kissinger and Indira Gandhi, July 7, 1971, New Delhi, India, *FRUS* 11 (1976): 221–226.

78. Memorandum of Conversation between Kissinger and Jagjivan Ram, July 7, 1971, *FRUS* E-7 (1969–1976).

79. Memorandum of Conversation between Kissinger and Ambassador Jha, Washington, DC, September 11, 1971, *FRUS* 11 (1969–1976): 407–409.

80. Seymour Hersh, *The Price of Power: Kissinger in the Nixon White House* (New York: Summit Books, 1983), 452.

81. Hemen Ray, *The Enduring Friendship: Soviet-Indian Relations in Mrs. Gandhi's Days* (New Delhi, India: Abhinav Publications, 1989), 15.

82. Surjit Mansingh, *India's Search for Power: Indira Gandhi's Foreign Policy, 1966–1982* (New Delhi, India: Sage, 1984), 135.

83. Memorandum from the Deputy Administrator of the Agency for International Development [Williams] to Secretary of State Rogers, Washington, DC, November 5, 1971, *FRUS* E-7 (1969–1976): 1–5.

84. Joseph Alsop, "US Role in South Asia," *Washington Post, Times Herald*, January 14, 1972.

* * * * *

85. Transcript of Telephone Conversation between the President's Assistant for National Security Affairs [Kissinger] and the Pakistani Ambassador [Raza], Washington, DC, December 8, 1971, *FRUS* E-7 (1969–1976).

86. Transcript of Telephone Conversation between Secretary of State Rogers and the President's Assistant for National Security Affairs [Kissinger], Washington, DC, December 23, 1971, *FRUS* E-7 (1969–1976): E-7.

87. Gul Hassan Khan, *Memoirs of Lt. Gen. Gul Hassan Khan* (Karachi, Pakistan: Oxford University Press, 1993), 328.

88. Telegram 19243, from the Embassy in India to the Department of State, December 15, 1971, *FRUS* E-7 (1969–76).

89. Conversation among President Nixon, his Assistant [Haldeman], and his Assistant for National Security Affairs [Kissinger], Washington, DC, December 15, 1971, *FRUS* E-7 (1969–1976).

90. John H. Gill, *An Atlas of the 1971 India-Pakistan War: The Creation of Bangladesh* (Washington, DC: National Defense University, Near East South Asia Center for Strategic Studies Occasional Paper, 2004).

91. Charles Mohrs, "Dacca Captured: Guns Quiet in Bengali Area but War Goes on at Western…," *New York Times*, December 16, 1971.

92. Malcolm Browne, "West to Fight On: Yahya Calls for Help but Vows to Battle 'Alone If We Must'," *New York Times*, December 16, 1971.

Chapter Four: Picking Up the Pieces

1. Telegram from the Embassy in Pakistan to the Department of State, Islamabad, Meeting with Bhutto, December 20, 1971, *FRUS* 11 (1969–1976): 858–861.

2. Telegram from the Embassy in Pakistan to the Department of State, for Deputy Asst. Secretary Van Hollen, February 17, 1972, *FRUS* E-7 (1969–1976).

3. Telegram from the Department of State to the Embassy in Pakistan, March 23, 1972, *FRUS* E-7 (1969–1976).

4. Cable from the Embassy in Pakistan to the Department of State, April 4, 1972, *FRUS* E-7 (1969–1976).

5. Cable from the Embassy in Pakistan to the Department of State, Bhutto Looks to the Summit, June 22, 1972, *FRUS* E-7 (1969–1976).

6. A. R. Siddiqi, *The Military in Pakistan: Image and Reality* (Lahore, Pakistan: Vanguard Books, 1996), 223.

7. Ibid., 224.

8. Malcolm Browne, "The People Went to Mosques to Pray and Weep: India-Pakistan," *New York Times*, December 19, 1971.

9. Telegram 12542, from the Embassy in Pakistan to the Department of State, December 14, 1971, *FRUS* E-7 (1969–1976).

10. Browne, "The People Went to Mosques to Pray and Weep."

11. Conversation among President Nixon, his Assistant for National Security Affairs [Kissinger], and Secretary of State Rogers, Washington, DC, November 24, 1971, *FRUS* E-7 (1969–1976).

12. Ibid.

13. Ibid.

14. Telegram 227784, from the Department of State to the Embassy in Pakistan, December 18, 1971, *FRUS* E-7 (1969–1976).

15. Malcolm Browne, "Bhutto Tries to Put the Pieces Together," *New York Times*, December 26, 1971.

16. Telegram from the Embassy in Pakistan to the Department of State, Islamabad, Pakistan, Conversation with Pres. Bhutto Wednesday Evening, December 22, December 23, 1971, *FRUS* 11 (1969–1976): 869–872.

17. Backchannel Message from the Ambassador to Pakistan [Farland] to the President's Assistant for National Security Affairs [Kissinger], Islamabad, Pakistan, January 13, 1972, *FRUS* E-7 (1969–1976).

18. Malcolm Browne, "Bhutto a Whirlwind on Mission to Restore a Shattered Pakistan," *New York Times*, January 19, 1972.

19. Robert La Porte Jr., "Pakistan in 1972: Picking Up the Pieces," *Asian Survey* 13, no. 2 (February 1973): 187–198.

20. Ibid., 187–188.

21. James Michener, "A Lament for Pakistan," *New York Times*, January 9, 1972.

22. "Mr. Bhutto's New Pakistan," *New York Times*, December 22, 1971.

23. C. L. Sulzberger, "Bhutto Wants a Defense Pact with US," *New York Times*, February 13, 1972.

24. Telegram 1581, from the Embassy in Pakistan to the Department of State, February 17, 1972, *FRUS* E-7 (1969–1976).

25. Anwar H. Syed, "Z. A. Bhutto's Self-Characterizations and Pakistani Political Culture'," *Asian Survey* 18, no. 12 (December 1978): 1260.

26. Telegram 2213, from the Embassy in Pakistan to the Department of State, March 10, 1972, *FRUS* E-7 (1969–1976).

27. Telegram 1834, from the Embassy in Pakistan to the Department of State, February 25, 1972, *FRUS* E-7 (1969–1976).

28. Memorandum from Secretary of State Rogers to President Nixon, President Bhutto's Proposals for Closer Military Collaboration, Washington, DC, March 17, 1972, *FRUS* E-7 (1969–1976).

29. "New Friends, Neglected Loves," *New York Times*, February 24, 1972.

30. Memorandum for the President's File, Washington, DC, February 3, 1972, *FRUS* E-7 (1969–1976).

31. Transcript of Telephone Conversation between Secretary of State Rogers and the President's Assistant for National Security Affairs [Kissinger], Washington, DC, March 29, 1972, *FRUS* E-7 (1969–1976).

32. Memorandum of Conversation between Nixon, Kissinger and Aziz Ahmed, Washington, DC, March 29, 1972, *FRUS* E-7 (1969–1976).

33. Letter from Pakistani President Bhutto to President Nixon, Rawalpindi, Pakistan, April 18, 1972, *FRUS* E-7 (1969–1976).

34. National Intelligence Estimate, "Pakistan: Short-Term Problems and Prospects," May 5, 1972, *FRUS* E-7 (1969–1976).

35. Zulfikar Ali Bhutto, *If I Am Assassinated...* (New Delhi, India: Vikas Publishing House, 1979), 130.

36. "India and Pakistan: Show the Way," *Washington Post, Times Herald,* July 8, 1972.

37. Telegram 32, from the Embassy in Pakistan to the Department of State, January 2, 1973, *FRUS* E–7 (1969–1976).

38. Memorandum from Harold Saunders and John Holdridge of the National Security Council Staff to the President's Assistant for National Security Affairs [Kissinger], Washington, DC, November 8, 1972, *FRUS* E-7 (1969–1976).

39. Telegram 4533, from the Embassy in Pakistan to the Department of State, June 4, 1973, *FRUS* E-7 (1969–1976).

40. Telegram 4712, from the Embassy in Pakistan to the Department of State, June 8, 1973, *FRUS* E-7 (1969–1976).

41. Memorandum from the President's Assistant for National Security Affairs [Kissinger] to President Nixon, Washington, DC, March 7, 1973, *FRUS* E-7 (1969–1976).

42. Department of State, "Issues and Talking Points—Bhutto Visit," July 1973, in *The American Papers: Secret and Confidential India, Pakistan, Bangladesh Documents, 1965–1973,* ed. Roedad Khan (Karachi, Pakistan: Oxford University Press, 1999), 960.

43. Memorandum of Conversation, Washington, DC, September 18, 1973, *FRUS* E-7 (1969–1976).

44. Ibid.

45. Ibid.

46. Cable from Embassy in Iran to Department of State, "Secretary Connally Travel: Memorandum of Secretary Connally's Meeting with President Bhutto at the Presidential Palace in Rawalpindi on July 6, 1972," July 8, 1972, *FRUS* E-7 (1969–1976).

47. "Bhutto and US—Assistance without Arms," editorial, *Los Angeles Times*, September 19, 1973.

48. "Mr Bhutto's Visit," *Washington Post, Times Herald*, September 22, 1973.

49. Memorandum of Conversation, Washington, DC, September 19, 1973, *FRUS* E-7 (1969–1976).

50. W. Eric Gustafson, "Economic Problems of Pakistan under Bhutto," *Asian Survey* 16, no. 4 (1976): 373.

51. Anwar H. Syed, "Pakistan in 1976—Business as Usual," *Asian Survey* 17, no. 2 (1977): 188.

52. Ibid.

53. Department of State, Bureau of Intelligence and Research, "Pakistan and the Middle East: An Assessment of Military Ties," June 15, 1973, in Khan, *The American Papers*, 937–943.

54. Memorandum from the Director of the Bureau of Intelligence and Research to Director of Central Intelligence, "Prospects of an Indian Nuclear Test," February 23, 1972, *FRUS* E-7 (1969–1976).

55. Ibid.

56. "India Joins the Club," *Los Angeles Times*, May 21, 1974.

57. Cable from Embassy New Delhi to Department of State, "India's Nuclear Explosion: Why Now?" May 18, 1974, *FRUS* E-7 (1969–1976).

58. Telegram 5623, from the Embassy in Pakistan to the Department of State, June 12, 1974, *FRUS* E-7 (1969–1976).

59. Cited in Kausar Niazi, *Zulfikar Ali Bhutto of Pakistan: The Last Days* (New Delhi, India: Vikas, 1992), 99.

60. Memorandum of Conversation between Kissinger and Aziz Ahmed, Washington, DC, September 30, 1974, *FRUS* E-7 (1969–1976).

61. Memorandum of Conversation, Islamabad, Pakistan, October 31, 1974, *FRUS* E-7 (1969–1976).

62. Memorandum of Conversation, Washington, DC, February 5, 1975, *FRUS* E-7 (1969–1976).

63. National Security Decision Memorandum 289, Washington, DC, March 24, 1975, *FRUS* E-y (1969–1976).

64. Telegram 10198, from the Secretary's Delegation in Alexandria, Egypt, to the Embassy in Pakistan, August 30, 1975, *FRUS* E-7 (1969–1976).

65. Memorandum of Conversation, New York, September 30, 1975, *FRUS* E-7 (1969–1976).

66. "Halting Pakistan," *New York Times*, February 25, 1976.

67. Letter from President Ford to Pakistani Prime Minister Bhutto, Washington, DC, March 19, 1976, *FRUS* E-7 (1969–1976).

68. Memorandum of Conversation, Washington, DC, September 11, 1976, *FRUS* E-7 (1969–1976).

69. Memorandum of Conversation between Secretary of State Vance and State Department Officials, "Non Proliferation: Next Steps on Pakistan and Brazil," January 7, 1977, National Security Archives.

70. Bhutto, *If I Am Assassinated*, 59.

71. Memorandum of Conversation, Islamabad, Pakistan, October 31, 1974, *FRUS* E-7 (1969–1976).

72. Biographic Sketch General Mohammad Zia ul Haq, August 1988, Defense Intelligence Agency, National Security Archives.

73. Inter-Services Intelligence, Top Secret Paper for Prime Minister, "General Elections," October 5, 1976.

74. Memo from Warren Christopher to Carter, "Reprocessing Negotiations with Pakistan: A Negotiating Strategy," April 2, 1977, Secret, National Security Archives, Record Group 59, Department of State Records, Records of Warren Christopher, 1977–1980, box 17, January–December 1977.

75. Lewis Simons, "Pakistan Spurred by Tear Gas Decision, Seen Reconsidering Ties…," *Washington Post*, April 27, 1977.

76. Lewis Simons, "Pakistani Outraged: Bhutto Says US Is Trying to Oust Him," *Washington Post*, April 29, 1971.

77. James Markham, "Bhutto Presses Political Attack as Clashes Continue," *New York Times*, May 1, 1977.

78. White House Sit Rep Memorandum, Top Secret, June 13, 1977, National Security Archives.

79. Clifford Manshardt, "In Pakistan, Politics Becomes a Holy War," *Los Angeles Times*, May 3, 1977.

80. "Pakistan Awaits a Rebirth," *Los Angeles Times*, July 7, 1977.

Chapter Five: A Most Superb and Patriotic Liar

1. Vernon Walters, Cable from Embassy Islamabad to State Department, "My First Meeting with President Zia," July 5, 1982, and "My Final Meeting with President Zia," July 6, 1982," National Security Archives.

2. Cable from Embassy Pakistan to State Department, "Pakistan Nuclear Issue: Meeting with General Zia," October 17 and 25, 1982, National Security Archives.

3. Memorandum from Secretary of State George Shultz to President Reagan, "How Do We Make Use of the Zia Visit to Protect Our Strategic Interests in the Face of Pakistan's Nuclear Weapons Activities," November 26, 1982, National Security Archives.

4. Douglas Brinkley, ed., *The Reagan Diaries: Ronald Reagan* (New York: Harper Collins, 2007), 117.

5. Bernard Weinraub, "US Withholds Sale of Jets to Pakistan," *New York Times*, June 3, 1977.

6. Memo from US Embassy Islamabad to Secretary State, Reply re: Secretary of State Letter to Embassy in Paris on Pakistan Reprocessing Issue, April 1978, National Security Archives.

7. Feroz Hassan Khan, *Eating Grass: The Making of the Pakistani Bomb* (Stanford, CA: Stanford University Press, 2012), 6.

8. U.S. Embassy Islamabad Cable 7591 to State Department, "Pakistan Reprocessing Plant: USG Stipulation," August 5, 1978, Secret, National Security Archives.

9. Memorandum from US Embassy Islamabad to State Department, "Nuclear Reprocessing," August 6, 1978, Secret, National Security Archives.

10. Transcript of Interview to Bernard Nossiter, *Washington Post*, April 25, 1978, in Muhammad Zia-ul-Haq, *President of Pakistan General Zia ul Haq: Interviews to Foreign Media*, vol. 1 (Islamabad, Pakistan: Directorate of Film and Publications Ministry of Information and Broadcasting, 1983), 96. The *Post* published only part of the quote in a story on May 1, 1978, titled, "Pakistani Chief Denies Political Ambition."

11. Memorandum from US Embassy Islamabad to Secretary of State, June 1978, "No Evidence of Afghanistan Opposition Coalition in Pakistan," National Security Archives.

12. "US to Renew Aid to Pakistan," editorial, *Washington Post*, August 25, 1978.

·····

13. Ian Stephens, *Horned Moon: An Account of a Journey through Pakistan, Kashmir, and Afghanistan* (London: Chatto and Windus, 1953), 108.

14. John C. Griffiths, *Afghanistan: Key to a Continent* (Boulder, CO: Westview Press, 1981), 154.

15. Mohammad Asghar Khan, *Generals in Politics: Pakistan 1958–1982* (New Delhi, India: Vikas Publishing, 1983), 71.

16. Selig S. Harrison, "How the Soviet Union Stumbled into Afghanistan," in *Out of Afghanistan: The Inside Story of the Soviet Withdrawal*, eds., Diego Cordovez and Selig S. Harrison (New York: Oxford University Press, 1995), 15.

17. Memo from Embassy Islamabad Cable to State Department, "Ambassador's Talk with General Zia," September 5, 1978, National Security Archives.

18. "Congressional Consultations on Pakistan," State Department from Newsom to US Embassy Vienna, September 15, 1978, Secret, National Security Archives.

19. CIA Study, "Re: Pakistan Strong Motivation to Develop Their Nuclear Capability," April 26, 1978, National Security Archives.

20. "Congressional Consultations on Pakistan."

21. From US Embassy Paris to State Department, October 22, 1978, "Pakistan Ambassador to France Hardlines on Reprocessing Plant," National Security Archives.

22. Memo for Director, CIA from John Despres, National Intelligence Officer for Nuclear Proliferation via Deputy Director for National Foreign Assessment [and] National Intelligence Officer for Warning "Monthly Warning Report—Nuclear Proliferation," December 5, 1978; Memo from John Despres, NIO for Nuclear Proliferation, to Interagency Intelligence Working Group on Nuclear Proliferation, "Monthly Warning Report—May Soon Acquire All the Essential Components for a Plant," January 18, 1979, National Security Archives.

23. Cable from Embassy Islamabad to State Department, "Pakistan Nuclear Program: Technical Team Visit," February 27, 1979, National Security Archives.

24. Cable from Embassy Islamabad to State Department, "Pakistan's Nuclear Program: Hard Choices," March 5, 1979, National Security Archives.

25. Memorandum from Harold Saunders and Thomas Pickering to Secretary of State, "A Strategy for Pakistan," March 5, 1979, National Security Archives.

26. Cable from Embassy Islamabad to State Department, "Nuclear Aspects of DepSec Visit Discussed with UK and French Ambassadors," March 7, 1979, National Security Archives.

27. Memorandum of the Presidential Review Committee Meeting, "Pakistan," March 9, 1979, National Security Archives.

28. Robert Trumbull, "Pakistan Denies It Plans A-bomb, Denounces Washington Aid Cut-Off," *New York Times*, April 8, 1979.

29. "Pakistan and the Bomb," *Washington Post*, April 9, 1979.

30. Memorandum from Anthony Lake to Secretary of State, "The Pakistan Strategy and Future Choices," September 8, 1979, National Security Archives.

31. Cable from Embassy New Delhi to State Department, "India and the Pakistan Nuclear Problem," June 7, 1979, National Security Archives.

32. Seymour Topping, "Zia Denies Pakistan Builds Nuclear Bomb and Urges US to Resume Aid," *New York Times*, September 23, 1979.

33. Transcript of Interview to Sig Gissler, *Milwaukee Journal*, January 18, 1979, in Zia-ul-Haq, *President of Pakistan General Zia ul Haq*, vol. 2, 31.

34. Transcript of interview to Peter Collins, Columbia Broadcasting Service, February 14, 1979, in Zia-ul-Haq, *President of Pakistan General Zia ul Haq*, vol. 2, 76.

35. Dennis Kux, *The United States and Pakistan, 1947–2000: Disenchanted Allies* (Washington, DC: Woodrow Wilson Center Press, 2001), 241.

36. Ibid.

37. Peter Niesewand, "Guerillas Train in Pakistan to Oust Afghan Government," *Washington Post*, February 2, 1979.

38. Robert Michael Gates, *From the Shadows: The Ultimate Insider's Story of Five Presidents and How They Won the Cold War* (New York: Simon and Schuster, 1996), 143–144

39. Ibid.

40. See George Crile, *Charlie Wilson's War: The Extraordinary Story of the Largest Covert Operation in History* (New York, Grove Press, 2007). A movie was also made, based on the book. Both project Texas Congressman Charlie Wilson as the hero who enabled the Afghan Mujahideen to defeat the Soviets by securing large-scale funding for the war from the US Congress.

41. Gates, *From the Shadows*, 144.

42. Dānishjūyan-I Musalmān-I Payraw-I Khatt-I Imām, *Documents from the US Espionage Den*, quoted in Hafizullah Emadi, *State, Revolution, and Superpowers in Afghanistan* (New York: Praeger, 1990), 112.

43. Michael T. Kaufman, "Body of 2nd American Is Found in Islamabad Embassy," *New York Times*, November 23, 1979.

44. Ibid.

45. Kux, *The United States and Pakistan*, 244–245.

46. Lieutenant General Fazle Haq, interview with author, Islamabad, September 8, 1988.

47. President Carter's Secretary of State, Cyrus Vance, was among those who had refused to consider the April 1978 coup that brought the PDPA to power as part of a Soviet agenda for the region. See Cyrus R. Vance, *Hard Choices: Critical Years in America's Foreign Policy* (New York: Simon and Schuster, 1983), 384.

48. President Carter, Remarks at Foreign Policy Conference for Editors and Broadcasters on February 22, 1979, *Public Papers of the Presidents of the United States: Jimmy Carter 1979*, vol. 1 (Washington, DC: US Government Printing Office, 1980), 316.

49. President Carter, Remarks at a White House Briefing for Members of Congress, *Public Papers of the Presidents of the United States: Jimmy Carter 1980*, vol. 1 (Washington, DC: US Government Printing Office, 1981), 40.

50. President Carter's Letter on Soviet Invasion of Afghanistan, 1980, National Security Archives.

51. Memo from Brzezinski to Carter, Reflections on Soviet Intervention in Afghanistan, December 26, 1979, National Security Archives.

52. Memorandum on National Security Council Meeting, Iran, Christopher Mission to Afghanistan, SALT and Brown Trip to China, January 2, 1980, National Security Archives.

53. Zbigniew Brzezinski, *Power and Principle: Memoirs of the National Security Adviser, 1977–1981* (New York: Farrar Strauss Giroux, 1983), 449.

54. Memo from Secretary of Defense Harold Brown to Ambassador-at-Large Gerard C. Smith, Enclosing Excerpts from Memoranda of Conversations with Geng Biao and Deng Xiaoping, and January 7 and 8, 1980, January 31, 1980, National Security Archives.

55. Vance, *Hard Choices*, 389.

56. Michael T. Kaufman, "Pakistan Is No Longer the Ardent Suitor, but the Prize," *New York Times*, September 28 1980.

57. Transcript of Interview with Arnaud de Borchgrave, *Newsweek*, January 1980, in Zia-ul-Haq, *President of Pakistan General Zia ul Haq*, vol. 3, 5.

58. Stuart Auerbach, "Pakistan Is Reluctant to Accept Limited US Arms Pledge," *Washington Post*, January 6, 1980.

59. Brzezinski, *Power and Principle*, 448.

60. Ibid.

· · · · ·

61. Ibid., 148–149.

62. Stuart Auerbach, "Pakistan Seeking US Guarantees in Formal Treaty," *New York Times*, January 18, 1980.

63. William Branigin, "Pakistan Seeks Billions in US Aid," *Washington Post*, January 23, 1980.

64. Auerbach, "Pakistan Seeking US Guarantees in Formal Treaty."

65. Transcript of Interview with Bill Redeker, *ABC News*, March 8, 1980, in Zia-ul-Haq, *President of Pakistan General Zia ul Haq*, vol. 3, 136.

66. Transcript of Interview with Michael Kaufman, *New York Times*, September 23, 1980, in Zia-ul-Haq, *President of Pakistan General Zia ul Haq*, vol. 3, 299.

67. Ibid.

68. "Quick, Say the Pakistanis," editorial, *Washington Post*, January 9, 1980.

69. "Asia Needs Help, Not A-Bombs," editorial, *New York Times,* January 22, 1980.

70. Cable from Ambassador Goheen [New Delhi] to Secretary of State, "Indian Foreign Minister Expresses 'Grave Concern' Over US Moves to Rearm Pakistan," January 24, 1980, National Security Archives.

71. Transcript of Interview with Indian Journalist Kuldip Nayar, January 29, 1980, in Zia-ul-Haq, *President of Pakistan General Zia ul Haq*, vol 3, 43.

72. "Uneasy about South Asia," editorial, *Washington Post*, February 3, 1980.

73. "Afghanistan: Soviet Invasion and US Response," Congressional Research Service, Issue Brief, January 10, 1980, National Security Archives.

74. Cable from State Department to Embassy Switzerland et al., "Non-Proliferation Policy and Renewed Assistance to Pakistan," January 30, 1980, National Security Archives.

75. "The Carter Corps at the Pass," editorial, *New York Times*, February 7, 1980.

76. "Drawing the Line," editorial, *Washington Post*, March 9, 1980.

77. "No Peanuts for Pakistan," editorial, *New York Times*, March 10, 1980.

78. Michael T. Kaufman, "Pakistan Shapes Foreign Policy with an Eye on Saudi Funds," *New York Times*, March 22, 1980.

79. Memorandum from Special Assistant for Nuclear Proliferation Intelligence to Director of Central Intelligence, "Warning Report—Nuclear Proliferation," April 30, 1980, National Security Archives.

80. Philip Sherwell, "How Joanne Herring Won Charlie Wilson's War," *Telegraph*, London, June 7, 2013.

81. Gates, *From the Shadows*, 197.

82. Cable from Ambassador Hummel to Secretary of State, "President Zia ul Haq on Afghanistan," March 28, 1981, National Security Archives.

83. "Slow on Pakistan," editorial, *Washington Post*, March 25, 1981.

84. Cable from Secretary of State to Embassy Islamabad, "Visit of Pakistan Foreign Minister," April 1981, National Security Archives.

85. Cable from Secretary of State to All Embassies, "US Policy Towards Pakistan," April 1981, National Security Archives.

86. Ibid.

87. Summary of Special Assistant for Nuclear Proliferation Intelligence, National Foreign Assessment Center, Central Intelligence Agency, to Resource Management Staff, Office of Program Assessment et al., "Request for Review of Draft Paper on the Security Dimension of Non-Proliferation," April 9, 1981, National Security Archives.

88. Transcript of Interview to Barry Came, *Newsweek*, May 14, 1981, in Zia-ul-Haq, *President of Pakistan General Zia ul Haq*, vol 4, 172.

89. Ibid.

90. Transcript of Interview to Bernard Falk, *BBC TV*, May 28, 1981, in Zia-ul-Haq, *President of Pakistan General Zia ul Haq*, vol. 4, 188.

91. Juan de Onis, "US and Pakistanis Reach an Agreement on $3 Billion in Aid," *New York Times*, June 16, 1981.

92. Kux, *The United States and Pakistan*, 258.

93. Judith Miller, "U.S. Cites Pakistan Pledge Not to Make Nuclear Arms," *New York Times*, June 25, 1981.

94. "Arms for Pakistan," editorial, *Washington Post*, September 19, 1981.

95. "Pakistan's Choice: Aid or a Bomb," editorial, *New York Times*, October 2, 1981.

96. Letters to the Editor, *New York Times*, August 26, 1981.

97. Cable from Department of State to Embassy in London, "Pakistani Efforts to Procure Nuclear-Grade Calcium from France," 1981, National Security Archives.

98. Gates, *From the Shadows*, 199.

99. Ibid., 252.

100. Ibid., 251.

101. Ibid., 320–321.

102. Mohammed Yousaf and Mark Adkin, *Afghanistan—The Bear Trap: The Defeat of a Superpower* (Havertown, PA: Casemate, 2001), 79.

103. Ibid., 81.

104. Ibid., 96.

......

105. Note for [name excised] from [name excised], "State/INR Request for Update of Pak SNIE, and Assessment of Argentine Nuclear Program," June 4, 1982, National Security Archives.

106. Michael T. Kaufman, "In India: Sikhs Raise a Cry for Independent Nation," *New York Times*, August 16, 1982.

107. William Stevens, "Indira Gandhi Calls Rebellion 'Under Control'," *New York Times*, June 14, 1984.

108. Sanjoy Hazarika, "Indians Say Exiles in Europe and US Stirred Sikh Revolt," *New York Times*, July 11, 1984.

109. William Stevens, "In Pakistan, Islam Leaves Little Room for Freedom: Riots Challenge Zia," *New York Times*, August 28, 1983.

110. Fred Hiatt, "Weinberger, in Pakistan, calls Riots 'Internal Problem'," *Washington Post*, October 1, 1983.

111. "Reagan Warned Pakistanis on Nuclear Project," *Washington Post*, October 26, 1984.

112. Cable from Defense Intelligence Agency to [excised location], "Pakistan-China: Nuclear Weapons Production and Testing," December 7, 1985, National Security Archives.

113. Steve Coll, *Ghost Wars: The Secret History of the CIA, Afghanistan and Bin Laden from the Soviet Invasion to September 10, 2001* (New York: Penguin, 2004), 165.

114. Gates, *From the Shadows*, 427.

115. Philip Taubman, "Soviet Lists Afghan War Toll: 13,310 Dead, 35,478 Wounded," *New York Times*, May 26, 1988.

116. Yousaf and Adkin, *Afghanistan*, 28.

117. Ibid., 105.

118. Zia-u-Haq's interview with Selig Harrison, published in *Le Monde Diplomatique*, cited in Coll, *Ghost Wars*, 175.

119. Coll, *Ghost Wars*, 181.

Chapter Six: Denial and Double Game

1. Letter from Secretary of State James A. Baker III to Prime Minister Nawaz Sharif to author, dated May 10, 1992, in the author's possession.

2. Ambassador Nicholas Platt's talking points for meeting with Prime Minister Sharif, May 1992, in author's possession.

3. Author's notes of meeting at the prime minister's house on May 18, 1992.

* * * * *

4. Biographic Sketch Maj General Hamid Gul, January 1989, Defense Intelligence Agency, National Security Archives.

5. See Christina Lamb, *Waiting for Allah: Pakistan's Struggle for Democracy* (New Delhi, India: Viking, 1991), 47, and Iqbal Akhund, *Trial and Error: The Advent and Eclipse of Benazir Bhutto* (Karachi, Pakistan: Oxford University Press, 2000), chs. 4 and 5 for details of the limits on Bhutto's power set by President Ishaq Khan and General Beg.

6. Barbara Crossette, "Gandhi Visit to Pakistan: Hopes for a New Era," *New York Times*, December 29, 1988.

7. John Kifner, "Bhutto Ousts Powerful Intelligence Chief," *New York Times*, May 26, 1989.

8. George H. W. Bush, "Remarks Following Discussions with PM Benazir Bhutto of Pakistan," June 6, 1989, The American Presidency Project, presidency.ucsb.edu.

9. "Ms Bhutto Makes Her Case," *New York Times*, June 12, 1989.

10. Dennis Kux, *The United States and Pakistan, 1947–2000: Disenchanted Allies* (Washington, DC: Woodrow Wilson Center Press, 2001), 306–307.

11. Ibid., 299.

12. Ibid.

13. Lawrence Ziring, "Pakistan in 1990: The Fall of Benazir Bhutto," *Asian Survey* 31, no. 2 (February 1990): 114.

14. Steve Coll, "Pakistan's Army Deep in Politics; Generals' Objectives Remain Unclarified," *Washington Post*, August 9, 1990.

15. "Defeat for Democracy in Pakistan," *New York Times*, August 9, 1990.

16. See Azhar Sohail, *Agencio ki Hukoomat* [in Urdu, "Government by Covert Agencies"] (Lahore, Pakistan: Vanguard, 1993), 37–49.

17. For excerpts from the filings by General Beg and General Durrani before Pakistan's Supreme Court, see Ardeshir Cowasjee, "We Never Learn from History," *Dawn*, August 11 and 18, 2002. Also see "Beg Says He Is Not Answerable to Court," *Dawn*, February 25, 1997.

18. Kux, *The United States and Pakistan*, 308.

19. Ibid., 309.

20. Ibid., 308–309 and 318.

21. Ibid., 312.

22. Ibid., 309.

23. Steve Coll, "Intrigue Permeates Pakistan: A Political Culture of 'Shadow Games'," *Washington Post*, December 15, 1991.

· · · · ·

24. Strobe Talbott, *Engaging India: Diplomacy, Democracy and the Bomb* (Washington, DC: Brookings Press, 2004), 22.

25. Ibid., 24.

26. From Joint Staff HQs DC to DIA DC, "Pakistan Weapons Acquisition Efforts," June 20, 1991, Department of Defense, National Security Archives.

27. William J. Clinton, "Statement on the Apprehension of Ramzi A Youssef," February 8, 1995, The American Presidency Project, presidency .ucsb.edu.

28. Cable from [Excised] to Ron McMullen [Afghanistan Desk], "Developments in Afghanistan," December 5, 1994, National Security Archives.

29. Ahmed Rashid, *Taliban: Islam, Oil and the New Great Game in Central Asia* (New York: I. B. Tauris, 2000), 45.

30. John F. Burns, "Pakistan Shifting Stance on Hard-Line Afghans," *New York Times*, March 27, 1996.

31. "The 9/11 Commission Report," 9-11commission.gov/report/911 Report.pdf, 124.

32. Cable from State Department to US Consulate Karachi, "The Harakat-ul-Ansar—The Pakistan Dimension [Excised]," March 29, 1995, National Security Archives.

33. Ibid.

34. Central Intelligence Agency, Report, "Harakat ul-Ansar: Increasing Threat to Western and Pakistani Interests," August 1996, National Security Archives.

35. William J. Clinton, "Statement on the Terrorist Attack in Pakistan," March 8, 1995, The American Presidency Project, presidency.ucsb.edu.

36. "Death in Pakistan," *Wall Street Journal*, March 10, 1995.

37. John War Anderson and Kamran Khan, "Pakistan Shelters Islamic Radicals; Militant Groups Train Warriors in Camps Near Afghan Border," *Washington Post*, March 8, 1995.

38. Ibid.

39. Cable from Special Mission UNSMA [UN Special Mission to Afghanistan] to US Mission at the UN, "Present Pakistani Initiatives in Afghanistan" October 30, 1997, National Security Archives.

40. "The Karachi Killings," editorial, *Wall Street Journal*, November 13, 1997.

41. Cable from Embassy [Islamabad] to Department of State, "Afghanistan: [Excised] Describes Pakistan's Current Thinking" March 9, 1998, National Security Archives.

······

42. Cable from Secretary of State [Secretary Albright] to Embassy Islamabad, Pakistan: Ghauri Missile Flight, April 8, 1998, Wikileaks, http://wikileaks.org/cable/1998/04/98STATE62472.html.

43. Nathan Glazer, "Why Arm Pakistan?," *New York Times*, April 13, 1998.

44. John F. Burns, "India Sets 3 Nuclear Blasts, Defying a Worldwide Ban; Tests Bring a Sharp Outcry," *New York Times*, May 12, 1998; "India Carries Out 2 More Atom Tests Despite Sanctions," *New York Times*, May 14, 1998.

45. Dan Balz, "U.S. Urges Pakistan to Forgo Tests; Clinton Pleas Issued as Nation Seems Set on Nuclear Exercise," *Washington Post*, May 18, 1998.

46. Talbott, *Engaging India*, 57.

47. Memorandum from State Department to the White House [Berger], "Secretary's Morning Summary," May 13, 1998, National Security Archives.

48. Talbott, *Engaging India*, 59–61.

49. Ibid., 59–61.

50. Ibid., 62–63.

51. Ibid.

52. Cable from Embassy Islamabad [Amb Simons] to Department of State, "Prime Minister Succumbs to Domestic Pressure and Pakistan Conducts Five Nuclear Tests," May 28, 1998, Wiki.

53. Cable from Embassy [Islamabad] to Department of State, "Bad News on Pak Afghan Policy: GOP [Government of Pakistan] Support for the Taliban Appears to Be Getting Stronger," July 1, 1998, National Security Archives.

54. Cable from Embassy [Islamabad] to Department of State, "Afghanistan: Evidence Not There to Prove Assertions That Pak Troops Have Been Deployed to Assist Taliban in the North," August 6, 1998, National Security Archives.

55. Ibid.

56. Bill Clinton, *My Life* (New York: Alfred Knopf, 2004), 745–746.

57. Ibid.

58. Ibid.

59. Ibid., 748.

60. Cable from Embassy [Islamabad] to Department of State, "Afghanistan: Reaction to U.S. Strikes Follows Predicable Lines: Taliban Angry, Their Opponents Support U.S.," August 21, 1998, National Security Archives.

61. Kamran Khan and Pamela Constable, "Pakistanis Reportedly Killed in Raids," *Washington Post*, August 22, 1998; Pamela Constable, "U.S. Strike Is Blow to Pakistan's Rulers," *Washington Post*, August 26, 1998.

62. To the Secretary of State from Assistant Secretary of State for South Asian Affairs Karl F. Inderfurth, "Pakistan: Reaction to Afghanistan Strikes," August 21, 1998, US Department of State, National Security Archives.

63. To the Secretary of State from Assistant Secretary of State for South Asian Affairs Karl F. Inderfurth, "Pakistan: Reaction to Afghanistan Strikes," August 21, 1998, US Department of State, National Security Archives.

64. Howard B. Schaffer and Teresita C. Schaffer, *How Pakistan Negotiates with the United States* (Washington, DC: US Institute of Peace, 2011), 175.

65. Cable from Embassy [Islamabad] to Department of State, "Ambassador Reviews Again GOP [Government of Pakistan] Policy on Afghanistan," January 7, 1999, National Security Archives.

66. Kenneth J. Cooper, "India, Pakistan Kindle Hope for Peace; Leaders Meet Near Border After Symbolic Bus Trip, Pledge to Resolve Disputes," *Washington Post*, February 21, 1999.

67. William J. Clinton, 'Statement on a Meeting of the PMs of India and Pakistan," February 22, 1999, The American Presidency Project, presidency.ucsb.edu.

68. Bruce O. Riedel, *American Diplomacy and the 1999 Kargil Summit at Blair House* (Philadelphia, PA: Center for the Advanced Study of India, 2002).

69. Clinton, *My Life*, 800–802.

70. Riedel, *American Diplomacy*.

71. Clinton, *My Life*, 802.

72. "Dangerous Coup in Pakistan," editorial, *New York Times*, October 13, 1999.

73. "Pakistan and the Senate," editorial, *Wall Street Journal*, October 15, 1999.

74. Steven Weisman, "Pakistan's Dangerous Addiction to Its Military," *New York Times*, October 17, 1999.

75. Ibid.

76. Richard N. Haass, "Pakistan: Democracy Is Not Everything," IntellectualCapital.com, November 11, 1999.

77. Robert C. McFarlane, "The Uses of a Coup," *New York Times*, October 14, 1999.

78. Talbott, *Engaging India*, 190.

79. Ibid.

80. Ibid., 190–191.

81. Clinton, *My Life*, 830–833.

82. William J. Clinton, "Television Address to the People of Pakistan from Islamabad, Pakistan," March 25, 2000, The American Presidency Project, presidency.ucsb.edu.

83. Cable from Department of State to Embassy Islamabad, "Pakistan Support for Taliban," September 26, 2000, National Security Archives.

84. Ibid.

85. Cable from Department of State to US Mission, "U/S Pickering Discusses Afghanistan, Democratization and Kashmir in NY with [Excised]," November 20, 2000, National Security Archives.

86. Condoleezza Rice, *No Higher Honor: A Memoir of My Years in Washington* (New York: Crown Publishers, 2011), 24.

87. Ibid., 65.

88. Dick Cheney, *In My Time: A Personal and Political Memoir* (New York: Threshold Editions, 2011), 418.

89. Rice, *No Higher Honor*, 62.

90. Cable from Embassy [Islamabad] to Department of State, "Staffdel Focuses on Afghanistan at MFA," August 30, 2001, National Security Archives.

91. Cable from Deputy Secretary Armitage to Ambassador Chamberlin, "Deputy Secretary Armitage's Meeting with Pakistan Intel Chief Mahmud: You're Either with Us or Against Us," September 12, 2001, National Security Archives.

92. Cable from US Embassy [Islamabad] [Amb Chamberlin] to Department of State, "Musharraf: We Are with You in Your Action Plan in Afghanistan," September 13, 2001, National Security Archives.

93. Pervez Musharraf, *In the Line of Fire: A Memoir* (New York: Free Press, 2006), 200–207.

94. George W. Bush, *Decision Points* (New York: Crown Publishers, 2010), 188.

95. See President's Address to the Nation, September 19, 2004, available at Government of Pakistan, infopak.gov.pk/President_Addresses/presidential_addresses_index.htm.

96. US Embassy [Islamabad], Cable, "Mahmud Plans 2nd Mission to Afghanistan," September 24, 2001, National Security Archives.

97. US Embassy [Islamabad], Cable, "Mahmud on Failed Kandahar Trip," September 29, 2001, National Security Archives.

98. Paul Watson, "A Revolving Door for Pakistan's Militants," *Los Angeles Times*, November 17, 2002.

* * * * *

99. John Lancaster and Kamran Khan, "Extremist Groups Renew Activity in Pakistan," *Washington Post*, February 8, 2003.

100. Jay Solomon, Zahid Hussain, and Keith Johnson, "Despite U.S. Effort, Pakistan Remains Key Terror Hub," *Wall Street Journal*, July 22, 2005.

101. Bush, *Decision Points*, 211–212.

102. Rice, *No Higher Honor*, 442.

103. Bush, *Decision Points*, 213–214.

104. Cheney, *In My Time*, 523.

105. David Sanger, "Cheney Warns Pakistan to Act Against Terrorists," *New York Times*, February 27, 2007.

106. Cable from Embassy [Islamabad] to Department of State, Bhutto's Homecoming, October 18, 2007. Wikileaks, http://wikileaks.org/cable/2007/10/07ISLAMABAD4472.html.

Chapter Seven: Parallel Universes

1. Jiang Zemin, "Carrying Forward Generations of Friendly and Good-Neighborly Relations and Endeavoring Towards a Better Tomorrow for All," December 2, 1996, Ministry of Foreign Affairs, Government of China, http://www.fmprc.gov.cn/eng/wjb/zzjg/yzs/gjlb/2757/2758/t16111.htm.

2. Eric Schmitt, "Plan Would Use Anti-Terror Aid on Pakistani Jets," *New York Times*, July 24, 2008.

3. Ibid.

4. "Deal Lets U.S. Drones Strike Bin Laden; Musharraf Agreement Limits Pentagon," *Washington Times*, July 2, 2008.

5. Cable from Ambassador Washington to Foreign Secretary, Durrani Meeting with Rice, December 19, 2008. Author's papers.

6. Bob Woodward, *Obama's Wars* (New York: Simon and Schuster, 2010), 46–47.

7. Zahid Hussain, "Pakistani Firing Exposes Rift Over Mumbai Probe," *Wall Street Journal*, January 9, 2009.

8. "Release of Proliferator of Nukes a Risk, Says U.S.; Pakistani Court Frees Rogue Scientist," *Washington Times*, February 7, 2009.

9. "Face Down Pakistani Army," *USA Today*, April 1, 2009.

10. Pamela Constable, "Pakistan's Plans for New Fight Stir Concern; Swat Refugees, Others Question Move to Battle Insurgents in Tribal South Waziristan," *Washington Post*, June 24, 2009.

11. "Mrs. Clinton in Pakistan," *New York Times*, October 30, 2009.

*****

12. Mark Landler, "Clinton Arrives in Pakistan to Confront Rising Anti-Americanism," *New York Times*, October 28, 2009.

13. Letter from President Obama to President Zardari, November 11, 2009, author's papers.

14. Woodward, *Obama's Wars*, 302.

15. Peter Shanker, "Inside the Situation Room: How a War Plan Evolved," *New York Times*, December 6, 2009.

16. James Traub, "After Cheney," *New York Times*, November 29, 2009.

17. David Ignatius, "A Threat's New Face," *Washington Post*, May 5, 2010.

18. Julie Ray and Rajesh Srinivasan, "Pakistanis Criticize U.S. Action That Killed Osama Bin Laden," Gallup World, May 18, 2011, www.gallup.com/poll/147611/pakistanis-criticize-action-killed-osama-bin-laden.aspx.

19. "U.S. Image in Pakistan Falls No Further Following bin Laden Killing," Pew Global Attitudes Project, June 21, 2011, http://www.pewglobal.org/2011/06/21/u-s-image-in-pakistan-falls-no-further-following-bin-laden-killing.

20. Julian E. Barnes, Matthew Rosenberg, and Adam Entous, "U.S. Accuses Pakistan of Militant Ties," *Wall Street Journal*, September 23, 2011.

Acknowledgments

President Asif Zardari and Prime Minister Yusuf Raza Gilani made it possible for me to serve as Pakistan's ambassador to the United States and supported me under difficult circumstances, as did Bilawal Bhutto Zardari, who seems set to continue his family's tradition of public service.

US Senators John Kerry, John McCain, Joseph Lieberman and Mark Kirk helped me get out of Pakistan safely when, after resigning as ambassador, I faced a lynch-mob and false accusations.

The late Ambassador Richard Holbrooke and Marc Grossman were diplomats of distinction from whom I learned a lot. Anne Patterson and Cameron Munter, as my American counterparts, and Pakistani Foreign Secretary, Salman Bashir, helped me not only in doing my job as ambassador but also in understanding the complexities of the US-Pakistan relationship.

Howard and Teresita Schaffer, Marvin Weinbaum, Stephen Cohen, Bruce Riedel, Lisa Curtis, William Milam, Robert Hathaway, George Perkovich, Ashley Tellis, and Mark Siegel helped me clarify some of my concepts as did my colleagues at Boston University, Andrew Bacevich, Erik Goldstein, and Stephen Kinzer. Encouragement from Ken Weinstein, Lewis Libby, and Hillel Fradkin of Hudson Institute was invaluable.

The idea of this book was first mooted by Clive Priddle at Public Affairs, who was most supportive as editor, backed by an excellent team including Christine Marra and Jaime Leifer. It was a blessing to have the backing of Andrew Wylie, book agent extraordinaire.

· · · · ·

Shuja Nawaz of the Atlantic Council helped me in settling on the title.

Dr. Aparna Pande, friend and colleague at Hudson Institute, helped me with research, especially as I sought archival material from original sources. A scholar in her own right, she has been especially valuable in organizing the inputs from many volunteer students and interns. Among these, Jamil Ahmed Hasan stands out for his diligence.

Some of my students at Boston University took time to help me track down dates, references, and facts with the sole objective of expanding their knowledge. These include Aarthi Gunasekaran, Annis Saniee, Christine Clarke, Cody Marden, Jillian Petrie, Kelsea-Marie Pym, Rachel Traver, Zack Swan, and Zain Homaeer.

My children Huda, Hammad, Maha, and Mira were helpful by letting their father spend an entire year on this book without complaining about parental inattention.

I would like to add that the views in this book, as well as any mistakes or errors, are solely my responsibility.

Index

······

·····

......

. . . . .

＊＊＊＊＊＊

......

· · · · ·

......

About the Author

Husain Haqqani was Pakistan's ambassador to the United States from 2008 to 2011. A trusted adviser to the late Pakistani prime minister Benazir Bhutto, Ambassador Haqqani is a professor at Boston University and director for South and Central Asia at the Hudson Institute as well as coeditor of the journal *Current Trends in Islamist Ideology.* He has written for the *Wall Street Journal, New York Times, Boston Globe, Financial Times, International Herald Tribune,* and more. Follow him on Twitter: @husain haqqani.